best new poets
2010

best new poets

2010

CLAUDIA EMERSON, EDITOR

Jeb Livingood, Series Editor

This book was published by Samovar Press LLC, Charlottesville, Virginia,
in cooperation with *Meridian*, www.readmeridian.org.
For additional information on *Best New Poets*,
see our Web site at www.bestnewpoets.org.

Text set in Adobe Garamond Pro

Printed by Bailey Printing, Charlottesville, Virginia

ISBN 13: 978-0-9766296-5-8

ISSN 1554-7019

Contents

Introduction ix

Mary Angelino, Helping My Father Write His Father's Eulogy 1

Kara van de Graaf, Poem at the Bottom of the Allegheny River 2

Eleanor Smith Tipton, Wheel and Shadow 4

Lisa Fay Coutley, My Lake 6

Tracey Knapp, Inheritance 8

Linda S. Gottlieb, Green Knife-Sharpening Car 11

Hailey Leithauser, The Moon Speaks of Polar Bears 12

Matthew Kelsey, Frost Heave 14

M. Ann Hull, The Stutterer 16

Chloe Honum, Spring 18

Joshua Rivkin, Pastoral 19

Stephen McDonald, Stories 20

Brent Newsom, Esther Green Moves Out of the Sunset Acres Mobile
    Home Community 22

Joanna Pearson, After a Molar Pregnancy 25

Megan Grumbling, Leaving the Room 26

Stephanie Pippin, Afterimage 28

Nathan McClain, Landscape with Goats 30

Erin Gay, Portrait Sealed in an Apothecary Jar 32

Sharon Fain, Angola, 2002 34

Todd Dillard, Brother Mailed His Thumb 37

Jeff Baker, April Blizzard 38

Eugenia Leigh, Every Hair on Your Head 40

Sarah Sousa, Leaving Maine... 42

Brandi George, Dear Beauty 44

Adam Houle, The Reddish Cur 46

Steven C. Brown Jr., Penumbra 48

Angie Macri, A Song for Fever 50

Rebecca Lehmann, The Factory, An Elegy in Six Parts................................. 51

Melanie McCabe, Paperboy 58

Eric Smith, Story Problems 60

Teresa Breeden, Waiting on Spring... 63

Jake Ricafrente, The Funeralgoers 64

Graham Hillard, What the Ground Gives... 69

dawn lonsinger, The Economist's Daughter 70

Stephen Ackerman, A Small Obsession 72

Sheri Allen, June Arrival, Gainesville.. 74

Benjamin Pryor, New Year's Resolve 75

Meighan Sharp, Habitats.. 76

Emily Louise Smith, After Reading about How to Attract
    Martins to Gourd Houses.. 78

Sarah J. Wangler, A Bawl-Ass Remembers Her Childhood 79

Douglas S. Jones, Drinking Slow, Waiting for Weather 82

Kate Angus, Inside My Sleep 84

Iain Haley Pollock, Upon Irremediable Shores, Those Who Never Had Time 86

Monika Zobel, On the Corner of Guilt and Ash 88

Kai Carlson-Wee, Thresher 90

Luke Johnson, Remembering the Old Testament while Walking the Dog 92

James Arthur, Independence.. 93

Rachel Langille, Telescope 94

Matthew Ostapchuk, Eulogy for the Method 95

Alison Palmer, Vertigo 97

CONTRIBUTORS' NOTES 101

ACKNOWLEDGMENTS 113

PARTICIPATING MAGAZINES 115

PARTICIPATING WRITING PROGRAMS 123

Introduction

Welcome to *Best New Poets 2010*, our sixth installment of fifty poems from emerging writers. In these pages, the term "emerging writer" has a narrow definition: here, it means someone who has yet to publish a book-length collection of poetry. Like the rules for many anthologies, that one is, perhaps, arbitrary. But the main goal of *Best New Poets* is to provide special encouragement and recognition to new poets, the many writing programs they attend, and the magazines that publish their work. And, of course, to deliver an accessible, eclectic sampling of emerging poets to you, the reader.

From April to May of 2010, *Best New Poets* accepted nominations from each of the above sources. For a small reading fee, writers could upload two poems as part of our open competition. A month earlier, writing programs from around the United States and Canada sent free nominations of up to two writers, whom *Best New Poets* later solicited for work. And the anthology also asked literary magazines across North America to send two of their best recent poems by writers who met our definition of "emerging." We asked that the poems submitted either be unpublished or published after April 1, 2009. So, not only do new writers appear in this anthology, but you are also seeing some of their latest work.

In all, we received over 1,500 submissions, most of them containing two poems, for a total of roughly 2,800 individual poems. Six dedicated readers blindly ranked these submissions, sending 185 manuscripts to this year's guest editor, Claudia Emerson, who selected the final fifty. Our initial readers—Evan Beaty, Joe Chapman, George David Clark, Julia Hansen, Terence Huber, and Wanling Su—deserve special thanks. All are practicing poets, and as with prior editions, they worked hard to include not only poems they liked, but also those that they thought might interest a reader with different tastes.

Claudia Emerson and I are pleased with the result. A few reviewers have generously compared this book to *Best American Poetry* or the Pushcart series, but those anthologies are in a different league when it comes to contributors. You will not see the poems of Mary Oliver, Ted Kooser, Louise Glück, or Billy Collins in our pages. Yet, this book is not meant as some sort of literary comment: *More emerging poets in the best-ofs!* Instead, this book began simply because emerging fiction writers had a venue for their work in the annual series edited by John Kulka and Natalie Danford, but emerging poets did not. It seemed like a slightly different model might make a poetry equivalent viable, even at a turbulent time in publishing. Through modest entry fees from our open competition, broad distribution by the University of Virginia Press, and growing bookstore sales, we have been able to break even for six years now. We know *Best New Poets* remains a minor league venture, strictly AAA ball. But in this little championship series, more than a few of our contributors show flashes of professional talent, knocking poems out of the park. Our mission is to be one snapshot of poetry as it exists today and give our readers a glimpse of what tomorrow might hold.

So, here we are, six years in, and by the time this edition reaches bookstores, our calls for *Best New Poets 2011* will go out. Batter up.

—*Jeb Livingood*
University of Virginia

Mary Angelino

Helping My Father Write His Father's Eulogy

Instead of *uneducated*, write *immigrant*,
instead of *mason*—
artist with brick and stone.

If you say *worked hard, always
food on the table,* you won't need
to say *poor.*

He'd want the Psalm read first
to get it out of the way.

End with the time
he drove to that mansion,
the fence white as a rich man's teeth,

just to show you the tile rooftop,
blue as a thousand passports
cut from the sky.

—Nominated by the University of Arkansas–Fayetteville

Kara van de Graaf

Poem at the Bottom of the Allegheny River

Nothing miraculous. Maybe colder
than you thought, maybe darker,

maybe so dim you have to give up
seeing altogether, the way over centuries

certain fish on the bottoms of caves turned
pale as corpses, forfeited the luxury

of eyes. But it wouldn't matter. Here,
the surface is all lies, the moon halved

and distant, some neon streetlamp
that comes on like clockwork.

There's no mistaking the world
is shifting. The surface gluts back

on itself all day long, rocking,
as if trying to remember something

simple, something close—the time of day,
the drawn out syllables of its own name.

But the lesson of water is forgetting,
is taking any name at all. You know this

like a promise in the grayed brain,
a message bearing over you in waves

until you are swayed, until
you yield, malleable, and fine as silt.

—Nominated by the University of Wisconsin–Milwaukee

Eleanor Smith Tipton

Wheel and Shadow

—After Giorgio de Chirico

A statue looking into the horizon,
the sun coming or going. Its hand, not flesh:
upturned. A row of arches receding

into smokestacks without smoke. The train that is
or is not arriving. Its steam uplifted. Nothing
but an engine car glimpsed through the acute

angle of a colonnade. I can hear the dull ring
of an iron bell building from within the frame
like one whose synapses reach

for a phantom limb and feel its pulse
in an image traced by air. My body,
this derangement of alleles

into skin and crevice, now feels like
a child with a red wheel and shadow.
The mind sputters and burns

like a dusty stage lamp. I can see
my father's blue truck, his tool shed,
spreading across this day's grey edge.

The dinner bell (stilled) beside the magnolia tree.
My father driving, driving, driving,
cannot see his face, cannot hear his whistle.

And someone, my mother, (it must be)
when she was happy and poor, calling his name
until her voice becomes a glove nailed to the wall.

—Nominated by George Mason University

Lisa Fay Coutley

My Lake

My lake has many rooms and one, which is red
with a door that's always open but chained.
My lake owns boxing gloves. She owns lingerie.
She can swing, she can cha-cha, she can salsa
and tap but refuses a simple slow dance. My lake
learned early to rest the needle without a scratch.
She has been classically trained in lovemaking.
When she wants to ride a rollercoaster, she does
it alone. When she lets her hair down, men go
blind. My lake doesn't take any shit. She wears
stilettos in ice storms, does crosswords in pen.
She eats red meat. Her porch needs painting,
her flowers need weeding, but my lake reads
palms in twelve different languages. If my lake
puts her hand to your chest, she decides. At times,
whole days can pass when she won't let anyone
near her. She freezes just before she murders
her own shore. It's been years, and still my lake
won't name the delicate sound of ice taking,
then brushing away. She might say it's the train
of a wedding dress, or the rain falling on a glass

slipper. There are times she sees the grace of two loons gliding—their bodies a duet over breaking water, and she slows herself. She makes a cradle.

Tracey Knapp

Inheritance

I've been checking on your cats as you asked,
watering the plants that have since outgrown
their rotting baskets, and just today I noticed the skin

of mold festering on the old pot of coffee.
It reminded me of a field of algae on the pond out back
beyond the ruined railroad ties of this place,

once our grandma's house where her dogs
uprooted deer bones and nuzzled each other's butts
under a dim swarm of bees choking themselves

on pollen. We used to walk out back in the faltering
light and you pretended you were the mom
who let me sleep on the rocks and eat dirt.

I was always in your context—me, the shy one,
you with the freckled lips, your saggy hand-me-down
swimsuits, how our father loved you so effortlessly.

Remember when it downpoured and we were still up
in the old oak, the thunder throwing us around?
I might have cried or screamed in fear but there you were,

your large eyes electric with thrill, your fist
holding mine as the wet leaves stuck to our thighs
and we clung to the slippery trunk, laughing like crows.

How I was just your sister then, not the younger one
reflecting back our differences like a carnival mirror.
Never mind the blackberry thorns still stuck

in my palms from a little shove at the pricker bush.
Whatever. Nothing could fix my sullen face
like your hand pulling me over the neighbors' fence,

us both falling backwards into the waist-high grass.
Later, I loved your quiet devotion to my ankle
as you tweezed a drunken tick. Its ballooned body

popped between your fingers and we gasped at the blood.
Sometimes I followed you out back while our parents slept—
watched while your teenage boyfriend hauled the rotting logs

and threw them on the fires. Do you remember lying
down in the leaves and telling me to get lost?
which I always sort of did—your voice

lowly murmuring me away, your hair bright and full,
the light of the shimmering embers, his tan body
arcing over you. Sisters can make you feel so

small sometimes. Older now, and I'm still
exaggerating our differences: your chirpy laugh,
my combat boots. But despite your perfect breasts,

I can still sit out here on the lawn and drink the last
of the beer you left since he slipped you into his white Cadillac,
a giant envelope on softened wheels ripping down

the dirt roads and off into something like a sunset.
I have waited for you past the stars rising and the days
have dropped down before me, asked me knee-bent:

what do I own and who owns my life? I beg myself
for something other than my own words to answer: the crickets'
cyclic hymn, your hands braiding my hair behind me.

Linda S. Gottlieb

Green Knife-Sharpening Car

Women come out to greet him, armloads of boning knives,
scissors, sometimes an ax and often more than one cleaver.
They want to hurry to him, but the driveways are long
and their limbs bare and full of blades.
Where the backseat would have been,
his all-day whetstone, his feet foot-grind wheel,
and those women. They lean into the shade of his roof,
and watch sparks slick like skin under a sheet.
Inside our house, Uncle Bob hones knives on the edge
of a bone china plate, one from my mother's wedding set.
Father strops them done. My uncle calls me to him,
we need you close by us, closer,
and holds my arm above the elbow, hard.
When they have enough of me, when they stay dull,
I slow to my room, lie down on carpet, on damp
stomach, count coins into stacks, flatten bills, tight-clutch
cutlery hidden under my bed. Full flush with dollars
and dull utensils, I run to the man outside, his car, to wait my turn.

—Nominated by Johns Hopkins University

Hailey Leithauser

The Moon Speaks of Polar Bears

Some things are better defined
by what they are not,
as when snow heaping the world

replaces the world, becoming
no longer a rooftop, no longer a narrow
gravel shoreline or road,

even in times, in places,
no longer the black breathing
of the sea.

In this way the polar bear
stealing her difficult, beautiful life
from the ridges

and drifts, the colorless
plateau around her,
teaches her young to hunt

by sliding her belly
flat along the frozen light,
blunting her cloudlike

respiration, covering
with one comic paw
the dark flesh of her nose,

so well suited to artifice
that the oily
seals collecting the ice

are pulled by an intimate
landscape, soundless
and ravenous and white.

—Nominated by *Agni*

Matthew Kelsey

Frost Heave

Small stones crown the soil. Mayapple, brown
seeds of buttonbush crushed and the primrose

crimped in the yard beside the drive. Preparing to leave,
I think of you, mother, voice through which plants

catch as you recite them like an apology—
false violet, choke cherry, trembling aspen, vetch. Everything

seems vulnerable in the slush, the hobblebush,
the mess of seasons turning, as if sense

can be made from this place when put behind us, this
town we call a city, the Mohican cave long shut down,

and the falls we named ourselves after
dammed up and quiet at the foot of the mill.

Home is where the start is, only. I trust weeds
to overgrow their beds when I'm gone. I trust

in the end of things. Lovely for our names, if not
for some design, we will lose and lose again, then

become something unbecoming, unmoving, a list.
We will swear by the garden we lie beneath.

Clots of hosta, creepers, blue flags left
to surrender, crutch of silver maple, pinched

nerves of rhododendrons, mulch turned up
by the rain that starts like an engine and hisses

as it falls. Or, simply, it is raining. I am still
trying to leave. There is no perfect metaphor

for this, no word to wave off with.
No one means go when they say it.

M. Ann Hull

The Stutterer

        Loopscoopandpull,
        my tongue a reefknot, sheepknot,
        sheepshank.
The doctors
        a nauticalseascape
said it,
        on the wall
the doctors said it was my brain thinking
faster than my tongue could touch,
            deaffingerfast,
        the words reefknot,sheepknot,sheepshank.
I never said noose.
The doctors said it
        sails stitched of diploma paper
as though it explained what I wasn't saying.
        I never said nooseno.

In my bedroom, I made my dolls talk as women do,
            deaffingerfast,
until my mother's headache *Melissa,*
I love you, but you have to stop ached
        from bloody sunrise
        to a ring of blood on the moon.

In the classroom, I *Melissa, we like you but you…*
                  wouldn't say a word,
            I licked instead the salt of
            phoneme seas, palatal ks of
            keel in practice, practice,
                  and never said No.

In the teacher's room, I
                  never said my father
said he didn't love my mother with his hands
though his throat uttered words of other. I
            tied up tightly into myself
            bezoar balls of babydollhair
                  until I spat up strangle. I never
                  said noose. I never said he couldn't,
could ring his hands, reefknot,
              sheepknot, sheepshank into a bellknot,
ringing us home.

At home, my brain thinking faster than my mouth,
an extra bone I never stopped gnawing, I was
            a shark with freshcaughtkill
            who would not share a drop.

The doctors said I would
grow into my talk.
                  I never said No,
                  I never said helpherhelpher,
              I let the drowned alone.

Chloe Honum

Spring

Mother tried to take her life.
The icicles thawed.
The house, a wet coat
we couldn't put back on.

Still, the garden quickened,
the fields were firm.
Birds flew from the woods'
fingertips. Among the petals

and sticks and browning fruit,
we sat in the grass and
bickered, chained daisies, prayed.
All that falls is caught. Unless

it doesn't stop, like moonlight,
which has no pace to speak of,
falling through the cedar limbs,
falling through the rock.

Joshua Rivkin

Pastoral

You. The waves belly up to sand. *No You.* The ducks dive. *You.* City kids. They kick a starfish between them. *Bravado*, wrote a friend, *is the work of the gods.* We're fickle as coastlines. A woman with gray hair and binoculars walks over and picks up the sea star—she knows about these things—her fingers fit neatly in the space between the animal's body and arms. She shows them what they couldn't know by looking at the topside, it's curve and spike, defense and shimmer: nothing is alive inside. *Here, you can hold it if you want.* Hollow as wind off the bay. Empty vessel, empty room. Cavafy: rooms inside rooms, left vacant by bodies and left full by time: three wicker chairs, two yellow vases, the mirrored wardrobe, the lover's bed, and the afternoon light slipping from wall to wall to wall—all gone, all here. Past the waves, more waves. The woman leaves the kids to argue over their treasure: take it home or leave it. He holds the ocean to his ear. An arriving surf, a bird's wanting call, a world beyond this one. How lush this absence, how full is this room. Cavafy: *They must still be around somewhere, these old things.* How we try to leave them. How they call us back: *You. You. You.*

Stephen McDonald

Stories

Saturday mornings I surfaced to voices
of children in the other room, then sank again,

slipped into the green and brown algae-bloom
of sleep, the world above growing darker,

the stories fainter, until I couldn't breathe—
didn't want to anyway…Disappearances:

The way Chaucer's life ended, no record
of how or where, of funeral or burial.

The way Bierce passed into silence
beyond Chihuahua, or Weldon Kees,

his empty car at one end of the Golden Gate.
Once, in a visitors' center at a women's prison,

I read a child's storybook to inmates,
illustrations blue and gold cradled in my palms—

a bear, a mouse—wide-open eyes of lifers
brimming at the well of story, arms wrapped

around each other, the dried flower of cheek
against cheek, the way my sister one day

after school pressed her face to mine, whispered
the story of a grimy man who'd followed

her home on a bicycle, weaving like a drunk
from street to gutter, muttering his lewd

invitations, how our father, alarmed,
patrolled the streets for weeks, searching

for a monster, she admitted years later,
she'd created from nothing. Would it surprise

you to hear she had come to believe her own
story? That for years a man with teeth broken

and yellow had cycled through her dreams?
Perhaps you have seen him—as have I.

Today, in a shed behind a church, I sit
at a splintered table, shovels and hoes

hanging from hooks, voices rising like golden
fish in a dark pond. I have surfaced again.

I have come to hear the stories, to tell
my own, to see if by coming I will come to.

Brent Newsom

Esther Green Moves Out of the Sunset Acres Mobile Home Community

1.
Every day, more faded ghosts
of family past: last week,
cleaning out a drawer, photos
I didn't know you kept. You and me
holding cane poles with bluegill on the lines,
you beaming while I squint
into the sun; Easter, me and our girls
dolled up in white straw hats,
matching floral dresses I sewed
from *McCall's* patterns; our youngest
graduating elementary the year before
she passed. And one
before kids, *The Queen*
inked on back in blue.

2.
Weekends, England's queen camps out
in Windsor Castle, the Union Jack
flying high to show she's home.

On the pristine lawn, she lets loose
whichever four corgis she's brought along.
All this I learned from the satellite's
Biography channel, which you would never watch
with me. *People's private lives,*
you'd say and rise, head outside
for a smoke. But what's private
about being queen? If you were here
you'd listen to what I liked the best:
a whole room in the state apartments
covered with portraits. Alive with spirits.

3.
No one's left for me to rule
inside the wood-grain walls
of our double-wide kingdom:
the girls off making their own babies
with boyfriends or common law husbands;
you gone. Even without our furniture's
sagging fleur-de-lis, I could read
our history there—a brown crest
in the carpet where our oldest bled
after busting her head on the table's edge,
the lines in the avocado vinyl where,
for each night's supper, you scooted in.

4.
Raise a flag; make it black.
Your insurance bought this two-bedroom:
a brand new oven, my first lawn,

a pecan tree. But a scratch in the wood floor
is just a scratch. The walls are blank
as an empty gravestone, so I tape up
a photo—the one with the bluegill—
then set to unpacking, you
beaming down at me.

Joanna Pearson

After a Molar Pregnancy

Little no-child, wicked womb-fruit,
I grew you in your muscle suit,
my hidden chamber. There was blood,
cold jelly, sonograms: I understood
what you were not. Imposter,
snow blur on the screen, yet faster
than a baby fattening, you crept,
a boneless nightmare, while I slept,
and gobbled at the pith of me.
You blew my belly to its tympany;
with tissue fistfuls, clustered grapes,
shaped my silhouette—it apes
a fecund one, a waiting mother.
But you are no one, and no other
life is housed here, doleful mess
of giddy blebs, translucent flesh,
yet still I listen carefully and murmur
nothings to your ghostly human brother.

Megan Grumbling

Leaving the Room

This is the trick: Get out of where you are
in your deliberate home—kitchen gestalt

in paring knife, colander, clocksure ribs
of juicer, every perfect thing in synch

and place, spigot and looking glass; bookshelves
that loom the living room—and limn yourself

into the doorway, a safe place to fail
against, neither this room nor that. Now splay

soles into dovetails, hands to jamb. Exert
flush full against the frame. You will yield first,

but wait—hold it a spell. Hold hard. Quake. Tick
off sixty down to naught. This is the trick

the young play on themselves, seeking a swerve
from known to nigh, ceding to ghost stunt, nerve

and reflex. Once the countdown swoons to none,
release your stance, loose self, tilt shelves, welcome

the phantom rising: two freed arms in flight
from sill and you, will shilling its own sleight.

—Nominated by *Memorious*

Stephanie Pippin

Afterimage

In Pompeii every girl is a fresco—
her right hand held in front of her stomach,
her left arm bent at the elbow.
Closed in her robe's smooth
volutes, she gives no hint of how
it must have sounded

so like the neighbors breaking
each other again. Song
of black-eye, song of fist.
Song of sometimes you make me
a little bit crazy, sometimes
you make me insane.

The lost are like this. Misheard,
slightly bent, a faint
assault on my dreaming.

It is perilous to be resilient
and a little sentimental.
It is enough to know

the clouds came down
on shuttered rooms. Then
the tremble, then the hush.

How can I be rid of these
swans painted on plaster,
this sky of promiscuous wings,
when I still see them
deckle-edged and rolling with smoke.
Their jeweled eyes lamp the ash.

Nathan McClain

Landscape with Goats

> *—after Felix Meseck*

I.)

We had entered a time
Of famine. The few
Crops nodded in the wind

Like withered old men
Who couldn't remember

Anything but themselves
Nodding, nodding & not
Knowing what they were

Saying yes to—I was
Saying yes to our bodies

Holding water in the absence
Of flesh. You were saying
Yes to feeling large & empty

As the eyes of an ocean.
A bird we couldn't name

Sat on a branch every morning
Heavy with the news of spring
Being gone. We found

Two goats roaming, their tongues
Worn from wearing

Trees down to the water
Feeding their leaves. They were
Sick & began eating one

Another, as though they were
Their own medicine.

II.) *Reprise*

We wondered how long we had
Been sitting across from each other
At the kitchen table with nothing
Between us.

Erin Gay

Portrait Sealed in an Apothecary Jar

In the backyards of my youth, I was in love with all of my sisters. It was a fence we cut out of paper, drawings of morning glory vines, those muted trumpets. The pharmacist collected our pillow secrets and strung them around strangers' necks.

Strangers jealous to break the roots and make their own tea. Lovelorn: you poured water until there was nothing to taste.

There is a mineral spring I follow back to the heat where orchids grow, the slow pouting of lower lips.

I was a fern / I was a release. Sarsaparilla. Sassafras.

I was a bramble.

We were wild among the thousand irises. Catalogued in lithographs from those mornings we lay still enough to outline.

Flora: it was a long drive before I found you again under the July rot, that porous heat, we rubbed the pollen into my lace. We were bee lovers, holding the stingers between our lips, our helmeted warriors pulling away. We were swollen, swelling.

Those lavish toxins—swimming in our own treatises on the intricate weave of vessels knotted in our hearts.

We were gold leaf pressed between pages of the apothecary's handbook. We were the years painted on the insides of jars, we were the wax seal with our own initials.

Debts: those jars we buried under an ordinary field.

Sharon Fain

Angola, 2002

1.

I watched children in the streets
near my daughter's flat and marveled
at my inability to make things
even the slightest bit better for them.

Successful escapees from war,
they foraged beneath market stalls
for fruit and slivers of roasted meat,
then slept side-by-side in stairwells
or close to trash fires in vacant lots.

Now peace had come. They wanted to go home,
washed their shirts beneath spigots
in the municipal garden
where cape jasmine and hibiscus bloomed.

I was used to being necessary
but in that country of the young,
that country of few survivors,

I was old and suspect
walking the cracked pavement,
graffiti scrawled in Portuguese or Umbundu
mysterious as markings on the moon.

2.

My daughter showed me her statistics—
malaria, polio, land mines, dysentery.

We were out on the Ilha, at Club Miami,
owned, as so many things were,
by relatives of the country's president.
Ten U.S. dollars to use a beach chair,
the customers mainly locals, but a few aid workers
and some oil rig guys down from Cabinda,
lifting glasses of Castle lager, talking price per barrel.

Most people didn't talk, just closed their eyes.
That mile-long, breezy sand bar—
the closest thing to not being in Africa at all.

It was the year my grandchild was born,
grew chubby and thrived, a fearless one,
in love with sand, its grittiness against damp skin.
My daughter drank limonada, sighed.
Gulls strutted along the seawalls
pulling tiny crabs from beneath stones.

Then as if she had decided something, the baby
for the first time crawled away from us,
moving fast toward the water.
She would not be deterred.
I jumped and danced and waved my arms
back and forth in front of her,
laughed when she laughed, made the sea
unreachable. That was something I could do.

Todd Dillard

Brother Mailed His Thumb

Brother mailed his thumb home from the war. I kept it in my coat pocket. It wiggled against my side during choir practice, crawled back and forth across my desk in class.

Other children had similar gifts: Billy ate soup from his sister's shoulder blade, the quiet girl cupped an ear in her palms like the Eucharist.

The war continued: newspapers spelled Winning with a million words, no mention of a prize.

Meanwhile, the thumb slowed, hardened into a rock. I rolled it like a marble across the sidewalk until it smoothed into a piece of chalk, used it to scratch my height on my bedroom door.

It was the season to meet under the kissing tree. Billy etched names on its trunk with a white needle, confessed he was renouncing all soups. I held the quiet girl's hands in mine, slowly drew close to her dust-caked lips.

Jeff Baker

April Blizzard

White whips of spindrift
                    beneath the street lights' fission—
a snowdrift climbs the door (one dare not open) like a cresting
wave—
          and though the softened light inside their hulls
suggests a giddy warmth,
                  the buses sign OUT OF SERVICE
and quit their routes.
               The blocky ghost of a mailbox haunts
the corner where steam breaks
                  from the mouth of a manhole.
When it's like this,
             the body dallies too sweetly with its lead
shadow and the mind contracts like a dwarf star—densethought.
Outside, the white branches snap—
                novas of downed
power lines—and the body's osseous ideogram must fold
into its sleep.
          When it's like this, the postman comes
approaching the darkened windows.

                              Is it difficult to believe

green shoots have pushed up

                        beneath the banks of snow

and that, like so, our dreads and joys record themselves

upon a single ground?

                    Postcard and postcard and postcard

fills up these idling trucks parked side by side.

                            Tomorrow

a blue suitcase, hidden beneath the junipers,

will throw itself open.

                Tomorrow birdsong,

                          the reappearance

of a child's wagon covered by snowplows,

                        nature loosening

itself like a muscle that can kill.

                      Tomorrow a warm breeze

across a windowsill littered with capsized flies and

robins hopping

              their shabby goddamn scansion in the grass.

Eugenia Leigh

Every Hair on Your Head

> *Every hair on your head is counted.*
> *You are worth hundreds of sparrows.*
> —Sparklehorse

—For Mark Linkous, RIP

The day you pushed a bullet through your heart,
the length of a day on earth shortened by a millionth of a second.

That same day, a NASA satellite captured an image of a dust storm,
Chile withstood its one hundred thirtieth aftershock in a week, and I
glimpsed a bird, twitching

on the floor of a Brooklyn metro station. Its eyeballs
bulged as if to literally absorb the ocular world

and I shuddered away. For hours, I saw that flinching
creature in my mind. I saw hundreds of similar birds
shimmering into the station to lie

next to it—a quilt of silvery bodies tiled wing to wing. On good days,
I want to be saved. Most days, I want
every savior in our hell—so they'll know
torment in the bloodstream—death's whistling, ceaseless,
blurring the cleanest heartbeats.   My first time, I was thirteen.

I tested five pills. My stomach barely ached, I ate ramen, lived, solved
math problems. But for days before that, I envisioned my body
smeared. Inside out. A swarthy, dazzling canvas.

What I wouldn't give to graze that silence.

Did you do it standing up
or crouching?   Which was the bigger surprise—
                        the gun punching   or the angel catching you?

Sarah Sousa

Leaving Maine

I thought of the abandoned farmhouse
in the woods where we found the red couch
spilling its white plush, spiked
all over with porcupine quills.
We stole the floorboards
for the cabin we were building
in your mother's backyard, you lowering
them to me one by one
through an upstairs window.
There aren't manuals on how to be so poor.
We imagined fixing up the house,
pruning the small orchard. The kitchen sink drained
through a pipe in the wall; we'd use the water
for our garden. We even made a plan
to find the owner, ask if he would sell
the place, cheap. For the time being, we took
what we needed: a box of canning jars,
a shelf covered in aged floral wallpaper
to hold my cookbooks; the flowers' black
centers like ink bleeding through.
I thought of Japanese landscape painting:

crooked branches and orange blossoms. Birds
perched and alighting like blossoms.
We would be the smudges
on the side of a distant mountain.

Brandi George

Dear Beauty,

You are a child's marble face, glued lips,
blush of twilight at his throat; blood—
how the whole earth can fit inside its color;
cut flowers—cheerful snap
of limb from body; waiting,
like falling. And isn't it a cold river,
the bottom untouched by a human foot?

Create in me blue spruce, trillium, limestone.
Let me be mountains.

The purple phlegm of a ghost; my shut heart;
my shut, watery heart; that woman's hands
on my chest—her spinning crown; the caw
of tires as Mother speeds away; Psalms—
let the bones you have crushed arc
around my bed with wings outstretched,
whisper like wind through leaves.

Grandmother, imagine your daughter's dark eyes
a demon's—your husband who crept

inside your daughter's dream-skin;
a slick, silt-footed nightmare—always a mirror's
breath from inside me; insects impaled
with pins; keys buried in the ditch; phantoms
with mouths like wilting petals.

Of all the gates to heaven, I choose an eye:
Formidable iris, unhinge. Horses tumble
through clouds as I tumble through daylight.
May it never end, this feathered thing.

Adam Houle

The Reddish Cur

Out she clambers
from beneath the keel-up canoe
left to rot in switch grass

and is not the lone fox the cops
first thought. Agents, noose snares
and tranquilizers, voices

that fracture the radio wire
converge. All these trappings
of capture after a woman

is yoked down on a dead-end
Georgia road by a pack of dogs
gone mad for lack of collars,

lack of names. After the first lunge
there's no quit. They mauled the man
who hoped to bring her home.

The disastrous plays good odds.
Then happens. Then happens again.
The rest is aftermath, and that jaw-snap

dance of teeth and fur rises as one
to meet the county's men
sent to collect and kill.

They rise as one except that one
reddish cur, who looks back, then leaves
past spindled trees behind the canoe,

slinks and disappears into shadows
hemmed by splintered fence posts.

—Nominated by Texas Tech University

Steven C. Brown Jr.

Penumbra

The rain jars are all filled up.
The yard's almost potable
with bright wet bowls.
Dogs, bulking like potatoes,
lap spores from off their drinking holes.

Clouds collect, flake, and fold
the sun to wincing
silkworms in the trees
where evening rests its injured elbows.

I've mistaken the habits of this hour—
the mayflies wilding wetly
on the sidewalk kliegs, the cast
of a soft windowlight
like gods in the dogs' mouths.

Water deepens every ordinance of dirt,
every high-and-dry.
So the daughters of this world
spit dimes into their flowerpots

where rings on rings rinse
orbital, with rhythms of inconsequence,
except that each ring
makes new welcome to the ends.

And near the porch's bulbshine,
the sons reach out
to touch a simple fluttering,
only to see
the bones within their hands.

Angie Macri

A Song for Fever

Your new word today is *hot*, for dishwasher steam,
for fire on the TV exploding in South St. Louis, live,
helicopters hovering and no one knowing why or what
is burning. Midmorning, you stand and cry, Motrin
in its fifth hour and your truck not turning right
and your pen not drawing right. You tuck your forehead
under my chin so that your lashes open into the hollow
of my throat, with my voice and pulses. Your breaths
rapid under my hands. I hold you and promise, you
will feel better, and I drop medicine like neon into
your mouth and give juice from cups plastic with puppies
until you sleep fitful as a leaf or decide to run again,
despite fever, despite the ozone alert, trying the doorknob
and saying, *I go*. You stop just once to call a rose the sun.

—Nominated by *Southern Indiana Review*

Rebecca Lehmann

The Factory, An Elegy in Six Parts

1. The Managers

The Managers are giving silver dollars to our children,
are telling them that if they are good, they can have our jobs
once we've died. Inside the Factory we step on the steel
grating of the stairs tenuously, we operate with levers
and cogs, with finger-stained red buttons that read:
Push here in case of emergency. We dream of pitch blue sunsets
at night, of our children skipping ropes woven from reedgrass
in the center of a deserted parking lot. All their feet
lifting at the same time, all their reed ropes whooshing
against the pristine concrete, the silver dollars flipping
in their pockets—one coin per pocket, one pocket per child.

2. Call and Response

Manager: The motor smoked and tilted, unexpectedly.

Me: I sat on the chinked-metal mat and broke the socket wrench.

Manager: The conveyor belt twisted out of shape.

Me: The long ditch grass where your feet step.
In the Factory, in the darkness, I am wondering how to name
the next passage of time.

Manager: Iridescent and beating to get to you.

Me: Even at this hour when the pavement has cooled.
None of my thoughts powerful, none moved the leaf flow.

Manager: I have given you the warning.

Me: The rest of the clunky machinery slid
through my fingers: my summer slip,
the red rose necklace, the two horse hitch.

Afterword: It's my own headache, caught up with me.
That's what the Managers tell me,
shaking their fists over fuck-wit fires.

3. Managerial Meeting

Factory A:
Output as maximal. No kerchiefs. No hazing.
No vending of hotdogs on Factory grounds.
Manufacture of: Holiday napkins, paper towel,
toilet paper (ass wipe—chortle, chortle), cocktail
napkins, scented and colored toilet paper (chortle—
ass wipe), Fourth of Juuuu-ly red-white-&-blue
napkins and paper towels with firework imprint
patterns, disposable paper bibs with front pockets
to catch spilled food from baby's mouth.

Factory B:
Output as efficient. More levers needed and
conveyor belt 11847c in need of repair. Gum
banned on Factory grounds. Manufacture of:
paper hospital gowns, paper booties, tampons
and sanitary napkins (cunt rags—chortle, chortle),
disposable diapers, paper coffee filters, sterile
paper hospital sheets, paper targets for shooting
ranges in shape of deer heads, paper targets for
shooting ranges in shape of human torsos,
disposable paper drinking cups with butterfly
pattern or alternate space ship pattern for boys.

Summation:
Calculation of losses: tax deductible and plashing.
Calculation of net gains: calculation compromised
by faulty abacus and lack of accurate statistics.
Calculation of employee breast size: adequate
(chortle, chortle).

4. Randall's Lament

Funny the colors that flow from our mouths,
quaking and pressed to the whitewashed walls.
The Managers all on balconies parading.
Dear Beatrice, I cannot feel your hand
in mine any more. Please send word if you are
still all okay. Found a bundle of toothpicks
under the machine from Todd's bad habit
of chewing them and spitting them.
Now Todd is being reprimanded. Polish
the gleaming metal until it says I love you.
Ammonia as a hard-strung savior. Dear Beatrice,
The children paraded past the window
this morning. Where are you now?
Todd is missing a tooth. The way to salvation
to admit guilt and culpability. So say
the Managers, all mighty and around us.
They are all sparkling and laughing
in their white coats and shined shoes. I think
they must be made of the dust of the universe,
the very best dust of the very biggest bang.

Beatrice's reply: Dear Randall, I am a cadet
in red and am all day feeling like swimming
in the pulp vats. And yesterday a man
was fished out like nothing, drowned.
Our Managers are also a-sparkle. Wave
to the children when they pass the next time,
and remember I am only six times six.

5. A Trial Is a Way to Find Guilt

Find me wicked or don't.
As the solution to a problem,
with streamers. At the old
park, the stranger on the car's
hood, the bloated water tower,
bold black letters spelling
the Factory's name. The teenagers
ready to take my place, eager,
and some in suits, and some
in coveralls. The noose. The pinecones
and puffball mushrooms
arranged as a crown. The squirrels
watching from the oaks. If I say,
This is what we were, the Managers
respond, So be it. The switch
on my back and on your back.

If I say, Mercy, the Managers
respond, Let the worker
swing from the neck until dead
or bluing. The grass bulging
fingers reaching for my feet.
The sky like a bathtub
emptying, the sun a glob
of blond hair clogging its drain.

6. Memo to All Workers

If we, Managers, supervise the crease machine.
If you, workers, operate on multiple levels.
If kerchiefs are banned on Factory grounds.
If each conveyor belt ticks along smoothly.
If there is no incident of ruckus among you.
If the windows are blackened. If the windows
are opened. If air conditioning is installed.
You will not mention Todd or toothpicks.
You will not mention Beatrice and Randall.
You will not cover your breasts with baggy
T-shirts any longer but will wear requisite
uniforms without complaint, unless you are
men, and then T-shirts are okay for now.
You will not mention the park. Your children
marching past the windows every morning
and afternoon, the sight of their cuffed
socks and saddle shoes. You will not steal
sanitary napkins from the cunt rag production
area of Factory B. You will hum the national
anthem while you work. On key. Not in F,
but in F-sharp because sharps are happy.
You will wear work gloves when necessary.
You will tell us, the Managers, that we look
very nice when we are supervising your work
or walking on the balconies above you.
You will not get headaches. You will not
get headaches. You will not get headaches.
You will practice reverence, and it will flood

you like coolant, like the river below the Factory,
overflowing with rain, covering your former homes.

—Nominated by *Contrary*

Melanie McCabe

Paperboy

At twelve, I could only see the seventeen-year-old boy
as a gift. A fluke from God. More real to me

now than his face—his bicep in the twilight, his stack
of undelivered *Evening Stars*, my shoe

stubbing at the shafts of grass that violated
the driveway bricks. I have no memory of language—

only of loitering, lingering far past curfew to circle
each other as leaf-cindered air turned gray, as

the huge shadow of the hickory, cut from sudden
streetlight, swallowed us from view.

What words did I say that made him return, dusk
after dusk, throughout that smoky autumn?

My mother was lost in steam, stirring. My father fell
asleep beside his Manhattan, the half-read mail.

I dawdled along the yard's perimeter, knowing longing
without knowing what I longed for. The voice

that rose in him was bass—my own voice,
vibrato. I was reedy—a flute. A straw. Desire

outstripped my body. His bones were tall—head
lost in the hickory limbs. He smelled of something

I knew. Like nothing I knew. He came to me
from the top of the street. He lived nowhere

I'd ever been. But every morning I split his window
with dangerous light. I lodged like a splinter in his day.

There was nothing to see and no one saw it. In fireplaces,
crumpled news crackled and lit; red embers breached

the chimneys. Something broken beat and beat the air—
a shutter, unhinged—a warped door that wouldn't close.

Eric Smith

Story Problems

Let's start with two trains
  clattering out of two stations
    nearly two thousand miles apart,
miraculously
on time, twinned steel skins
  winking in early light
    beneath two skies textbook
in their cloudy- and blue-ness.

The trains' passengers
  and related baggage are equal
    in number. Their respective conductors
are of similar weight
and jocularity.
  Assume wind speed, elevation
    and the demands of
small children remain constant.

Train A sheds the platform's
  nervous buzz, the waving hankies
    of tearful grandmas,

and angles southward.
B will head north, leaving
  behind a gaggle of
    stewards in white gloves
bored and anachronistic.

Let's say I'm on A,
  juddering along at 55
    through every inbred speed trap
mud-bogged dirt track hell
with combo liquor store-
  slash-post office. Here,
    rust red tracks clatter through
unkempt hills dotted with herds

of single-wide trailers.
  B leaves later with you on it,
    an arrow hitting 70
through interstitial
countryside quilted with
  brittle wheat chevrons.
    Shorebirds have followed you.
The sun's disc tills the horizon.

But before day dies,
  too tired for any more puzzles,
    take what we know. Let's work this out
hypothetically.
Given distance, time,
  and where we want to be,

in which one-horse whistle stop
does the story end? Let's say

you've been given me,
    the ever-variable x—
        ex-boy, ex-toy, execrable
break-up mixtape maker.
Diagram the poor ex-
    cuses I'll cram through
        the mail slot.

Or roughly halfway
    look up as our trains pull out,
        leaving from some Podunk Nowhere,
and we happen to catch
glimpses of each other
    on separate trains,
        our angles of coincidence
equaling the sum of longing.

Or there's an accident.
    A lineman got his signals crossed
        and flipped the track switcher too soon.
News crews eat it up.
One train plus one train
    equals one train. Today
        equals one burning
field, my hand plus or minus yours.

Teresa Breeden

Waiting on Spring

This torn and flattened brush
last year's tumbleweeds
that failed to tumble, leavings
of the desert, a rash
raised from dust,
the hum of recycled air, a catch
in my lover's inhale, the fold
inside what isn't said—
consider
how time unfolds truth, the crane
again only paper,
creased from a bird's barreling heart, the heart
failing to tumble, the leavings, the hum, the burden
of soil under the rain—
rash, unfastened—
crocus, wild sage.

Jake Ricafrente

The Funeralgoers

> *—for L.*

> *Only two things do not do to me,*
> *Then I will not hide myself from You:*
> *Withdraw Your hand far from me,*
> *And let not the dread of You make me afraid.*
> *—Job 13:20–21*

1. *Before the Service*

The minor deaths of fall accumulate.
Outside, unfastened from their old-growth roots,
The unfashionably-colored leaves fall straight
To the ground. Inside, the men adjust their suits:

They tighten their ties in the foyer, they yank
Their sleeves, they refold handkerchiefs, and tease
Each other about golf handicaps and swank
New Saabs. They toss around their idle-ese

Until the women, dressed in matching greys
And blacks, begin to weep while recollecting
L.—Wife, Mother, Friend—in abject praise.
The children stop. The double doors protecting

Us from them are shut, per our request,
So we have time before we lay her to rest.

2. *In the Hospital*

We took our time when putting her to rest
In the well-attired hospital room where "Get
Well Soon!" mylar balloons, pots of wilting
Forget-me-nots gave way to bedpans, compressed
O_2, and extra emesis basins set
Beside the bed. Three ladies sat by, quilting

From poplin aprons, pleated skirts, black crepe
Blouses—and not her assless gowns—a relic,
A future's artifact, Plan B. They saved
The scraps for batting, learned to stitch, used tape
To pattern from her estate-sale plates, those angelic
Pink figures on the rim. Some broke. L. braved

It all, said, "Suffer the little children." So quietly
Each woman filled a pocket, purse, or planner
With hems from her old clothes, laced them in shoes,
Tied them on husbands' wrists, as Christmas tree
Trimmings, around her bed rails when she began her
Treatment: keepsakes they had to know they'd lose.

3. *Snapshots*

The VHS is damning: him in Ray-
Ban aviators, white tux on their big day,
While she wore shoulder pads the size of sails.
The garter mid-air. The crasher who caught her bouquet.

Her daughter's first dance, first homecoming, first prom:
L. took-in, altered, glued ribbons to a mum
("Go Bulldogs!"). She slipped a twenty-dollar bill
Into her daughter's purse and signed it, "Love, Mom."

The holiday's black-tie *Simbang Gabi*:
Though prepared for by a stirring homily
About love, she was always moved to tears
By the words, "Do this in remembrance of me."

4. *En Route*

When the radio preacher says he knows the way
Is narrow, I wonder if "he" means God. The street
I'm on—one-lane, skid-marked, de-paved by wear—
Stretches Emmaus-long, and I drive while rain
Drips honey-like down "Slow" signs, a rustworn shed,
And billboards selling yesteryear's delights:

Tall Coca-Cola bottles, glass Christmas lights,
The Avon lady's seasonal array
From '91 (her full bouffant, her "Red
Earth" lips), and *The Morning Talk with Pastor Pete*.

The road is slick, like Pastor's Pete campaign
For us, the listeners, to "Prepare

For Jesus!" Inside my car, the stagnant air
And preacher's voice return me to a night's
Events, ten years before: To the refrain
Of *Hallelujah!*, *Amen!*, and "Trust and Obey,"
I stepped into the waters to repeat
My birth, accepting death and life, blood shed

For me, the genesis, a widow who bled
For years until she touched a hem, and a stair-
case meant to climb straight up to heaven. *Sweet*
Mercy! Praise! Not much done with schoolyard fights
Or Ninja Turtle action figures, I went the way
Of parents, siblings, L.—to whiten my stains.

Years later, L.'s thinning body wracked by pain-
staking doses and biopsies, we spread
That quilt across her bed in a display
Of faith. We laid our hands on her (in prayer)
And drizzled oil, yet nothing but the night's
Sleep came. Now, I drink my bourbon neat,

Replace the bottle beneath my bucket seat,
And drive, alone, past fallow fields and grain
Silos emptied of harvest. The rain recites
Its rage against the bright "Road Narrows Ahead"
And cuts the radio's reception. I near
The gathered milling near the chapel, and grey

Noise fills the car. Soon, side-by-side in pews, our sights
On L., we'll note the weeping and flat piano strains.
For now, I stare at my Maker's Mark and shake my head.

5. *The Service*

"She's gone to meet her Maker." Some shake their heads
At this and cry. Some twist frayed fabrics around
Their wrists and shuffle feet and pray the threads
Won't break. Inside the chapel, faces stare
At the lilies, mums, and roses that surround
Deincarnated L. and light the room.

We're hushed. Her daughter's smudged mascara brocades
Her cheeks. As the congregation—men in shades,
Muted children, and women smoothing out their gloom
With handkerchiefs—begins "Our Father," I
Turn away, retreat outside, ask *Why?*—
My seventy times seven times—in prayer.

For now, the world holds its breath. What's left awaits
The deaths that former, finer fall accommodates.

Graham Hillard

What the Ground Gives

After the topsoil had gone, washed away
by a crisp autumn of rain, stones migrated

to the surface and sat like dead testaments
in the clay, their faces aching for the sun.

The smoothness of them—things from the earth
should be rough and unknowable—surprised me,

and I pried one loose, a massive rock, and held it
to my nose, inhaling... fire? root? wood-smoke?

Or winter, settling in the throat like pepper,
coarse on the tongue like sand. There is

the possibility, after all, that we are alone.
I will take what the ground gives.

dawn lonsinger

The Economist's Daughter

Wherever she goes, trees follow, flash their blank
greenback hands in deaf applause, nervous

excitement, as if to flag her down or surrender,
as if to imply a state of emergency, carve up the wealth

of light, but she walks through the forest
that clumps around her like it's the biggest nothing

to note. Despite this ticker-tape parading,
she skips to the slow messy churning

of her own heart. She shies away from addition
but gathers lilacs in her skirt, arcs her back into

a bridge to broaden her own custody. She seems
confident that her interest will not falter.

She tells her father that in her dream there was enough
water for everyone to go swimming, but

he only hears a faint fraction. He's too busy
listening to registers humming, money heaping

like bees to the hive. Her dreams may be instrumental
since he's always on the lookout for an apt metaphor—

"The economy is a small girl in the blight of morning;
it's an ocean, the tossing about of slippery schools

of glittery fish; it's butter—smeared, whipped, melting.
The economy is bubble, crater, rocket, a green shoot."

She has gone outside again, into the glut of spindly things,
amid the dim cloying microbes poised over the dumb yard.

He's trying to coin just the right phrase, to say succinctly
what we are about to lose. He's pacing, thinking things

can't get more fraught, but when he looks out the window
he sees all the leaves suddenly drop down around her

softly like play money. It is the most beautiful schism,
a plunder he can not name. He can see in her eyes—

all spark and slalom—that she is not easily enumerated.
She is a bright light in a landscape of numbers;

when she smiles the zeroes flower into lust.

—Nominated by the University of Utah

Stephen Ackerman

A Small Obsession

He could ride a bicycle backwards and when he did
"He thought he was the cat's meow," his wife said.
Thank you for my eyes, thank you for opening my eyes.
Thank you for my idyllic childhood, long summer days
Outdoors and food in the kitchen, your glove oiled
To dark chocolate, it folds like a book, old, soft leather first baseman's
Mitt, foundered on a reef of grief when you died,
One extra large sob at your wake and several years
Of intermittent self-pity of which I am proud.
Thank you for adultery, it makes life vivid as when
I kicked the grill in the garage and one triangular leg
Impaled the sheet rock and there hung, waiting
For summer, for skewed suburban summer, for skewered
Idyllic summer. Oh, thank you for my eyes! Which weep,
Which are hazel like your wife's eyes, which wear glasses
To read the fine print, which is where beauty is, in the text
And in the footnotes, in the woven sheets with the high
Thread count, in a firm handshake (for which I must thank you).
They are a foreign race to me, who shake hands diffidently.
Were their fathers not Marines? Did they have idyllic childhoods
With long summer days and fathers who worked

And came home from work and played catch and read
The paper, days so long the mail was delivered twice
And so long ago that actual letters arrived, morning and
Afternoon, punctuated by the dash of lunch
On the run, screen door slapping the frame.
You introduced the world to me, in all its
Famous complexity, but only after providing
The simplicity of long summer days,
Deep woods, slow currents, open fields, cobalt clouds.
This poem is a coffin, and a resurrection.
To mourn the dead is not a small obsession.

Sheri Allen

June Arrival, Gainesville

The Midwest was a month behind you.
Fallen oranges moldered underfoot.
Your teeth shook from cicadas' crescendos.
An earthworm wide as a finger unfanned
over its pulsing vein, reminding you
of your lover across the Mississippi.
Oily leaves crowded in. Wherever you walked,
something at the edge of your vision moved
faster than you. Breathing the heavy air,
you dreamt of open sky, but your skin could not
forget where it was in this brutal abundance.

Benjamin Pryor

New Year's Resolve

Recalling things I need to fix in brittle January,
       shingles and soffit gone mossy, I rub
              my jackknife sharp on a whetstone dug

from grandfather's creek. Porch sitting.
       Imperial pines like threatening sky poles.
              Iced star thistle and spare brushstrokes

in branches moved by winter wind,
       sundown light cached with quickness
              to arrive. A squirrel shuttling leaves

in a terracotta pot reminds me of beer cans
       left there at Thanksgiving—I guzzled
              peace behind the house when parents

drove down to feast, the charity in this.
       I tote frozen cans to the bin at the road
              and see a crippled deer commanding a herd,

his front leg jutting awkwardly mid-stride.
       He leads a scattering in the secrecy of my woods—
              they follow his lack of hesitation closely.

Meighan Sharp

Habitats

1.
When asked about his favorite creature
at the zoo, my son replies, *that statue
of the turtle*, and I wonder if we've lived
in the city too long. From our window,
all winter, we've watched the padlocked Shrine lot
empty and fill—mostly colorful flocks
of old people perched on the stairs, flapping
and chittering, and once a parade train, trapped
clowns peering out their windows at the rain.
And we glanced back from our glass shell, the chain
of the fence and barbed wire between us. But three
thick oaks huddle on the pavement's periphery;
when snow comes, the blacktop's history
as a field blooms, and birds find what it used to be.

2.
After watching chickadees shimmy and thrum
the spiked wire again, my son and I, stunned
by the spark of March's warm days, the last
blackened patches of retreating snow, cast

our eyes up Mill Mountain. I think he needs
the zoo, the playground sprouting plastic trees,
the gaudy watch of the neon star. But,
no—he wants a green hill where he can cut
dead sticks, balance tree bark roofs over
toys shut inside all winter. He plucks clover.
We nestle our heads on the hill's fertile
slope; the ants make their way to his hair. He
curls his face to my stomach, asks me
to block the sun, to pretend he's still a turtle.

Emily Louise Smith

After Reading about How to Attract Martins to Gourd Houses

I, too, long to dive into a pool of sky, mayflies
and stinkbugs on my lips. All the good songs

are like purple clouds with a pulse. I think of home
as a familiar hole. By now I've swallowed my share

of sand, a baby tooth once, whole worlds
I'd imagined for us. Aren't all apartments

openings for sadness? And doesn't a songbird
nest inside of every hollow tear?

Sarah J. Wangler

A Bawl-Ass Remembers Her Childhood

Hen pecks blonde skull, mistakes me for corn silk.
I run, blood in eyes, to Daddy's embrace.
I lie in a hayfield, squish wild strawberries
Between gums & upper lip, call it mumps.
Border collie, mean from years of cow herds,
Stands over me, tears off bits of cheek.
Hungry growls like purrs escape his beard.
Push my bike up the yard, look as garbage
Man dumps our trash in his compactor & crash
Into mom's tractor-tire flowerbed.
Smash my mouth into gripless handlebar.
Crash, cry hand over mouth, show off red teeth.
My lip's no longer attached to my gums.
At the dentist, we learn that I am hard.
I carry ginger water for a ride
Around the field, sit on tractor fender.
Watch a New Holland hay mower spit fawn hunks
Like leg, bone, hock—beat on Daddy's back
When he doesn't hear me shout, *Stop, Daddy*.
A brother teaches me to sink or swim:
Throws me from pontoon boat in fifteen foot

Deep seaweed, snapper, & snake infested water.
Watch Daddy clip tails off border collie
Pups, crocodile tears on my raw cheeks.
Like Stubby, my attacker, they're worth more
Tailless. Grubby toddler hands reach up to
Squeeze Daddy's five-o-clock shadow. I say,
You cut off one more tail & I'll choke you.
I lose an incisor: string & slammed door.
My gray tabby cat Buffy gets hit by
The hay mower while I pull weeds in the beans
& watch Daddy cut hay. Chunks of her dry
In the sun. Crows peck bits from rows of clover.
When it rains, I become a zoo animal,
Captured under bars of a mattressless
Burnt orange pullout couch by brothers.
A rooster chases me out of his coop,
Toes bloodied. Birds are slaughtered with hatchet,
Hung on wire to drip. A rented plucker
Whirrs. I jump on the trampoline, watch, dread
Breezy metal scream, feathers whirl from pink
& white bodies. A gust of wind blows me,
In midair, off the tramp & I land hard,
Ankle broken: late again to supper.
I ride on an unloaded hay wagon,
Scootch off while it moves, hope to look cool.
Dangle from waistband caught on nail, dangle
While tires crunch stones, my jeans rip. Brothers
Stop Daddy—I earn the Indian name
Hung By Butt for this, nee Little Fawn.
Run, leave an ice-cream pail of blackberries

For the blackbear & her cubs, pedal two
Miles home, vessels in my lungs burst.
I breathe tinny blood, gulp water, lead Dad
& gun to a honeytree, then bears' den.
I can honey like I can chicken: hot.
We don snowsuits in May, sneak into steers'
Pens with Mom's camera, ride rodeo til
Wind's knocked from me, slink home with bluer backs.
We tie bulls' tails, hide torn flesh in rafters.
Rotted boards support roofs for haymow forts.
Minnie Mouser has a bum ovary,
Pregnant every heat cycle, she miscarries
Every other batch. Dad thinks she's dying.
A brother shoots my cat, dumps her body.
They tell me she ran away, but I know.
I find her in the swale, soggy & gnawed.
Bury her with dried stump of kitten cells.
I stay gone, a ruddy fawn bedded down
In a patch of wild berries. Farmwork waits
For no-one but some afternoons, a brother
Finds me, his lips also strawberry red.

Douglas S. Jones

Drinking Slow, Waiting for Weather

We drop ice in warm water
To hear the obsidian crack
Split silence in our hands.

This storm floats like a jellyfish,
Dropping its invisible veil of weight.

We drink with the speed of Sunday,
Count two water rings on the table
And play a game of numerology:

Parking tickets, days since your birthday,
Chickens in Carbon County…

Staring through my glass, another world,
Almost blind, curves like a tall man
Drinking from a fountain.

A strong wind picks up in prairie grass,
Takes the blooms from snail vines.
Clouds gather their voices,

Shout across darkened fat.
A spit of lightning
One alligator…
Two alligator…

Distance cracks against our roof.

Kate Angus

Inside My Sleep

You wrote three poems
to explain your absence. Someone else
was a broken red cup

on the floor. This collection of words
arrived this morning as if a train
inside me had carried them from a deep forest

to a city closer to the surface layers
where the outside world
always tugs on my skin. Other words

have less direction but are a feeling
more like a concrete thing. Absence
is also a razor—pliable silver blade in the mouth. Nesting

is a curled fetal motion, the tiny "g"
the umbilical cord hanging down. If a word is a sound
then "asp" is a hissing

slither around the corner
in the dark. "Hasp" is not just a door lock
but air's rattle in an old man's mouth—

this is a little like dying
and so are the stagnant ponds that fester within. Bogs
where the water has no current. Algae blooms

a wild bilious green. Dragonflies skim
over the surface, shimmer
eye-blue as bluebottle flies do when,

trapped on the wrong side of the window,
they hurl themselves over
and over again against glass.

—Nominated by The New School

Iain Haley Pollock

Upon Irremediable Shores, Those Who Never Had Time

We see the hunt of a cardinal, male,
more flamboyant for digging in the snow
after seeds set loose in the blizzard.

In the powder's mute and stop-motion, nothing
but the beating of the clock, replica of Victoria Station,
1905. Here's the real memory: on Olvera Street

I bought a marionette of Pancho Villa
riddled with nine bullets. And the false:
during my ninth birthday party, I swung

at a piñata mâchéd into Christ's burning heart
crowned with a thicket of blackberry thorns.
If we broke open this heart with a broomstick,

what sweetness would fall into the dust?
Does it matter that my family has no history

of senility or dementia? The women,
those with no fondness for tobacco,
live forever. The men die of mustard gas,

the Old Crow brand of bourbon, arrest—
cardiac or criminal. Oh, but my mother jigged
with Jim Crow once, first little black girl

to sit downstairs, not in *nigger heaven*, and butter
her face with popcorn at *That Darn Cat!*,

the Lee Theater, Hampton, Virginia.
Me, how will my first be diagnosed?
And the real: *Batter my Wounded Knee*. And
the false: *Bury my heart at three person'd God.*

Monika Zobel

On the Corner of Guilt and Ash

I lived two bus stops
from forgiveness.

On Wednesdays we confessed
        our sins to the butcher.
                Then prayed
to the blade steak.

Night was a lost boot,
        day had moved
                on, barefoot.

I went to school
        in abandoned
swimming pools,

studied the cracked
        tiles on the steps—

learned how to say
>   *I want to be one*
>>   in fragments.

We kept an owl as a pet
>   so we knew when night fell.
>>   The ocean always responded
with rejection letters.

When the windows grew
>   shut with moss,
>>   I took the bus
two stations south.

Kai Carlson-Wee

Thresher

There has to be a tree. There has to be
a sky. There has to be a chicken-hawk
skating the dust rising out of a thresher.
A ploughboy walking with a turtle
in the head-high corn. There has to be a pool
with a swirly slide entering the water.
A chain-link cut by the field where I took
Kerri-Ann to the river when the river
was flooded. A burnt knife lettering
her knee. And a song being played—
All the girls are gone, All the head-strong
good country girls are gone—from the window
of a painted Accord. Her father standing drunk
in the screen porch watching us dance.
There has to be light falling into his body.
And a muskie we pull from the mud puddles
under the tracks. A reason we throw it
in the pool where it wobbles and floats
in the shivering wave-lines. Her father still
watching us dance in his sleep. There has to be
a fight, a cross-fade of landscape surrounding

those liquor-marked breaths. Him catching
her thigh. The two of them wishing to god
they were drunker. And the black lines
of telephone wires rise quiet as old men
or grocery store crosses. The scarecrow
in silhouette losing its face in the hyper-
colored dust and the clouds. There has to be
light. And a circling car. And a song
moving out of his body like something
he names. A chicken-hawk rising
on dust trails over the ditch where the boy
now plays. The river still flooded,
the dissipated clouds in the late-day in awe
of their own color fading. There has to be
a flood. And a promise of love. And a fish
in the pool, and the pool gone dark
where the turtle glides under the leaves.

Luke Johnson

Remembering the Old Testament while Walking the Dog

Cobwebs pearl on the hedge-top while the dog
leans on the roots. This part of morning it's just us
and the old-timers taking our walks, a light frost

still dusting the shadowed half of the yard,
sunlight brimming over roofs newly shingled
since the windstorm last month brought down

a live power line into a pile of leaves,
whipping up a wildfire. Then, the whole valley
smelled like a woodstove during a white winter,

smoke drifting for the sky like morning fog
lifting—What does it mean to be holy, to be
in one place thinking of another, to hear a voice

come from something burning, something alive
fizzling away?—one of those mornings, the only sound
came from a woodpecker hammering an oak tree.

I stood still, listening, straining to hear the fire.

James Arthur

Independence

We are famous friends, here to get drunk,
stoned, here for the fireworks,
the night of Independence Day.

Ovals spawning xeroxed ovals across a gassy sky,
each boom pursuing its fiery halo. *Happy marriage!,*
someone cries. *I do, I don't,*
                                    I might someday.
Here's to the stars and bars!
To my bed, and you having nowhere else to go—

bring a kiss, not your clothes … *To the sky!,*
bright as a bottle shard … To optimism,
                and all the states, even the boring ones.

I know you … the skin graft on your cheek,
your lost dog, your *can't-sleep*. I might as well
be your own hand. Jesus Christ!—

take off his ring, keep it off,
and put a ring on me.

Rachel Langille

Telescope

> *The blank pages of the book are so bright they almost pour up from themselves.*
> —Nancy Eimers

Towel spread on the grass those almost thirty years ago, early
June garden, when I looked up from a sun-dazzled page
toward the house and checked the time—
two children on their way from school, the baby upstairs napping,
her second-floor windows high above
our valley of streams and ferns. I feel still that exact

warmth of sun on skin, heat rising from earth
and page and the shimmer inside the freckled
rhododendron blossoms, close to the water's edge. I knew
my marriage empty, though it wouldn't end
for twenty years: goldfish finning intentionless
through sunlit green

in the lower pond—his absence then
to Germany, England, Ottawa. Goldfish stir these shadows
still, as I dream at night of children mixing pine-cone
soup in sand pails, while I sing and set out evening
dinner on a blanket, lighting candles in that courtyard garden
beneath the first moon-edge we start to see.

Matthew Ostapchuk

Eulogy for the Method

My grandmother explained to me
how the window frame warped
when the grand piano was forced
through by men with biceps the size
of railway cars because the space
between the front door and the stairs
was too tight for goliaths and genius.

She told me how as a little girl
she beheld the rise and fall
of an empire borne on the back
of a tortoise; how the children
lined up in the street, sticks like
rifles on their shoulders, paraded
as the creature, exhausted, hauled

the deadweight into the sea. She
told me how age had turned
her poems to dust, the letters
calcified, and how tiny cities sprung
up on the remains of every period,

oceans around the corpse of every
comma, and if she listened closely

there was celebration. The apartment
manager found her body, dressed
in clothes once fine, ivory lace now
an argyle of dust and paisley stains
of mildew. There was a note pinned
to her favorite hat, the one that looked
like an elephant's foot, which read:

I have witnessed a century of rot
from the perspective of a worm.
Cleaning out from under the antique
Sheraton chaise after the funeral,
I found her treasures: a brandy bottle;
ticket stubs for a theater that never
existed; a black pearl; two dead birds.

Alison Palmer

Vertigo

The rivers have jumped ship.

I know my place among the missing.

Huddled in my home, the water
is cold at my feet. The wooden rafters
sink from weight. And I wait.

This is the last day for walking
the ground. The cemetery,
lithe, its stones afloat.

Here come the deadened ones,
the gone too early, too late.

A concrete bassinet with chiseled
baby inside rests outside my door.

I watch through the window.
The living make their way
to higher ground, as the dead

take their lead from the water.
I open the door, signal to a man on
a raft, his family in tow.

This is more than lightness. This
is more than mere sorrow.
This is the world saying, here,
here is your way to travel.

—Nominated by *FIELD*

Contributors' Notes

STEPHEN ACKERMAN's poems have appeared in *The Antioch Review, Boulevard, Columbia Review, Lana Turner, Mudfish, Partisan Review, Ploughshares, Salamander, Seneca Review,* and *upstreet*. He holds a BA from Columbia University, an MA from Johns Hopkins, and a JD from Boston University School of Law. He has worked since 1989 as an attorney in the Legal Counsel Division of the New York City Law Department.

SHERI ALLEN received her MFA from the University of Florida and is currently a doctoral candidate at the University of Cincinnati, where she recently won honorable mention for the Jean Chimsky Poetry Prize. Her work is forthcoming in *Birmingham Poetry Review* and has appeared in *Subtropics, Image, Boulevard, Poetry Southeast,* and *The Sagarin Review*. She also translates medieval and renaissance-era kabbalistic rabbinic Hebrew poems into contemporary English.

MARY ANGELINO is in the MFA program at the University of Arkansas in Fayetteville. She has been published in *Diagram* and *Measure*, and is a poetry editor for the online journal *Linebreak*.

KATE ANGUS's work has appeared in *Barrow Street, Subtropics, Gulf Coast, North American Review, Third Coast, Mid-American Review, Barrelhouse,* and *Poet Lore*, among other places. She has a MFA in poetry from The New School and teaches at Gotham Writers' Workshop and LIM College. She lives in New York.

JAMES ARTHUR'S poems have appeared or are forthcoming in *The New Yorker, The New Republic, The Southern Review, Ploughshares, New England Review*, and *Narrative*. He has received a Wallace Stegner Fellowship, the Amy Lowell Travelling Poetry Scholarship, and a Discovery/The Nation Prize. His first book, *Charms Against Lightning*, is forthcoming from Copper Canyon Press.

JEFF BAKER was raised in the mountains of Tennessee, near the birthplace of the Cherokee genius Sequoyah. He has degrees from Tennessee Tech and the Iowa Writers' Workshop. Recently, his poems have appeared in *Blackbird, Copper Nickel,* and *The Cream City Review*. His book of poems has been a finalist for The National Poetry Series and The Bakeless Prize.

TERESA BREEDEN loathes winter—not in a sighing, swooning, beleaguered way, but in a sackcloth, teeth-gnashing, hair-tearing way. "Waiting on Spring" is about wading through the dead-time. A recipient of the 2007 Nevada Arts Council Fellowship, and a member of Ash Canyon Poets, Teresa's poetry has found homes in various journals and anthologies, including *California Quarterly, Mid-America Poetry Review, Ruah*, and *White Heron*. Her two best poems are her children.

STEVEN C. BROWN JR's poems were recently paired with Jerry Uelsmann's photography in a book titled *Moth and Bonelight*, published by 21st Editions in 2010. Individual poems have appeared in the *Indiana Review, Asheville Poetry Review, Barrow Street,* and *Measure*. Currently, Brown is a PhD student in Harvard's History of American Civilization Program. He also blogs on photography and poetry at www.sublimophile.blogspot.com.

KAI CARLSON-WEE was born in Minneapolis, Minnesota, in 1982, in a plain white room overlooking the Mississippi river. During high school he spent his time rollerblading and listening to a boombox in his parents' three car garage. After moving to California and failing to become a professional skater, he went back to school and began writing poetry. His work has appeared or is about to appear in *Miracle Monocle, Forklift Ohio,* and *Many Mountains Moving.* He is currently the design editor for the journal *Devil's Lake,* and is working on an MFA at the University of Wisconsin–Madison.

LISA FAY COUTLEY's chapbook, *In the Carnival of Breathing,* won the Fall 2009 Black River Chapbook Competition and is forthcoming from Black Lawrence Press in mid-2011. *Back-Talk,* her first chapbook, won the 2009 *ROOMS* chapbook contest and was released by Articles Press in 2010. She received her MFA from Northern Michigan University, where she was poetry editor for *Passages North,* and she is currently a vice-presidential fellow in the PhD program at the University of Utah.

TODD DILLARD received his MFA from Sarah Lawrence College. His work has appeared in *Lumina, Sub-Lit, NANO Fiction, Pebble Lake Review,* and elsewhere. His chapbook, *The Drowned Hymns,* is available from Jeanne Duval Editions. He lives in Brooklyn, where he is working on a book about a boy with a balloon for a head.

SHARON FAIN started writing poetry late, after her children were grown. Recipient of the Robinson Jeffers Tor House Prize, she is also the author of *Telling the Story Another Way,* which won the Pudding House Press Chapbook Prize. Her work has appeared in *Nimrod, Poetry East, The Literary Review, Spoon River Poetry Review, Arts & Letters, Southern Humanities Review* and other publications. Honors include a Pushcart nomination, a Marin Arts Council grant, a Paumanok Visiting Writer Award, a Visiting Reader appointment at the Poetry Center of Chicago, and residencies at Blue Mountain Center, I-Park, Byrdcliffe and the Anderson Center. Retired from the Counseling Department at City College of San Francisco, she lives part of the year in Ghana, enjoying time with her grandchildren.

ERIN GAY received her MFA in creative writing at Syracuse University. Her chapbook, *Portrait from the Tiniest Window,* was published by *Mid-American Review* (Fall 2006).

Other work has appeared in *Cake Train, Field, New Ohio Review, Ontario Review, Phoebe,* and *Web Conjunctions,* among others.

BRANDI GEORGE's poems, which have been nominated for a Pushcart Prize and the Ruth Lilly 2010, have appeared or are forthcoming in *Cimmaron Review, Fugue, Harpur Palate, The Dirty Napkin,* and *Quercus.* Brandi currently resides in Tallahassee, where she is finishing her MFA at Florida State University.

LINDA S. GOTTLIEB studied fiction writing at Princeton University before going on to receive her MFA in poetry from Johns Hopkins University, where she currently teaches creative writing. Born and raised in New York City, she splits her time between Baltimore and New York. "Green Knife-Sharpening Car" is her first published poem.

MEGAN GRUMBLING's work has appeared or is forthcoming in *Poetry, The Southern Review, The Iowa Review, The Antioch Review, The Indiana Review,* and other journals. She was awarded a Ruth Lilly Poetry Fellowship from the Poetry Foundation and received the Robert Frost Foundation Award for Poetry. She teaches writing at the University of New England and Southern Maine Community College, serves as reviews editor for the poetry and arts journal *The Café Review,* organizes literary events in a former Danish-Lutheran church for the non-profit Mayo Street Arts, and is theater critic for the *Portland Phoenix.*

GRAHAM HILLARD lives in Nashville, Tennessee, and teaches at Trevecca Nazarene University. His work has appeared widely, in such journals as *The Oxford American, Tar River Poetry,* and *Puerto del Sol.*

CHLOE HONUM's poems have appeared in *The Bellingham Review, Poetry, The Paris Review,* and elsewhere. She received a Ruth Lilly Fellowship from the Poetry Foundation in 2009. She currently lives in Provincetown, Massachusetts.

Born in Green Bay, Wisconsin, ADAM HOULE is a PhD student at Texas Tech University and holds an MA from Northern Michigan University. His work has appeared or is forthcoming in *AGNI* online, *Southeast Review, Meridian, Dogs Singing* (SalmonPoetry 2010), and elsewhere.

M. ANN HULL was a former poetry editor of *Black Warrior Review* and is currently an MFA candidate at the University of Alabama where she is the festival co-coordinator for Slash Pine Press. Her poems have most recently appeared in *Barrow Street, 32 Poems*, and *Quarterly West*.

LUKE JOHNSON is the author of *After the Ark* (NYQ Books, forthcoming 2011). His work has recently appeared in *32 Poems, Beloit Poetry Journal, Crab Orchard Review, Greensboro Review*, and elsewhere. He is a recent graduate of the MFA program at Hollins University and has received awards from the Academy of American Poets and the *Atlantic Monthly*, as well as a Tennessee Williams Scholarship from the Sewanee Writers' Conference. This is his second appearance in *Best New Poets*.

DOUGLAS S. JONES earned his MFA in creative writing from Arizona State University where he was the 2005 Theresa A. Wilhoit Fellow chosen by C.D. Wright. In 2007 he served as poet-in-residence at the University of Durham, England. His chapbook, *No Turning East*, is available from Pudding House Publications.

MATTHEW KELSEY's poems have appeared in *Clarion* and *Center*. He received his BA from Boston University and recently completed his MFA at the University of Washington. He currently lives in Seattle.

TRACEY KNAPP grew up in the Hudson River Valley of New York State, and currently lives in San Francisco. Her poems have appeared in numerous publications, including *Connotation Press: An Online Artifact, The Minnesota Review* and *Best New Poets 2008*.

Rachel Langille was born in Halifax, Nova Scotia, and raised in southwest Detroit. She holds a BA in Asian Studies, with a concentration in Chinese Language and Literature, an MA in English, and an MFA in Creative Writing (Vermont College of Fine Arts, 2007). Currently, she lives in Dearborn, Michigan, and teaches literature, creative writing, and composition courses at Mott College, in Flint. Her work has appeared in *Blue Earth Review, Comstock Review, English Journal, Iron Horse, Louisiana Literature, The MacGuffin, The Mochila Review, The Peralta Press, The Wallace Stevens Journal,* and other literary magazines, as well as in the anthology *I Have My Own Song for It: Modern Poems of Ohio* (University of Akron Press).

Rebecca Lehmann is originally from Wisconsin. Her poems have been published or are forthcoming in *Denver Quarterly, Tin House, The Iowa Review, The Gettysburg Review, Conduit,* and other journals. She holds an MFA from the Iowa Writers' Workshop, has been a Resident at The Millay Colony for the Arts, and is currently a PhD candidate at Florida State University, specializing in poetry and literary theory.

Eugenia Leigh is a Korean American poet born in Chicago. She holds an MFA in poetry from Sarah Lawrence College, and has led writing workshops for high school students and incarcerated youths. Eugenia received the *Poets & Writers Magazine*'s 2010 Amy Award, and and her poems have appeared or are forthcoming in *Kartika Review, The Los Angeles Review, The November 3rd Club,* and *Relief Journal,* among other publications.

Hailey Leithauser has recent or upcoming work in the *Gettysburg Review, Iowa Review, Pleiades, Poetry,* and *Best American Poetry 2010.* She recently won the Virginia Art of the Book Chapter Verse Contest, and her winning poem will be published as a limited edition broadside.

Dawn Lonsinger received her MFA from Cornell University, and is currently pursuing a PhD at the University of Utah. Her poems have appeared in *New Orleans Review,*

Sonora Review, Subtropics, Colorado Review, and elsewhere. She is the recipient of a Pushcart Prize, four Dorothy Sargent Rosenberg Prizes, Smartish Pace's Beullah Rose Poetry Prize, and a Fulbright Fellowship. Her chapbook, *the linoleum crop,* was chosen by Thomas Lux as the winner of the 2007 Jeanne Duval Editions Chapbook Contest; and her second chapbook, *The Nested Object,* was published in 2009 by Dancing Girl Press.

ANGIE MACRI's recent poems appear in *Crab Orchard Review, Quiddity,* and *roger,* among other journals, and her work was featured in *Spoon River Poetry Review.* She holds an MFA from the University of Arkansas and was awarded an individual artist fellowship from the Arkansas Arts Council. She lives in Little Rock with her husband and four children and teaches at Pulaski Technical College.

MELANIE MCCABE is a high school English and creative writing teacher in Arlington, Virginia. Her work has appeared on *Poetry Daily,* as well as in *The Georgia Review, The Massachusetts Review, CALYX, Barrow Street, Quarterly West, Nimrod, Harpur Palate, The Evansville Review,* and numerous other journals. Work is forthcoming in *The Cincinnati Review* and *Shenandoah.* She won second prize in Literal Latte's 2009 poetry contest and was a finalist for the 2009 Pablo Neruda Prize. Her manuscript *History of the Body* was a finalist for both the May Swenson Award and the Walt McDonald First-Book Prize from Texas Tech University.

NATHAN MCCLAIN currently lives and works in Los Angeles. His poems have recently appeared or are forthcoming in *Water-Stone Review, RHINO, Boxcar Poetry Review, Barn Owl Review,* and *Redactions: Poetry & Poetics.*

STEPHEN MCDONALD's poems have appeared in *RATTLE, The Crab Creek Review, Spillway, Blue Unicorn, The Sow's Ear Poetry Review, Passager, Pinyon, The Cresset,* and other journals. He was a finalist in the 2008 Sow's Ear Poetry Awards, received honorable mention in the 2006 *Passager* poetry competition, and was a semi-finalist in the 2004 Dana Awards and in the 2007 Finishing Line Press chapbook competition. His chapbook, *Where There Was No Pattern,* was published by Finishing Line Press in 2007. His book *House of Mirrors* will be published by Tebot Bach Press in 2011. He is an English professor and administrator at Palomar College in San Marcos, California.

BRENT NEWSOM's poems have appeared or are forthcoming in *The Southern Review, Subtropics, Cave Wall, New Delta Review,* and *Tar River Poetry,* among others. *America* magazine awarded him their 2009 Foley Poetry Prize. A doctoral student in English at Texas Tech University, he has spent 2010 on a Fulbright grant in Hangzhou, China, with his wife and son.

MATTHEW OSTAPCHUK is a graduate of the creative writing program at Chester College of New England and is pursuing his MFA at Hollins University. His poetry has appeared in *Collective Fallout, OVS Magazine, Splinter Generation,* and *Soundzine.* He is the editor of *Two-Bit Magazine.*

ALISON PALMER received her MFA from Washington University in St. Louis where she was nominated for the 2007 and 2008 AWP Journals Project. She graduated from Oberlin College with a BA in Creative Writing and was awarded the Emma Howell Memorial Poetry Prize. She has a poem forthcoming in *Used Cat,* and she has recently published in *The Laurel Review, Cannibal,* and *FIELD.*

JOANNA PEARSON was included previously in *Best New Poets 2005.* She completed her MD at the Johns Hopkins University School of Medicine and her MFA at The Johns Hopkins University Writing Seminars. Her poems have appeared recently in *Blackbird, The New Criterion, Tar River Poetry, Gulf Coast,* and others. She is currently a resident physician at Johns Hopkins.

STEPHANIE PIPPIN lives in St. Louis, Missouri.

IAIN HALEY POLLOCK lives in Philadelphia and teaches English at Chestnut Hill Academy. He earned an MFA from Syracuse University and is a former Fellow with the Cave Canem Workshop. His poems have appeared previously in *American Poetry Review, Boston Review,* and *Callaloo.*

BENJAMIN PRYOR's work has appeared in *The Oxford American, The Southern Review, Cimarron Review, Quarterly West, Subtropics, MiPOesias, The Wallace Stevens Journal, Dark Sky Magazine,* and *The North Carolina Literary Review,* among others. He lives in Chapel Hill.

JAKE RICAFRENTE holds an MFA from The Johns Hopkins University. His poems have appeared or are forthcoming in *The Cincinnati Review, Barrow Street, South Carolina Review,* and elsewhere.

JOSHUA RIVKIN's poems have appeared in or are forthcoming from *Virginia Quarterly Review, The Kenyon Review, Harvard Review, The Southern Review, AGNI Online, The Missouri Review,* and elsewhere. He has received fellowships from the Inprint-Brown Foundation, the Bread Loaf Writers' Conference, a travel fellowship to the Krakow Writer's Seminar, and a Wallace Stegner Fellowship in Poetry from Stanford University. He lives in California.

MEIGHAN SHARP grew up in pre-Microsoft Redmond, Washington, and lived in Oregon, South Carolina, and Kentucky before moving to southwest Virginia. She is an MFA candidate at Hollins University, where she serves as a teaching fellow and an assistant poetry editor for *The Hollins Critic.* Her work has appeared in *The Spoon River Poetry Review.* She lives in Roanoke with her husband and son, both of whom kindly tolerate her inclination to collect intriguing pieces of trash.

EMILY LOUISE SMITH's poems have appeared in *Columbia Poetry Review, Front Porch, The Journal, Smartish Pace,* and *Tar River Poetry,* among others. She has been awarded fellowships from the Virginia Center for the Creative Arts and the Hub City Writers Project in South Carolina, where she served as the 2006–07 writer-in-residence. She teaches publishing arts at the University of North Carolina Wilmington and is a founding editor of Lookout Books.

ERIC SMITH received an MFA from the University of Florida and an MA from Northern Michigan University. His poems appear or are forthcoming in *Green Mountains Review* and *Five Points*. He teaches at Marshall University and is the managing editor for *Cellpoems*.

SARAH SOUSA is a poet living in western Massachusetts with her husband and two sons. She received an MFA in poetry from the Bennington Writing Seminars. Her poems have appeared in literary journals including: *Smartish Pace, Spire Press, White Pelican Review*, and *Amoskeag: The Journal of Southern New Hampshire University*, as well as the Maine anthology *A Sense of Place*. Her book manuscript *To Stave Off Disaster* was a semi-finalist for the 2009 University of Akron Book prize and a finalist for both the 2010 Astrophil Press book prize and the John Ciardi Prize. She has poems in the current issues of *Weave, Inertia,* and *Eudaimonia* and a poem forthcoming in *Clare Magazine* of Cardinal Stritch University.

ELEANOR SMITH TIPTON is the poetry editor of *So to Speak: A Feminist Journal of Language and Art* and an MFA candidate at George Mason University. She is the recipient of the Virginia Downs Poetry Award, and her poetry is published in *Front Porch* and forthcoming in *Pleiades: A Journal of New Writing*.

KARA VAN DE GRAAF is a doctoral student in English and creative writing at University of Wisconsin–Milwaukee where she also serves as an assistant editor at *The Cream City Review*. She received her MFA in poetry from the University of Pittsburgh. Her poems are forthcoming in *Ninth Letter* and *Indiana Review*.

SARAH J. WANGLER is an MFA candidate in poetry at Oklahoma State University, and she holds an MA in English from Northern Michigan University. Her work has appeared recently in *The Superstition Review, Di Mezzo Il Mare, Cardinal Sins,* & elsewhere. She is an editorial assistant for the *Cimarron Review.*

MONIKA ZOBEL was raised in northern Germany and has been living in the United States since 2001. She expects to receive her MFA in creative writing from San Diego State University spring 2011. For the past two years, she has been working as a contributing editor at *Poetry International.* Her translations of Gottfried Benn, Bertolt Brecht, Paul Celan, and Günter Eich are forthcoming in issue 17 of *Poetry International.* Her own poems are forthcoming in *Zoland Poetry* and *Blue Moon Literary & Art Review* and have appeared online at *Counterexample Poetics.*

Acknowledgments

Stephen Ackerman's "A Small Obsession" previously published by *upstreet*.

Kate Angus's "Inside My Sleep" previously published by *Poet Lore*.

Lisa Fay Coutley's "My Lake" previously published by *Cave Wall*.

Sharon Fain's "Angola, 2002" previously published by *The Atlanta Review*.

Megan Grumbling's "Leaving the Room" previously published by *Memorious*.

Graham Hillard's "What the Ground Gives" previously published by *Regarding Arts and Letters*.

Chloe Honum's "Spring" previously published by *Poetry*.

Adam Houle's "The Reddish Cur" previously published by *The Southeast Review*.

Luke Johnson's "Remembering the Old Testament While Walking the Dog" previously published by *Third Coast*.

Douglas Jones's "Drinking Slow, Waiting for Weather" previously published by *The Fiddlehead*.

Tracey Knapp's "Inheritance" previously published by *Connotation Press: An Online Artifact*.

Rebecca Lehmann's "The Factory, An Elegy in Six Parts" previously published by *Contrary*.

Hailey Leithauser's "The Moon speaks of Polar Bears" previously published by *Agni*.

dawn lonsinger's "The Economist's Daughter" previously published by *IOU: New Writing on Money* (Concord Free Press).

Angie Macri's "A Song for Fever" previously published by *Southern Indiana Review*.

Melanie McCabe's "Paperboy" previously published by *Literal Latte*.

Alison Palmer's "Vertigo" previously published by *FIELD*.

Joshua Rivkin's "Pastoral" previously published by *Kenyon Review Online*.

Participating Magazines

32 Poems Magazine
P.O. Box 5824
Hyattsville, MD 20782
www.32poems.com

AGNI
Boston University
236 Bay State Road
Boston, MA 02215
www.bu.edu/agni

Alaska Quarterly Review
University of Alaska, Anchorage
3211 Providence Drive
Anchorage, AK 99508

Alligator Juniper
Prescott College
220 Grove Avenue
Prescott, AZ 86301
www.prescott.edu/alligator_juniper

Anti-
4237 Beethoven Avenue
Street Louis, MO 63116
anti-poetry.com

The Antioch Review
Antioch College
P.O. Box 148
Yellow Springs, OH 45387
www.antiochreview.org

Arsenic Lobster
1830 W. 18Th St
Chicago, IL 60608
arseniclobster.magere.com

Arts & Letters
Georgia College & State University
Campus Box 89
Milledgeville, GA 31061
al.gcsu.edu

Bamboo Ridge:
    Journal of Hawaii Literature and Arts
P.O. Box 61781
Honolulu, HI 96839-1781
www.bambooridge.com

Bat City Review
The University of Texas at Austin
Department of English
1 University Station B5000
Austin, TX 78712
www.batcityreview.com

Bellevue Literary Review
NYU School of Medicine
550 First Avenue, OBV-A612
New York, NY 10016
www.BLReview.org

Beloit Poetry Journal
P.O. Box 151
Farmington, ME 04938
www.bpj.org

The Bitter Oleander
4983 Tall Oaks Drive
Fayetteville, NY 13066-9776
www.bitteroleander.com

Black Warrior Review
University of Alabama
Box 862936
Tuscaloosa, AL 35486
bwr.ua.edu

Boston Review
35 Medford St.
Suite 302
Somerville, MA 02143
bostonreview.net

Boxcar Poetry Review
Boxcar Poetry Review
510 S. Ardmore Ave. Apt 307
Los Angeles, CA 90020
www.boxcarpoetry.com

Cave Wall
P.O. Box 29546
Greensboro, NC 27429-9546
www.cavewallpress.com

Cerise Press
P.O. Box 241187
Omaha, NE 68124
www.cerisepress.com

Colorado Review
Colorado State University
The Center for Literary Publishing
9105 Campus Delivery / Dept. of English
Fort Collins, CO 80523-9105
coloradoreview.colostate.edu

Contrary
3133 S. Emerald Avenue
Chicago, IL 60616
www.contrarymagazine.com

Dappled Things
2876 S. Abingdon Street, C-2
Arlington, VA 22206
www.dappledthings.org

The Dead Mule School of Southern Literature
Second Street
Washington, NC 27889
helenl.wordpress.com

Fence
Science Library 320
University at Albany
1400 Washington Avenue
Albany, NY 12222
www.fenceportal.org

FIELD: Contemporary Poetry and Poetics
Oberlin College Press
50 North Professor Street
Oberlin, OH 44074
www.oberlin.edu/ocpress

Florida Review
University of Central Florida
English Department
P.O. Box 161400
Orlando, FL 32816-1400
www.flreview.com

The Georgia Review
University of Georgia
285 S. Jackson Street
Athens, GA 30602-9009
www.thegeorgiareview.com

The Gettysburg Review
Gettysburg College
300 N. Washington Street
Gettysburg, PA 17325-1491
www.gettysburgreview.com

Gold Wake Press
5 Barry Street
Randolph, MA 02368
goldwakepress.org

The Greensboro Review
University of North Carolina, Greensboro
MFA Writing Program
3302 Moore Building
Greensboro, NC 27402-6170
www.greensbororeview.org

Guernica
395 Fort Washington Ave., Apt. 57
New York, NY 10033
www.guernicamag.com

Hampden-Sydney Poetry Review
Hampden-Sydney College
Box 66
Hampden Sydney, VA 23943
www.hsc.edu/academics/poetryreview

Harvard Review
Harvard University
Lamont Library
Cambridge, MA 02138
hcl.harvard.edu/harvardreview

Hayden's Ferry Review
Arizona State University
The Virginia G. Piper Center for
    Creative Writing
P.O. Box 875002
Tempe, AZ 85287-5002
www.haydensferryreview.org

The Hudson Review
684 Park Avenue
New York, NY 10065
www.hudsonreview.com

I M A G E
3307 Third Avenue West
Seattle, WA 98119
www.imagejournal.org

Indiana Review
Indiana University
Ballantine Hall 465
1020 E. Kirkwood Ave.
Bloomington, IN 47405-7103
www.indianareview.org

The Iowa Review
University of Iowa
308 EPB
Iowa City, IA 52242-1408

Juked
110 Westridge Drive
Tallahassee, FL 32304
www.juked.com

The Kenyon Review
Kenyon College
Finn House
102 W Wiggin St.
Gambier, OH 43022-9623
www.kenyonreview.org

Lyric Poetry Review
P.O. Box 2494
Bloomington, IN 47402
www.lyricreview.org

The MacGuffin
Schoolcraft College
18600 Haggerty Road
Livonia, MI 48152
www.macguffin.org

Memorious:
    A Journal of New Verse and Fiction
3424 Brookline Avenue, Apt 16
Cincinnati, OH 45220
www.memorious.org

Michigan Quarterly Review
University of Michigan
0576 Rackham Building
915 East Washington Street
Ann Arbor, MI 48019-1070
www.umich.edu/~mqr

Mid-American Review
Bowling Green State University
Department of English
Box W
Bowling Green, OH 43403
www.bgsu.edu/midamericanreview

The Minnetonka Review
P.O. Box 386
Spring Park, MN 55384
www.minnetonkareview.com

New Orleans Review
Loyola University
Box 195
Loyola University
New Orleans, LA 70118
www.neworleansreview.org

Nimrod
The University of Tulsa
800 S. Tucker Dr.
Tulsa, OK 74104-3189
www.utulsa.edu/nimrod

Northwest Review
University of Oregon
5243 University of Oregon
Eugene, OR 97403
nwr.uoregon.edu

Pank
Michigan Tech
1400 Townsend Dr.
Department of Humanities
Houghton, TX 49931
www.pankmagazine.com

Pleiades
The University of Central Missouri
Department of English and Philosophy
Martin 336
Warrensburg, MO 64093
www.ucmo.edu/englphil/pleiades

Ploughshares
Emerson College
120 Boylston St.
Boston, MA 02116
www.pshares.org

Poemeleon: A Journal of Poetry
www.poemeleon.org

Prairie Schooner
University of Nebraska–Lincoln
201 Andrews Hall
P.O. Box 880334
Lincoln, NE 68588-0334
prairieschooner.unl.edu

Rattle
12411 Ventura Blvd
Studio City, CA 91604
www.rattle.com

Raving Dove
P.O. Box 28
West Linn, OR 97068
www.ravingdove.org

River Styx
Big River Association
3547 Olive Street Suite 107
Saint Louis, MO 63103
www.riverstyx.org

Salamander
Suffolk University English Department
41 Temple Street
Boston, MA 02114
www.salamandermag.org

The Scrambler
834 Walker St.
Woodland, CA 95776
www.thescrambler.com

The Seattle Review
University of Washington
Box 354330
Seattle, WA 98195-4330

Seneca Review
Hobart and William Smith Colleges
Pulteney Street
Geneva, NY 14456
www.hws.edu/SenecaReview

Sentence
Firewheel Editions
Box 7
181 White St.
Danbury, CT 06810
www.firewheel-editions.org

Shenandoah
Washington and Lee University
Mattingly House
2 Lee Avenue
Lexington, VA 24450-0303
shenandoah.wlu.edu

Silenced Press
449 Vermont Place
Columbus, OH 43201
silencedpress.com

Southern Indiana Review
University of Southern Indiana
College of Liberal Arts
8600 University Boulevard
Evansville, IN 47712
www.southernindianareview.org

The Southwest Review
Southern Methodist University
6404 Hilltop Lane, Room 307
P.O. Box 750374
Dallas, TX 75275-0374
www.smu.edu/southwestreview

Sou'wester
Southern Illinois University
Dept. of English Language & Literature
Box 1438
Edwardsville, IL 62026-1438
www.siue.edu/ENGLISH/SW

Street Petersburg Review
Box 2888
Concord, NH 03301
www.stpetersburgreview.com

Stirring : A Literary Collection
Sundress Publications
323 Oglewood Ave
Knoxville, TN 37917
www.sundress.net/stirring

Subtropics
University of Florida
English Dept. P.O. Box 112075
Gainesville, FL 32611
www.english.ufl.edu/subtropics

Third Coast
Western Michigan University
Department of English
Western Michigan University
Kalamazoo, MI 49008-5331

Unsplendid
c/o Douglas Basford
169 Mariner St., Apt. 2
Buffalo, NY 14201
www.unsplendid.com

upstreet
Ledgetop Publishing
P.O. Box 105
205 Summit Road
Richmond, MA 01254-0105
www.upstreet-mag.org

Waccamaw
Department of English
Coastal Carolina University
Conway, SC 29526
www.waccamawjournal.com

Willow Springs
501 N Riverpoint BLVD Ste. 425
Spokane, WA 99201-3903
willowsprings.ewu.edu

The Yale Review
Yale University
P.O. Box 208243
New Haven, CT 06520-8243

ZYZZYVA
P.O. Box 590069
San Francisco, CA 94159-0069
www.zyzzyva.org

Canada

Apple Valley Review:
  A Journal of Contemporary Literature
c/o Queen's Postal Outlet
Box 12
Kingston, ON K7L 3R9
www.applevalleyreview.com

Event
Douglas College
P.O. Box 2503
New Westminster, BC V3L 5B2
event.douglas.bc.ca

Participating Writing Programs

MFA Program in Creative Writing
American University
Department of Literature
4400 Massachusetts Avenue N.W.
Washington, DC 20016

University Creative Writing Program
Arizona State
Creative Writing
English Department
Tempe, AZ 85287

Middlebury College
The Bread Loaf Writers' Conference
Kirk Alumni Center
Middlebury, VT 05753
www.middlebury.edu

Program in Literary Arts
Brown University
Box 1923
Providence, RI 02912
www.brown.edu/Departments/Literary_Arts

Creative Writing Program
Colorado State University
Department of English
359 Eddy Building
Fort Collins, CO 80523-1773

MFA in Creative Writing–Poetry
Columbia College Chicago
600 South Michigan Avenue
Chicago, IL 60660
www.colum.edu/academics/
    english_department/poetry/mfa.php

School of the Arts
Columbia University Writing Division
415 Dodge Hall
2960 Broadway, Room 400
New York, NY 10027-6902

Creative Writing Program
Inland Northwest Center for Writers
501 N Riverpoint Blvd Suite 425
Spokane, WA 99202
ewumfa.com

MFA in Creative Writing
Emerson College
120 Boylston Street
Boston, MA 02116-1596
emerson.edu

Fine Arts Work Center in Provincetown
24 Pearl Street
Provincetown, MA 02657
www.fawc.org

MFA Program in Creative Writing
Florida International University
Department of English
3000 N.E. 151st Street
North Miami, FL 33181

Department of English
Florida State University
Williams Building
Tallahassee, FL 32306-1580
english.fsu.edu/crw/index.html

Creative Writing Program
George Mason University
4400 University Drive
MS 3E4
Fairfax, VA 22030
creativewriting.gmu.edu

Creative Writing Program
Hollins University
P.O. Box 9677
Roanoke, VA 24020

MFA Program
Hunter College
68th and Lexington
New York, NY 10065

The Writing Seminars
The Johns Hopkins University
081 Gilman Hall
3400 North Charles Street
Baltimore, MD 21218-2690
writingseminars.jhu.edu

Writing Program
Kalamazoo College
English Dept.
1200 Academy St.
Kalamazoo, MI 49006
www.kzoo.edu/programs/?id=12

Creative Writing Program
Kansas State University
Department of English
108 ECS Building
Manhattan, KS 66506
www.ksu.edu/english/programs/cw.html

English Department
Louisiana State University
260 Allen
Baton Rouge, LA 70803
english.lsu.edu/dept/programs/
    creative_writing

Program in Creative Writing
McNeese State University
P.O. Box 92655
Lake Charles, LA 70609
www.mfa.mcneese.edu

Creative Writing Program
Minnesota State University, Mankato
230 Armstrong Hall
Mankato, MN 56001
www.english.mnsu.edu

Department of English
New Mexico State University
Box 30001
Department 3E
Las Cruces, NM 88003-8001
www.nmsu.edu

Graduate Writing Program
The New School
66 West 12th Street, Room 505
New York, NY 10011

Graduate Program in Creative Writing
New York University
58 W. 10th St
New York, NY 10011

MFA in Creative Writing
North Carolina State University
221 Tompkins Hall
Box 8105
Raleigh, NC 27695
english.chass.ncsu.edu/creativewriting

Creative Writing Program
Ohio State University
Department of English, 421 Denney Hall
164 West 17th Avenue
Columbus, OH 43210-1370
english.osu.edu/programs/creativewriting/
    default.cfm

Creative Writing
Ohio University
360 Ellis Hall
Athens, OH 45701
www.english.ohiou.edu/cw

MFA Creative Writing Program
Old Dominion University
5th floor, Batten Arts and Letters Building,
Hampton Boulevard
Norfolk, VA 23529
al.odu.edu/english/mfacw

Master of Fine Arts in Creative Writing
Pacific University
2403 College Way
Forest Grove, OR 97116
www.pacificu.edu/as/mfa

MFA in Creative Writing
Pennsylvania State University
Department of English
S. 144 Burrowes Building
University Park, PA 16802

Master of Fine Arts Program
San Diego State University
Department of English and
    Comparative Literature
San Diego, CA 92182

Office of Graduate Studies
Sarah Lawrence College
1 Mead Way
Bronxville, NY 10708-5999

MA in English, Creative Writing
Southeastern Missouri State
MS 2650, English Department
Cape Girardeau, MO 63701

Program in Creative Writing
Syracuse University
Department of English
401 Hall of Languages
Syracuse, NY 13244-1170

Creative Writing Program
Texas A&M University
Deptartment of English
Blocker 227 – TAMU 4227
College Station, TX 77843-4227

MFA Program in Creative Writing
Texas State University
Department of English
601 University Drive, Flowers Hall
San Marcos, TX 78666
www.txstate.edu

Creative Writing Program
Texas Tech University
English Department
Lubbock, TX 79409-3091
www.english.ttu.edu/cw

Fairbanks Program in Creative Writing
University of Alaska
Department of English
P.O. Box 755720
Fairbanks, AK 99775-5720
www.uaf.edu/english

Creative Writing Program
University of Arizona
Department of English
Modern Languages Bldg. #67
Tucson, AZ 85721-0067
cwp.web.arizona.edu

Program in Creative Writing
University of Arkansas
Department of English
333 Kimpel Hall
Fayetteville, AR 72701
www.uark.edu/depts/english/PCWT.html

Creative Writing Program
University of Denver
Department of English
2140 South Race Street
Denver, CO 80208
www.du.edu/english/gradcwr.html

MFA@FLA
University of Florida
Department of English
P.O. Box 11730
Gainesville, FL 32611-7310
www.english.ufl.edu/crw

Creative Writing Program
University of Hawaii
English Department
1733 Donaghho Road
Honolulu, HI 96822
www.english.hawaii.edu/cw

Creative Writing Program
University of Houston
Department of English
R. Cullen 229
Houston, TX 77204-3015

Creative Writing Program
University of Idaho
Department of English
Moscow, ID 83843-1102
www.class.uidaho.edu/english/CW/
    mfaprogram.html

Program for Writers
University of Illinois at Chicago
Department of English MC/162
601 South Morgan Street
Chicago, IL 60607-7120
www.uic.edu/depts/engl

Program in Creative Writing
University of Iowa
102 Dey House
507 North Clinton Street
Iowa City, IA 52242

MFA Program
University of Kansas
Wescoe Hall
Lawrence, KS 66405
www2.ku.edu/~englishmfa

Creative Writing Program
University of Maryland
Department of English
3119F Susquehanna Hall
College Park, MD 20742
www.english.umd.edu/programs/
    CreateWriting

MFA Program for Poets and Writers
University of Massachusetts
452 Bartlett Hall
130 Hicks Way
Amherst, MA 01003-9269
www.umass.edu/english/eng/mfa

Master of Fine Arts in English
University of Mississippi
Bondurant Hall C135
P.O. Box 1848
University, MS 38677-1848
www.olemiss.edu/depts/english/
    mfa/home.htm

Program in Creative Writing
University of Missouri–Columbia
Department of English
107 Tate Hall
Columbia, MO 65211
www.missouri.edu/~cwp

MFA in Creative Writing Program
University of Missouri–St. Louis
Department of English
8001 Natural Bridge Road
St. Louis, MO 63121
umsl.edu/~mfa

Creative Writing Program
University of Nebraska, Lincoln
Department of English
202 Andrews Hall
Lincoln, NE 68588-0333

MFA Writing Program
University of North Carolina, Greensboro
3302 HHRA
P.O. Box 26170
Greensboro, NC 27402-6170
www.mfagreensboro.org

Department of English
University of North Texas
1155 Union Circle #311307
Denton, TX 76203-5017
www.engl.unt.edu/grad/grad_creative.htm

Creative Writing Program
University of Notre Dame
356 O'Shaughnessy Hall
Notre Dame, IN 46556-0368
www.nd.edu/~alcwp

MFA in Writing Program
University of San Francisco
Program Office, Kalmanovitz Hall 302
2130 Fulton Street
San Francisco, CA 94117-1080

MFA Program
University of South Carolina
Department of English
Columbia, SC 29208

Graduate Program Creative Writing
University of South Florida
Department of English, CPR 107
4202 E. Fowler Avenue
Tampa, FL 33620
english.usf.edu/graduate/concentrations/
    cw/degrees

Michener Center for Writers
University of Texas
J. Frank Dobie House
702 East Dean Keeton Street
Austin, TX 78705
www.utexas.edu/academic/mcw

Creative Writing Program
University of Texas at Austin
1 University Station B5000
English Department
Austin, TX 78712

Creative Writing Program
University of Utah
255 South Central Campus Drive
Room 3500
Salt Lake City, UT 84112

MFA in Creative Writing
University of Wisconsin-Madison
Department of English
600 N. Park St.
Madison, WI 53706
www.creativewriting.wisc.edu

Creative Writing Program
University of Wisconsin–Milwaukee
Department of English
Box 413
Milwaukee, WI 53201

Creative Writing Program
University of Wyoming
Department of English
P.O. Box 3353
Laramie, WY 82071-2000
www.uwyo.edu/creativewriting

Unterberg Poetry Center/Writing Program
92nd Street Y
1395 Lexington Avenue
New York, NY 10128
www.92Y.org/poetry

Master of Fine Arts in Writing
Vermont College
36 College Street
Montpelier, VT 05602
www.vermontcollege.edu

MFA in Creative Writing Program
Virginia Commonwealth University
Department of English
P.O. Box 842005
Richmond, VA 23284-2005

Creative Writing Program
Wayne State University
English Department
5057 Woodward Ave., 9th floor
Detroit, MI 48202

Creative Writing Program
West Virginia University
Department of English
P.O. Box 6296
Morgantown, WV 26506-6269
www.as.wvu.edu/english

MFA in Creative and Professional Writing
Western Connecticut State University
181 White St.
Danbury, CT 06810
www.wcsu.edu/writing/mfa

Graduate Program in Creative Writing
Western Michigan University
Department of English
6th Floor Sprau
Kalamazoo, MI 49008-5092

Whidbey Writers Workshop
P.O. Box 639
Freeland, WA 98249
www.writeonwhidbey.org/mfa

Canada

Creative Writing Program
University of British Columbia
Buchanan E462-1866 Main Mall
Vancouver, BC V6T 1Z1
www.creativewriting.ubc.ca

MA in English, Literature,
    and Creative Writing
University of Windsor
2-104 Chrysler Hall North
Windsor, ON N9B 3P4
web4.uwindsor.ca/units/english

How to Study in College

EIGHTH EDITION

Walter Pauk
Cornell University, Emeritus

Ross J. Q. Owens

Houghton Mifflin Company
Boston   New York

Overview

To the Instructor of the Eighth Edition　　　　　　　　ix
To the Student　　　　　　　　　　　　　　　　　　xvii

Part I　Permanent Skills　　　　　　　　　　　1

1　Setting Goals　　　3
Establish some goals to add meaning—not only to your studies, but also to your life.

2　Controlling Your Time　　　21
When you develop ways to save time and stick to a schedule, you can control this precious resource.

3　Staying Focused　　　45
If you can't keep your mind on your work, all your efforts at learning will be wasted.

4　Defending Your Memory　　　59
With forgetfulness waging a constant war against your memory, the only way to succeed is to fight back.

5　Managing Stress　　　83
There are commonsense ways to avoid, cope with, and prepare yourself to face stress.

Part II　Enrichment Skills　　　　　　　113

6　Improving Your Reading　　　115
A faster pace and increased comprehension are what most of us look for in reading improvement.

7　Building a Lasting Vocabulary　　　131
When you combine the right kind of tools with genuine interest, you'll wind up with a vocabulary that lasts.

8 Thinking Visually   **159**
*Information can make a different kind of
sense when you look at things from a visual
perspective.*

Part III   Note-Taking Skills   181

**9 Adopting a
   Note-Taking Mindset**   **183**
*To gain full benefit from a lecture or read-
ing assignment, you need to be warmed up
and ready.*

10 Taking Effective Notes   **205**
*All the valuable information you read or
hear will be lost without a system for jotting
things down.*

11 Mastering Your Notes   **243**
*Reviewing, reciting, and reflecting team up
to make key ideas a permanent part of your
knowledge.*

Part IV   Test-Taking Skills   263

12 Managing Test Anxiety   **265**
*What's the simple solution to the appre-
hension that often accompanies tests?
Preparation!*

13 Answering Objective Tests   **283**
*Objective tests may come in different flavors,
but they all draw on the same fundamental
approach.*

14 Tackling Essay Tests   **305**
*Answering essay questions effectively
combines systematic test taking with basic
writing skills.*

Appendix: Answers   **323**

Index   **327**

Contents

To the Instructor of the Eighth Edition   *ix*
To the Student   *xvii*

Part I   Permanent Skills   1

1   Setting Goals   3

Marching to Your Own Rhythm   4
Resisting the Tug of the Crowd   5
Harnessing the Power of "Imaging"   6
Pursuing Quality Instead of Quantity   6
Changing the Meaning of GPA   10
Defining a Goal   10
Devising a Plan   12
Taking Action   13
FINAL WORDS   16
HAVE YOU MISSED SOMETHING?   16
WORDS IN CONTEXT   18
THE WORD HISTORY SYSTEM   19

2   Controlling Your Time   21

Saving Time   22
Finding "Hidden" Time   22
Changing Your Time Habits   24
Sticking to a Schedule   27

Dividing Your Time into Blocks   28
Thinking in Terms of Tasks   34
FINAL WORDS   39
Ten Valuable Tidbits About Time   39
HAVE YOU MISSED SOMETHING?   40
WORDS IN CONTEXT   42
THE WORD HISTORY SYSTEM   43

3   Staying Focused   45

Eliminating Distractions   47
Reducing External Distractions   47
Discouraging Internal Distractions   50
Cultivating Concentration   51
Making Lists   51
Taking Breaks   52
Maintaining a Balance   52
FINAL WORDS   54
HAVE YOU MISSED SOMETHING?   54
WORDS IN CONTEXT   56
THE WORD HISTORY SYSTEM   57

4 Defending Your Memory   59

Making an Effort to Remember   62
Avoiding Pseudo-Forgetting   62
Finding a Reason to Remember   62
**Setting the Size and Shape
of Your Memories**   64
Limiting What You Choose to Learn   65
Arriving at Meaningful Patterns   65
Strengthening Memories   66
Connecting New Memories to Old   66
Using Recitation to Rehearse   73
Allowing Memories Time to Jell   75
Studying in Short Periods   75
Coming to Terms with Plateaus   77
FINAL WORDS   77
HAVE YOU MISSED SOMETHING?   77
WORDS IN CONTEXT   80
THE WORD HISTORY SYSTEM   81

5 Managing Stress   83

Eliminating Avoidable Stress   84
Discouraging Procrastination   85
Minimizing Multitasking   87
Sidestepping Common Stressors   90
Improving Your Attitude   91
Learning to Relax   92
Improving Your Self-Esteem   94
Taking Control of Your Life   95
Following a Healthy Routine   97
Developing Good Eating Habits   98
Improving Your Sleep   101
Getting Some Exercise   106
FINAL WORDS   108
HAVE YOU MISSED SOMETHING?   108
WORDS IN CONTEXT   110
THE WORD HISTORY SYSTEM   111

Part II   Enrichment Skills   113

6 Improving Your Reading   115

Learning the Limitations of Speed   116
Watching Your Eye Movements   116
Hearing Your Silent Speech   118
Keeping Comprehension in Mind   119
Allowing Time for Consolidation   120
Developing Ways to Pick Up the PACE   120
P: Increasing Your Preparation   120
A: Determining Your Altitude   121
C: Reading in Clusters   123
E: Drawing on Experience   125
FINAL WORDS   126
HAVE YOU MISSED SOMETHING?   127

WORDS IN CONTEXT   128
THE WORD HISTORY SYSTEM   129

7 Building a Lasting Vocabulary   131

Harnessing the Power of Interest   132
Choosing the Right Tools   135
Learning from a Dictionary   135
Preserving Your Words on Index Cards   143
Exploring Your Personal Frontier   145
Understanding How Words Are Learned   146
Recognizing Frontier Words   147
Applying the Frontier System   148

Treating Words Like Chemical Compounds 148
Learning Roots and Prefixes 148
Using the Fourteen Master Words 151
Appreciating the Value of History 152
Finding Books That Tell the Stories of Words 153
FINAL WORDS 154
HAVE YOU MISSED SOMETHING? 155
WORDS IN CONTEXT 157
THE WORD HISTORY SYSTEM 157

8 Thinking Visually **159**

Using Your Whole Brain 160
Improving Your Understanding 161

Making Your Memory Stronger 161
Reading Pictures 161
Using the OPTIC System 162
Learning the Language of Graphs 162
Watching Out for Distorted Data 166
Writing in Pictures 169
Adding Illustrations to Your Notes 169
Turning Abstract Ideas into Maps 172
FINAL WORDS 176
HAVE YOU MISSED SOMETHING? 176
WORDS IN CONTEXT 178
THE WORD HISTORY SYSTEM 179

Part III   Note-Taking Skills **181**

9 Adopting a Note-Taking Mindset **183**

Preparing to Read 184
Getting Acquainted with Your Textbook 184
Surveying Specific Assignments 190
Preparing to Listen 192
Using Triple-A Listening 194
Setting the Table for the Next Lecture 198
FINAL WORDS 200
HAVE YOU MISSED SOMETHING? 200
WORDS IN CONTEXT 202
THE WORD HISTORY SYSTEM 203

10 Taking Effective Notes **205**

Starting with a System 207
Using the Cornell System 207
Marking Your Textbook 212

Gathering Information 215
Being Inquisitive 215
Following the Signs 219
Recording Efficiently 226
Dealing with Special Cases 227
Pulling Things Together 233
Leaving Lectures 233
Finishing Readings 233
Summing Up 234
FINAL WORDS 236
HAVE YOU MISSED SOMETHING? 237
WORDS IN CONTEXT 240
THE WORD HISTORY SYSTEM 241

11 Mastering Your Notes **243**

Reviewing to Cement Understanding 244
Targeting Key Ideas with the Q System 244
Seeing the Big Picture with Summaries 248

Reciting to Strengthen Memories   250
Reciting Out Loud   251
Reciting by Writing   251
Reflecting to Add Wisdom   252
Making the Case for Reflection   253

Using Techniques to Help You Reflect   254
FINAL WORDS   256
HAVE YOU MISSED SOMETHING?   258
WORDS IN CONTEXT   260
THE WORD HISTORY SYSTEM   261

Part IV   Test-Taking Skills   263

12   Managing Test Anxiety   265

Preparing Yourself Academically   266
Starting Early   266
Staying on Top of Your Coursework   267
Organizing Yourself   267
Cramming Systematically   272
Preparing Yourself Mentally   274
Finding Out About the Exam   275
Getting Acquainted with the Test Site   275
Maintaining a Positive Attitude   276
FINAL WORDS   278
HAVE YOU MISSED SOMETHING?   278
WORDS IN CONTEXT   280
THE WORD HISTORY SYSTEM   281

13   Answering Objective Tests   283

Choosing Effective Study Methods   284
Using the Q System   284
Becoming a Study "Switch Hitter"   284
Understanding Each Question Type   285
Separating True from False   285
Choosing the Right Answer   286
Finding the Best Match   289
Completing a Sentence   291
Moving Systematically Through the Test   292
Reading Before You Answer   293

Marking Methodically   297
FINAL WORDS   298
HAVE YOU MISSED SOMETHING?   299
WORDS IN CONTEXT   302
THE WORD HISTORY SYSTEM   303

14   Tackling Essay Tests   305

Moving Systematically Through the Test   306
Reading Before You Write   306
Jotting Before You Answer   307
Mapping Out Your Time   307
Knowing the Basics of Writing an Essay   308
Understanding Each Question
   with Precision   308
Supplying the Correct Answer   308
Supporting Your Points   310
Operating Under Time Constraints   311
Getting Right to the Point   311
Organizing Your Essay Carefully   314
Keeping Your Writing Neat   317
FINAL WORDS   318
HAVE YOU MISSED SOMETHING?   318
WORDS IN CONTEXT   320
THE WORD HISTORY SYSTEM   321

Appendix: Answers   323
Index   327

To the Instructor of the Eighth Edition

Students who are seeking help are not primarily interested in theory, and most of them have little patience with merely inspirational talk. They want practical instruction on how to succeed academically. They want something that they can readily understand and apply and that works. After a week of classes, they discover that the hit-or-miss tactics that got them through high school are grossly inadequate and inefficient at the competitive college level. So they turn to us for help.

Let's then teach these students proven techniques for studying and learning.

How to Study in College is brimming with exciting techniques, based on widely tested educational and learning theory, that have already helped myriad students. But the tail of theory is never allowed to wag the practical, feet-on-the-ground dog. While theory is always implicit and is sometimes given in enough detail to explain the rationale behind a particular technique or reassure the skeptic, it is never presented without explicit applications and never used simply as exhortation. After all, the person who needs penicillin is hardly cured by learning the history of antibiotics!

Because it is so crucial that students learn for the long term, we are wholeheartedly against techniques that stress mere memorization. Such techniques fill the mind with "knowledge" that melts away after a test and leaves learning still to be done. The techniques presented in this book result in real learning. And real learning, like a real diamond, lasts.

Finally, no textbook—no matter how complete or current—is truly useful if it is boring, confusing, or excessively difficult to read. We have worked hard to keep this book well organized and clear, maintaining a conversational tone so that reading it is like having a sincere, person-to-person chat.

What's Different in the Eighth Edition?

In this new edition, one completely new—and very important—thrust has been added. In addition, valuable changes and adjustments have been made throughout to material retained from the previous edition.

New! Questions in the Margins

The Cornell System, with its extra wide margin designed for jotting cues to use for recitation, has been around for more than forty years and served the test of time. But over time, our thinking about exactly what belongs in this margin has evolved. Initially it was keywords or phrases, but with memory research demonstrating the advantage of recall over mere recognition, we began to suggest using questions as an alternative to keywords. Why? Because formulating questions requires more than extracting a word or phrase from a paragraph's main idea; it actually encourages students to *think* about what's truly important in each paragraph. We call this use of marginal questions the Q System.

Of course, coming up with questions isn't always easy. We know that. While it is possible to extract a keyword or phrase almost mechanically, to arrive at a question you must truly understand a paragraph's meaning. We firmly believe this extra struggle is worth it, but understand how students who are unaccustomed to formulating questions may be reluctant or unsure of how to do so. That is why in this edition we have added questions in the margins throughout the text of this book.

This simple but dramatic step has the potential to revolutionize the way in which this book can be used as a study aid.

1. *It supplies concrete examples of how the main ideas can be used to formulate questions.* Students who are reluctant to use the Q System or unsure of how to begin now have page after page of examples to show them how it is done.
2. *It provides a built-in means for reviewing and reciting the book's important ideas.* By covering the text with a sheet of paper and using the Q System questions as cues, students will be able to more readily master the important material in each chapter.
3. *It offers an advantage over end-of-chapter summaries.* Unlike the summaries in previous editions, which could sometimes be hobbled by a shortage of space, the Q System questions provide a thorough review of every chapter. And because the questions are located alongside the paragraphs they refer to rather than at the end of the chapter, students always have the option of "drilling down" into a particular paragraph when curiosity or confusion leads them to conclude that the main idea alone is not enough.

4. *It provides an additional "entry point" for each chapter.* The approach that one student takes to learning new material may differ dramatically from that of another. The Q System recognizes the diversity of learning styles by providing another "route" for navigating the important ideas of a chapter. It is now possible to walk through each chapter, using the questions as landmarks.

Finally, although we feel that this new approach to *How to Study in College* is a breakthrough, we recognize that there may be some who would prefer to read, study, or teach the book "the old-fashioned way," without the benefit of the Q System's marginal questions. It is for this reason that we have made the questions ever-present but relatively unobtrusive. Rather than breaking up the text with questions, we have moved them off to the side and chosen a typeface and font size that don't dominate each page, thus making them a little easier to ignore if you should so choose. The slight increase in the book's size and the inclusion of marginal questions should in no way be construed as a change in the book's fundamental purpose and tone. *How to Study in College* is definitely not a workbook. It remains a book devoted to providing commonsense advice, systems, and techniques supported by in-the-field experience and established research.

New! Improved Navigation

The popularity of the World Wide Web has taught us a great deal about the way in which we approach the things we read. Internet experts refer to "navigation" to describe the way in which readers move through material to find the information they need. To that end, the standard table of contents can be helpful in pointing you to the precise page of a chapter or section you seek, but as that table of contents gets longer and more detailed another important element is lost: its ability to show you at a glance the overall organization of the textbook. Rather than simplifying our detailed table of contents to provide this valuable bird's-eye view, we've included two contents: one that resembles the table of contents from previous editions and another that provides a broad outline of the book's contents and includes a helpful summary sentence for each chapter. Both should enable you to "navigate" this book even more effectively.

We've applied this same thinking to bolstering the book's index, enabling you and your students to take several paths to pinpoint some of the book's key ideas.

New! Integrated Computer Information

Since the release of the seventh edition of *How to Study in College*, computers and the Internet have been so utterly integrated into classrooms and college that including a separate chapter on computers would seem as pointless as devoting a separate chapter to using a pen or a pencil. Instead, all references to computers and the Internet—and there are a lot of them—are incorporated into the book as a whole, occurring at logical and appropriate points throughout the book instead of in a separate chapter at the end. For those instructors and students who still feel the need to read their computer-related information in one parcel, there remains a more conventional chapter on computer use available on the ClassPrep CD and website.

New! Multitasking Advice

A number of recent books have reported on the breakneck pace of modern life. Others have talked about the immense amount of information that we are expected to process in a typical day. Many of us attempt to cope with this speed and overload by multitasking—that is, routinely doing two or more things at once. A new section in Chapter 5, "Managing Stress," discusses the effects and the pitfalls of this very modern phenomenon and offers some commonsense ideas for coping.

New! Revised Nutritional Information

Food is your fuel. What you eat can affect both your academic performance and your ability to withstand stress. Since the publication of the seventh edition, doctors, nutritionists, and the popular press have been reexamining some of the fundamental beliefs about what you should and shouldn't be eating. This new edition integrates some of their findings into commonsense recommendations for nutritional guidelines that will steel you against the inevitable demands of academic life.

New! The PACE System for Reading Improvement

Despite overwhelming scientific evidence, speed-reading courses continue to collect money from well-intentioned students who mistakenly believe that they will be able to defy anatomical reality and read at rates of thousands and even tens of thousands of words per minute. It's a myth that just won't die. In this edition—as in previous ones—we systematically lay out the reasons why most of these claims are physically impossible. What we've added in the eighth edition is the PACE approach—a systematic approach to improving your reading that counteracts the tantalizing claims of the speed-reading salespeople.

New! Consolidated Note-Taking Information

Taking notes in a lecture can be superficially quite different from taking notes for a textbook assignment. Yet despite some key distinctions, the two activities fundamentally share a great deal in common. Rather than teaching textbook and lecture note taking separately as we have in the past, we've combined the discussion of both, stressing the similarities of both systems in the hopes of making the process of note taking and mastery easier to learn and to remember. Chapters 9, 10, and 11 systematically take you through the before, during, and after of the note-taking process.

Valuable Features Retained

- Both the **Words in Context** and the **Word History System** sections remain in this edition. Because words are the building blocks of thinking, it is essential that students be given a variety of opportunities to add to and strengthen their vocabularies. Unfortunately, not all students have an instant affinity for learning new words. And as instructors know all too well, it is often the approach, not the ultimate goal, that can lead to indifference and even resistance in some students. The Words in Context, by dissecting the remarks of modern thinkers and leaders, provides a level of relevance that makes learning words more meaningful, while the Word History System bolsters the impact of each word with a fascinating explanation and a compelling image.
- In this edition, as in recent ones, "concept maps" provide a graphical means of summarizing chapter content. It would be good to remind the students that much can be gained from these maps, both before reading the chapter and, perhaps even more, after reading the chapter. Before reading, students can acquire advance *organizers,* which, according to David P. Ausubel, can help them learn and remember material they encounter in the chapter itself. After reading the chapter, the concept maps provide a bird's-eye view of the entire chapter, showing the main concepts with linking lines that establish relationships.
- Each "Have You Missed Something?" chapter quiz includes questions to reinforce students' understanding of key concepts. And once again, the rationale for these questions is not to test but rather to teach. If the chapter is read with care and understanding, any student should achieve a perfect score.

Ancillary Materials

This edition is supported by a number of ancillaries that are designed to reinforce and enrich the basic book.

The **Instructor's Resource Manual** provides information on preparing your syllabus, extra multiple-choice questions for each chapter, questions for discussion, and reproducible masters relating to the concepts found in the text.

The **Houghton Mifflin ClassPrep CD-ROM** offers not only an electronic version of much of the content found in the Instructor's Resource Manual, but also a number of additional resources, including chapter-by-chapter **Power-Point slides**, sample tests, and other supplementary tools that will assist you in using this text to its fullest extent. Also available on this CD are supplementary chapters dealing with a number of specialized skills including writing a research paper, studying foreign languages, studying literature, studying science, studying mathematics, and using the computer. Many of these assets are also available on the instructor's website for this text.

The title-based student website features an interactive version of the Frontier Word System from the text, online versions of the text exercises including additional questions for review, web links exercises to aid students in building their vocabulary, as well as the supplementary chapters.

The **Houghton Mifflin Assessment and Portfolio Builder CD-ROM** provides a bridge between the valuable skills and concepts in this book and the demands of the workplace. Students may use this tool to build their portfolio by responding to questions in the Personal, Interpersonal, Career, and Community modules and by reflecting on their skills, attitudes, values, and behaviors. The Accomplishments Report will summarize the results of their responses and can be used as a starting point for creating a résumé or preparing for interviews. Equipped with their accomplishments report, students are then invited to explore Houghton Mifflin's web-based **Career Resource Center** for more tips, exercises, articles, and ideas to help them succeed. (This tool can be shrink-wrapped with your text.)

ACKNOWLEDGMENTS

Sincere words of thanks go to those who are permanently linked to this book: the late Henry F. Thoma and Ian D. Elliot.

Sincere thanks also go to the contributors of material in previous editions: Professors Harrison A. Geiselmann, Kenneth A. Greisen, and Jane E. Hardy, all of Cornell University; Professor William G. Moulton of Princeton University; Professor James A. Wood and Dr. Nancy V. Wood, both of the University of Texas at El Paso.

In addition, Walter Pauk remembers the valuable contributions made by Professors Mike Radis and Ron Williams of Pennsylvania State University as well as Professor Carol Kanar of Valencia Community College.

Ross Owens is especially grateful to Gwinn Owens and to Joan Quirie Owens, who instilled in him at a very early age a thirst for knowledge and a genuine love of learning, and also to Julie, who provided inspiration and encouragement throughout the process of revising this book. But above all, thanks go to Walter

Pauk himself, a loyal friend and wonderful mentor, who truly is the embodiment of this book's plain-spoken, clear-thinking, well-meaning wisdom.

At Houghton Mifflin we would like to thank Mary Finch, Shani Fisher, and Andrew Sylvester for their editorial support of our work. We would also like to thank Shelley Dickerson, Sarah Ambrose, Keith Fredericks, and Nancy Benjamin for their time and contributions in seeing this new edition to its completion.

We would also like to thank the reviewers of previous editions, as well as these reviewers of the present eighth edition for their helpful suggestions:

Cecilia Brewer, University of Missouri–Kansas City
Lucy Brooks, Wabash College, IN
Julie Colish, University of Michigan–Flint
Susan Farmer, William Rainey Harper College, IL
Karen Goode-Bartholomew, St. Norbert College, WI
Rita Karr, Brunswick Community College in Supply, NC
Patsy Krech, University of Memphis, TN
Jane Lehmann, Elgin Community College, IL
Nita McMillan, Southwest Tennessee Community College
Janet Zupan, University of Montana

And finally, in this edition, as in the seven previous ones, Walter Pauk offers very special thanks to his students:

"I am eternally grateful to my many students who have taught me much—so that I may pass on a little more to others."

W. P.
R. J. Q. O.

To the Student

The desire for learning and the thirst for self-improvement are incredibly powerful impulses. Time and again they have dramatically altered individual lives and even changed our collective history. Helen Keller was unable to hear or see and yet she still learned to read and to communicate with extraordinary eloquence. Booker T. Washington, born into slavery, made a five-hundred-mile trek to high school in order to get the education he craved. More recently, Ben Carson made a U-turn away from what seemed like a dead-end life in a poor Detroit neighborhood by reading two books a week and ultimately earning a scholarship to Yale before going on to medical school and becoming the head of pediatric neurosurgery at the prestigious Johns Hopkins Hospital. And finally, there's the well-known story of Abraham Lincoln, whose willingness to walk twenty miles to borrow a book eventually put him on a path to the U.S. presidency.

Maybe you know someone like Keller, Washington, Carson, or Lincoln. Perhaps their stories share some similarities with your own. If so, you know firsthand how the desire to learn can give you the strength to start projects and to steadfastly see them through to a fulfilling finish. In college, few qualities will serve you better than a deep-rooted will to succeed. After all, on a cold winter morning, it's far easier to get out of bed if you want to ace a mid-term than if you don't really care about your performance!

How This Book Is Organized

The fourteen separate chapters in the eighth edition of *How to Study in College* have been clustered into four distinct parts that are designed to make the book even easier to follow.

Part I: Permanent Skills addresses fundamental competencies that are essential in college and beyond. You don't need to be a student to benefit from learning how to set goals (Chapter 1), control time (Chapter 2), stay focused (Chapter 3), defend your memory (Chapter 4), and manage stress (Chapter 5). And if you are a student, these are skills that you will be carrying with you for the rest of your life. That's why we call them permanent skills.

Part II: Enrichment Skills deals with the words and pictures we use to communicate. By the time you reach college, you should be competent in communicating in words and to some degree in images. But competency and excellence aren't the same. You can enrich your verbal skills by improving your reading (Chapter 6) and bolstering your vocabulary (Chapter 7). And you can become more image-savvy by thinking visually (Chapter 8).

Part III: Note-Taking Skills is as straightforward as it sounds. The three chapters in this part follow the before, during, and after of taking notes, namely the preparation you should do to gear up for note taking (Chapter 9), the particulars you need to take notes effectively regardless of whether they're in a lecture or for a textbook reading (Chapter 10), and the skills you'll require to review your notes and master them (Chapter 11).

Part IV: Test-Taking Skills fast-forwards to the event that accounts for a lion's share of academic anxiety and a significant portion of your grade: exam week. It offers commonsense advice for managing test anxiety (Chapter 12) and then zeroes in on the two main flavors of college-level tests: objective (Chapter 13) and essay (Chapter 14).

Using This Book

No matter what academic goals you've set for yourself, this book can help you achieve them. In theory, there is no limit to learning and no limit to how you can improve your natural abilities to understand the material you study. By applying the techniques presented here, you will quickly begin to improve as a student, making your college experience a rewarding one.

How to Use This Book's Marginal Questions

If you've already had an opportunity to flip through this book, then you have almost certainly noticed something a little unusual about it. Running along the outside of each page in the marginal area that is blank in most books is a series of questions, one for each important paragraph.

No single academic skill is more important than the ability to ask and answer questions. Questions are what make learning come alive. They activate inert facts and turn them into vibrant ideas. If questions aren't a key component of your studying, there's a chance that you aren't truly learning.

How to Study in College has stressed the importance of questions for quite some time, but in this edition we've taken things an important step further by making questions a regular feature of every page. What should you do with these questions? As it happens, they have a number of potential uses.

Use them as examples. If asking questions is already a part of your learning process, then their importance is already clear to you. But for students who are new to asking questions, this approach may seem a little awkward and strange. We understand that. And that's one of the primary reasons we've included our own questions in the margins of this book: to provide you with real examples of the kinds of questions you'll want to be pondering as you're reading along.

Use them as motivators. As you move through each chapter assignment, how can you be sure you've actually understood what you've read? One way is by asking questions. Before you read each paragraph, ask yourself the question in the margin. Then make it a kind of mini goal to see if you can answer it as you read. If you find it a struggle to answer the question, you may want to read the paragraph again. (If you still can't answer a question after additional tries, you may want to get help from your instructor.) If you find it easy to answer the question, then you're probably picking up the paragraph's important information. That realization should provide motivation to read on and unlock the meaning of each new paragraph in a similar fashion.

Use them as a reviewing aid. After you've finished a page or, if you prefer, the entire chapter, go back and cover up the text of each page with a blank sheet of paper, leaving only the marginal questions uncovered. Then systematically read each question and try to answer it from memory and in your own words. Either recite your answer out loud or jot it down on the blank sheet you're using to cover up the text. Once you've provided your answer, check your work by comparing your response to the actual text.

Use them as a navigational tool. If you're returning to a chapter to look up a specific passage or to confirm a particular fact, it helps to be able to go directly to the information you're seeking rather than having to reread large portions just to find what you're looking for. Chapter and section titles help you in this effort, but they only go so far. The marginal questions give you a quick sense of what each important paragraph is addressing.

Not all books have questions in the margins, of course. In fact, most don't. But the value of learning with a book that has the questions already supplied is that you can then apply this approach to your other textbooks. Your efforts should lead to true comprehension and mastery.

How to Use the "Have You Missed Something?" Questions

The end-of-chapter questions are designed to teach, not test; you'll find no trick questions and no traps to lead you to an incorrect answer. Take each question at face value and answer it to the best of your ability. Use any incorrect answers you give as opportunities to reread the pertinent portion of the chapter. By rereading and rethinking the question and answer, you will greatly strengthen your understanding of the entire concept. Answers to these questions are located in the appendix.

How to Use the Vocabulary-Building Components

The final pages of every chapter are devoted to vocabulary building. There you'll find "Words in Context," a series of quotations that can be instructive, inspiring, and sometimes even amusing. In each quotation, one or more words is italicized. You are asked to select from three options the word that most nearly reflects the meaning of the italicized word. This is not a test; rather, the purpose is to expose you to words in a real-world context. You may select unfamiliar words for further study. Familiar words will provide reinforcement for your existing vocabulary.

Finally, at the end of each chapter, a single word is pictorially presented in a way that is both highly interesting and incisively memorable. Without a historical background, a word, like a gas-filled balloon, usually floats freely out of sight and out of mind. But once it is anchored to its colorful origins, a word should always remain with you. For example, the history of the word *tantalize* at the end of Chapter 1 is portrayed by King Tantalus. Just out of reach of his parched lips is a pool of fresh water that recedes whenever he tilts his head to drink. Just out of his grasp is a branch of succulent fruit that draws back whenever he tries to pull it toward him. It's hard not to sense his profound frustration. The picture makes a memorable mental impression that the word *tantalize* means "to excite (another) by exposing something desirable while keeping it out of reach." The Chinese adage that "a picture is worth a thousand words" proves itself again.

A wide and precise vocabulary is really the main ingredient or quality that provides all of us with the endless ability for better thinking and judgment in all phases of life—personally, socially, and professionally.

Discover Your Own Resources

"Know thyself" is wise advice for a student poised at the path that leads to an academic goal. Development of your skills begins with understanding your personal learning style and study skills. By identifying your preferences and strengths, you can zero in on the best study skills techniques for you.

The following list can help you identify your basic learning style. For each item, circle the letter that best matches your style. Keep your responses in mind as you read this book.

Learning Styles Self-Assessment

1. I study better (a) by myself; (b) in groups; (c) in a combination of the two.
2. I remember best when I've (a) *heard* something; (b) *read* or *seen* something; (c) *done* something active, such as problem solving.
3. I think I'm (a) better with facts, such as names or dates; (b) better with concepts, ideas, or themes; (c) about the same with both.
4. I learn better when I read (a) slowly; (b) quickly; (c) either way.
5. I study more efficiently in (a) one solid study period; (b) small blocks of time.
6. I work (a) well under pressure; (b) poorly under pressure.
7. I work (a) quickly, for short periods of time; (b) at a steady, slower pace for longer periods of time.
8. I (a) do learn best in a structured setting, such as a classroom or laboratory; (b) do not learn best in a structured setting.
9. I think that the greatest strength of my learning style is _____.
10. I think that the greatest weakness of my learning style is _____.

FIGURE 1

The Nine-Dot Problem
Connect these dots by drawing four straight lines without taking your pencil from the paper and without retracing any lines. The solution appears on page xxiii.

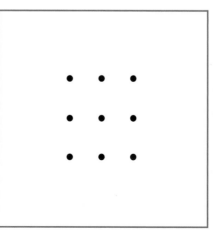

You'll improve your chances of success if you balance this knowledge of your learning style with a willingness to remain flexible. For example, you may be thinking, "It's true. I'm a sprinter who begins working with a burst of energy and then slacks off. That's the way I've always been. How can I possibly change?" Or you may believe that studying all night is an effective way of coping with a tight schedule and that you have no need for a more conventional strategy. These ways of thinking probably feel comfortable, but they may have created blind spots in your view of studying. To get a sense of how blind spots can limit you, try to solve the problem shown in Figure 1. Odds are that a blind spot will prevent you from solving it. Yet once you see the solution, you'll probably say, "How easy! Why didn't I think of that tactic myself?"

A Second Chance

The Nine-Dot Problem (Figure 1) not only demonstrates a point, but it is also an excellent learning device. For instance, although very few students have solved the puzzle, they nevertheless have learned to break out of the conventional-thinking mold and let their minds rove more freely, which leads to more innovative and imaginative approaches to solving problems.

To prove that you, perhaps, have learned a great deal from this one puzzle, apply your newfound knowledge to the problem shown in Figure 2.

FIGURE 2

The Puzzle of Squares
How many squares are there in this figure? The solution appears on page xxiv.

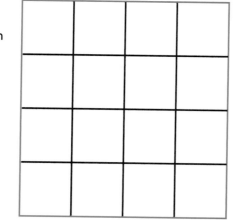

FIGURE 3
Answer to the Nine-Dot Problem
Begin at the top left corner and follow the arrows.

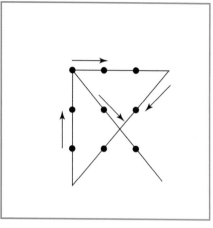

Take Advantage of This Book's Additional Resources

A number of this book's important skills and systems are enriched and brought to life on our website. You'll have an opportunity to boost your vocabulary skills with electronic flash cards, to test your knowledge and comprehension with additional questions, and to customize and print out your own copies of the time- and task-based schedules discussed in Chapter 2. You can also learn more academic strategies in online supplementary chapters on writing a research paper, studying foreign languages, studying literature, studying science and mathematics, and using a computer for school. To visit the *How to Study in College* website, go to http://collegesurvival.college.hmco.com/students.

Take Advantage of Your School's Resources

College or university website   It's a rare college these days that doesn't have a website. What sort of information do these sites contain? That's going to vary widely depending on the college. Some have simply converted the text of their college catalog into an online form. Others provide elaborate and interactive repositories of information that keep you up to date on a variety of college news and often enable you to conduct some transactions that might otherwise need to be done by mail, over the phone, or in person. Regardless of the scope of your college's site, it is often a good place to start. Check the site's FAQs (Frequently Asked Questions) to see if your concern has already been addressed.

College catalog   General information about your college's requirements, policies, programs, and services appears in the college catalog. Even if your college provides this information on its website, it still helps to have a hard copy of the catalog handy during the first weeks of classes to remind yourself of requirements and deadlines to be met.

Student handbook   The student handbook provides information about your school's procedures, regulations, and code of conduct. It may also describe the school's requirements for good academic standing and graduation. For details or for specific department requirements, consult your department office or your academic adviser.

Admissions or registrar's office   You can find answers to questions about grades, transcripts, and college requirements in the admissions or registrar's office. Admission to college and registration for courses begin with this office.

Office of financial affairs   For answers to questions about scholarships, loans, and grants, contact the financial affairs office. You will come here to pay fees and fines and to pick up your checks if you are in a work-study grant or program. If you want a part-time job on campus for which you must qualify on the basis of your financial status, you will fill out application forms in this office.

Career development and placement office   If you want help choosing a major or setting a career goal, contact the career development and placement office. People in this office can administer various interest, personality, and skills assessment tests to help you determine the kind of work for which you are best suited. They can help you find jobs on and off campus. Some career development centers sponsor on-campus recruitment, inviting businesses to interview prospective graduates and aiding them in submitting applications and résumés. After graduation, you can file a résumé in the placement office if you want your school's help with landing a job.

FIGURE 4
Answer to the Puzzle of Squares: 30 squares.

1×1 Squares	16
2×2 squares	9
3×3 squares	4
4×4 squares	1
Total squares	30

Academic advising office or counseling department Academic and guidance counselors can help you with everything from choosing the right course to solving personal problems that prevent you from meeting your academic goals. The academic office or counseling department may be part of the admissions office, or it may be a separate department. In many colleges students are assigned to an adviser or a counselor who follows their progress throughout their college careers.

Student health center If you become ill, you can go to a doctor at the health center. The health center may have a pharmacy and may provide a limited amount of hospital care. Some mental health services may be available through this center, through the office of a school psychologist or psychiatrist, or through a peer counseling group. The health center may also refer students to an agency outside the college.

Student government association Working with the dean of students, the student government association sponsors student activities such as intramural events, dances, special-interest organizations and clubs, and other social and academic events. (Joining a club or taking part in campus events is a good way to meet other students who share your interests.) In addition, your student government may publish a weekly bulletin or a student handbook that summarizes college requirements and resources.

Student publications The college newspaper or literary magazine offers contributors unique opportunities for self-expression and provides readers with information and entertainment. Serving on the editorial staff of one of these publications may also fulfill some journalism or English requirements.

Learning lab or skills center You may turn to the learning lab or skills center for help in improving your study, reading, writing, math, or computer skills. Whether you are required to spend time in a lab because of your performance on a college skills assessment test or you choose to go on your own, take full advantage of the opportunity to gain the skills you need.

Special student services Veterans, students with physical or learning disabilities, minority students, international students, and students who are economically disadvantaged may need the special assistance of a trained support group to meet their academic goals. If you think you qualify for these services, ask your counselor or adviser about them. Your college may also offer services such as off-campus residence listings.

Athletics office   A listing of the college's athletic programs and events is available in the athletics office. This is the office to visit if you are interested in participating in sports.

Resident assistant   For on-campus students, resident assistants (RAs) can be a great source of information about campus services. Although RAs are not professional counselors, they have recently been through many of the experiences you're undergoing and can probably direct you to the campus office best suited to your needs.

Final Words

Our ultimate goal in this book is to provide you with tools, skills, and systems that will lead to self-sufficiency. Or, as Ralph Waldo Emerson once expressed it: "The best service one person can render another person is to help him help himself."

Permanent Skills

1   Setting Goals

2   Controlling Your Time

3   Staying Focused

4   Defending Your Memory

5   Managing Stress

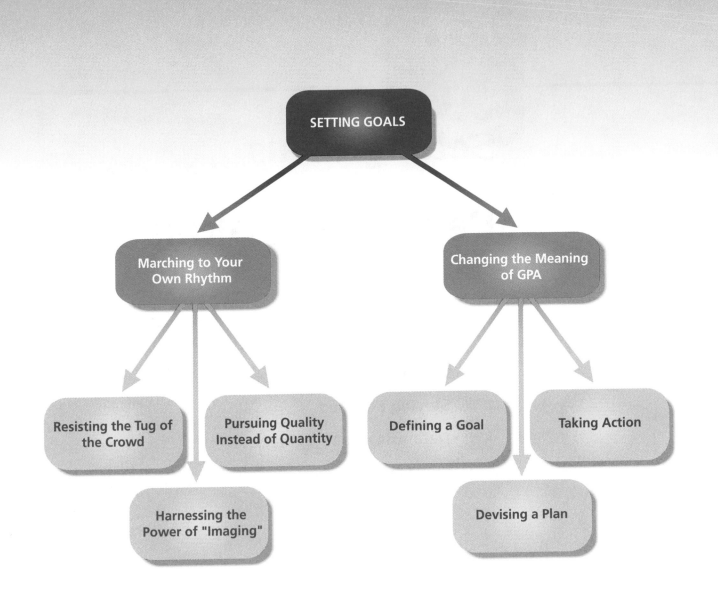

Setting Goals

*Most of us go to our
graves with our music still
inside us.*

Oliver Wendell Holmes
(1809–1890), American
physician and writer

There's something deep inside each of us that yearns for fulfillment. We were meant for something to which our nature inclines. But what? No one really knows. So, you yourself must dig. Dig—but for what? Start by digging for happiness. Ask, "What kind of work would I be happiest in? Doesn't it make sense that every day's work should be a joy?" In this chapter, you can begin to focus your life as you read and think about:

- **Marching to Your Own Rhythm**
- **Deciding What Would Make You Happy**
- **Redefining GPA**

What are the risks of having no goal?

Goals bring meaning to life; otherwise, life can be aimless. Viktor Frankl's research revealed these stark data:

> When 60 students were asked why they had attempted suicide, 85% said the reason had been that "life was meaningless."[1]

How do goals go beyond simple survival?

Goals have to go beyond earning your "bread and butter," as is shown in the following slice of human life:

> Governments, guided by social scientists, used to say that if you just improve the socio-economic status of the people, everything will be OK, people will become happy. The truth is that as the struggle for survival has subsided, the question has emerged: survival for what? Ever more people today have the means to life, but no meaning to live for.[2]

How do goals relate to purpose?

Goals and purpose breathe meaning into life. Goals and purpose form the psychological underpinnings of our individual lives. There's power in purpose, as is shown in this excerpt:

> We cannot have deep and enduring satisfaction unless we have self-worth. We cannot have self-worth unless our lives are an earnest attempt to express the finest and most enduring qualities that we are aware of. Purpose is an important condition for an enduring satisfaction with life.[3]

Marching to Your Own Rhythm

What was Thoreau's advice?

The nineteenth-century American writer, philosopher, and naturalist Henry David Thoreau famously wrote:

> If a man does not keep pace with his companions, perhaps it is because he hears a different drummer. Let him step to the music which he hears, however measured or far away.[4]

[1]Viktor Frankl, an Austrian psychiatrist and psychotherapist, created the theory of Logotherapy, which states that a person's primary motivation is his or her search for meaning in life.

[2]Richard J. Leider, *The Power of Purpose* (San Francisco: Berrett-Koehler Publishers, 1997), p. 35.

[3]Ibid.

[4]Henry David Thoreau, *Walden and Resistance to Civil Government,* 2nd ed. (W. W. Norton, 1992), p. 217.

How can you bring meaning into your life?

This doesn't mean, as some have suggested, that you need to be an outcast or iconoclast or that you have to live alone in the woods of Walden Pond, as Thoreau once did. Many people who are intricately woven into the fabric of society still manage to adhere to ideals that they have sharpened and defined on their own. To bring meaning into your life, you must decide on your own goal. Avoid the trap of surrendering to the expectations of others instead of pursuing a goal that is personally meaningful.

What role should friends and family play in your goals?

This doesn't mean that you shouldn't discuss your goals with friends and family. It is helpful to ponder their thoughts and advice. But process these through your own brain cells and heart cells, and then make a decision, which must be your very own. Above all, set your own pace instead of marching along with the crowd.

Resisting the Tug of the Crowd

What happens when people think as a crowd instead of individually?

When you become part of the crowd, your individual thinking is replaced by crowd psychology. Here's how Gustave LeBon, a French social scientist, described crowd psychology:

> The most striking peculiarity presented by a psychological crowd is the following: Whoever be the individuals that compose it, however like or unlike be their mode of life, their occupations, their character, or their intelligence, the fact that they have been transformed into a crowd puts them in possession of a sort of collective mind which makes them feel, think, and act in a manner quite different from that in which each individual of them would feel, think, and act were he in a state of isolation.[5]

What did Gould observe about the psychology of a crowd?

LeBon's observations about crowds were adopted and furthered by Edson Gould, one of the most respected names on Wall Street, who used this easily visualized example to illustrate how the individual is almost powerless to resist the powerful magnetism of the crowd:

> You're *alone* in an empty movie theater and hear the cry of "fire." You look around, see no flames, smell no smoke, you *calmly walk* to the nearest exit. But, repeat the same cry of "fire" (again without flames visible or the smell of smoke) in a *crowded* theater and once the *crowd* starts *running* for an exit, you'll find *yourself running,* too. That's crowd psychology.[6]

What should you guard against in crowd psychology?

Don't let crowd psychology rob you of your independence or rob you of your freedom to think and decide individually. In sum, preserve yourself as a

[5]Quoted in Dan Sullivan, *The Chartist* (December 30, 1997): 4.

[6]Quoted in Edson Gould, *Findings and Forecasts* (New York: Anametrics, 1974).

sovereign individual so that, for better or for worse, you are the ruler of your career and destiny.

Harnessing the Power of "Imaging"

In what way does a goal go beyond a statement?

A goal is much more than just a simple statement. Actually, it's a vivid dream that has been mentally acted and reenacted. What lawyer hasn't first imagined presenting a closing argument to judge and jury? What business executive hasn't imagined outlining an exciting plan to staff members seated around the board of directors' table?

What is Peale's explanation of imaging?

Although *imagined* is generally used to denote imagination, in his landmark book *Positive Imaging* Norman Vincent Peale used the word *imaging* to convey a much deeper concept:

> Imaging consists of vividly picturing, in your conscious mind, a desired goal or objective, and holding that image until it sinks into your unconscious mind, where it releases great, untapped energies.[7]

How does imaging your goal affect it?

So, if we think deeply enough and image vividly enough about what we want to do with our lives, our whole being can be energized. Peale, who is one of the most widely read inspirational writers of all time, goes on to say,

> There is a powerful and mysterious force in human nature that is capable of bringing about dramatic improvement in our lives. It is a kind of mental engineering. . . . In imaging, one does not merely think about a hoped-for goal; one "sees" or visualizes it with tremendous intensity. Imaging is a kind of laser beam of the imagination, a shaft of mental energy in which the desired goal or outcome is pictured so vividly by the conscious mind that the unconscious mind accepts it and is activated by it. This releases powerful internal forces that can bring about astonishing changes in the life of the person who is doing the imaging.[8]

Pursuing Quality Instead of Quantity

How has money affected the way we define our goals?

Over time, Peale's pristine image of a goal has been diluted by the dollar sign. Everyone, it seems, is out to make money. Look at the crowds thronging the race tracks, the casinos, the state lotteries, and even the frequently bubbling stock market. Apparently this "money idea" has steadily seeped into the career

[7]Norman Vincent Peale, *Positive Imaging.* Copyright © 1982. Published by Fleming H. Revell, a division of Baker Book House. Reprinted with permission.

[8]From Norman Vincent Peale, *Positive Imaging.* Copyright © 1982. Published by Fleming H. Revell, a division of Baker Book House. Reprinted with permission.

goals of students. According to a poll conducted by consulting firm KPMG (Klynveld, Peat, Marwick, Goerdeler), New York, three out of four college students expect to become millionaires.[9]

What advice does John Rau give his students?

The siren song of money may be difficult to ignore, but is it really the key to happiness or the true mark of success? John Rau, who has been the CEO of three corporations, dean of Indiana University's business school, and no stranger to success himself, offers a straight-shooting sanity check for students who are thinking of sacrificing quality in the pursuit of quantity. "Unless you're doing the stuff you like," he cautions, "you can burn out."[10]

What does Dr. Williams conclude about defining your goals?

In line with Rau's succinct pronouncement, Dr. David Williams pulls no punches. Few people know more about "burnout" than medical doctors. After years of treating people who were experiencing burnout, Dr. Williams wrote this compelling article on choosing a career that will enhance the possibilities of living a healthier life.

What Do You Want to Be When You Grow Up?

If you're like me, the last time someone asked you this question was quite some time ago. Most of us guys probably responded with something like a fireman, forest ranger, cop, race car driver or even the President. I'm not being sexist (I'm not even sure there was such a word when someone last asked me the question), but if you're female you probably answered the above question with occupations like a model, flight attendant, school teacher or movie star. You chose these answers because at the time you thought these endeavors would be enjoyable. You could visualize being happy. Maybe a more appropriate question than "What do you want to be when you grow up?" would have been "What would make you happy?" And since the answer to this question changes throughout your life, it's a question we really need to ask ourselves more often.

When was the last time you actually got away by yourself and seriously thought about what you needed to be happy? Maybe it's time to do so.

As hectic as life has become, we see happiness as a luxury. Surveys have shown that most people really don't believe it's possible to be happy the majority of the time. They think that true happiness is an unobtainable goal. It's an unpredictable, fleeting sensation over which one has little control. But accepting this idea, that you have no or little control over your own happiness, can have serious health consequences. Happiness is just as important, if not more so, to good health as proper nutrition and adequate exercise. Happiness is a powerful healing force. On the opposite

[9]Pamela Sebastian, *The Wall Street Journal* (March 25, 1999), p. A1.

[10]Quoted in Hal Lancaster, "Managing Your Career," *The Wall Street Journal* (May 6, 1997), p. B1.

side of the coin we have stress. There seems to be an inverse relationship between stress and happiness. In other words, less happiness leads to more stress. And stress can be an extremely powerful destructive force. Stress is one of the best examples of the power the mind can have over the body.

In animal studies, French researchers at the University of Bordeaux have recently shown that depression and anxiety in adults can be a direct result of placing the mother under stress prior to birth. Stress causes the adrenal glands to produce more of the "stress hormone," corticosterone. Corticosterone easily passes from the mother to the fetus through the placenta. Consistently high levels of corticosterone desensitize brain receptors, altering the feedback system and making it more difficult to shut down the excess corticosterone production. After birth these receptors in the brain remain desensitized, which can lead to suppression of the immune system, depression and anxiety later in life. *(J Neurosi 96;15[1 Pt1]:110-6.)*

In an amazing study recently performed at Columbia University, New York, researchers found that young girls who suffer from undue stress grow up to be 5 cm. (2 in.) shorter than their happier contemporaries. Stress stunts their growth by depressing the levels of growth hormone in the body.

Volumes have been written on the detrimental effects of stress. And while I won't bore you with all the detailed research here, stress has been linked to everything from asthma and cardiovascular disease to cancer and practically every disease in between. The point to be made here is that happiness replaces and counteracts stress. Probably more than any other single factor, discovering and acting on what makes you happy can improve both the quality and length of your life.

Over the next few hours, days and weeks, I urge you to invest some time in seriously deciding what you want out of life. What would make you happy? I am not talking about what would make you happy for a moment or a day, but instead, what you want and need to be happy for the long term. I can assure you it will be one of the most productive things you will ever do.

Discovering what it would take for you to be happy is, without a doubt, one of the most powerful tools you'll ever possess. It defines your basis for living. It gives you a purpose and provides the answers to life's day-to-day problems. It almost miraculously provides direction at each of life's crossroads. It crystallizes and clarifies your day-to-day goals and activities. It allows you to focus your talents and energies toward achieving the rewards that are most important to you.

If you can't honestly verbalize what you *need* to make you happy, you're going to wander aimlessly throughout life. The clock keeps ticking whether you decide to answer "what would make me happy" or not. Instead of participating and reveling in life, you end up simply reacting to situation after situation. You unquestionably embrace the idea that your own happiness is out of your control. You then begin to believe that it will suddenly appear just as soon as someone or something in your life changes. Unfortunately, that's like playing the state lottery. Your chances of getting hit by lightning are far better than finding real happiness and meaning in your life.

Most of us (I'm as guilty as anyone, if not more so) have a tendency to take life much too seriously. When we were younger it was easier to be less serious. It reminds me of a Bob Dylan song, in which he says, "If you ain't got nothing, you ain't got nothing to lose." The older and more responsible we become, the more we feel we have to lose. We begin to perceive changes in our lives as risks rather than opportunities. As such, we try to avoid change. But in reality, change is not something over which we have any control.

I'm sure you've heard the saying that there are only two things you can count on: death and taxes. Well, there are actually a couple more. One is that your surroundings will change. Technology changes. Weather changes. People change. Everything changes. Always has. Always will. Accept it. Accept the fact that people and situations are *always* going to be changing throughout your life.

Fighting change is like swimming against the current in a river. You're so busy trying to keep your head above water that you never get a chance to see or enjoy what's on the bank. The quicker you accept the fact that everything will change, the quicker you can get out of the water. You can sit on the bank, relax for a moment and evaluate your surroundings. In a life that's always too short, you can then decide how best to spend your remaining time. This brings up the other thing you can always count on—the God-given, human ability to make choices.

Through changes in your thinking, your actions and your lifestyle, you can choose to live your life in a state of unhappiness or in a state of happiness. It's totally up to you.

Although it was several decades ago, I remember sitting at my desk in Mrs. Benger's first-grade class back in Friona, Texas. Above the chalkboard there were two large handwritten signs. One read, "Act the way you want to be and soon you'll be the way you act." It's probably one of the more lasting lessons I've learned in life thus far. (The other sign said, "One who thinketh by the inch and talketh by the yard should be kicketh by the foot." [I'm still working on that one.])

Before you can "act the way you want to be," and before you can expect to find happiness, you must answer that one simple question. "What would make me happy?" It's a difficult question, probably the most difficult you'll ever have to answer. Getting the answer will require some time and serious thinking. Strangely, there's no right or wrong answer. And even stranger is the fact that only you know the answer. Don't think of this as some kind of test. Nobody is going to give you a grade or set any time limits. The only way you can really fail is aimlessly wandering through life and simply not answering the question at all.

So "What do you want to be when you grow up?" "What would make *you* happy?"

Dr. David G. Williams, "What Do You Want to Be When You Grow Up?" from *Alternatives for the Health Conscious Individual* 6, no. 15 (September 1996): 119–120. Copyright © 1996, Mountain Home Publishing (800-527-3044). Reprinted with permission.

Changing the Meaning of GPA

What is the best way to become a success?

"If you want to make it in college, your GPA is the key." Students who tell you this are talking about your grade point average, your report card, the number of As and Bs you get in relation to the number of Cs, Ds, and Fs. Grades are certainly important, but they aren't as important as another GPA: your goal, your plan, and the action you take. If you really want to make it, *that's* the GPA you should strive for. If you are able to set a specific goal in your life, if you can come up with an efficient plan for that goal, and if you have the discipline to take action, there's an excellent chance that you will be headed down the road to success.

Defining a Goal

What is the purpose of a goal?

Where are you headed? That's the question that your goal is designed to answer. Imagine throwing ingredients into a mixing bowl without any idea of what you are making. Think of running around on the basketball court with no knowledge of the object of the game. The best cooks and the best basketball players know what they are doing and why they are doing it. They have a clear idea of where they are headed. In short, they have a goal in mind.

What kinds of things can be considered goals?

Although winning a basketball game and baking a cake can both be seen as goals, it can be easier to think of your goal as a kind of destination. A lot of our common expressions use this idea. "Making it to the top," "climbing the corporate ladder," and even "reaching for the stars" portray the goal as a place in the distance that you are trying to reach. Of course, some goals really are destinations. When American pioneers declared that their goal was "Pike's Peak or Bust" and tacked signs saying so to their wagons, they were talking about an actual destination hundreds of miles to the west and more than fourteen thousand feet above sea level. When President Kennedy made the moon the country's goal in 1961, he was aiming for a destination that was about 238,900 miles out into space.

Set Minor Goals

Are smaller goals useful?

Your life should be full of both major and minor goals. Most of us set minor goals all the time. Passing a test can be seen as a minor goal. So can completing a homework assignment or even finishing a chapter before dinnertime. Having minor goals can be a great help. Each time we reach a minor goal, we get a small sense of victory that helps spur us on toward something even bigger.

Notice in a basketball game how the crowd cheers and the scoring team's pace quickens each time a basket is made. Everyone knows that one basket by itself won't win the game, but when the score is added up, each basket can prove to be crucial. The same is true in school. Although no one has gained

---

A FAMOUS GOAL, PLAN, AND ACTION

The <u>Goal</u>

First, I believe that this nation should commit itself to achieving the goal, before this decade is out, of landing a man on the moon and returning him safely to earth.

President John F. Kennedy
before a joint session of Congress
May 25, 1961

The <u>Plan</u>

The Mercury Program:	Each rocket would send a single astronaut into space.
The Gemini Program:	Each rocket would send two men into space to orbit the earth, to practice docking with other spacecraft, and to test human beings' ability to withstand prolonged periods in space.
The Apollo Program:	Each rocket would send three men into space in order to leave the earth's orbit, to orbit the moon, and eventually to land on the moon and explore it.

The <u>Action</u>

The United States sent twenty manned flights into space between May 1961 and June 1969. In July 1969, eight years and two months after President Kennedy set the country's original goal, astronauts Neil Armstrong and Edwin "Buzz" Aldrin set foot on the moon and returned safely to earth.

---

success by virtue of a single test or paper, these little victories will add up and help you move toward your major goal. In the meantime, minor goals provide the encouragement you need to cheer yourself on and quicken your pace.

Set Major Goals

How do you choose your major goal?

Choosing a major goal will come naturally for some, while it may be an agonizing decision for others. For every person who says, "I've always wanted to be a doctor" or "I know that teaching others is what really matters to me," there are those who complain, "There's really nothing I'm interested in" or "I'm interested in practically everything; how am I ever going to choose?" Although goals may vary widely from person to person, they all grow out of the same source: the things we want and need. Therefore, choosing your goal means deciding what you value most in life.

How large should a major goal be?

Your major goal should be large and distant. It should be a target you can aim for, something to inspire you. Don't let short-term minor goals like finishing an assignment, passing an exam, and simply getting through the day mark the limits of your dreams. Aim high, but at the same time be sure that the goals you set are specific and distinct. Health, happiness, security, love, and money are all ideals that people aim for, but they are far too vague to be considered goals. On the other hand, "discovering a cure for cancer" and "becoming the best possible parent" are both admirable and specific goals that can help you approach the broad ideals we all share.

Make Your Goal Official

What should you do with your goal once you've chosen it?

If the goal you have chosen is a clear one, you should have no trouble writing it down. Goals that stay only in your head have too great a chance of remaining vague. Furthermore, once you write down your goal, that documentation can act as a constant reminder. If you're feeling discouraged, a quick look at your goal can inspire you. (That's what the signs on the covered wagons did.) And if for some reason you forget your goal, a written description can refresh your memory.

Are you stuck with a goal until you reach it?

The purpose of a goal is not to force you on a course that you don't want to follow; it is to give you a target so that your efforts can be more focused than they would be if you had nothing to aim for. Time and fate have a way of shifting our priorities. People change, and so do the things they view as important. If the goal you once wrote down no longer matches your ambition in life, come up with another goal to replace it.

Devising a Plan

How does your plan relate to your goal?

If you think of your goal as your destination, then a plan can be seen as the route that will take you there. Coming up with a plan is like drawing a map. You need to know where you are starting, where you are heading, and where you plan to stop along the way. Most goals will have several possible plans. The challenge comes in choosing the best one.

How can you choose the most efficient plan?

An efficient plan is a balancing act between what you need and want and what you are able to pay. Paying, as far as a plan is concerned, doesn't always mean money. It can mean time and energy as well. For example, a one-week plan for reviewing your notes is "too expensive" if the test is only two days away. In the same way, a plan that forces you to stay up all night will often cost too much because what you gain in knowledge you will lose in sleep. The most efficient plan will meet your goal without being too costly.

Shouldn't it be easy to tell which plan is the most efficient?

The best plans aren't always obvious from the outset. For example, many students approach an exam by answering questions as soon as they receive the test. Given the time limit, that plan may seem to make sense, even though it's actually a bad idea. The most efficient strategy is to read the exam directions, look over all the questions, and even come up with a time plan before answering a single question. The first plan is fast but reckless, whereas the second is steady and dependable. Now you have a more structured and efficient approach to test taking. When you make an effort to devise a systematic plan, you will usually gain more bene-fits than you would with a hastily drawn up strategy.

What sort of impact should flexible thinking have on your goal?

Devising the best plan can require flexible thinking. For example, when you look at a map, you may conclude—as commercial airline navigators once did—that the best way to get from Amsterdam to Tokyo is to head in an easterly di-rection along what is known as the Mediterranean route. But look at a globe instead of a map, and your perspective may change. Rather than heading east on the Mediterranean route, commercial planes going from Amsterdam to Tokyo now fly north! That's right. They take what is known as the "polar route," flying over the North Pole to Alaska, and then west to Tokyo—for a sav-ings of roughly fifteen hundred miles! The lesson is this: After you've decided on a goal, work vigorously to accomplish it, but keep looking for ways of achieving the goal more efficiently, perhaps from a different angle.

When is a good plan the wrong plan?

No single plan will work for every goal, and few plans are flexible enough to work for several goals. Using the wrong plan can be inefficient and sometimes even comical. Perhaps you remember the folktale about the lazy son who gets scolded by his mother for losing the money he received as payment from a local farmer. "Next time you get paid," she tells him sternly, "be sure to carry it home in your pocket." But the following day the boy goes to work for a dairy farmer who pays him with a pail of milk instead of money. Anxious not to anger his mother, the boy dutifully pours the milk into his pocket. Although his mother's plan was a good one, it could work only when used in the right circumstance. The same idea applies to your study plans. For example, writing out your notes in full sentences makes sense if the goal is to study a textbook assignment. But if you used the same plan for taking lecture notes, you'd move so slowly that you'd miss most of what the instructor said. The secret is to find a plan that fits the goal you have in mind.

What are the best plans for your own personal goal?

In the same way that good plans may not work for every goal, plans that work for most people may not always work for you. That's why the best way to come up with a plan for success is to balance wise advice with your own expe-rience. This book is full of plans for success and tricks of the trade. All of them have been proven to work, and most should work for you. Use trial and error to determine which plans work best for you, and be prepared to adapt some plans to better fit your needs. Even the best plans can fail if they are used too rigidly. Allow a little breathing room. If things go wrong, don't give up. Adjust and keep on going.

Taking Action

What is action?

Goals and plans won't do you any good unless you take some action. Action is the spark that brings your goal and plan to life. Without action, goals and plans are moot. You can decide you want to finish a book, and you can even plan the

---

THE <u>GPA</u> OF SUCCESS

<u>G</u>OAL—should reflect your wants and needs. Make it large and ambitious without being vague. Write it down!

<u>P</u>LAN—lists the route you plan to take in order to reach your goal. It should be efficient and specific. Good advice and personal experience combine to create the most effective plans.

<u>A</u>CTION—brings your goal and your plan to life. Requires confidence, self-discipline, and a power over procrastination.

---

pages that you need to read each day, but until you actually start reading, all your preparations will be pointless. In the same way, the goal to reach the moon and the plans for the spacecraft were impressive, but they didn't come to life until the first rocket left the launch pad and headed into space.

Overcome Your Obstacles

What prevents people from taking action?

Having a goal and a plan is no guarantee that you will take action. Procrastination stops many people from taking action. Procrastination is the tendency to put things off, to write that paper the night before it is due, to cram for a test instead of studying for it right from the start. Although it is just one of many common bad habits, procrastination may be the single greatest obstacle to success. It is also, as we'll see in Chapter 5, a prime source of stress.

How can you prevent procrastination?

The first step in fighting procrastination is to develop a goal and a plan. If you have a goal and a plan but you're still procrastinating, you should take aim at your excuses for not getting your work done. Dream up reasons why you can instead of reasons why you can't. That will often be all it takes to pull yourself out of the vicious circle of inactivity and low self-esteem and put yourself on the road to progress and success.

What does Peale say about taking action?

This chapter would not be complete without more wisdom from Norman Vincent Peale, who expresses the vital importance of *taking action* throughout the entire process of personal goal setting:

> I suggest that you write down what you want to do with your life. Until you write a goal, it is only a wish; written, it becomes a focused objective. Put it down on paper. When it is on paper, boil it down to a single sentence: what you want to do, exactly when you intend to start (which should be right now), exactly when you plan to achieve your goal. Nothing fuzzy or hazy. Everything sharp and clear and definite. No reservations or qualifications. Just one strong, simple, declarative sentence. . . . I want you to make half a dozen copies of that sentence and put them where you'll

see them at least three times a day. I want that pledge to sink down through all the levels of your conscious mind and deep into your unconscious mind, because that is where it will unlock the energies that you will need to achieve your goal.

If setting worthy goals is the first step on the road to success, the second is the belief—the conviction that you are capable of achieving those goals. There has to be in your mind the unshakable image of yourself *succeeding* at the goal you have set yourself. The more vivid this image is, the most obtainable the goal becomes.

Great athletes have always known this. The high jumper "sees" himself skimming over the bar; the place-kicker in football keeps his head down as he kicks, but in his mind's eye he holds the mental picture of what he wants to happen in the next few seconds. . . . The more intensely he images this before it happens, the higher his confidence in himself and the better his chances of making it happen.[11]

Put Theory into Practice

How can you use your understanding of goal, plan, and action?

Now that you have a clearer understanding of the role of a goal and the way in which a plan and action can turn a dream into reality, you are ready to put theory into practice by writing out your goal or goals. The following four steps are designed to help you in this process.

Step 1: Brainstorm. On a clean sheet of paper, do some brainstorming about your goals. Jot down possible goals or words about them that come to mind, and do so quickly and freely. Use brainstorming as an opportunity to explore any aspects of any goals you choose. Don't stop to correct your spelling, polish a phrase, reorganize your notes, or analyze a thought. Just keep going until you've jotted down all that you can think of about your possible goals. Next, look over what you've written, and group similar items. Formulate each group into a goal by writing a sentence that summarizes its main idea.

Step 2: Plan. Focus in on one of the goals you've arrived at, and write it down as a heading on clean sheet of paper. Beneath your goal, make a chronological list of all the steps you'll need to take in order to achieve it.

Step 3: List your strengths. On another sheet, jot down those academic and personal strengths that will help you achieve your goal. These could include skills you already have or classes you have taken as well as personal qualities such as discipline and perserverance.

Step 4: Assess your weaknesses. Identify any academic weaknesses (such as difficulty writing papers) or personal obstacles (such as financial, family, or health problems) that you will have to overcome to reach this goal, and either list them alongside your strengths or on a separate sheet of paper.

---

[11]From Norman Vincent Peale, *Positive Imaging.* Copyright © 1982. Published by Fleming H. Revell, a division of Baker Book House. Reprinted with permission.

What should you do after you've completed the steps?

Don't be surprised if you feel a great sense of relief once you've completed these steps. Even if you're not certain that your goal and your plan are precisely on target, at last you have something concrete that you can adjust and refine. You also have an excellent starting point for guidance and advice. Talk with your academic adviser or with a counselor in your school's career center. Don't underestimate the value of discussing your goals and your plans for achieving them. Get as much feedback as you can. Then, if necessary, modify your goals and plans into realistic, attainable maps for your future. By getting into the goal-setting mode, you can put yourself in control not only of your academic life but also of your life after college.

FINAL WORDS

What should you do if you're worried that your goals are going to change?

Goals can change. There's no rule that you can't rethink your objectives after you've defined them. One student seemed generally irked that she had to check in with an academic adviser before registering for her first semester of classes. She knew without a doubt that she wanted to go into dentistry and didn't feel that she needed advice from anyone. But the adviser pointed out something she had overlooked. She needed to take an English course in order to meet the college's distribution requirement. That course was a revelation. She fell in love with literature and shifted sharply toward a career in publishing, a goal she pursued with the same passion, determination, and planning that she had originally devoted to dentistry. Yes, goals can change. But that's no excuse to settle for murky, ill-defined objectives. The skills you develop and lessons you learn in defining your goals will serve you well, no matter where they wind up taking you.

HAVE YOU MISSED SOMETHING?

SENTENCE COMPLETION   *Complete the following sentences with one of the three words listed below each sentence.*

1. Based on many of our common expressions, it seems that a goal is considered a _____.

   promise   destination   liability

2. The best way to come up with a plan is to balance wise advice with your own personal _____.

   shortcomings   experience   success

3. Goals and plans won't do you any good without _____.

   action   education   discussion

MATCHING

In each blank space in the left column, write the letter preceding the phrase in the right column that matches the left item best.

_____ 1. Frankl

a. Warned that "burnout" may result if you aren't doing "the stuff you like"

_____ 2. Thoreau

b. Defined a clear goal of putting Americans on the moon and returning them safely to earth

_____ 3. LeBon

c. Suggested that we should regularly ask ourselves what would make us happy

_____ 4. Gould

d. Suggested that those who seem out of step may just hear a different drummer

_____ 5. Peale

e. Noticed the collective mindset that emerges when people become part of a crowd

_____ 6. Rau

f. Reported that 85 percent of students who attempted suicide said that "life was meaningless"

_____ 7. Williams

g. Used the shout of "fire" in a theater as an illustration of crowd psychology

_____ 8. Kennedy

h. Advocated vividly picturing a desired goal or objective in your conscious mind

TRUE-FALSE

Write T *beside the* true *statements and* F *beside the* false *statements.*

_____ 1. It's not a good idea to discuss your goals with close friends and family.

_____ 2. When you join a crowd, your individual thinking is replaced by crowd psychology.

_____ 3. Norman Vincent Peale was a nineteenth-century naturalist and philosopher who lived in the woods near Walden Pond.

_____ 4. The purpose of a goal is to give you an idea of where you are headed.

_____ 5. Health, happiness, and security are all excellent career goals.

MULTIPLE CHOICE

Choose the word or phrase that completes each sentence most accurately, and circle the letter that precedes it.

1. When it comes to setting goals, GPA stands for a goal, a plan, and an

a. acumen.

b. article.

c. average.

d. action.

2. Passing a test is generally considered to be a
   a. minor goal.
   b. major goal.
   c. common excuse.
   d. scholastic requirement.

3. Once you arrive at a goal, you should
   a. stick with it.
   b. keep it a secret.
   c. write it down as a reminder.
   d. come up with a backup goal.

4. Coming up with a plan is like
   a. running a race.
   b. building a fire.
   c. drawing a map.
   d. none of the above.

5. One of the greatest obstacles to success is
   a. procrastination.
   b. lack of money.
   c. education.
   d. boredom.

SHORT ANSWER   *Supply a brief answer for each of the following items.*

1. Explain Norman Vincent Peale's notion of "imaging."
2. Relate the story of the "polar route" to the discussion of planning.
3. Discuss the role of minor goals.
4. Elaborate on the four recommended steps for arriving at a goal.

WORDS IN CONTEXT

From the three choices beside each numbered item, select the one that most nearly expresses the meaning of the italicized word in the quote. Make a light check mark (✓) next to your choice.

Nothing in the world can take the place of *persistence*. *Talent* will not; nothing is more common than unsuccessful men of talent. *Genius* will not; unrewarded genius is almost a byword. Education will not; the world is full of educated *derelicts*. The slogan "Press on" has solved and always will solve the problems of the human race.

—Calvin Coolidge (1872–1933), thirtieth president of the United States

1. place of *persistence*   perseverance   principles   mottoes

2. *talent* will not   nobility   tradition   natural gift

3. *genius* will not   high aptitude   distinction   status

4. educated *derelicts*   snobs   vagrants   tycoons

Don't be afraid to take a big step. You can't cross a *chasm* in two small jumps.
—David Lloyd George (1863–1945), British statesman and prime minister

5. cross a *chasm*   river   gorge   peak

Call it what you will. *Incentives* are the only way to make people work harder.
—Nikita Krushchev (1894–1971), Soviet premier

6. *incentives . . .*   rewards   praise   punishment
   make people work harder

THE WORD HISTORY SYSTEM

Tantalize
to torment with the punishment of Tantalus

tantalize   TAN′-ta-lize′ *v.* To excite (another) by exposing something desirable while keeping it out of reach.

In Greek mythology, King Tantalus offended the gods and was punished in an extraordinary manner. He was placed in the midst of a lake whose waters reached his chin but receded whenever he attempted to allay his thirst. Over his head hung branches laden with choice fruit, which likewise receded whenever he stretched out his hand to satisfy his hunger. Tantalus became the symbol of such teasing, and his name is the root of our verb *tantalize*.

Reprinted by permission. From *Picturesque Word Origins* © 1933 by G. & C. Merriam Co. (now Merriam-Webster, Incorporated).

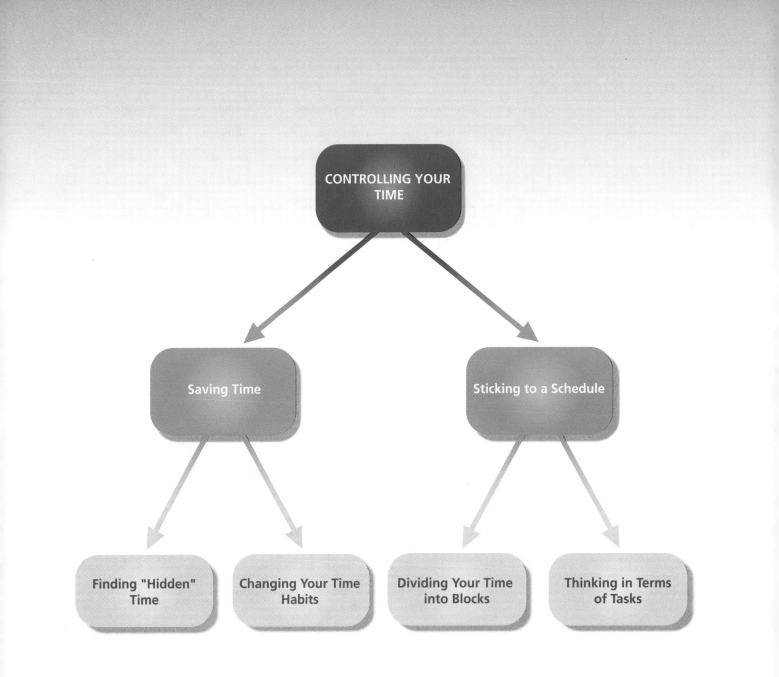

Controlling Your Time

Time flies, but that's no reason for you to go through each day simply "winging it." Through conscientious use of time and commonsense planning, you can make the most of your day. This chapter ticks off the important elements of time management, including:

- **Finding "Hidden" Time**
- **Changing Your Time Habits**
- **Dividing Your Time into Blocks**
- **Thinking in Terms of Tasks**

How important is time management to your academic success?

Time is a precious and irreplaceable commodity. As she lay on her deathbed, Queen Elizabeth I of England (1533–1603) reportedly said, "All my possessions for a moment of time." How you use time can determine your success or failure in college. If you use time wisely, you'll prosper. If you use it poorly, you'll fail in the job you came to do. That's why the management of time is the number-one skill to master in college.

What did the Fordham study find about how students use their time?

Yet students frequently squander time. A survey conducted at Fordham University found that college freshmen spent roughly one-third of their waking hours engaged in social activities or idle leisure during a typical weekday. This "free time" amounted to nearly twice the time they spent studying. And on the weekend the ratio of social and idle leisure time to study time for the same group was almost six to one!

How can you gain extra time?

Although the students in the survey seemed to waste time routinely, you needn't put yourself in the same position. You can gain extra time in two ways: (1) by doing a job in less time than usual, and (2) by taking control of your time. The first way requires you to study more efficiently, and this book provides a great many techniques to help you do just that. The second way requires you to save time by reclaiming "hidden" time and improving your time habits and to better manage your time by sticking to a schedule.

Saving Time

How can you put your time to better use?

All of us have claimed that we don't have enough time to accomplish what we need to do. But the fact is that everyone is allotted the same amount of time: twenty-four hours a day. Many of us allow a lot of this time to go to waste by failing to realize it is available in the first place. In addition, it's often our day-to-day habits, activities we no longer notice, that save time or waste it. You can put your time to better use by pinpointing areas of "hidden" time and cultivating time-saving habits.

Finding "Hidden" Time

What is "hidden" time?

There's a lot of valuable time in your day that is being overlooked, simply because you didn't realize it was time you could use. For those who flush tiny slivers of soap down the drain or toss small scraps of cloth into the wastebasket, there are others who combine those slippery bits and pieces into a whole new bar or stitch discarded shreds into a comfortable quilt. Think of all the time you spend standing in line or even waiting for a traffic light to change. If you could find ways to make use of this "hidden" time, you could almost certainly add hours to each week.

Carry Pocket Work

How does pocket work use hidden time?

Many situations may leave you with a few moments of unexpected free time—a long line at the bank or supermarket, a delayed bus or train, a wait at the doctor's office, a lunch date who arrives late. If you make a point to bring along a book, a photocopied article, index cards on which you've written key concepts, vocabulary words, or formulas, you'll be able to take advantage of otherwise frustrating experiences.

Use Your Mind When It's Free

When is your mind free for studying?

Some activities may afford an overlooked opportunity for studying if you're prepared. For example, if you're shaving, combing your hair, or washing dishes, there's no reason you can't be studying at the same time. Since many of us tend to "zone out" in such situations, they are excellent opportunities to use time that might otherwise be squandered. Attach small metal or plastic clips near mirrors and on walls at eye level. Place a note card in each clip. Do a problem or two in math or master some new vocabulary words as you eat a sandwich at work.

Record Study Information

How can recording information use hidden time?

Another way of using hidden time is by listening to information you've recorded on audiocassettes or MP3 files or burned onto CDs. Recorded information enables you to keep studying in situations where you're moving about or your eyes are otherwise occupied, such as when you're getting dressed or driving. In addition, recorded information can provide a refreshing change from written material.

Employ Spare-Time Thinking

What is spare-time thinking?

You can make the most of the moments immediately before or after class by recalling the main points from the last lecture as you're heading to class or by quickly recalling the points of a just-completed lecture as you're leaving class.

Use Your Subconscious

How can you use your subconscious to save time?

At one point or another, you have awakened during the night with a bright idea or a solution to a problem that you had been thinking about before bedtime. Your subconscious works while your conscious mind is resting. If you want to capture the ideas or solutions produced by your subconscious, write them down as soon as you wake up; otherwise, they'll be lost. Many creative people know this and keep a pad and pencil near their beds. For example, Nobel Prize winner Albert Szent-Györgyi said, "I go to sleep thinking about my problems all the time, and my brain must continue to think about them when I sleep because I wake up, sometimes in the middle of the night, with answers to questions that have been eluding me all day."[1]

[1]Originally published in *Some Watch While Some Must Sleep*, by William C. Dement, as a volume in The Portable Stanford series published by the Stanford Alumni Association. Copyright © 1972. Reprinted by permission of the Stanford Alumni Association.

Changing Your Time Habits

What's a good way to begin saving time?

Habits, by their very nature, are things we do routinely without even thinking. Most of us are unaware of our habits unless someone or something draws attention to them. A good way to take inventory of your time habits is by keeping a daily activities log. From the time you wake up to the time you go to sleep, note all your major activities, the time you started and finished each, and the time each activity consumed. With your day itemized on paper, you can gain a clearer picture of where your time is being spent and where it's being wasted. The activities log in Figure 2.1 shows one student's daily routine and how he decided to put his time to better use.

Figure 2.1
Record of One Day's Activities and Suggestions for Making Better Use of Time

Time Start	Time End	Time Used	Activity – Description	
7:45	8:15	:30	Dress	Paste index cards on mirror: laws of economics; psychological terms; statistical formulas. Study while brushing teeth, etc.
8:15	8:40	:25	Breakfast	
8:40	9:00	:20	Nothing	Look over textbook assignment and previous lecture notes to establish continuity for today's psychology lecture.
9:00	10:00	1:00	Psychology - Lecture	
10:00	10:40	:40	Coffee - Talking	Break too long and too soon after breakfast. Work on psychology notes just taken; also look over economics assignment.
10:40	11:00	:20	Nothing	
11:00	12:00	1:00	Economics - Lecture	
12:00	12:45	:45	Lunch	
12:45	2:00	1:15	Reading - Magazine	Rework the lecture notes on economics while still fresh in mind. Also, look over biology assignment to recall the objectives of the coming lab.
2:00	4:00	2:00	Biology Lab	
4:00	8:00	4:00	Work (includes ½ hour dinner break)	
8:00	8:50	:50	Study - Statistics	
8:50	9:20	:30	Break	Break is too long.
9:20	10:00	:40	Study - Statistics	
10:00	10:50	:50	Chat with Bob	Good as a reward if basic work is done.
10:50	11:30	:40	Study - Accounting	Insufficient time allotted, but better than no time.
11:30	11:45	:15	Ready for bed	While brushing teeth, study the index cards. Replace cards that have been mastered with new ones.
11:45	7:45	8:00	Sleep	

How can you use what you learn from your daily log?

Once you have the concrete evidence of a daily activities log before you, you can begin to eliminate your time-wasting habits and develop or reinforce the time-saving ones.

Defy Parkinson's Law

What can you learn from Parkinson's Law?

Parkinson's Law says that work expands to fit the time allotted.[2] To avoid running out of time, work Parkinson's Law in reverse: For each task, set a deadline that will be difficult to meet, and strive to meet that deadline. Each time you achieve your goal, reward yourself with some small but pleasant activity. Take a break. Chat with a friend. Stroll around the room. Have a special snack, such as a bag of peanuts (keep it in your desk, to be opened only as a reward). If you fail to meet a deadline, don't punish yourself. Just hold back your reward and set another goal. Positive reinforcement is powerful in effecting a change in behavior.

Obey Your Alarm Clock

Why is it so important to obey your alarm?

How many times do you hit the snooze button on your alarm clock before you finally get out of bed? Even one time is too many. Set your alarm for the time you want to get up, not for the time you want to start getting up. If you can't obey your alarm, you'll have a hard time sticking to your time schedule. After all, it doesn't even buzz.

Limit Your E-mail and Internet Time

What can you do to limit your e-mail and Internet time?

As marvelous as they both can be, e-mail in particular and the Internet in general can be tremendous "time sinks," swallowing up hours in a typical day. Rather than checking it constantly, designate specific times during the day when you read and send e-mail. It's true that e-mail has sped up communication, but it's a rare message that can't wait a few hours before being read or sent. The same applies to any Web surfing you may do, whether for schoolwork or pleasure. Time has a tendency to fly by as you click from one link to the next. You can help keep things under control by setting a timer when you surf and returning to your studies when the timer goes off.

Take "Time Out"

What is the value of taking time out?

Reward yourself with regular short breaks as you work. Learning in several small sessions, rather than in one continuous stretch, increases comprehension. In one study, students who practiced French vocabulary in three discrete sessions did 35 percent better on an exam than those who tried to learn the words in one sitting.[3] So take a breather for ten minutes every hour, or rest for five

[2]C. Parkinson, *Parkinson, the Law* (Boston: Houghton Mifflin, 1980).

[3]Kristine C. Bloom et al., "Effects of Massed and Distributed Practice on the Learning and Retention of Second-Language Vocabulary," *Journal of Educational Research* 74, no. 4 (March–April 1981): 245–248.

minutes every half-hour. Whichever method you choose, keep your breaks consistent. This way, you'll study with more energy and look forward to your regular rests. When you return to your desk, you'll find that you feel more refreshed.

Listen to Your Body

How can understanding circadian rhythms affect your scheduling?

All of us are subject to circadian rhythms. That is, we have periods when we're most wide awake and alert and other periods when we're sluggish or drowsy. In general, we're sleepiest a few hours before dawn and twelve hours later, in mid-afternoon. In keeping with these natural cycles, we're widest awake about every twelve hours, usually at mid-morning and again in mid-evening. Knowing this can help you plan the day's activities more strategically.

1. *Schedule cerebral tasks for mornings and evenings.* Reading, writing, problem solving, and other "thinking tasks" should be done when you're likely to be most alert.
2. *Save active behavior for mid-afternoon.* Fieldwork, lab work, exercise, and errand running are best done at this time of day, when more sedentary activities may make you feel drowsy. If you're not a heavy coffee drinker, a cup of coffee might get you through the afternoon slump.
3. *Resist the temptation to sleep in on the weekends.* Changing your sleep schedule on the weekends can have a chain reaction effect on the following week. You may find yourself feeling jet-lagged on Monday or Tuesday if you sleep in on Saturday or Sunday.
4. *Read in the morning; review in the afternoon.* Scientists have discovered that short-term memory peaks at about nine o'clock in the morning and that long-term memory is strongest at about three o'clock in the afternoon.

Keep a Notepad Handy

How can a notepad improve your time habits?

As we'll see in the next chapter, stray thoughts and worries can really cut into your ability to concentrate. They can also eat up valuable time. The best way to deal with these distractions is to get them out of your head and onto a piece of paper as quickly as possible, then return to your work. Writing these thoughts down can result in an additional time-saving bonus. Getting started is often the hardest part of shifting from one activity to another. Your jottings may provide a needed jump-start to overcome the inertia that seems to characterize the outset of a new activity. If so, they may save you some valuable time. Here is an example from the note pad of one student who, while working on a calculus assignment, came up with a topic for an upcoming paper. As soon as she finished her calculus, she was able to begin doing preliminary research on the topic without delay.

Call Prof. Singh about make-up test.
Check Campbell book for discussion of brain laterality.
What about "Earthquake Prediction" as possible paper topic?
Look up definitions for leftover vocabulary cards.
Tennis at 6 tonight, not 7!

Of course, although spontaneous scribblings can sometimes provide guidance as you're moving from one task to the next, a far better strategy is to come up with a schedule and stick to it.

Sticking to a Schedule

What is the function of a time schedule?

A time schedule is a game plan, a written strategy that spells out exactly what you hope to accomplish—during a day, a week, or even the entire term—and how you plan to do it. Committing yourself to planning and keeping to a schedule can seem a bit frightening at first, but following a schedule soon becomes a source of strength and a boon to your life. There are several benefits to a schedule.

How will a schedule provide greater control?

A schedule provides greater control.   A thoughtfully constructed time schedule can increase your sense of control in four ways. First, because your schedule is written down, your plans seem more manageable. You can start working without delay. Second, you know you'll study all your subjects—even those you dislike—because you've allotted time for them in your schedule. There's less of a temptation to skip disliked subjects when study time has already been allotted for them. Third, a schedule discourages laziness. You've got a plan right in front of you, and that plan says, "Let's get down to business!" Fourth, you can schedule review sessions right from the start and avoid last-minute cramming for tests.

How does a schedule encourage relaxation?

A schedule encourages relaxation.   At the same time, because your plan is written down instead of floating around in your head, your mind is freed for other things. There's no time wasted worrying about what to do next. It's all there on paper. There's no guilt either. Both work and play are written into your schedule. This means that when you take a break, you know you deserve it.

Why are some students reluctant to use time schedules?

Despite these benefits, many students are reluctant to start using time schedules. They feel not only that a schedule will do them little good but also that keeping track of time will turn them into nervous wrecks. Neither worry is warranted.

How does a schedule save you time?

A schedule saves time.   Yes, it takes time to devise a schedule, but that time is rewarded. You will be able to shift smoothly from one activity to another, without wondering what to do next.

How does a schedule provide freedom?

A schedule provides freedom.   Scheduling frees you from time's control. The people you see dashing from class to library to gym, or eating lunch on the run, are slaves to time. The students who schedule time, who decide how time will be used, are the masters of time.

In what way does scheduling increase flexibility?

A schedule increases flexibility.   Disorganized people often waste so much time that there's no room for flexibility. People who use schedules free their time for a variety of activities and are therefore more flexible.

Which schedule type is best: time-based or task-based?

If you are a full-time student or have considerable control over the hours in your day, your best bet is to rely on traditional schedules that divide your time into manageable blocks. If, however, you are juggling your academic life with the responsibilities of a job or the demands of raising a family, you're probably better off using schedules that focus on tasks instead of on time. Each approach has advantages, but both provide an opportunity to tackle tasks with a genuine game plan instead of flailing at them haphazardly.

Dividing Your Time into Blocks

What does the story of the sticks illustrate about time?

A father once tied a bundle of small, thin sticks together with a strand of twine, handed the bundle to his youngest son, and said, "Son, break these sticks in half." The boy used his hands and knees but could not break the bundle. Sadly, he handed it back to his father. Without a word, the father untied the twine, and using only his fingers, snapped each stick one by one.

What is the advantage of dividing your time into blocks?

When the sum total of your obligations and academic assignments seems overwhelming, it helps immensely to split them up into small, manageable units. By dividing each day into blocks, time schedules break up your responsibilities and allow you to deal with them one by one. Assigning a block of time to each activity ensures that you will work at peak efficiency.

What are the components of the three-part scheduling system?

Using time blocks, you can create a three-part scheduling system consisting of (1) a master schedule, (2) a weekly schedule, and (3) a daily schedule. Each plays an integral role in managing your time. The master schedule serves as a basic structure for organizing your activities; the weekly schedule adds specific details to the master schedule; and the daily schedule puts the weekly schedule into a portable form. Although each schedule performs a different function, all three follow the same basic scheduling guidelines:

What is the best way to use big blocks of time?

1. *Don't waste big blocks.* If you have a big block of time, use it for a big assignment. There's a strong tendency to say, "I'm going to get these smaller assignments out of the way before I tackle the big assignment." This is a poor decision. Instead, use the large block of time for a large and time-intensive assignment, and save your small assignments for the little slivers of time.

When it comes to studying, what is prime time?

2. *Study during prime time.* For most of us, prime time is daytime. In fact, research has shown that each hour used for study during the day is equal to an hour and a half at night. Even so, you may find that you have dead hours

during the day when you are less productive than you'd like to be. Schedule less-demanding tasks for these hours.

How does the type of class influence when you should study for it?

3. *Study before recitation classes and after lecture classes.* A study session before a recitation or discussion class (a foreign language course or a psychology seminar, for example) helps warm you up. When you walk into class, the material is fresh in your mind. For lecture classes, use the time immediately after class to fill in any gaps in your notes and to review the information you've just learned.

Why should you shy away from making your schedule too detailed?

4. *Don't let details tie your hands.* Account for all your time, but don't be overly detailed. The time you'd take to make an overly meticulous schedule can be better used in studying a subject directly, and the chances of your following such a strict plan are slim.

What sorts of nonacademic activities belong in your schedule?

5. *Include nonacademic activities.* Always set aside time for food, sleep, and recreation as well as the other activities of your life. Cheating yourself out of a meal, a good night's sleep, a swim, a family get-together, or a meeting with friends won't save you time in the long run. In fact, it may cost you time because all these activities are necessary for your overall mental and physical wellness. Make your plan for living, not just for studying.

Lay a Foundation with a Master Schedule

What is the purpose of the master schedule?

A master schedule provides an agenda of fixed activities around which your varying activities are arranged. Unless changes occur in your basic program, you need to draw up a master schedule only once per term.

What does a master schedule look like?

A master schedule grid lists the days of the week at the top and the hours of the day down the left side. The boxes in the grid are filled in with all your required activities: sleep, meals, job, regular meetings, community activities, sports, and, of course, classes. The empty boxes that remain represent your free time. Figure 2.2 provides an example of a typical master schedule.

How does a master schedule help?

A master schedule, on a five-by-eight-inch card taped over your desk or carried in your notebook, unclutters your mind. More important, it enables you to visualize actual blocks of time into which you can fit necessary activities.

Account for Changing Details with a Weekly Schedule

What is the purpose of a weekly schedule?

The weekly schedule takes over where the master schedule leaves off. To construct it, photocopy or print out another copy of your master schedule, and fill in the empty blocks with the activities you have planned for the upcoming week. If you have a math test on Friday, for example, you will need to schedule a little extra study time for math. Next week you may be assigned a research paper. If so, you'll probably want to leave space in your schedule for library or Internet research. The weekly schedule helps you adapt your time to your changing priorities. Keep it posted by your desk or pasted on the inside cover of your notebook.

Figure 2.2
A Master Schedule with Work

	Mon.	Tues.	Wed.	Thurs.	Fri.	Sat.	Sun.
7-8	←		Dress and Breakfast		→		
8-9	Bio-Sc		Bio-Sc		Bio-Sc	Dress & Breakfast	
9-10		P.E.		P.E.		P.E.	Dress & Breakfast
10-11	History		History		History		
11-12		Spanish		Spanish		Spanish	
12-1	←			Lunch			→
1-2	Math	Computer Lab.	Math	Computer Lab.	Math		
2-3	English		English		English		
3-4		Work-study Prog.		Work-study Prog.			
4-5	Work-study		Work-study		Work-study		
5-6							
6-7	←			Dinner			→
7-8							
8-9							
9-10							
10-11							
11-12	←			Sleep			→

A sample weekly schedule is shown in Figure 2.3. The lists that follow show how the guidelines for scheduling were used to set it up.

Monday Through Friday/Saturday

7–8 A.M.	Avoid the frantic dash and the gobbled (or skipped) breakfast by getting up on time.
12–1 P.M.	Take a full, leisurely hour for lunch.
5–6	Relax before dinner—your reward for a day of conscientious work.
7–9	Keep up with current notes and assignments through systematic studying.
9–10	To forestall cramming at quiz and examination times, give some time every day to a review of previous assignments and ground covered to date.
10	A cease-study time of 10 P.M. provides an incentive for working hard during the day and early evening.
10–12	Devote some time every day to reading books that truly interest you. Recreational reading and conversation help you unwind for a good night's sleep.

Tuesday/Thursday/Saturday

8–9 A.M.	Because chemistry (10–11) is your hardest subject, build your morning study program around it. An hour's study before class will make the class period more meaningful.
11–12 P.M.	Another hour's study immediately after chemistry class will help you remember the work covered in class and move more readily to the next assignment.

Special

Tuesday	2–5 P.M.	Library: paper
Sunday	7–9 P.M.	English paper

For some assignments you will need to schedule blocks of time to do research or to develop and follow up on ideas.

Saturday	From noon on, Saturday is left unscheduled—for recreation, for special projects to which you must devote a concentrated period of time, for extra work on difficult subjects, for thorough review.
Sunday	This is your day until evening. Study history before you go to bed because it is the first class you'll have on Monday morning.

Figure 2.3
A Detailed Weekly Schedule Based on a Master Schedule

Time	Mon.	Tues.	Wed.	Thurs.	Fri.	Sat.	Sun.
7-8	← Dress and Breakfast →						
8-9	History	Study Chem.	History	Study Chem.	History	Study Chem.	
9-10	Study History	Phys. Ed.	Study History	Phys. Ed.	Study History	Phys. Ed.	Religious Service, Recreation, Conversation, Recreational Reading
10-11	Study French	Chem.	Study French	Chem.	Study French	Chem.	
11-12	French	Study Chem.	French	Study Chem.	French	Study Chem.	
12-1	← Lunch →						
1-2	Math	Film-making	Math	Film-making	Math		
2-3	Study Math	Library: Paper	Study Math	↑	Study Math	Recreation, Conversation, Special Projects, Reading, Extra Work on Difficult Subjects Through Review	
3-4	Study English	Library: Paper	Study English	Chem. Lab.	Study English		
4-5	English	Library: Paper	English	↓	English		
5-6	← Recreation →						English Paper
6-7	← Dinner →						
7-8	Study English	Study Math	Study English	Study Math	Study English		English Paper
8-9	Study French	Study History	Study French	Study History	Study French		English Paper
9-10	Review English	Review French	Review History	Review Math	Review Chem.		Study History
10-11	← Recreational Reading →						
11-12	← Conversation, Sleep →						

Provide a Portable Game Plan with a Daily Schedule

What goes into a daily schedule?

A daily schedule is a brief yet specific list of the day's tasks and the time blocks you plan to accomplish them in. You should be able to fit all this information on an index card that you can carry around with you all day. Make up your daily schedule each night before you go to bed. Once you have put your worries and concerns on paper, your mind will be free for sleep. You will also have thought through your day and will be better prepared when the morning comes. Figure 2.4 shows one student's daily schedule and explains why it is effective.

Figure 2.4
A Daily Schedule

FOR MONDAY

8-9	Psychology - Review Chapter V and Lecture Notes
9-10	Psychology Lecture
10-11	Economics Lecture
11-12	Economics - Fix Up Notes, Begin Chapter VII
1-2	Campus Store - Pick Up Paper and Binder, Pen, Lead, Calculator
2-5	Engineering - Work on Assignment
5-6	Exercise - Tennis Court with Joan
7-10	Accounting and Math

Review: Just before class is a good time to review the high points of chapters previously studied. Also review the previous lecture for continuity.

Fix up notes: The very best time to fix up lecture notes, and review them simultaneously, is immediately after the lecture.

After lunch: This is a good time to give yourself a semi-break from academic work and do some necessary errands.

2-5 block: This a valuable block of time during which you should be able to read the assignment and work out the assigned problems without losing continuity.

Exercise: After an entire day with the books, some exercise and a shower will help put an edge on your appetite, as well as make a definite break between study during the day and study during the evening.

Breaks: Breaks are not listed. You judge for yourself when a break is best for you. Also, the break should be taken when you arrive at a good stopping point.

After dinner: Both subjects need unbroken time for efficient production. Use the block of three hours to do a balanced amount of work for each, depending on the assignments.

What are the pros and cons of special scheduling tools?

Use Scheduling Tools If You Feel Comfortable with Them

These days, you can choose from a growing variety of tools and utilities, from computer software to personal digital assistants to Internet applications to hefty loose-leaf notebooks, all designed to make scheduling your time both easier and more intelligent. These tools may provide the breakthrough that some students need to finally begin to appreciate the importance of keeping a schedule. For other students, they are an elaborate, costly, time-intensive distraction that does little to control or organize time. Index cards and blank sheets of paper may not be all that sophisticated, but they are extremely inexpensive and breathtakingly simple, and they can usually provide all you need to get a firm grasp on your available time. If you swear by your scheduling software or your store-bought appointment book, that's fine. As long as you keep in mind that your goal is managing time, you can make just about any system work. The essential component is not the tool, but rather the person who is using it.

Thinking in Terms of Tasks

When is it preferable to use task-based scheduling?

Because of the way a schedule based on time blocks divides the day into manageable bite-sized segments, it is often preferable for most students. But some of us don't have the luxury of predictably structuring our days from top to bottom. If your days are largely unpredictable or your free time is fluid, you may need schedules that emphasize tasks instead of blocks of time. In addition, long-term assignments, which can't always be squeezed into time blocks, may require a task-based approach.

How did Ivy Lee demonstrate the value of tasks?

Anyone who's ever had the satisfaction of systematically crossing items off a lengthy to-do list has at least an inkling of the effectiveness of a task-based approach. During the first half of the twentieth century, legendary management consultant Ivy Lee demonstrated just how effective—and lucrative—it could be to view things in terms of tasks.

Charles Schwab, then chairman of the Bethlehem Steel Company, challenged Lee: "Show me a way to get more things done with my time, and I'll pay you any fee within reason." Lee thought for a while, then said,

- Every *evening* write down the six most important tasks for the next day in order of priority.
- Every *morning* start working on task #1 and continue until you finish it; then start on task #2, and so on. Do this until quitting time and don't be concerned if you have finished only one or two tasks.
- At the end of each day, tear up the list and start over.

When Schwab asked how much he owed for this advice, Ivy Lee told him to use the plan for a few weeks, then send in a check for whatever he thought it was worth.[4] Three weeks later, Lee received a check for $25,000, which is equal to about $250,000 in today's dollars!

By using good judgment, you can allot the bulk of your time to getting top-priority tasks done, yet not ignore other tasks with due dates.

Of course, just as a daily schedule would provide only a limited view of your tasks, a single to-do list is not sufficient for a task-based approach to help you through the entire semester. Whether it hinges on time blocks or tasks, a three-part scheduling system still makes sense. If you're focusing on tasks, you'll need (1) a task-based master schedule and (2) a weekly assignment-oriented schedule in addition to (3) a daily to-do list.

Develop a Task-Based Master Schedule

A task-based master schedule enables you to keep track of one or more assignments or goals over an extended period of time. Figure 2.5 provides an example of a task-based schedule. Across the top of the schedule, instead of the days of the week, list the major goals you hope to accomplish or the assignments you plan to complete. Deadlines for subgoals may be written down the left side, where the hours of the day would normally be written in a standard master schedule.

Now divide each goal or long-term assignment into manageable subgoals. List them in a column beneath the task they refer to. For example, if you've been assigned a research paper, you may arrive at the following subgoals: do preliminary research, choose topic, plan outline, conduct research, complete first draft, and revise first draft. As you reach each milestone on the way to completing your assignment, cross it off your schedule. As you do, you provide yourself with visual evidence of and positive feedback for the progress you've made.

Make Your Weekly Schedule Assignment-Oriented

If the span of your goal or assignment is a week or less, you can use an assignment-oriented weekly schedule as a supplement to your master schedule. Figure 2.6 shows such a schedule. The format is simple. Draw a horizontal line to divide an eight-and-one-half-by-eleven-inch sheet of paper in half. In the top half, list your subjects, assignments, estimated study times, and due dates. Then, with the due dates and estimated times as control factors, check your master schedule for available time. Allocate enough hours to do the job, and write them on the appropriate line on the bottom half of the sheet. Stick to your schedule. As long as you give study hours top priority, your remaining hours will be truly free.

[4]T. W. Engstrom and R. A. Mackensie, *Managing Your Time* (Grand Rapids, MI: Zondervan, 1967).

What sort of schedules do you need for a task-based approach?

How does a task-based master schedule differ from a standard master schedule?

How do you divide your goals into subgoals?

When should you use an assignment-oriented weekly schedule?

Figure 2.5
A Task-Based Master Schedule

	Psychology Research Paper April 21	Train for Amateur Triathlon May 1	Self-Paced Computer Course
Feb. 7	Select Three Topic Ideas	Up Minimum to 60 Laps	Complete Ch. 1-3
Feb. 10	Do Preliminary Research	Try Ride Up Satyr Hill	
Feb. 14	Make Final Topic Choice	Run 30 Miles Per Week	Complete Ch. 4-6
Feb. 18	Complete Bibliography		
March 15	Finish First Draft		Mid-term Exam
March 18	Begin Rewriting		
April 21	Paper Due		Final

Figure 2.6
A Weekly Schedule Based on Assignments

Subject	Assignment	Estimated Time	Date Due	Time Due
Electronics	Chapter V - 32 pp. - Read	2 hr.	Mon. 13th	8:00
English	Paper to Write	18 hr.	Mon. 20th	9:00
Math	Problems on pp. 110-111	3 hr.	Tues. 14th	10:00
Industrial Safety	Make Shop Layouts	8 hr.	Fri. 17th	11:00
Computer Graphics	Generate Slide Presentation (2-4 slides)	6 hr.	Fri. 17th	1:00
Electronics	Chapter VI - 40pp. - Read	2 1/2 hr.	Weds. 22nd	8:00

Day	Assignment	Morning	Afternoon	Evening
Sun.	Electronics - Read Chap V English - Find a Topic			7:30-9:30 9:30-10:30
Mon.	English - Gather Notes Math - Problems		2:00-6:00	7:00-10:00
Tues.	English - Gather Notes Industrial Safety	8:00-10:00	3:00-6:00	7:00-10:00
Wed.	English - First Draft Computer Graphics		2:00-6:00	7:00-10:00
Thurs.	Industrial Safety English - Paper Computer Graphics	8:00-10:00	3:00-6:00	7:00-10:00
Fri.	English - Final Copy Electronics		2:00-6:00	7:00-9:30
Sat.				

Turn Your Daily Schedule into a To-Do List

How should you adjust your daily schedule when your time is unpredictable?

Your daily study schedule should simply be a list of things to do arranged in order of priority on an index card. In this case, assigning specific times is likely to lead to frustration.

Figure 2.7 shows a typical daily list. To be successful, you need a sense of urgency about referring to your list and studying whenever an opportunity presents itself. Cross off the tasks as you complete them.

Figure 2.7
A Things-to-Do List

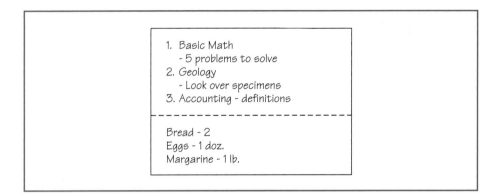

1. Basic Math
   - 5 problems to solve
2. Geology
   - Look over specimens
3. Accounting - definitions
- -
Bread - 2
Eggs - 1 doz.
Margarine - 1 lb.

What is the Pareto Principle?

Use the *Pareto Principle* to help draw up your list. Named after Vilfredo Pareto (1848–1923), an Italian economist and sociologist, the Pareto Principle states that the truly important items in any group constitute only a small number of the total items in the group. This principle is also known as the *80/20 rule*.[5]

What are some examples of the 80/20 rule?

For example, in almost any sales force, 80 percent of the business is brought in by 20 percent of the salespeople. In any committee, 80 percent of the ideas come from 20 percent of the members. In a classroom, 80 percent of the teacher's time is taken up by 20 percent of the students.

In any list of things to do, 80 percent of the importance resides in 20 percent of the list. In a list of ten items, 80 percent of the list's value lies in two items, which constitute 20 percent of the list. Because of the Pareto Principle, always list the most important items first. Then, if you accomplish only the first few items, you will have accomplished the most important tasks.

Keep the Pareto Principle in mind whenever you make up a list or a schedule or must decide which subject to study first. Apply the principle by listing first things first.[6]

[5]Reprinted with the permission of Scribner, a Division of Simon & Schuster, from *Getting Things Done*, Revised and Updated Edition, by Edwin C. Bliss. Copyright © 1976, 1991 by Edwin C. Bliss.

[6]B. Eugene Griessman, *Time Tactics of Very Successful People* (New York: McGraw-Hill, 1994).

FINAL WORDS

Why do people who understand the importance of time continue to waste it?

Let's face it. Most people understand the supreme importance of time and the value of sticking to a schedule, yet many of us continue to waste time needlessly. Why? Perhaps it is because we are human beings, not machines. Learning to use time wisely after years of wasting it doesn't happen by simply flipping a switch. Controlling your time is ultimately a matter of developing the right mindset. If the dying words of Queen Elizabeth and the compelling evidence of this chapter haven't been enough to convince you to change your time-wasting ways, perhaps the following tidbits about time will finally make things click.

Ten Valuable Tidbits About Time

1. One of America's greatest composers, jazz giant Duke Ellington still wasn't ashamed to admit that "Without a deadline, I can't finish nothin'."
2. If you've got a long list of things to do but you're spinning your wheels, start with the easier tasks. Getting one done makes the next one easier. Build momentum.
3. Be a contrarian. Go to the library when almost nobody is there. Get into the dining-hall line before the crowd. Get the reserved books before the line forms. The time you save will add up quickly.
4. Make decisions wisely by asking, "What are the alternatives?" Make a list of the alternatives, and then put pluses and minuses alongside them. Learn this process. It will save lots of time.
5. Don't spread yourself thin by attempting to become an "information junkie." This scattershot approach takes up a great deal of time and can still leave you feeling stressed and dissatisfied. Just make sure that you gain a firm grip on your own field.
6. A lot of time is lost by looking for misplaced notes, books, journals, and reports. Make an unbreakable rule: a place for everything, and everything in its place.
7. "Most people," says motivational speaker Anthony Robbins, "would not see an awful movie a second time, yet they play the same bad memories over and over again in their heads."
8. When you're really through studying, spend an extra fifteen minutes studying just an extra bit more.
9. If the thought of saving time sounds sensible but uninspiring, ask yourself this simple question: What do I want to save time for? Suddenly, the efficient use of time may take on a significance that it never had before.

10. A Sanskrit proverb puts everything in proper perspective:
    Today well lived
    Makes every yesterday a dream of happiness
    And every tomorrow a vision of hope
    Look well therefore to this day.

HAVE YOU MISSED SOMETHING?

SENTENCE COMPLETION   *Complete the following sentences with one of the three words listed below each sentence.*

1. A time schedule functions as a _____.

   reward   game plan   punishment

2. When it comes to studying, "prime time" is usually _____.

   daytime   mid-afternoon   flexible

3. A master schedule should normally be drawn up once a _____.

   day   week   term

MATCHING   *In each blank space in the left column, write the letter preceding the phrase in the right column that matches the left item best.*

_____ 1. Pocket work

_____ 2. E-mail

_____ 3. Master schedule

_____ 4. "Free time"

_____ 5. Pareto Principle

_____ 6. Szent-Györgyi

_____ 7. Parkinson's Law

_____ 8. Circadian

a. Work expands to fit the time allotted

b. Consumes a large portion of a typical first-year student's weekday

c. Nobel Prize winner who used sleep time to solve problems

d. Provides a basic structure for organizing the term's activities

e. Rhythms that influence your body's cycle of sleeping and waking

f. Productivity boon that can sometimes be a "time sink"

g. Supplies study material for unexpected free time

h. Also known as the 80/20 rule

TRUE-FALSE

Write T *beside the* true *statements and* F *beside the* false *statements.*

_____ 1. Taking breaks has a detrimental effect on comprehension.

_____ 2. Free time can often occur unexpectedly.

_____ 3. Using a time schedue can make you a slave to time.

_____ 4. Scheduling saves time that might otherwise be wasted.

_____ 5. An hour of daytime work is usually more productive than an hour at night.

MULTIPLE CHOICE

Choose the word or phrase that completes each sentence most accurately, and circle the letter that precedes it.

1. When your obligations and assignments begin to seem overwhelming, it helps to
   a. take a nap.
   b. divide your time into blocks.
   c. use Parkinson's Law.
   d. all of the above.

2. "Hidden" time is time that you
   a. aren't allowed to use.
   b. managed to overlook.
   c. reserve for recreation.
   d. leave off your schedule.

3. A good way to take inventory of your time habits is by
   a. checking your master schedule.
   b. asking an instructor to help you.
   c. keeping a daily activities log.
   d. none of the above.

4. The master schedule provides
   a. an alternative to a weekly schedule.
   b. an excuse for increased recreation.
   c. a basic structure for organizing your activities.
   d. a solution to the problem of hidden time.

5. A task-based schedule may be your best bet if
   a. your days are unpredictable.
   b. your free time is fluid.
   c. you have a full-time job.
   d. all of the above.

SHORT ANSWER *Supply a brief answer for each of the following items.*

1. What is the purpose of keeping a daily activities log?
2. In what ways does a schedule promote relaxation?
3. Explain the possible role of a note pad in controlling your time.
4. Discuss how to prepare a task-oriented master schedule.

WORDS IN CONTEXT

From the three choices beside each numbered item, select the one that most nearly expresses the meaning of the italicized word in the quote. Make a light check mark (✓) next to your choice.

Mathematics has given economics *rigor*, but *alas*, also *mortis*.
—Robert L. Heilbroner (1919–), American economist

1. *rigor*	strength	exactitude	precision
2. *alas*	sorrowfully	interestingly	happily
3. *mortis*	humanity	fear	death

Interest you owe works night and day, in fair weather and foul. Interest gnaws at a man's *substance* with invisible teeth.
—Henry Ward Beecher (1813–1887), newspaper editor and clergyman

4. man's *substance*	brain	worth	body

Of all the mysteries of the stock exchange, there is none so *inpenetrable* as why there should be a buyer for everyone who seeks to sell.
—John Kenneth Galbraith (1908–), Canadian-born American economist, writer, and diplomat (ambassador to India)

5. *inpenetrable*   incredible   inexplicable   important

"Involvement" in this context differs from "commitment" in the same sense as the pig's and the chicken's roles in one's breakfast of ham and eggs. The chicken was *involved*—the pig was *committed*.

—Anonymous

6. chicken was *involved*   primed   rejected   associated

7. pig was *committed*   solicited   included   affiliated

THE WORD HISTORY SYSTEM

Tally
a reminder of the early method of counting

tally   tal'-ly   *n.* 1. A reckoning or score. 2. A mark used in recording a number of acts or objects.

Tally goes back to the time when things were commonly counted by cutting notches in a stick of wood. The word was borrowed in Middle English as *taille*, from Old French *taille*, "a cutting." It was formerly customary for traders to have two sticks and to mark with notches on each the number or quantity of goods delivered, the seller keeping one stick and the purchaser the other. When such records came to be kept on paper, the same word was used for them; and it now means almost any kind of count or score.

Reprinted by permission. From *Picturesque Word Origins* © 1933 by G. & C. Merriam Co. (now Merriam-Webster, Incorporated).

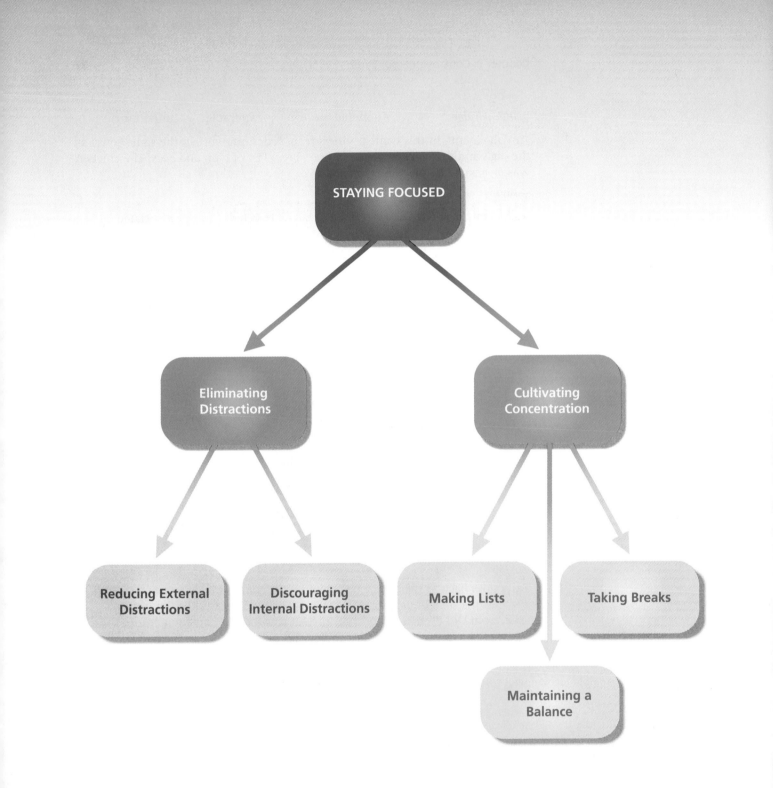

Staying Focused

*Consider the postage
stamp. It secures success
through its ability to stick
to one thing until it gets
there.*

Josh Billings (1818–1885),
pen name of Henry Wheeler
Shaw, American humorist

Everyone—from astronauts to athletes, from merchants to musicians—appreciates the value of being able to focus on the task at hand. Yet few of us know how to attain and then sustain this kind of concentration. Although concentration does not appear at the snap of the fingers, there are ways you can improve the conditions for concentration. To help you stay focused, no matter what your task may be, this chapter deals with:

- **Reducing External Distractions**
- **Finding a Place to Study**
- **Overcoming Internal Distractions**
- **Adopting Strategies for Concentration**

What are some examples of concentration?

Although concentration can sometimes be difficult to define, most of us know it when we see it. Watch a good bowler as she takes her position and directs all her thoughts on knocking down the pins at the end of the alley. Watch a quarterback as he focuses on getting a pass to an open receiver, even while linebackers rush in on him from several directions. That's concentration! Imagine becoming so absorbed in your textbook that you find yourself "talking" to the author: "That's not proof enough," or "Other writers explain it differently," or "I never thought about the problem that way before." Imagine studying your notes so intently that when you finally look up, you see that it's been two hours since you last checked the clock. That's concentration!

What makes concentration elusive?

Concentration is focused thinking. Just as light waves can be focused into a single powerful beam—a laser—concentration can focus the power of your thoughts, enabling you to think with greater precision and penetrate difficult ideas. But powerful as it can be, concentration has an elusive quality. In fact, concentration comes only when you don't think about it. Ironically, if you were thinking deeply about a subject and suddenly realized that you were concentrating, at that moment you would have broken your concentration. Such prolonged, undivided attention can be difficult to achieve. After all, in normal circumstances there are dozens of things competing for your attention. Thoughts and ideas constantly bang, rattle, and knock on the door of your consciousness, trying to gain entry.

What does Figure 3.1 tell us about concentration?

Figure 3.1 provides a vivid illustration of the natural tendency to divide attention. As you gaze at this picture, you'll probably discover that your visual focus is shifting every few seconds so that you first see a goblet, then two profiles, and then the goblet again. Once you're aware of both images, it is difficult for your eyes to focus on one and ignore the other. Similarly, it is hard for your mind to focus on one idea at a time. People who can focus exclusively on the task before them have a much better chance of completing that task more

Figure 3.1
A Goblet or Two Profiles?

quickly and accurately than those who divide their attention even when they don't mean to do so.

So how do you stay focused? Because you can't strive for concentration directly, you must instead try to improve the conditions that promote concentration. That involves eliminating distractions and adopting strategies to enhance concentration.

How can you concentrate if you can't do it directly?

Eliminating Distractions

What's the first step in eliminating distractions?

Trouble concentrating may come from external distractions, such as sights or sounds that compete for your attention, or from internal distractions, such as worries or daydreams. Once recognized, these obstacles to concentration can be overcome.

Reducing External Distractions

What is an external distraction?

Anything that stimulates your senses and in the process disrupts your concentration can be considered an external distraction. Study halls and living quarters are overflowing with such distractions, everything from banging doors to baking bread. To work in a way that is compatible with concentration, you need the proper environment as well as the right equipment.

Select the Proper Environment

What elements make up a proper study environment?

Your study environment should be used exclusively for study. In addition, it should be quiet and well lighted. You can take your work to a place that is already designed for study, or you can create your own study environment.

What is the best environment for study?

Find a Workshop   You'd be hard-pressed to find an environment more suitable for high-quality concentration than a library. It offers a minimum of nonacademic distractions, a quiet atmosphere (usually as a matter of policy), and sufficient lighting. Get in the habit of studying at the library right away, on the first day of class. Even the walk to the library can be used productively as a review session or a refreshing break.

Why is it important to use your study area for studying only?

Whether you choose to work in the library or somewhere else, make sure your study area is reserved for studying. Psychologists emphasize that a conditioning effect is created between the desk and you: If you nap or daydream a lot while sitting at the desk, the desk can act as a cue for napping or daydreaming. By the same token, if you read or work in bed, you make it difficult to work energetically and fall asleep easily. To avoid this negative conditioning, use your desk only for studying. When you feel the urge to nap or daydream, leave your desk to nap or daydream elsewhere.

What other steps can you take to ensure a proper study environment?

Your study area should be your workshop, a place where you feel secure and comfortable. You can ensure that you have the proper environment for study and concentration if you minimize visual distractions, avoid or eliminate distracting noises, refrain from playing music, beware of e-mail and the Internet, control the impulse to register distractions, and provide the area with plenty of light.

How can you reduce visual distractions?

Minimize Visual Distractions   A sheet of notes or a page from a textbook can seem dull compared with a glimpse of a softball game being played on a nearby diamond or a view of gently falling snow. To improve your chances of concentration, avoid competition for your eyes' attention. Study by a window so you can take advantage of the natural light, but keep your head turned away from the potentially distracting view. Of course, not all visual distractions lie on the other side of the windowpane. If your study area contains photographs you're liable to look at, gadgets you're likely to fiddle with, or books you'll be tempted to pick up and read, remove them until you have completed your work.

What can you do to eliminate noise when you study?

Eliminate Noise   If you need a quiet spot for efficient study, do your utmost to find one. Noise can be one of the most serious obstacles to effective study. Nothing is more wasteful than going over the same paragraph again and again because the noise makes it impossible to absorb what you are reading. If the library is the right place for you, make an effort to study there whenever you can. If you study at home, achieving quiet can sometimes be as simple as closing a door or inserting ear plugs.

Is music a distraction?

Turn Down the Loud Music   When studying, loud music, especially vocal music, can break your concentration. To keep your concentration from bouncing between the music and your books, you expend energy that could be put to better use. However, some students can tolerate music better than others. If you find music nonintrusive, then instrumental music—played softly—could form a pleasing background, and such a background can actually muffle some external, intermittent noises.

What can you do to prevent e-mail and the Internet from becoming distractions?

Beware of E-mail and the Internet   E-mail has been a tremendous boon to communication. And the Internet has opened vast avenues of information that were available only to experts just a decade or so ago. But when you're trying to concentrate, both e-mail and the Internet can be gigantic distractions. Unless you're working *on* your computer, you shouldn't be working *at* your computer. Avoid the temptation to surf or constantly check e-mail by keeping your screen out of your line of sight. If you *are* working on your computer, turn off your e-mail application and limit your Web surfing to the work at hand. If you're expecting important e-mail, set a timer for an hour or so, and work without interruption before checking. When the timer goes off, check for mail, then start the timer again.

What does the spider technique involve?

Try the Spider Technique   A vibrating tuning fork held close to a spider's web sets up vibrations in the web. After the spider makes a few hurried investigations and finds no fly in the web, it learns to ignore the vibrations. The next time you are studying in the library and the door opens, don't look up. Controlling your impulse to look up will disturb your concentration the first few times. But very soon, like the spider, you'll learn to ignore these external disturbances.

Use the Right Equipment

What is the most important piece of concentration equipment?

Because proper lighting is an important component of your study environment, the right light should head your list of equipment to promote concentration and reduce external distractions.

What is the best kind of light for studying?

Find the Right Light   Whether it comes from conventional lightbulbs, fluorescent tubes, or the newer compact fluorescent bulbs, the best light for study is bright, even, and steady (remember B, E, and ST).

Bright.   The emission of light is measured in lumens. For studying, you need at least 2,500 lumens. Two standard 100-watt bulbs (1,750 lumens each) will meet that requirement. So will a double-tube fluorescent lamp; it provides the same amount of light as two 100-watt incandescent bulbs and can last up to a hundred times longer!

Even.   Shadows in your work area or "hot spots" caused by glare will tire your eyes and make concentration difficult. Get rid of glare by shielding your lamp with a shade and by using a light-colored, nonglossy blotter on your desk. Eliminate shadows by using two lamps, fluorescent light, or diffuse light.

STeady.   A constant flicker will undermine concentration. If you use fluorescent light, try a double- or triple-tube lamp. These multitubed fixtures eliminate the natural strobe of fluorescent light. If you are using conventional (incandescent) light, make sure the bulb is screwed in properly.

What are the drawbacks of studying under bad light?

Good lighting makes for good studying. By contrast, poor lighting causes eyestrain, general tension, headaches, and sleepiness—irritations that interfere with concentration. If you study under good light but your eyes still bother you, have them examined by an ophthalmologist or optometrist. Clear and comfortable vision is essential to good studying.

What is the pencil technique?

Use a Pencil to Catalyze Concentration   A technique that does not fail is the simple, humble *pencil technique*. The technique is this: *Whenever you are working to learn, study with a pencil in hand. And use it!* For example, if you are reading a textbook chapter, stop after several paragraphs and very briefly, in your own words, write down the key points made by the author. If, after reading several paragraphs, you find that no words come to you, you have no recourse but to go back and read the passage again. This time, read with determination and concentration to make sure you learn the key points. The secret: Activity promotes and almost ensures concentration. The pencil provides the activity!

What is the best kind of chair for promoting concentration?

Find the Right Kind of Chair   More ink and more words have been wasted extolling the virtues of a straight-backed, hard-seated hickory chair than on any other single piece of study equipment. Forget it: Use a comfortable, well-cushioned chair. Staying awake or falling asleep does not depend on your chair; rather, it depends primarily on the method of study, your attitude and self-discipline, the light, and the room temperature. A hard, straight-backed chair can't take the place of these basic requirements.

How does a bookstand encourage concentration?

Use a Bookstand   An extremely practical piece of equipment is a bookstand. I don't mean a bookshelf or bookends; I mean a stand placed on your desk that holds the book in a tilted position and holds the pages down so that they do not flip over. A bookstand can work for you in many ways. First, and very important, it can give you a feeling of readiness to study—a feeling of being a scholar in the traditional sense. This alone is worth many times the price of the stand. Second, the stand provides physical freedom. It eliminates the strain of continually holding the book open, pressing down on two sides to keep the pages from flipping over, tilting the book to avoid the glare, and trying to find something heavy enough to hold the book open so you can free your hands to make notes. It permits you to sit back with arms folded, to contemplate and reflect on the meaning of what you are reading.

What other equipment can be helpful for concentration?

Keep Other Equipment Nearby   Other basic equipment that can help you study without interruption includes an up-to-date dictionary, a calculator, a clock, a calendar, paper, notebooks, paper clips, tape, rubber bands, pencils, pens, erasers, and index cards. If you make it a habit to keep your desk well stocked, you won't derail your concentration with unplanned emergency trips to obtain necessities.

Discouraging Internal Distractions

What are internal distractions?

Internal distractions are distractions that *you* create: daydreams, personal problems, anxiety, indecision, forgetfulness, and unrealistic goals. These distractions are as disruptive as the sights, sounds, and smells that make up the external variety, even though in this case the only one who is aware of them is you. Because internal distractions come from within, you have the power to eliminate or at least control them.

Use a Concentration Scoresheet

What is a concentration score-sheet?

Keep a sheet of paper handy. Whenever you catch your mind wandering, keep score by putting a check mark on the sheet. The mere act of doing this reminds you to get back to work. Students report that when they first tried this system, they accumulated as many as twenty check marks per textbook page, but after one or two weeks, they were down to one or two check marks per page.

How does keeping score help you concentrate?

The concentration scoresheet encourages self-observation. Making note of your breaks in concentration—when they happen, how often they occur, and what triggers them—will help you realize just how intrusive the lapses are and will enable you to gradually eliminate them.

Put Stray Thoughts on a Worry Pad

What is the purpose of a worry pad?

Although pleasant plans and diverting daydreams can be major sources of internal distraction, nagging worries and obligations can also take your mind off your work. The concentration scoresheet will alert you to these breaks in your attention, but it won't address the problems that prompted the distraction. To prevent the same worries from interfering with your concentration again and again, you must address them. A worry pad provides an excellent short-term solution to the problem.

How do you use a worry pad?

When an intrusive thought disrupts your concentration, write it down on your worry pad with the idea that you will attend to it just as soon as you get the chance. Then with your conscience clear and your bothersome thought recorded on paper, you can get back to the business of concentration. After you have finished studying, read over your list and give these concerns your full attention. If you cannot alleviate them yourself, get the help of friends or counselors.

Cultivating Concentration

What sorts of strategies will encourage concentration?

Although the best way to encourage concentration is usually to discourage distractions, you can also take positive actions to improve your concentration. Get into the habit of making lists, taking regular breaks, and maintaining a balance between the challenge of a particular assignment and your skill level.

Making Lists

What is the value of lists?

As we have seen, keeping random thoughts and information in your head instead of writing them down is a primary impediment to concentration. Lists allow you to free up your mind without losing important information. Use lists to remind yourself of day-to-day obligations and to catalog all the study equipment you're likely to need.

How can you prevent goals and appointments from distracting you?

Are hand-held computers good tools for keeping lists?

To avoid worrying about the possibility of missing personal appointments and forgetting those things you've set out to do, write them down on your daily schedule (see Figure 2.4, page 33). As a result, you will be able to shift smoothly from one activity to the next without breaking your concentration.

Some students may prefer to keep their lists on hand-held personal digital assistants (PDAs) that can be easily stowed in a pocket or purse. If you have a PDA and are comfortable using it, feel free to do so. But if you don't have a PDA, don't feel that you are somehow at a disadvantage. In general, it's quicker and more convenient to jot your list items down on an ordinary paper pad. PDAs excel when you've got information you want to keep around for an extended period of time, but they aren't usually as time-efficient for making short-term lists. The tiny typewriter keypads or the handwriting recognition software that some PDAs employ may be ingenious, but they aren't perfect, and they do take some practice. It's important not to let keeping your list become its own distraction. This can be a danger with a handwritten list, but it's an even greater risk with a PDA.

Taking Breaks

How important is it to take breaks?

Breaks can sometimes be as vital as the work itself. Although some students with short attention spans may be tempted to take a rest after only a brief time of working, others have the exact opposite problem. As tempting as it may be to put your nose to the grindstone and just keep working until all of your assignments are completed, this sort of strategy can often be a recipe for distraction and burnout.

What happens if you don't take breaks?

If you allow physical energy to build up unabated, your mind will race. If you keep repressing concerns that compete for your attention, those concerns will eventually triumph and scuttle your concentration. And if you persist in denying such a basic instinct as hunger, all you'll be able to think of is food.

What are the benefits of taking a break?

If, however, you take a few minutes to defuse these distractions, stand up and stretch, address a problem you've been avoiding, or grab a healthy snack to tide you over, you can return to your work ready to concentrate.

How often should you take breaks?

Breaks are essential. But like almost anything beneficial, they're susceptible to abuse. If you're making progress, it's important not to take an open-ended break that interrupts your momentum. And if you're not making progress, don't let a break serve as an excuse for evasion. Be as precise about allocating your breaks as you are about scheduling your work time. In general, keep a ratio of no less than five to one between work time and break time. In other words, work for fifty minutes and then take a ten-minute break. Or work for twenty-five minutes and take a break of five minutes.

Maintaining a Balance

How do you obtain the most rewarding kind of concentration?

Psychologist Mihaly Csikszentmihalyi believes that the most intense and rewarding kind of concentration (which he calls "flow") comes when you develop a balance between the challenge of the work you are doing and the level of skills you possess.[1] If the challenge of an assignment overwhelms your skill level, anxiety—not concentration—is likely to result. Conversely, if your skills are high but the assignment isn't challenging, you're apt to become bored and easily distracted. Finally, if both your skill level and the challenge of an assignment are low, you'll probably grow apathetic and have no desire to concentrate. Here are some strategies for boosting your skills and raising your interest level.

Find a Tutor

When should you get a tutor?

If you find yourself struggling with a subject, don't procrastinate. Before you reach the point of anxiety—or worse, apathy—get a tutor. Either go to the campus learning skills center or tutoring office, or find a classmate who has time to help you. In most cases, it won't take long before a tutor will pinpoint your problem, help you work it out, and send you off to tackle the rest of the term on your own.

Join a Study Group

What are the benefits of a study group?

Get together regularly with a small group of other students to discuss specific assignments and the course as a whole. During the give-and-take of the discussions, you are bound to learn a great deal; the subject may come alive, or the enthusiasm of some of the members may rub off on you. As you grow more familiar with the subject, your interest level will rise. The only prerequisite for a group meeting is that all members do their homework. Only then can each member become an active contributor.

Find an Alternate Textbook

How will an alternate textbook help?

If you're having a difficult time with a course, the textbook, not the subject, may be the source of your problem. A little investigating at a library or bookstore may turn up books in which other authors discuss the same topics in ways you find more accessible. After you have consulted some alternative books, read the material in your assigned textbook. The two texts may discuss the same topic, but your class will probably be focusing on aspects and approaches specific to the assigned text.

Use Programmed Materials and Workbooks

What do programmed materials provide?

If your skills don't seem to match the requirements of a course, you may need some extra practice. Programmed materials furnish questions and problems closely followed by their answers, thereby enabling you to teach yourself every incremental step of each lesson. These days, the most common programmed materials are found on Web sites or in specialized software, although some books operate using the programmed format as well. Workbooks provide

[1]Richard Flaste, "The Power of Concentration," *The New York Times Magazine* (October 8, 1989), p. 26.

exercises that apply the ideas explained in your textbooks. These study aids can help minimize the anxiety that arises from feeling uncertain about putting newly learned ideas to use. They can also stimulate your interest by helping you take what you've learned a step further.

Set Realistic Study Goals

How do realistic goals promote a balance?

Sometimes when the challenge of your work outstrips your skills, the problem lies with you and is easily remedied. For instance, don't expect to acquire a term's worth of skills in a few marathon study sessions. If you have done little or no studying up to now, change your habits gradually. Start by studying for only two hours on the first evening; then work up to longer sessions in which you'll be able to achieve increasingly larger goals.

FINAL WORDS

How is learning to concentrate like gardening?

Ultimately, learning to concentrate is like learning to be a good gardener. Anyone who has had experience raising flowers, fruits, or vegetables knows that you can't actually make them grow. The plant takes care of that, not you. All you can do is improve the conditions for growth. That requires skill, planning, and a little bit of luck. It's the same with concentration.

HAVE YOU MISSED SOMETHING?

SENTENCE COMPLETION   *Complete the following sentences with one of the three words or phrases listed below each sentence.*

1. Concentration is focused _____.

   light   thinking   intensity

2. The best light for studying is bright, even, and _____.

   strong   stylish   steady

3. It's important not to let your efforts at keeping a list become their own _____.

   distraction   advantage   list

MATCHING   *In each blank space in the left column, write the letter preceding the phrase in the right column that matches the left item best.*

_____ 1. "Flow"   a. Strategy for tuning out external distractions

                           b. Tires the eyes and makes concentration difficult

_____ 2. Library

_____ 3. Spider technique

_____ 4. Glare

_____ 5. Bookstand

_____ 6. Check mark

_____ 7. Worry pad

_____ 8. Reminder list

c. Provides physical freedom and promotes readiness

d. Can serve as a signal for broken concentration

e. Stopgap measure for dealing with internal distractions

f. Enables you to shift smoothly from one task to the next

g. Describes an especially rewarding kind of concentration

h. Best environment for high-quality concentration

TRUE-FALSE

Write T _beside the_ true _statements and_ F _beside the_ false _statements._

_____ 1. Concentration only occurs when you're not thinking about it.

_____ 2. Anything that stimulates the senses is a potential external distraction.

_____ 3. E-mail and the Internet both have a positive influence on concentration.

_____ 4. Whether you stay awake or fall asleep depends on the type of chair you use.

_____ 5. Working continuously without a break can result in distraction and burnout.

MULTIPLE CHOICE

Choose the word or phrase that completes each sentence most accurately, and circle the letter that precedes it.

1. Trouble concentrating is due primarily to
   a. internal and external distractions.
   b. boredom.
   c. anxiety.
   d. poor eyesight.

2. The face-goblet image in Figure 3.1 illustrates our natural tendency to
   a. forget faces.
   b. divide attention.
   c. recognize people.
   d. focus thoughts.

3. Although concentration is powerful, it is often
   a. unnecessary.
   b. elusive.
   c. underestimated.
   d. time consuming.

4. A concentration scoresheet is used to tabulate each time your mind
   a. wanders.
   b. focuses.
   c. improves.
   d. all of the above.

5. When the challenge is high but your skill level is low, you will probably experience
   a. concentration.
   b. boredom.
   c. anxiety.
   d. apathy.

SHORT ANSWER   *Supply a brief answer for each of the following items.*

1. Explain how smells can act as external distractions.
2. Discuss the conditioning effect that occurs when you use your desk only for studying.
3. Explain how a pencil can be used to promote concentration.
4. Describe strategies you can use to eliminate noise.

WORDS IN CONTEXT

From the three choices beside each numbered item, select the one that most nearly expresses the meaning of the italicized word in the quote. Make a light check mark (✓) next to your choice.

If I were asked to name the deadliest *subversive* force within capitalism, I would without hesitation name advertising.
—Robert L. Heilbroner (1919–), American economist

1. *subversive* force   underlying   substantial   corruptive

Marketing is merely a civilized form of warfare in which most battles are won with words, ideas, and *disciplined* thinking.

—Albert W. Emery (1923–), American advertising agency executive

2. *disciplined* thinking   informed   orderly   shrewd

Gentility is what is left over from rich ancestors after the money is gone.

—John Ciardi (1916–1986), American poet and critic

3. *gentility*   refinement   large debts   large family

The ideals which have lighted my way, and time after time have given me new courage to face life cheerfully, have been Kindness, Beauty, and Truth. The *trite* subjects of human efforts—possessions, outward success, luxury—have always seemed to me *contemptible.*

—Albert Einstein (1879–1955), German-born American theoretical physicist

4. *trite* subjects   concise   precise   unappealing

5. seemed . . . *contemptible*   temporary   despicable   probable

THE WORD HISTORY SYSTEM

Acumen
the sharpness of the mind

acumen a-cu'-men *n.*
Quickness, accuracy, and keenness of judgment or insight.

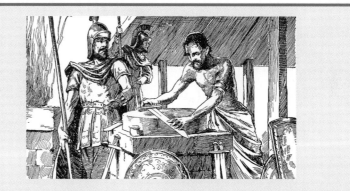

A keen mind may be likened to a sharp knife, which penetrates easily and quickly. For clean-cut action, both the knife and the mind-hr must be sharp. So it is natural that when a word was needed to denote the faculty of keen, penetrating thought, the Latin word for "sharpness" should be borrowed. *Acuere*, in Latin, means "to sharpen," and *acumen* means "sharpness." English borrowed *acumen* and used it figuratively for sharpness of the mind.

Reprinted by pemission. From *Picturesque Word Origins* © 1933 by G. & C. Merriam Co. (now Merriam-Webster, Incorporated).

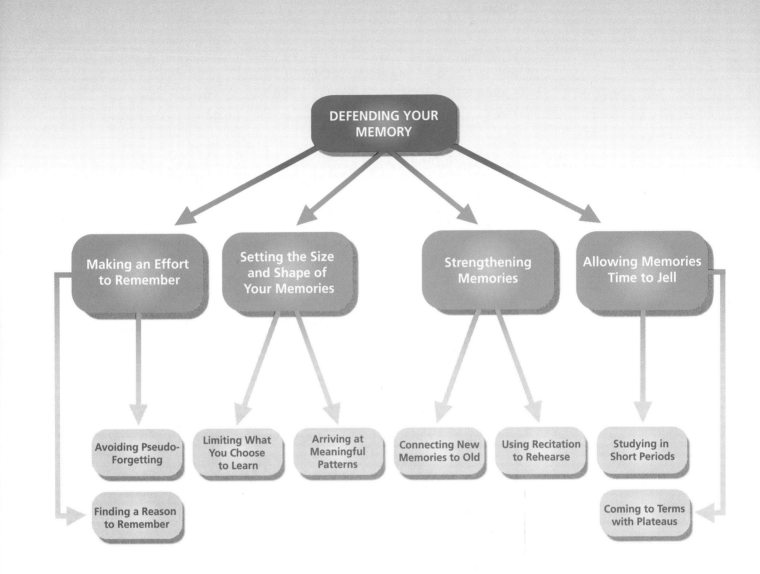

Defending Your Memory

Forgetting is like an ocean wave, steadily washing away what you've learned. You can't stop forgetting anymore than you can stop a wave. But you can reinforce what you've learned and strengthen your memories in the face of the incoming tide. To aid you in doing so, this chapter focuses on:

- **Making an Effort to Remember**
- **Setting the Size and Shape of Your Memories**
- **Strengthening Your Memories**
- **Allowing Memories Time to Jell**

Why is forgetting the biggest enemy of academic success?

There's a battle going on in your brain. You may not always be aware of it, but your memory is under constant assault from forgetfulness, the biggest single enemy of your academic success. Forgetting works both massively and rapidly to undo learning. In fact, research has shown again and again that when you learn something new you are likely to forget most of it in a matter of days.

What have experiments shown about forgetting?

In one experiment, people who read a textbook chapter forgot 46 percent of their reading after one day, 79 percent after fourteen days, and 81 percent after twenty-eight days. In other words, subjects could remember only slightly more than half of what they'd read the previous day; after less than a month, the information they were able to retain from their reading had dwindled to 19 percent.

Why is it harder to remember what you've heard than what you've read?

Forgetting's effect on reading can be pretty devastating. But it's even worse on listening. After all, unlike readers who can slow down, pause, reflect, and, if necessary, reread, listeners have no such luxury; they usually have just one chance to catch spoken words and ideas.

What did the Cambridge Psychological Society experiment conclude about forgetfulness?

For instance, in a classic experiment researchers secretly recorded a seminar held by the Cambridge Psychological Society.[1] Two weeks later, the society members who had attended the seminar were asked to write down all they could recall of it. The results were shocking. More than 90 percent of the points from the lecture had been forgotten or confused with the passage of time. The average proportion of specific points each member correctly recalled was 8.4 percent! Much of what members recalled was at odds with what had actually been said. Events were mentioned that never took place; casual remarks were embellished; points were reported that had only been hinted at. This learned group of psychologists forgot 91.6 percent of the specific points made in the seminar.

What is the cause of forgetting?

How does this happen? How can forgetting do so much damage in so short a time? Although the experts are divided on the answer, they have arrived at a number of theories (Figure 4.1).

What does fading theory suggest about forgetting?

Use it or lose it: Fading theory.   According to fading theory, the trace or mark a memory etches in your brain is like a path you make when you walk across a meadow. If you don't continue to walk over the path, grass will grow and obliterate your trail. In the same way, a fact that's learned but never used will become fainter until it is completely obliterated by forgetfulness.

How does retrieval theory differ from fading theory?

I know it's here somewhere: Retrieval theory.   Unlike proponents of fading theory, some psychologists believe that once a fact or idea is thoroughly learned, it remains a memory for life. According to retrieval theory, a forgotten fact hasn't faded; it has been misfiled in the vast storehouse of your mind. Whether the in-

[1]See Ian M. L. Hunter, *Memory: Facts and Fallacies* (Baltimore: Penguin, 1957), p. 83.

CHAPTER
4

Figure 4.1
Theories of Forgetting

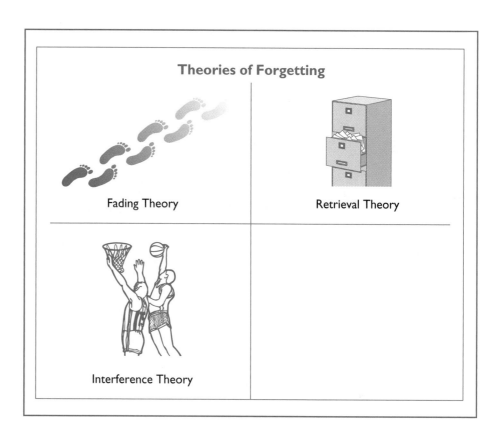

Theories of Forgetting

Fading Theory

Retrieval Theory

Interference Theory

formation has disappeared completely or has simply been misplaced, the net result is the same: Information you once learned and remembered has now been forgotten.

What is the idea behind interference theory?

Get outta my way: Interference theory. Interference theory suggests that memories are actually forced out, either by other memories or by your own efforts to eject them. Memories become like a bunch of competitive basketball players fighting for a spot beneath the basket. With *forward interference,* old memories elbow out new ones, making it harder to remember the things you've just learned. With *backward interference,* the situation is reversed; new memories push out older ones in an effort to clear a space for themselves. *Interactive interference* suggests that an older fact and a newer one gang up on a fact that falls in between. The middle fact usually gets squeezed out, but the remaining facts often get damaged in the process. Finally, there's *reactive interference,* which shows the importance that attitude plays. According to this theory, if you don't like or are bored with what you've learned, you sweep the memory away.

How can you defend your
memories from forgetting?

When you consider how much resistance your memories face, it's folly to as-
sume that something you've learned will still be there when you need it. You
can defend your memories by making an effort to remember, by setting the size
and shape of your memories, by working to strengthen your memories, and by
giving them time to jell.

Making an Effort to Remember

How does effort affect your
memory?

To remember something, you have to make a conscious effort to learn it. If you
don't learn new information in the first place, it isn't really yours to forget. And
even if you do learn new information, it won't stay with you very long unless
you're convinced that it's worth hanging onto. The effort you initially make de-
termines whether you'll remember what you've heard or read for a lifetime or
forget it in a matter of seconds.

Avoiding Pseudo-Forgetting

What is pseudo-forgetting?

Whenever you cannot remember a name, a telephone number, a fact, an idea, or
even a joke, it's quite natural to say, "I forgot." Yet forgetting may not have any-
thing to do with your problem. You may never have learned the information in
the first place. This phenomenon is known as pseudo-forgetting. The word *pseudo*
means "false" or "phony." Thousands of instances we blame on forgetting are ac-
tually a result of this "phony forgetting."As the poet Oliver Wendell Holmes suc-
cinctly put it, "A man must *get* a thing before he can *forget* it."

How can you guard against
pseudo-forgetting?

If an idea or a fact is to be retained in your memory, it must be impressed on
your mind clearly and crisply at least once. A record of that idea or fact must be
laid down in your brain before you can truly recall or forget what you've learned.

Finding a Reason to Remember

What effect does intention have
on memory?

If you can find a reason for holding on to information you've learned, you have
a much better chance of remembering it. In a carefully designed study, re-
searchers showed how intention can influence the life span of a memory. Two
groups of students were asked to master identical material. The only difference
was that those in the first group were told to remember the material for only a
single day, while those in the second group were instructed to master it for re-
call after two weeks.[2] The difference in intention had a noticeable effect. Al-
though the two groups studied the same material in a similar fashion, after two

[2]H. H. Remmers and M. N. Thisted, "The Effect of Temporal Set on Learning," *Journal of
Applied Psychology* 16 (June 1932): 257–268.

weeks the students who had intended to remember over the long term retained more than the students who had intended to hang on to what they had learned for only a day.

Of all the sources of motivation, interest is the strongest. If you could study all subjects with motivated interest, you would not have to worry about your final grades. When you are naturally interested in a subject, you have no problem. If, however, you are not naturally interested, try to combat boredom by artificially creating interest. Once you begin to learn something about a new subject, the chances are great that you will find it genuinely interesting. Use the power of interest to work *for* you, not against you.

Whether genuine interest or simple academic survival serves as your motivation, when you hear or read information you want to hold onto, there are ways to strengthen your intention to remember, so that what you've learned will be recalled:

Pay attention.   If you're distracted while you're trying to learn, it's unlikely you'll remember anything. Therefore, make a point of minimizing distractions as you read your assignments or listen to lectures.

Get it right the first time.   False ideas and misunderstood facts can hang on as tenaciously as information you learn correctly. Therefore, it pays to be attentive when you learn something new. For example, many people incorrectly pronounce the word *nuclear* (NEW-clee-er) as "NEW-cue-ler." One look at the word shows you that this pronunciation is incorrect. But if you learn a word incorrectly, you'll have difficulty replacing the old memory with the correct pronunciation.

Make sure you understand.   Ideas that aren't clear to you when you read or hear them won't miraculously jell and become clearer in your memory. You cannot fashion a lucid, correct memory from a fuzzy, poorly understood concept. Therefore, don't hesitate to ask the instructor to explain any point that you are not clear on. And don't be reluctant to read and reread a passage in your textbook until you're sure you fully grasp its meaning.

Interestingly, the same motivation that enables you to remember can also help you forget. Recall that reactive interference theory suggests that we have a tendency to "tune out" information that bores or bothers us. But motivated forgetting can be used positively to clear your mind of information you no longer need to retain.

This conscious intention to forget is well demonstrated by servers in restaurants. They exhibit a remarkably good memory for what their customers have ordered up to the moment the bill is paid. Then experienced servers jettison the entire transaction from their minds and give their full attention to the next customer. Just as they intend to remember, so they intend to forget.

This idea of intending to forget explains why Albert Einstein, unquestionably one of the great minds of the twentieth century, was nonetheless unable to provide his home telephone number from memory. He saw no point in clogging his mind with simple numbers that could easily be stored in an address book, so he purposely forgot them.

Setting the Size and Shape of Your Memories

What are the limits to our memory?

The forgetting that many of us practice instinctively seems to imply that there is a limit to how much we can remember at once. In 1956 psychologist G. A. Miller produced scientific support for this notion. In his article "The Magical Number Seven, Plus or Minus Two," Miller points out that most people are able to hold only seven items in short-term memory at one time. The size of each item, however, can be virtually unlimited as long as the information in it is meaningfully organized. For example, you couldn't expect to remember the following thirty-one items:

aabceeeeeeeilmmmnnnoorrrssttuvy

How does organization help memory?

But if you organized these items in a meaningful way—as words—you could reduce the number of items to seven and increase your odds of remembering them:

You	can	learn	to	remember	seven	items.
1	2	3	4	5	6	7

As Miller explains, "Our language is tremendously useful for repackaging material into a few chunks rich in information."[3]

How important was Miller's article in the study of learning and memory?

Although its profound importance wasn't immediately recognized by all, Miller's article has had a dramatic influence on the study of learning and memory. Looking back, Jerome Bruner, a prominent psychologist and former director of Harvard University's Center for Cognitive Studies, paid tribute to Miller and his ground-breaking work.

> I think if there were a retrospective Nobel Prize in Psychology for the mid-1950s, George Miller would win it hands down—and on the basis of one article, "The Magic Number Seven, Plus or Minus Two."[4]

[3]G. A. Miller, "The Magical Number Seven, Plus or Minus Two: Some Limits on Our Capacity for Processing Information," *Psychological Review* 63 (March 1956): 81–97.

[4]Jerome Bruner, *In Search of Mind* (New York: Harper & Row, 1983), p. 97.

What is the lesson from G. A. Miller's research?

The lesson to be learned from Miller's research is this: Improve your chances of remembering by being selective about what you learn and by making sure that what you do choose to remember is meaningfully organized.

Limiting What You Choose to Learn

What were the conclusions from Ebbinghaus's most famous experiment?

Long before Miller's discussion of the "magical number seven," Hermann Ebbinghaus (1850–1909), a German psychologist, spent more than twenty years investigating forgetting and the limits of memory. In his most famous experiment, he counted the number of trials required to learn a series of six nonsense syllables (such as *bik, luf, tur, pem, nif,* and *wox*). He then counted the number of trials required to learn a series of twelve such syllables. Ebbinghaus's tabulations yielded surprising results: The number of trials required to memorize twelve syllables was fifteen times greater than the number required to learn six syllables.[5] So, for example, if it took four minutes to memorize six syllables, it would take an hour to memorize twelve.

What does Ebbinghaus's research tell us about mastering textbook and lecture material?

Granted, Ebbinghaus dealt only with nonsense syllables, but his careful research still teaches a valuable lesson that can be applied to both textbook and lecture material: To improve your chances of remembering what you've learned, you must condense and summarize. In practical terms, this means picking out the main ideas from your lecture and textbook notes and leaving the supporting materials and examples aside. Once you have selected the important points from what you've read, you should be able to memorize them in a manageable amount of time.

What is another benefit of limiting what you learn?

Another beneficial by-product that comes from limiting what you learn is that in making the choice of what to keep and what to forget you'll be strengthening your overall understanding of the material. In other words, you can't really tell what idea is worth saving and what is worth deleting without having a basic understanding of both. As you'll see in Chapter 11, a method called the Silver Dollar System that is specfically designed to condense your notes provides an opportunity to make what you've learned a permanent part of your knowledge.

Arriving at Meaningful Patterns

How does organizing affect retrieval?

The papers on your desk are easier to keep track of if you organize them into groups and put them into file folders. A textbook is easier to understand because the information in it has been divided into chapters. A single item is easier to find in a supermarket because the products have been grouped together

[5]Matthew High Erdelyl, "Commentary: Integrating Dissociations Prone Psychology," *Journal of Personality* 62, no. 4 (1994): 669–680.

and arranged in different aisles. If you had to look for a jar of peanut butter in a supermarket where the items were randomly placed, you might give up the search.

How should you organize a list of items you need to remember?

The same idea applies to memories. When you have a large list of items to remember, try to cluster similar items around a natural heading or category. Once clustered and categorized, the items will resist the decaying power of forgetting. Just as the stem holds together the individual grapes, so categories and clusters hold together individual facts and ideas. This hanging together is especially useful during an exam: Remembering one item from a cluster is usually the key to remembering all the items. For example, it would take a long time to memorize by rote the following words, which you might encounter in a geology course:

slate	diamond	sapphire
bronze	lead	aluminum
iron	marble	silver
emerald	steel	brass
gold	limestone	ruby
granite	platinum	copper

But when these words are organized into categories and are clustered as shown in Figure 4.2, memorization is relatively easy and remembering is strong.

Strengthening Memories

What can you do to help strengthen your memories?

The stronger a memory is, the longer it lasts. If you reinforce new ideas by connecting them to ideas already in your memory, and if you conscientiously use recitation to rehearse what you've learned, that result should be strong enough to stand up to forgetting.

Connecting New Memories to Old

What is the role of association in memory?

The famous line "No man is an island" applies to memories as well. An idea that stands alone is not likely to be recalled because the ideas you remember are woven into a network that connects a single memory with hundreds and often thousands of other memories. The more connections there are in the network and the stronger those connections are, the better the chance for recall.

Figure 4.2

The Category and Cluster System of Organizing Items

Source: Figure from *Psychology: An Introduction*, Sixth Edition, by Jerome Kagan. Copyright © 1988. Reprinted with permission of Wadsworth, a division of Thomson Learning: www.thomsonrights .com. Fax 800-730-2215.

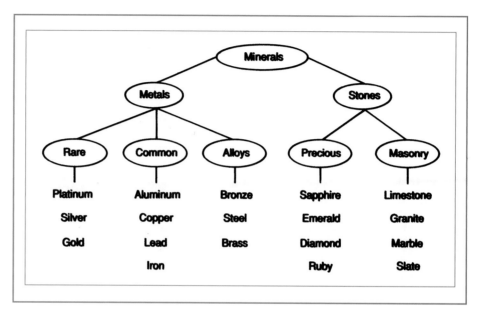

When are connections made automatically?

Sometimes connections are made automatically, as in the case of traumatic events. Most people easily recall, for example, where they were and what they were doing when they learned of the attack on the World Trade Center in 2001 or when the space shuttle *Challenger* exploded in 1986. In these cases, you instantly connect the memory of the event with the memory of where you were.

What can you do to deliberately create associations?

But in normal circumstances, relying on your memory to automatically make these connections is risky. If you want to improve your chances of remembering something, you must make a real effort to link what you've learned to your memory network. You can strengthen the staying power of information when you add it to your memory by consciously making either logical or artificial connections.

Make Logical Connections

How do you establish logical connections for memories?

Consider how you can recall the written directions to a friend's house by keeping in mind a map you once saw or how you can strengthen your memory of the bones of the body by recalling a diagram of a human skeleton. These are examples of logical connections you make to improve your recall. The best ways of strengthening your memory network through logical connections are by building on your basic background and by using images to support what you're trying to remember.

How does background help strengthen memory?

Build on Your Basic Background   The principle behind basic background is simple but powerful. Your understanding and memory of what you hear, read, see, feel, or taste depend entirely on what you know, on what you already have in your background. Some of this information has been with you for years, whereas other parts of it may be just seconds old. When listening to a speaker, you understand his or her points as long as you can interpret them in light of something you've already learned. When you make connections this way, you increase the power of your memory.

What are ways of building a solid background?
Why are basic courses so important?

Here are some concrete steps to help you build a solid background:

Give basic courses the attention they deserve.   Many students make the mistake of thinking that the basic courses they take in their first year of college are a waste of time. Yet these introductory courses create the background essential for all the courses that follow. Indeed, each student's professional life begins with first-year courses.

How can you consciously link new information to old?

Make a conscious attempt to link what you learn to what you already know.   When you learn something new, ask yourself questions such as "How does this relate to what I already know?" and "How does this change what I already know?"

How can your instructor help your background?

Ask an instructor to explain what you don't understand.   At times an entire class can hinge on a single point. Miss that and you miss the purpose of the class. Don't feel hesitant or shy about asking an instructor to go back over a point you can't quite get a fix on. After all, the instructor is there to help you learn.

How do pictures strengthen memories?

Strengthen memories with pictures.   Another way of reinforcing what you've learned is by creating a picture of it. Whether you draw the new information on paper or simply visualize it in your mind, you add an extra dimension to your memory. After all, only one-half of your brain thinks in words; the other half thinks in pictures. When you convert words into pictures, you are using both sides of your brain instead of just one.

A student who attended a lecture on amoebas included a sketch of this one-celled organism in her notes (see Figure 4.3). The combination of words and picture gave her a clearer understanding of the subject than she would have gained from relying exclusively on written information. When a question about amoebas appeared on a test, the student handled it easily by recalling the picture she had drawn.

What do you do with material that doesn't seem to lend itself to drawing?

Even when material doesn't lend itself to drawing, you can still devise a mental image. According to Dr. Joseph E. Shorr of the Institute of Psycho-Imagination Therapy in Beverly Hills, California, "The human memory would be worthless without the capacity to make mental pictures." Almost any memory can be turned into a mental image. If you need to remember, for example,

Figure 4.3
Structure of the Amoeba

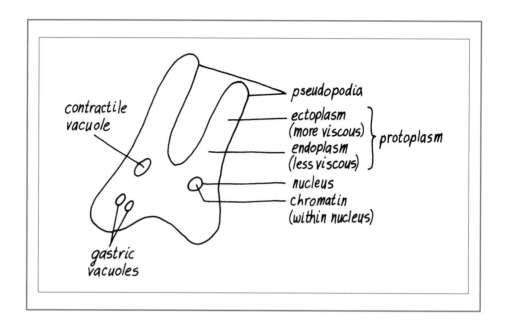

that Abraham Lincoln was born in 1809, you can picture a log cabin with "1809" inscribed over the doorway. The image you recall doesn't have to be especially detailed; it only has to be strong enough to jog your memory. (Chapter 8 provides a detailed discussion of how to tap into your natural ability to think visually.)

Make Artificial Connections

What is an example of an artificial memory connection?

Strong connections don't always have to be natural or logical ones. They can be completely artificial. After all, what natural link is there between the word *face* and a group of musical notes? Yet many beginning music students rely on this word to help them recall the notes written in the spaces of the treble clef (F, A, C, E).

Such connections are by no means limited to music. Suppose you have just been introduced to a man named Mr. Perkins. To remember his name, you immediately associate it with a coffeepot *perking.* You even visualize the perking pot and smell the aroma of freshly brewed coffee. What you have done is tie *new* information (Mr. Perkins) to *old* information (perking coffeepot) that is already well established in your memory. When you meet Mr. Perkins at some future time, you will recall the perking coffeepot, which will prepare you to say, "Hello, Mr. Perkins. Nice to see you again."

What do most memory tricks rely upon?

The majority of memory tricks (known as *mnemonic devices*) rely on such artificial connections.

How prevalent are mnemonic devices?

Use Classic Mnemonic Devices   Nearly everyone employs at least one or two mnemonic devices to recall specific hard-to-remember facts and information. Probably the most widely used mnemonic device is the old jingle by which many of us keep track of the irregularities in the calendar:

> Thirty days hath September,
> April, June, and November.
> All the rest have thirty-one,
> Except February alone.

Rivaling this days-in-the-month mnemonic is one for spelling:

> *i* before *e* except after *c*
> or when sounding like *a*
> as in *neighbor* and *weigh*

Many people have their own personal mnemonics, such as "Surround the *r* with *a* for the word *separate*."

Why do mnemonics work?

As we've already learned, the cardinal rule for dealing with masses of information is to make sure the information is organized in a meaningful way. A mnemonic device is an organizational system, pure and simple. It is an ordinary means to an important end. Gerald R. Miller conducted a study to evaluate the effectiveness of mnemonic devices as aids to study.[6] He found that students who used mnemonics raised their test scores by as much as 77 percent!

Is there a risk to using mnemonics?

Miller recognizes that the use of too many mnemonics can overload the memory. Nevertheless, he argues that learning a large number of mnemonics well creates no greater hazard than learning a large amount of material in the traditional way. Here's a sampling of some classic mnemonics you may have encountered:

Spelling.   The greatest number of mnemonic devices are aids to spelling. Here's how to remember the correct way to spell two words that confuse many students:

> A princi<u>pal</u> is a <u>pal</u>.
> A princi<u>ple</u> is a ru<u>le</u>.

Why is it especially important to memorize mnemonics thoroughly?

If you use classic mnemonic devices to help recall information, make certain you memorize the sentence, word, or jingle thoroughly. The slightest error can

[6]Gerald R. Miller, *An Evaluation of the Effectiveness of Mnemonic Devices as Aids to Study,* Cooperative Research Project no. 5-8438 (El Paso: University of Texas Press, 1967).

throw you off completely. For example, some algebra students use the FOIL method to remember the order for multiplying a binomial: First, Outer, Inner, Last. But if you recall the wrong word instead, say, FILE, you wind up hopelessly confused.

Biology. The first letters of the words in the following sentence stand for the major categories and subdivisions of the animal world—kingdom, phylum, class, order, family, genus, species, and variety:

Kings Play Cards On Fairly Good Soft Velvet.

Astronomy. Most people, when pressed, can name the nine planets. But how about listing them in order? (Mercury, Venus, Earth, Mars, Jupiter, Saturn, Uranus, Neptune, Pluto.)

My Very Educated Mother Just Sent Us Nine Pizzas.

History. The royal houses of England (Norman, Plantagenet, Lancaster, York, Tudor, Stuart, Hanover, Windsor) are difficult to remember without the help of a mnemonic device:

No Plan Like Yours To Study History Wisely.

Medicine. Even doctors and pharmacists use memory systems to help keep certain chemicals straight. To distinguish between cyanates, which are harmless, and cyanides, which are extremely poisonous, they use this device:

-ate, I ate; *-ide,* I died.

What can you do to remember information that doesn't have a common mnemonic device?

Devise Your Own Mnemonics Associating new information logically is generally better than doing so artificially, and truly knowing something is always better than using a system to remember it. But if you're required to learn facts that you can't connect with your memory network and that have no classic mnemonic, you may want to invent your own mnemonic device to help yourself remember.

What are the two steps for creating a keyword mnemonic?

Keyword mnemonic.[7] Connecting a man named Perkins with a perking coffeepot provides a good example of a *keyword mnemonic* in action. The procedure for devising a keyword mnemonic has two steps, a verbal step and a visual step.

[7]The keyword mnemonics section is based on a discussion in K. L. Higbee, *Your Memory: How It Works and How to Improve It,* 2d ed. (New York: Prentice-Hall, 1988).

What is involved in the verbal step?

1. *The verbal step.* Find a familiar word or phrase that sounds like the word you are trying to remember. This is your keyword. For the name *Perkins* the keyword is *perking*.

What do you do in the visual step?

2. *The visual step.* Connect your keyword with what you want to remember. For example, form a mental image of Mr. Perkins's face on a perking coffeepot. Then when you see him again, you'll recall that image, which will remind you of his name.

What are some common uses for keyword mnemonics?

The keyword system isn't limited to helping you remember the names of people you meet. It also comes in handy for remembering vocabulary from a foreign language. For example, if you want to recall the French word for "butter," *beurre,* connect it with a keyword like *burr,* or *brrr,* and then link the two with a visual image, a pat of butter covered with burrs or a stick of butter wearing a parka and shivering (brrr!).

What is a create-a-word mnemonic?

Create-a-word mnemonic.   The letters of a "created" word can be used to help you remember important information. What if you needed to remember the Great Lakes, for example: Lake Superior, Lake Erie, Lake Michigan, Lake Huron, and Lake Ontario?

What are the steps in creating a mnemonic word?

To devise a *create-a-word mnemonic,* proceed as follows:

1. Underline the keyword in each item. (Superior, Erie, Michigan, Huron, Ontario.)
2. Write down the first letter of each keyword. (S, E, M, H, O.)
3. Create a word or several words from the first letters of the keywords. If the order of the elements isn't important, try rearranging the letters until they spell a word or words. (HOMES.)
4. If possible, make a link between your keyword and the idea for which it acts as a mnemonic. ("The HOMES along the Great Lakes must have a beautiful view.")

Your mnemonic may be a real word or a word you just made up. If you use a made-up word, be sure you have some means of remembering it.

In what cases is a create-a-sentence mnemonic preferable to a create-a-word one?

Create-a-sentence mnemonic.   If the order of the items you want to remember is important, the create-a-sentence mnemonic is often more flexible than the create-a-word mnemonic. For example, if you need to remember the Great Lakes from west to east (Lake Superior, Lake Michigan, Lake Huron, Lake Erie, Lake Ontario), HOMES won't help you. But a create-a-sentence mnemonic will.

Here are the steps for devising a create-a-sentence mnemonic:

What are the steps for a create-a-sentence mnemonic?

1. Underline the keyword for each item. (Superior, Michigan, Huron, Erie, Ontario.)

2. Write down the first letter of each keyword. (S, M, H, E, O.)
3. Construct an easy-to-remember sentence using words whose first letters are the same as the first letters of the keywords. (Super Machine Heaved Earth Out.)
4. Devise a sentence that relates to the information you want to remember. ("Five large lakes in the middle of the country almost make it seem as though a super machine heaved earth out.")

Why is creating a sentence mnemonic sometimes easier than creating a word or two?

In general, creating a simple sentence is easier than taking the first letters from your keywords and turning them into a word or two, especially if the order of the points has to be maintained. Of course, if the initial letters are mainly consonants, both methods can be difficult. To circumvent the problem of having too many consonants, try to choose some keywords (or synonyms of the keywords) that begin with vowels.

What is at the heart of most commercial memory courses?

Employ Commercial Memory Methods Most commercial memory courses rely on something called "the peg." This system for memorizing items in sequence employs a master list of words that act as hooks or pegs on which to hang the information you want to remember. A peg word often rhymes with the number it stands for. For example, one is bun, two is shoe, three is tree, and four is door. To remember a group of items, you associate them with the peg words, often by conjuring up bizarre images.

How would you remember a shopping list using a commercial memory system?

For example, if you want to remember a shopping list consisting of butter, sugar, and sausage, you might visualize a pound of butter melting atop a gigantic bun, a shoe filled with loose sugar, and a sausage as tall as a tree. Then when you arrive at the supermarket, you run through the peg words in sequence (bun, shoe, tree) and recall the item with which each is associated.

What are the drawbacks of the peg system?

Although the peg system may help out in a pinch, it definitely has drawbacks: It works with only one list at a time; it may cause interference; and it does little to reinforce information in your long-term memory.

Using Recitation to Rehearse

Why is recitation so vital to strengthening your memory?

No single activity is more important in strengthening your memory than recitation. That's because recitation forces you to think seriously about what you've read or heard. This deep thinking (experts call it *deep cognitive processing*) is the key to making memories last. To reap the benefits of recitation, you need to know what reciting involves. It also helps to learn why reciting works.

What Recitation Involves

How do you recite?

Reciting simply involves reading a passage in a book or a line of your notes and then repeating it from memory, either out loud or by writing it. Whether you recite out loud or in writing, your goal should be to use your own words rather than parroting what you've just read. Recitation isn't about memorizing words. It's about comprehending ideas. Chapter 11 explains in detail how you can use recitation to master the notes you've taken from lectures or textbook assignments.

Why Recitation Works

What is the secret behind recitation?

Whether you recite by speaking or by writing, the effect on your memory is basically the same. Recitation strengthens the original memory trace by prompting you to think actively about the new material. It gets both your body and your mind involved in the process of learning. It supplies immediate feedback so you can test yourself and check your progress. And it motivates you to continue reading.

How does reciting encourage participation?

Reciting Encourages Participation   Reading is not the same as comprehending. It's possible, for example, to read a book aloud to a child without paying attention to the story. Likewise, if you're having a tough time concentrating, you can read every word on a page and still not understand or even recall what you've read. To truly comprehend what you've read, you need to know both what the words say and what they mean. When you recite, you make yourself stop and wonder, "What did this just say?" You're transformed from a detached observer into a participant. The physical activity of thinking, pronouncing, and hearing your own words involves your body as well as your mind in the process of learning. The more physical senses you use in learning, the stronger the memory will be.

How does recitation provide feedback?

Reciting Provides Feedback   Reciting not only gets you involved in your reading; it also demonstrates how involved you are. Rereading can give you a false and dangerous sense of confidence. It takes a lot of time and leaves you with the feeling that you've been hard at work, yet it provides no concrete indication of what you're learning. When test time comes, you may blame your mental blanks on test anxiety or on unfair questions when the real culprit is ineffective studying. Unlike rereading, reciting lets you know right away where your weaknesses lie. As you finish each paragraph you find out whether you understand what you've just read. This gives you a chance to clarify and solidify information on the spot, long before you're tested on it.

How does recitation supply motivation?

Reciting Supplies Motivation   Because it gets you involved and checks your progress regularly, recitation provides motivation for studying. And motivated interest promotes stronger memory. If you struggled to extract the information from a paragraph you just read, you may be motivated to get the point of the next paragraph more easily. If you had no trouble finding the meaning in that paragraph, the momentum of your reading may serve as motivation.

Allowing Memories Time to Jell

Why don't new ideas instantly become part of your memory?

How did a mountain climber's injury demonstrate consolidation?

What are the similarities between human memory and a computer's memory?

What does consolidation tell us about study strategies?

What is distributed practice?

The fact that recitation helps new information jell hints at another aspect of memory: New ideas don't instantly become part of your memory. Your memory needs time to consolidate what you've learned.

A dramatic illustration of memory's need to consolidate comes in a story of a mountain climber who fell and hit his head. Although the man was not permanently injured, he couldn't remember falling. In fact, he couldn't recall anything that had happened to him in the fifteen minutes *before* the accident. Why not? According to the principle of consolidation, the climber's memories before the accident had not had a chance to consolidate. As a result, when the climber hit his head, those unfinished memories were lost.[8]

Although analogies between humans and machines can only be taken so far, your short-term memory shares some interesting similarities with DRAM, the dynamic random access memory (often just referred to as RAM) of a personal computer. If your computer crashes a few minutes after you started typing a paper or letter, there's a good chance that all your work up to that point will be lost. That's because it existed only in dynamic memory and had yet to be transferred to a disk where it could be stored permanently. This explains the advice of many experienced computer users to "save often and always." When you save a file, you move the information from the short-term temporary storage of DRAM to the long-term storage of a disk. Similarly, when you allow time to consolidate your memories, you move them from the limbo of your short-term memory to the stability of your long-term memory.

This principle helps explain why in most cases the most effective way to study is in short blocks of time instead of in one long stretch. An understanding of consolidation will help you live through those frustrating times when you don't seem to retain what you're studying.

Studying in Short Periods

In *distributed practice*, you engage in relatively short study periods broken up by rest intervals. In *massed practice*, you study continuously until the task is completed. A number of studies have demonstrated that several short "learning

---

[8]R. S. Woodworth and H. Schlosberg, *Experimental Psychology*, rev. ed. (New York: Holt, Rinehart & Winston, 1954), p. 773.

What effect did distributed practice have on learning French vocabulary?

What effect did distributed practice have on reading comprehension?

What are some other advantages of using bite-sized study sessions?

In what situations is massed practice superior to distributed practice?

sprints" are more productive than one grueling, long-distance study session. This is sometimes known as the "spacing effect."

For example, Kristine Bloom and Thomas Shuell gave two groups of high school French students twenty new vocabulary words to learn. The first group used massed practice, studying all the words in a single thirty-minute session. The second group spent the same amount of time on the words but spread the sessions over three consecutive days, studying ten minutes per day. When tested immediately after they had completed their practice, both groups remembered roughly the same number of words (sixteen). But when the test was readministered four days later, the massed group had forgotten nearly half of the words, while the distributed group was able to recall all but five.[9]

In an extensive experiment, researchers D. Krug, T. B. Davis, and J. A. Glover examined the effects of massed and distributed practice on a reading comprehension task and found that distributed practice led to better performance.[10]

The memory's need to consolidate information seems to play a key role in explaining why distributed practice is superior to massed practice. Other advantages also support these bite-sized study sessions:

Periodic "breathers" discourage fatigue. They refresh you both physically and emotionally.

Motivation is stronger when you work in short blocks of time. The end of each session marks a minivictory that provides momentum and a sense of accomplishment.

Distributed practice wards off boredom. Uninteresting subjects are easier to take in small doses.

In spite of all the advantages of distributed practice, massed practice is superior in a few cases. For instance, when you are writing the first draft of a paper, massed practice is often essential. You have organized your notes in stacks; discrete bits of information are waiting in your mind like jigsaw-puzzle pieces to be fitted together; and the organizational pattern of your paper, though dimly perceived, is beginning to take shape. To stop working at this point would be disastrous. The entire effort would collapse. So in such a circumstance, it is far more efficient to overextend yourself—to complete that stage of the process—than to take a break or otherwise apply the principle of distributed practice.

[9]Kristine C. Bloom and Thomas J. Shuell, "Effects of Massed and Distributed Practice on the Learning and Retention of Second-Language Vocabulary." *Journal of Educational Research* 74, no. 4 (1981): 245–248.

[10]D. Krug, T. B. Davis, and J. A. Glover, "Massed Versus Distributed Repeated Reading: A Case of Forgetting Helping Recall?" *Journal of Educational Psychology* 82 (1990): 366–371.

Coming to Terms with Plateaus

What is a learning plateau?

No two people learn at exactly the same rate, yet the learning patterns of most people are similar. We all experience lulls in our learning. Progress is usually slow and steady at first; then for a period of time there might be no perceptible progress even though we are making a genuine effort. This "no-progress" period is called a *learning plateau*. After days, weeks, or even a month of effort, a surprising spurt in learning suddenly occurs and continues until another plateau is reached.

What is the best way to deal with a learning plateau?

When you reach a plateau, do not lose heart. Plateaus are a normal part of learning. You may not see any progress, but learning is still occurring. Once everything is in place, you'll be rewarded for your effort.

FINAL WORDS

How has Alzheimer's disease affected our attitude toward memory?

Alzheimer's disease has recently shifted a great deal of attention to human memory. People—especially older people—worry even more than they once did when a name or a piece of information slips their minds. Some make changes in their diet or lifestyle in the hope of forestalling or turning back the dreaded disease. The fear is understandable, and the attention to health and good habits is commendable. But the preciousness and precariousness of memory is nothing new. Memory has always been a vital component of our humanity, and it deserved our care, our respect, and our attention long before the emphasis turned to Alzheimer's. That is something we should never forget.

HAVE YOU MISSED SOMETHING?

SENTENCE COMPLETION   *Complete the following sentences with one of the three words listed below each sentence.*

1. G. A. Miller's Magical Number Seven theory teaches the importance of _____.

    numbers   selectivity   reciting

2. Your brain's short-term memory can be compared to a computer's _____.

    mouse   monitor   DRAM

3. No single activity is more important in strengthening your memory than _____.

    reviewing   reciting   reflection

MATCHING

In each blank space in the left column, write the letter preceding the phrase in the right column that matches the left item best.

_____ 1. Listening

_____ 2. Fading

_____ 3. Interest

_____ 4. Einstein

_____ 5. Clustering

_____ 6. Ebbinghaus

_____ 7. Feedback

_____ 8. Consolidation

a. Enables large amounts of information to be more readily remembered

b. Illustrated by the story of the injured mountain climber

c. Even more susceptible to forgetting than reading is

d. Measured the time it took to remember a series of nonsense syllables

e. Theory that says we need to rehearse the information we want to retain

f. Provided when you recite information either out loud or on paper

g. Strongest form of motivation for remembering information

h. Used motivated forgetting to free his mind of unnecessary information

TRUE-FALSE

Write T *beside the* true *statements and* F *beside the* false *statements.*

_____ 1. When you learn something new, you are likely to forget most of it in a matter of days.

_____ 2. To remember something, you have to make a conscious effort to learn it.

_____ 3. Incorrect information can last as long in memory as correct information.

_____ 4. Strong, memorable connections between ideas always have to be logical.

_____ 5. Commercial memory courses often rely on a method called "the wizard."

MULTIPLE CHOICE

Choose the word or phrase that completes each sentence most accurately, and circle the letter that precedes it.

1. Restaurant servers frequently use
   a. fading theory.
   b. motivated forgetting.

c. pseudo-forgetting.

d. mnemonic devices.

2. The "basic background" memory principle reinforces the importance of

a. getting it right the first time.

b. introductory classes.

c. pseudo-forgetting.

d. condensing and summarizing.

3. Memory acquires an extra dimension when information is

a. written on note cards.

b. drawn or visualized.

c. reread or recited.

d. condensed or reduced.

4. Mnemonic devices are

a. computer programs.

b. memory aids.

c. research instruments.

d. learning theories.

5. Reciting should always be done

a. out loud.

b. silently.

c. from memory.

d. on paper.

SHORT ANSWER

Supply a brief answer for each of the following items.

1. Explain how reciting provides motivation.
2. Compare the merits of massed and distributed practice.
3. What does retrieval theory suggest about our memories?
4. Provide illustrations of G. A. Miller's Magical Number Seven theory.

WORDS IN CONTEXT

From the three choices beside each numbered item, select the one that most nearly expresses the meaning of the italicized word in the quote. Make a light check mark (✓) next to your choice.

Business has two basic functions: marketing and *innovation*. Marketing and innovation produce results: All the rest are "costs."

—Peter Drucker (1909–), American business philosopher and author

1. *innovation*   improvements   research   new ideas

Customers deserve the very best. It would be helpful if everyone in business could, to *paraphrase* the American Indian expression, walk a mile in their customer's moccasins.

—Norman R. Augustine (1935–), American author and chairman, Martin Marietta Corporation

2. *paraphrase* the expression   quote   reword   relate

I want this team to win. I'm *obsessed* with winning.

—George Steinbrenner (1930–), American executive, owner, New York Yankees baseball team

3. *obsessed* with winning   concerned   possessed   neutral

War is a series of *catastrophes* that results in a victory.

—Georges Clemenceau (1841–1929), French statesman

4. series of *catastrophes*   battles   tactics   disasters

THE WORD HISTORY SYSTEM

Broker
originally, a retail vendor of
wine

broker   bro'-ker *n.* 1. One
that acts as an agent for others,
as in negotiating contracts,
purchases, or sales, in return
for a fee or commission. 2. A
stockbroker.

The modern *broker* who engages in large-scale financial operations takes his
name from a humble origin. *Broker* (spelled in Middle English *brocour*)
appears to be derived from Old French *broquier* or *brokier,* dialect for *brochier,*
"a broacher," "one who broaches or taps" a cask to draw off the liquor. The
modern verb *broach,* besides meaning "to tap" a cask, is used in a figurative
sense of "to open," as in "the subject was *broached.*" So the original *broker*
was a retail vendor of wine, and later, any small retailer, middleman,
peddler, or agent in general, as a pawn*broker.* More dignified commodities,
such as stocks and bonds, have in modern times dignified the *broker* and
his occupation.

Reprinted by permission. From *Picturesque Word Origins* © 1933 by G. & C. Merriam Co. (now
Merriam-Webster, Incorporated).

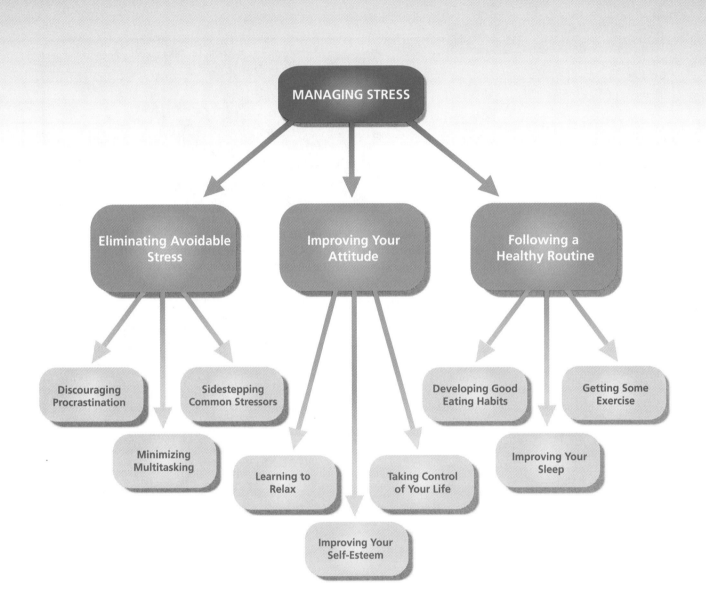

Managing Stress

Life is a journey, not a guided tour.

Anonymous

Stress, writes Dr. Hans Selye, a pioneer in its study, is "the spice of life or the kiss of death—depending on how we cope with it."[1] Unfortunately, most of us cope with it poorly. We worry too much, criticize too much, get angry too often, and become too tense. But if you can learn to deflect the stress that comes your way, you can thrive as a student and as a human being. This chapter helps you manage stress by focusing on:

- **Eliminating Avoidable Stress**
- **Improving Your Attitude**
- **Following a Healthy Routine**

[1]Hans Selye, "How to Master Stress," *Parents* 52 (November 1977): 25.

When can stress be a good thing?

Mere mention of the word *stress* is enough to make most people anxious. It brings to mind images of frayed nerves, shortened tempers, and rising blood pressure. But being under stress isn't always a bad thing. In fact, stress can prompt us to respond effectively to a tough situation, to rise to the occasion when a paper comes due or a test is handed out. According to Marilyn Gist, a professor at the School of Business Administration of the University of Washington, "A certain amount of stress is healthy and beneficial; it stimulates some to perform, makes them excited and enthusiastic."[2]

What is the medical definition of stress?

"Stress," according to Dr. Hans Selye, "is the nonspecific response of the body to any demand made upon it."[3] In other words, it is the body's attempt to adjust to a demand, regardless of what the demand may be. You undergo stress when you run or walk at a brisk pace. Your body responds to the demand for more oxygen by increasing your breathing and causing your heart to beat faster. Yet most people view exercise not as a source of stress, but as a means of stress relief. Likewise, watching a quiz show or doing a crossword puzzle can be considered stressful. In each case, the brain responds with increased mental activity. Yet most people undertake these activities specifically for relaxation.

What makes stress a problem?

The problem is that we don't always respond to the sources of stress (known as *stressors*) in a positive fashion. If instead of running for exercise, you're racing to catch a bus, or instead of solving a crossword puzzle, you're struggling with a math test that you didn't study for, your reaction is apt to be quite different. Rather than experiencing the exhilaration of exercising or the stimulation of solving a puzzle, you may wind up feeling exhausted or intimidated.

How can we better manage stress?

That's the two-sided potential of stress. Instead of compelling us to rise to the occasion, stress can sometimes plunge us into a sea of anxiety, worry, hostility, or despair. The way we respond to stress, whether we use it as a boon or a burden, depends on two major factors: our overall approach to life, and the number of stressors we face at any one time. To better manage the stress in your life, it helps to eliminate the avoidable sources of stress, improve your overall attitude, and maintain a healthy routine.

Eliminating Avoidable Stress

What can you do to eliminate avoidable stress?

Not all stress is unavoidable, of course. But a lot of it is. You can work to eliminate needless stress by discouraging procrastination, by minimizing most multitasking, and by sidestepping some of the other common sources of stress.

[2]Quoted in Pam Miller Withers, "Good Stress/Bad Stress: How to Use One, Lose the Other," *Working Woman* (September 1989): 124.

[3]Hans Selye, *Stress Without Distress* (New York: J. B. Lippincott, 1974), p. 27.

PEANUTS reprinted by permission
of United Features Syndicate, Inc.

Discouraging Procrastination

How can you avoid procras-
tination?

"Nothing [is] so fatiguing as the eternal hanging on of an uncompleted task."[4]
These words of William James, distinguished American psychologist, strike at
the hearts of us all. Everyone has had bouts with procrastination. The best way
to avoid future ones is to learn why people procrastinate and what you can do
to prevent procrastination.

Learn Why You Procrastinate

What are the common sources
of procrastination?

There's no single explanation for why people procrastinate. Nevertheless, many
of the stressors already discussed in this chapter can trigger procrastination.
Here's a list of common sources:

How does fear of failure
prompt procrastination?

Fear of failure.   Many students hesitate to begin a task because they're afraid
they won't be able to complete it successfully. Have some faith in yourself.
Think back to past successes, and realize that if you've achieved success before,
you can achieve it again. If you've failed in similar situations in the past, think
of times when you've succeeded in other areas and apply the confidence you
gained then to the present.

Why would fear of success
make you put things off?

Fear of success.   Some students put tasks off because they are afraid of succeed-
ing. A person might be afraid of success for at least two reasons. First, successful
people are a minority. There is a kind of loneliness in success. Some students
unconsciously procrastinate because they don't want to be resented by people
who aren't as successful. Second, success brings responsibility and choices.
When a person succeeds, doors suddenly open. That should be good news, but
some students view these opportunities as threats and burdens instead of chal-
lenges and choices. The solution involves a shift in attitude—to embrace success
instead of fleeing from it.

[4]Criswell Freeman, ed. *Wisdom Made in America* (Nashville, TN: Walnut Grove Press,
1995), p. 97.

What's at the heart of the prob-
lem of lack of time as a cause of
procrastination?

Lack of time.   If you used all the time you've been spending worrying about the time you don't have, you'd be well on your way to completing the task you've been putting off. This is a problem of control. Realize that how you budget your time is up to you. If you feel in control, you'll find it easier to complete the jobs that need to be done.

Why does poor organization
sometimes lead to procrastina-
tion?

Poor organization.   Perhaps you begin each day determined to get started on that task you've been putting off. But when nighttime comes, you find that despite your best intentions, you didn't get around to it. If that's your trouble, the cause may be a lack of priorities and/or poor organization. Draw up a to-do list and use the Pareto Principle (explained in Chapter 2) to help you put your priorities in perspective.

Devise Ways to Prevent Procrastination

Although the roots of procrastination are varied, the following methods of preventing procrastination should work regardless of the cause:

With so many sources of
procrastination, what's the
solution?
How does publicizing your
plans discourage procras-
tination?

Make your plans a part of the public record.   When you have a job that has to be completed or a goal that you want to reach, write it down. Or announce your intentions to close friends or family members. For example, "I plan to finish the bibliography for my research paper this weekend." Once you've made your intentions official, you're less likely to put them off. Procrastinators commonly fall into the habit of deceiving themselves, but they are less likely to deceive the people around them.

How do progress checks keep
procrastination from getting out
of hand?

Step back and check your progress from time to time.   One way many people procrastinate is by getting needlessly entangled in the details of their work. If, as you're working, you periodically step back and measure your progress, it will be easier to tell if you've gotten unnecessarily bogged down. If you discover that you have, you should be able to pick up your pace so you can reach your goal in the allotted time.

What is the five-minute plan?

Use the five-minute plan.   William J. Knaus, author of *Do It Now: How to Stop Procrastinating,* recommends what he calls the "five-minute plan."[5] Tackle a long-neglected task by agreeing to work on it for only five minutes. When the five minutes are up, decide whether you want to keep going. You usually will. The hardest part of almost any job is getting started. The five-minute plan takes the sting out of that painful first step.

How can you use momentum
to halt the progress of procras-
tination?

Let your momentum work for you.   If you've successfully completed a task you were anxious to finish, let your momentum carry over to an activity that you

[5]Quoted in Emrika Padus, *The Complete Guide to Your Emotions and Your Health* (Emmaus, PA: Rodale Press, 1986), p. 393.

CHAPTER 5

aren't as enthused about. Your extra energy can help you get started on the dreaded task, and once you've begun (the hardest part), completion will become much easier.

Why is a timer more effective than a watch for beating procrastination?

Use a timer instead of a watch. Clock-watching is a time-honored technique of perpetual procrastinators. If you want to keep to a schedule but avoid disrupting your concentration by constantly checking your watch or clock, use a timer instead. Many watches come with them. If your watch doesn't have one, an ordinary kitchen timer should do.

How can being specific prevent you from putting things off?

Be specific. A task is almost always more intimidating and stressful when it looms large and undefined. Instead of constantly telling yourself, "I've got to start writing that research paper," zero in on a specific aspect of your paper, such as choosing the topic or compiling a working bibliography. Suddenly your goal becomes more concrete, more doable, and thus much easier to complete. Or as James R. Sherman, author of *Stop Procrastinating*, puts it, "A job well-defined is a job half done."[6]

What happens when you verbalize your reasons for procrastination?

Verbalize your excuses. You may think you've got perfectly good reasons for putting off what needs to be done. If you let your excuses see the light of day by writing them out or explaining them to a friend, you'll often find that your reasoning isn't nearly as logical as you'd thought.

How does imagining success fight procrastination?

Visualize success or completion. Take a moment to imagine yourself accomplishing a task, passing a test, or achieving a goal. Through visualizing, you chart a course in your mind's eye. That course gives you a tangible game plan. The positive outcome you've imagined provides an incentive to follow that course until you reach the point of completion.

Minimizing Multitasking

What is multitasking?

If you're doing research for a term paper, answering e-mail, listening to the radio, and finishing your lunch all at once or in rapid succession, you're almost certainly multitasking. *Multitasking* means working on several tasks simultaneously or rapidly shifting back and forth between them. The term comes from computer operating systems, which are able to keep several applications running at the same time. The difference, of course, is that people are not machines. Sometimes mistakenly held up as a model of efficiency, multitasking is not only less productive than working on one task at a time, but it's also a

[6]James R. Sherman, *Stop Procrastinating* (Los Altos, CA: Crisp Publications, 1989), p. 38.

troubling source of stress.[7] Luckily, there are a handful of simple steps you can take to avoid it.

Multitasking Makes You Less Productive

Why does multitasking make you less productive?

Dividing your brain power between several tasks at once has a predictable effect. As a study published in the *Journal of Experimental Psychology* concludes, people who multitask are less efficient than people who don't. According to the study's coauthor, Dr. David Meyer, "There's scientific evidence that multitasking is extremely hard for somebody to do, and sometimes impossible."[8]

What are the costs of multitasking?

Of course, in spite of the evidence, thousands of people continue to multitask and would appear to be doing so successfully. "It doesn't mean you can't do several things at the same time," says Dr. Marcel Just, codirector of the Carnegie-Mellon University's Center for Cognitive Brain Imaging "But we're kidding ourselves if we think we can do so without cost."[9] According to studies by Dr. Just, Dr. Meyer, and others, those costs include forgetfulness and difficulties in concentrating.[10]

How does multitasking result in forgetfulness?

Forgetfulness. Chronic multitaskers often feel that their memories are failing them when in fact the converse is true: They are failing their memories. As we read in Chapter 4, you need consolidation time to ensure that you'll remember what you've learned for any length of time. Multitasking monopolizes this valuable consolidation space with additional activities that make forming a permanent memory trace more difficult.[11]

What is it about multitasking that makes concentration difficult?

Difficulty in concentration. Similarly, in Chapter 3, we learned how distractions—both internal and external—can undermine the mind's ability to stay focused. Multitasking frequently supplies both types of distractions. Dr. Meyer points out that "no matter how hard you try, you will never be as good multitasking as you are concentrating on one [task]."[12]

---

[7]Christina Tibbits, "Just Throw Multitasking Out Your Window of Work," *Austin Business Journal* (online), June 10, 2002, available at http://austin.bizjournals.com/austin/stories/2002/06/10/smallb3.html.

[8]Sue Shellenbarger, "Juggling Too Many Tasks Could Make You Stupid," *Wall Street Journal Online* (February 28, 2003), available at http://www.careerjournal.com/columnists/workfamily/20030228-workfamily.html.

[9]Ibid.

[10]John McChesney, "Minds Weren't Made for Multitasking," interview with Dr. Michelle Weil, *Hot Seat* (November 5, 1997), available at http://hotwired.lycos.com/synapse/hotseat/97/44/transcript2a.html.

[11]Shellenbarger, "Juggling Too Many Tasks."

[12]Amanda S. Fox, "Tallying the Cost of Doing Too Much," *CIO Magazine* (March 15, 2000).

Multitasking Increases Stress

Why does multitasking increase stress?

Not surprisingly, the drain on productivity results in an increase in the potential for stress.[13] You are compelled to struggle against the inevitable pseudo-forgetting that occurs and fight to maintain your concentration in a climate of relentless distractions. Moreover, multitasking forms an unhealthy alliance with two major culprits in stress, procrastination and loss of control, and can sometimes start you on a vicious cycle of insomnia as well.

What is the connection between multitasking and procrastination?

Procrastination. That other notorious source of self-imposed stress, procrastination, often works hand in hand with multitasking. After all, one technique that procrastinators frequently use to put off assignments is to shift back and forth between several tasks instead of focusing on a single one. Avoid multitasking and you may succeed in discouraging procrastination in the same stroke.

Why does multitasking sometimes lead to a loss of control?

Loss of control. As we'll learn, your sense of control can have a dramatic effect on your level of stress. Students, even overworked students, feel less stress when they are able to maintain a sense of control over what they are doing. Multitasking robs you of that control. All your activities and obligations are moving targets, and thus maintaining equilibrium becomes difficult for most and impossible for some.

How can multitasking lead to insomnia?

Insomnia. People who multitask—or attempt to—are often compelled to shift into a kind of mental overdrive that doesn't necessarily downshift when the day's work is done.[14] "Part of what's happening," says Michelle Weil, coauthor of the book *Technostress*, "is that we're overstimulating our physiological capabilities as well as our cognitive capabilities, and this leads to sleep interruption, the waking in the middle of the night, where it feels like your brain's just firing off ideas."[15] As we'll see later in this chapter, sleep loss not only results from stress, but can in turn be the source of *more* stress.

Multitasking Can Be Minimized

What can you do to minimize multitasking?

Obviously, some multitasking is arguably beyond your control. If you're in the middle of an assignment and the phone rings or someone comes to your door, it's natural to want to answer. But most factors that lead to multitasking are well within the realm of your control. You can avoid the stressful pitfall of multitasking by planning your day carefully, by making a point to finish one task before beginning another, and by keeping a pad handy to deal with the distractions that may lead to multitasking in the first place.

[13]Larry Rosen and Michelle Weil, "Multitasking Madnesss," *Context* (Fall 1998), available at http://www.contextmag.com/archives/199809/InnerGameOfWork.asp.

[14]McChesney, "Minds Weren't Made for Multitasking."

[15]Ibid.

Why does a plan discourage multitasking?

Plan your day.   Use the time-based scheduling outlined in Chapter 2 to inoculate yourself against multitasking. If each block of time has a specific task associated with it, you're less likely to bounce back and forth between several tasks.[16]

What can you do to make sure you work to completion?

Work to completion.   Don't start a new task until you've finished the old one.[17] This may be difficult with long-term tasks. But with short-term tasks, it should be achievable. If you do have a task that is stretched out over a longer period of time, try to create subtasks that you can tackle and complete before moving on.

What does a nearby pad do to prevent multitasking?

Keep a pad handy.   Here's another tip that comes from Chapter 3. The "worry pad" that is designed to serve as a temporary holding area for pending ideas and concerns can also be used to arrest early impulses to multitask. It's common to "task-shift" when there's a concern that "if I don't take care of it now, I never will." That's an understandable worry with a simple solution. Write it down, and get back to the task at hand. When you've finished the first job, you'll have the pad to remind you of what to do next.

Sidestepping Common Stressors

What are some other tips for sidestepping stress?

Although procrastination and multitasking may be two of the bigger avoidable causes of stress, there a number of other minor sources that can be sidestepped relatively easily. Here are some suggestions for doing so:

Wake up a half-hour earlier.   If you find yourself skipping breakfast or taking your last bite just as you race out the door, you're starting your day on a stressful note. Although getting an adequate amount of sleep is crucial, waking up a half-hour earlier than usual won't significantly affect your sleeping habits but can do wonders to ease the pace of your morning preparations.

Allow yourself plenty of travel time.   High-strung travelers are easily aggravated by slow drivers or long traffic lights. But slow drivers and long lights are facts of every commute. Factor them into your travel time.

Never wait empty-handed.   The stress that comes from standing in line or waiting in traffic stems from boredom and from irritation about wasting time. Both problems have the same easy solution: Have a book to read or some notes to review the next time you're kept waiting, and the time will fly by. Simply listen-

---

[16]Rosen and Weil, "Multitasking Madness."

[17]Ibid.

ing to the radio while waiting may be relaxing for some, but in general it won't provide the same sense of accomplishment.

Eat dinner early.   If you eat at a college dining hall, it's usually wise to get there early. The trivial but real stress that comes from waiting in line, searching for a seat, or racing to get a second helping before the kitchen closes can be eliminated if you show up soon after the dining hall opens. Whether you eat your meals at home or at school, an early dinner gives you more time before bed to be productive.

Don't take your work to bed with you.   Your bed is for relaxation. Don't mix your mind's signals by turning it into an auxiliary workspace. If you establish a clear boundary between where you work and where you sleep, your work will become more productive, and your sleep will be more restful. And both activities will tend to improve your approach to life's stressors.

Stay calm, cool, and in queue.   Try this Buddhist "loving kindness" meditation to help maintain a positive attitude while waiting in ticket or baggage lines. Take a few deep breaths and say these words slowly and silently several times: "May I be peaceful. May I be happy. May I be free from harm." Then say this blessing for each person in line one by one: "May you be peaceful," and so on. By the time you've reached the front of the line, you'll likely feel more generous and forgiving.[18]

Improving Your Attitude

What did James, Lange, and Peale suggest about attitude?

Although you can't turn away disaster simply by keeping a smile on your face, there are now abundant indications that your overall attitude can have a powerful influence on the outcome of potentially upsetting or stressful situations. The first evidence was offered near the end of the nineteenth century, when American philosopher and psychologist William James and Danish psychologist Carl Lange simultaneously developed a remarkable theory of emotion. You don't cry because you're sad, they suggested. You're sad because you cry. This revolutionary reversal of the apparent cause and effect of emotions briefly sent the scientific community into an uproar. As the twentieth century progressed, the controversial proposal, known as the James–Lange theory, was scoffed at by most members of the mainstream scientific community and was advocated instead by "inspirational" writers and speakers such as Dr. Norman Vincent Peale,

[18]Andrew Weil, "A Healthier Way to Fly," *Self Healing* (August 2000).

How did one study test the effect of facial expressions?

who championed the virtues of "positive thinking." Now the James–Lange theory has been vindicated, and Peale's ideas, bolstered by recent scientific evidence, have garnered mainstream defenders.

As part of a study conducted by Paul Ekman, Robert W. Levenson, and Wallace V. Friesen at the Department of Psychiatry of the University of California, San Francisco, subjects were given specific instructions for contracting various facial muscles to imitate six basic emotions: happiness, sadness, disgust, surprise, anger, and fear.[19] Instead of being told, for example, to "look scared," the subject was instructed to "raise your brows and pull them together, now raise your upper eyelids and stretch your lips horizontally, back toward your ears."[20] Expressions were held for ten seconds, while electronic instruments measured the subjects' physiological responses.

What effect did the facial expressions have on the subjects' bodies?

The results were fascinating. Simply imitating an emotional expression was enough to trigger the physiological changes normally associated with that emotion. The most interesting contrast was between expressions for anger and for happiness. The average subject's heart rate and skin temperature increased more with anger than they did with happiness. Yet the subjects weren't truly angry or happy: They were just imitating the expressions associated with the two emotions.

How can you improve your attitude?

We can conclude from this study that simply putting on a happy face may make you feel happier and that taking a dim or overly pessimistic view can lead to the discouraging outcome you expected. But managing stress shouldn't simply be a fuzzy-headed smile-at-all-your-troubles strategy. Improving your attitude should be done systematically by learning to relax, by improving your self-esteem, and, above all, by *taking control of your life*.

Learning to Relax

What does relaxation *mean?*

The regular use of relaxation techniques, according to studies at the Mind/Body Medical Institute of Harvard Medical School, reduces stress and the prevalence of stress-related illness.[21] But many of us don't consider using such techniques because we misinterpret what the word *relaxation* means. Relaxation doesn't necessarily mean that you're about to fall asleep. In fact, some World War II pilots used relaxation techniques not to prepare themselves for sleep or to "take it easy," but to stay alert and avoid fatigue during bombing missions.[22]

[19]Paul Ekman, Robert W. Levenson, and Wallace V. Friesen, "Autonomic Nervous System Activity Distinguishes Among Emotions," *Science* 221 (1983): 1208–1210.

[20]Ibid., p. 1208.

[21]Stephanie Wood, "Relax! You've Earned It," *McCall's* 118 (July 1991): 50.

[22]Edward A. Charlesworth and Ronald G. Nathan, *Stress Management* (New York: Atheneum, 1984), p. 41.

What effect does relaxation have on your muscles?

Nor is *relaxation* a synonym for lethargy. "Relaxation," wrote psychologists Edward A. Charlesworth and Ronald G. Nathan in *Stress Management,* "simply means doing nothing with your muscles."[23] Relaxation is relief from wasted effort or strain, an absence of tension. Indeed, explains author Emrika Padus, "Tenseness wastes energy; tenseness causes anxiety. . . . The best performances come when the mind and body are *floating,* enjoying the activity just as we did when we were young children, completely absorbed in the experience and unaware of any consequences of the actions. This is true relaxation."[24]

What techniques can you use to encourage relaxation?

There's nothing mystical about relaxation. Two simple techniques—breathing deeply, and using progressive relaxation—can help you get the hang of this life-sustaining practice.

Breathe Deeply

What is the connection between the way you breathe and how you feel?

There is a strong connection between the way you breathe and the way you feel. When you're relaxed, your breaths are long and deep, originating from your abdomen. When you're anxious, your breathing is often short and shallow, originating from high in your chest.

What have experiments shown about the effect of rapid breathing?

The link between breathing and emotion operates in both directions. Just as the way you feel affects the way you breathe, the way you breathe affects the way you feel. A handful of experiments have established this connection. Dr. James Loehr found that when relaxed subjects were asked to take short, rapid, and irregular breaths for two minutes—in other words, to pant—nearly everyone interviewed felt worried, threatened, and panicky.[25] Simply by imitating the response of an anxious person, the subjects had made themselves anxious.

How can experiments about rapid breathing promote relaxation?

Luckily, this principle can be used to encourage relaxation as well. By breathing slowly, steadily, and deeply and by beginning your breaths in your abdomen instead of up in your chest, you can encourage a feeling of relaxation. So just before an exam, an interview, or a dental appointment, when your palms are sweating, your body is tense, and your breath is short and shallow, try the count-of-three method to induce a more relaxed state. Count slowly and calmly through each step:

What are the steps in the count-of-three relaxation method?

1. Inhale slowly through your nose while silently counting to three.
2. Hold your breath for the count of three.
3. Exhale slowly through your nose while silently counting to three.

[23]Ibid., p. 42.

[24]Padus, *Complete Guide to Your Emotions and Your Health,* p. 490.

[25]James E. Loehr and Peter J. McLaughlin, with Ed Quillen, *Mentally Tough* (New York: M. Evans and Company, 1986), pp. 141–142.

4. With your breath expelled, count to three.

5. Repeat steps 1 to 4 several times. (Once you have the rhythm, you need not continue counting; but maintain the same timing and the same pauses.)

Use Progressive Muscle Relaxation

When can you use progressive muscle relaxation?

A big advantage of the count-of-three method is that it can be done inconspicuously almost anywhere, including in an exam room. But if you have some time, a quiet place, and a little privacy, you may want to try progressive muscle relaxation (PMR), a method for systematically tensing and relaxing the major muscles in your body.

What is the history of PMR?

PMR was developed more than seventy-five years ago by Edmund Jacobson, a doctor who saw the connection between tense muscles and a tense mind. PMR works by helping you become aware of the difference between how your muscles feel when they're tensed and how they feel when they're relaxed.

What are the steps involved in progressive muscle relaxation?

Start PMR by assuming a comfortable position, either sitting or lying down, and by closing your eyes. Make a tight fist with your right hand, and at the same time tense your right forearm. Hold this position for five seconds, feeling the tension in both your hand and arm, and then slowly release that tension, letting it flow out of you as you unclench your fist. Repeat the procedure with your left hand, noting the difference between how this hand feels tensed compared with your right hand and arm, which are now relaxed. Continue by separately tensing your shoulder muscles, your neck, and the muscles in your face. Then start with your feet and toes, moving up each leg; finish by tensing the muscles in your abdomen and chest. Once you've tensed and released every muscle group in your body, take a moment to savor the overall feeling of relaxation. Then open your eyes and end the exercise.

Improving Your Self-Esteem

What is self-esteem?

Self-esteem is your personal assessment of your own value. Unfortunately, many of us are our own toughest critics. We overlook our positive attributes and forget our successes, emphasizing our shortcomings instead and providing ourselves with a silent but constant stream of discouraging dialogue. The stress that results from this inner discouragement is far worse than criticism from a nagging parent, an insulting instructor, or an overly demanding boss.

What can you do to improve your self-esteem?

A healthy level of self-esteem is crucial to keeping stress at bay. If your self-esteem needs improvement, rewrite the potentially destructive inner dialogue that haunts you throughout the day and take some time to dwell on your successes.

Rewrite Your Inner Dialogue

What's the first step in rewriting your inner dialogue?

You can't rewrite your inner dialogue unless you've seen the script. So, the first step in eliminating the destructive thoughts that undermine your self-esteem is to become aware of them.

What should you do when your self-talk turns negative?

Most of us talk silently to ourselves almost continually. Psychologists commonly refer to this inner conversation as *self-talk*. Although you may have learned to ignore the sound of your self-talk, the effect it has on your overall attitude can still be damaging. So when you enter a new situation or are faced with a difficult challenge, take a moment to express your apprehensions to yourself. Then listen to your self-talk. Whenever you have a negative thought, counteract it with a positive one. Remember that the thoughts you have are your own and are under your control. You can open the door of your mind to whatever thoughts you want. Admit only the positive ones, and leave the negative ones out in the cold.

Build on Your Success

How do you build on your past success?

All of us have experienced success at one time or another. When you feel your self-esteem slipping, remember when you did a job you were proud of, when you overcame an obstacle in spite of the odds, or when everything seemed to go smoothly. It helps to congratulate yourself from time to time, to put yourself in an achieving frame of mind so that you can achieve success again.

Taking Control of Your Life

How does self-esteem relate to your sense of control?

One of the results of increased self-esteem is an increased sense of control, a quality that both medical doctors and psychologists are finding can have a measurable effect on your physical well-being and state of mind. According to the *Wellness Letter* from the University of California, Berkeley, "A sense of control may, in fact, be a critical factor in maintaining health."[26] When you're in control, you act; you set your own agenda instead of reacting to the wishes or whims of others or resigning yourself to what we often call "fate."

Appreciate the Significance of Control

How did Norman Cousins use control to change his life?

In the early 1960s writer and magazine editor Norman Cousins was stricken with a painful life-threatening illness. Determined not to let the illness control his life and sentence him to death, Cousins fought back. He watched movie comedies, one after another. The laughter the films elicited made the sleep that had eluded him come more easily and ultimately reversed the crippling illness.[27] In fact, the results so impressed the medical community that Cousins, who had no medical background, was awarded an honorary degree in medicine by the Yale University School of Medicine and was appointed adjunct professor in the School of Medicine at the University of California, Los Angeles.

[26]"Healthy Lives: A New View of Stress," *University of California, Berkeley, Wellness Letter* 6, no. 9 (June 1990): 4.

[27]*Managing Stress—From Morning to Night* (Alexandria, VA: Time-Life Books, 1987), p. 21.

What quality do many sur-
vivors of stress share?

Norman Cousins is not the only person who has demonstrated the impor-
tance of a sense of control. Author Richard Logan investigated the lives of peo-
ple who were able to survive extreme stress—such as imprisonment in a
concentration camp—and found that they all had at least one quality in com-
mon: a belief that their destiny was in their own hands. In other words, they
had a sense of control.[28]

What did one experiment show
about the relationship between
control and the hormone
cortisone?

The importance of control was reinforced in a study that provided a physio-
logical insight into the phenomenon. When your body is under stress, your
adrenal glands release *cortisone,* a hormone that in small doses can fight allergies
and disease but that in larger amounts can impair the body's ability to fight
back. When the two groups of employees who made up the study worked al-
most to the point of exhaustion, only one group experienced a significant in-
crease in cortisone production. Those employees with high levels of cortisone
had jobs that allowed them very little control. Employees who experienced no
increase in cortisone held positions with a high level of control.[29]

What are the long-term effects
of lack of control?

Lack of control can result in a sense of helplessness almost guaranteed to
bring about the frayed nerves, tense muscles, and overall feeling of panic nor-
mally associated with short-term stress. If these conditions persist, they can
have an adverse effect on your body's immune system, making you more sus-
ceptible to illness. Robbed of your sense of control, you not only react instead
of acting but also overreact. Turned outward, this overreaction may surface as
anger. Turned inward, it can lead to fear, anxiety, and general depression.

How did a button affect the
stress level of office workers?

In *The Joy of Stress,* Dr. Peter Hanson described an experiment in which two
groups of office workers were exposed to a series of loud and distracting back-
ground noises. One group had desks equipped with a button that could be
pushed at any time to shut out the annoying sounds. The other group had no
such button. Not surprisingly, workers with the button were far more produc-
tive than those without. But what's remarkable is that no one in the button
group actually *pushed* the button. Apparently, the knowledge that they could
shut out the noise if they wanted to was enough to enable them to work pro-
ductively in spite of the distractions. Their sense of control resulted in a reduc-
tion in stress and an increase in productivity.[30]

Understand How Attitude Affects Control

As a student, how can you gain
a better sense of control?

Dr. Hanson's story of the control button underscores an important element of
control: Taking control is primarily a matter of adjusting your attitude. As a stu-
dent, you can achieve a sense of control by changing the way you view your
courses, assignments, and exams.

[28]Mihaly Csikszentmihalyi, *Flow: The Psychology of Optimal Experience* (New York: Harper &
Row, 1990), p. 203.

[29]Robert M. Bramson, *Coping with the Fast Track Blues* (New York: Doubleday, 1990), p. 217.

[30]Peter Hanson, *The Joy of Stress* (New York: McMeel & Parker, 1985), pp. 15–16.

What can you do to change your attitude about your classes and assignments?

Taking control of your classes and assignments means viewing them as choices instead of obligations. The stressed-out, overwhelmed student looks to the next lecture or reading assignment with dread. The student who feels in control (and feels confident as a result) understands that attending lectures and completing assignments are a matter of choice and that the benefits derived from both are not only practical but also enjoyable. According to psychologist Mihaly Csikszentmihalyi, "Of all the virtues we can learn, no trait is more useful, more essential for survival and more likely to improve the quality of life than the ability to transform adversity into an enjoyable challenge."[31]

Learn to Cope with Out-of-Control Circumstances

What's a good way to cope with out-of-control circumstances?

Clearly, a great many situations in life are out of your control. But even in unavoidable or unpredictable situations, you can still exercise some degree of influence. Psychologists have found that as your coping resources increase (both in number and variety), so does your sense of control. Thus, a person with multiple coping strategies, instead of just one plan, is better able to adapt to the inevitable surprises that can accompany almost any undertaking.

How can you increase your sense of control over an upcoming exam?

For example, you have no control over whether an upcoming exam will be made up of essay or multiple-choice questions. If the instructor doesn't tell you which type it will be, you can increase your coping resources by preparing for both types of questions. Then, regardless of the type the instructor chooses, you will be ready. You will have a feeling of control.

How can you apply a sense of control to mundane annoyances?

The same strategy can be applied to a number of mundane situations that often generate unwanted stress. An unexpected line at the bank or the grocery store can leave you feeling helpless and anxious. You can't make the line disappear or move more quickly, but you can control the situation by reading a book or reviewing a set of vocabulary cards while you wait. As you can see, even a small degree of control can be used to minimize a large amount of stress.

Following a Healthy Routine

What can you do to your physical self to minimize the effects of stress?

Stress isn't all in your head. It has a noticeable effect on your body and can often be avoided through changes in your physical routine. If you make a concerted effort to improve your sleep, develop good eating habits, and get some exercise, you'll make yourself more stress-resistant and decrease your chances of being subjected to stress in the first place.

[31]Csikszentmihalyi, *Flow*, p. 200.

Developing Good Eating Habits

How are stress and eating interconnected?

There is a destructive, cyclical nature involving stress and eating that you want to work hard to avoid. If you develop poor eating habits, the negative effect on your body may make you more susceptible to stress. And there's ample evidence that a by-product of stress is poor eating habits. Because stress is so demanding, your body needs extra energy to address it. According to Dr. Robert Sapolsky, we expend between 10 and 23 percent of our energy on digestion.[32] It's not surprising, then, that when your body undergoes stress it often robs energy from the digestive process. In response to stress, CRF (corticotropin releasing factor) shuts down your digestion. This not only accounts for the lack of appetite, but also for the dry mouth that many of us experience in a stressful situation. But stress also triggers glucocorticoids, which enter your bloodstream at a slower pace. Whereas CRF depresses your appetite, glucocorticoids actually stimulate it and, according to Sapolsky, serve as the means for recovering from the stress response.[33]

How does the length of the stress affect your appetite?

How can you break the cycle of stress and bad eating habits?

"Thus, lots of short stressful events should lead to overeating," Dr. Sapolsky explains, "while one long, continuous stressor should lead to appetite loss."[34]

If you're overfed or undernourished, you may be putting an extra strain on your body that could be resulting in stress. And with that, the cycle continues. The way to break this vicious cycle is by taking time out for meals, rather than letting stress dictate whether you eat, and by eating in a way that counteracts stress instead of contributing to it.

Take Time Out for Meals

How do erratic meal schedules affect stress?

Stress can diminish or deplete certain vitamin and mineral supplies. An erratic meal schedule can aggravate this problem. According to nutritionist Jane Brody:

> Millions of Americans have fallen into a pattern of too-late-for-breakfast, grab-something-for-lunch, eat-a-big dinner, and nibble-nonstop-until-bedtime. They starve their bodies when they most need fuel and stuff them when they'll be doing nothing more strenuous than flipping the TV dial or pages of a book. When you think about it, the pattern makes no biological sense.[35]

What's the best way to restore a sensible eating routine?

The simplest way to put some sense back into your eating routine is by beginning each day with breakfast. Breakfast stokes your body's furnace so you have

[32]Robert M. Sapolsky, *Why Zebras Don't Get Ulcers* (New York: W. H. Freeman, 1998), p. 64.

[33]Ibid., p. 78.

[34]Ibid., p. 79.

[35]Jane E. Brody, *Jane Brody's Good Food Book* (New York: W. W. Norton, 1985), p. 187.

energy to burn for the rest of the day. Lunch and dinner simply throw a few coals on the fire; breakfast gets that fire burning.

Meals not only provide needed nutrients; they also supply you with a necessary break from the stresses of school or work. Here are some stress-relieving suggestions for mealtime:

What are some other nonnutritional benefits of meals?

Why is it a bad idea to work while you eat?

Don't work as you eat. Time will have been wasted, and you won't have gained the break you deserved when you sat down to eat. As a result, you'll probably feel more stressed than you were before you ate.

What is the difference between eating quickly and rushing your meal?

Eat quickly, but don't rush. There's a difference. If you have a lot of work to do, you won't have time for a leisurely lunch. But if you keep one eye on your sandwich and the other on the clock, you'll increase your chances of getting indigestion and stress without significantly speeding up your meal.

Eat the Right Foods

What were the drawbacks of the USDA's food pyramid?

In the last decade there has been a major reexamination of the United States Department of Agriculture's dietary recommendations, which are embodied in the famous food pyramid. Apparently in an effort to provide consumers with a simple, easy-to-follow set of guidelines and to prevent elevated cholesterol levels and heart disease, the USDA may have initially oversimplified its advice. People who saw the pyramid or read the recommendations were likely to conclude that fat is bad and that complex carbohydrates are good. That's only partially true. Not all fats are bad, and not all complex carbohydrates are good. The reality is a little more complicated, and there have been calls among doctors and nutritionists to rebuild the famous pyramid to reflect this. In an article published in 2003 in *Scientific American*, two professors at Harvard Medical School, Walter C. Willett and Meir J. Stampfer, set out to do just that. Their conclusions helped clarify and refine the original USDA recommendations.[36]

What is the simple math behind calorie consumption?

Curb Your Consumption of Calories Strictly speaking, fat doesn't make you fat. Calories do. The confusion lies in the fact that there are more calories in a gram of fat than in the same amount of protein or carbohydrate. Thus, some people overcompensate by avoiding fats and piling up calories from proteins and carbohydrates instead. Ultimately, it's a matter of simple math. If you consume more calories than you use up, you will gain weight. If you burn up more than you consume, you will have a "caloric deficit" and will lose weight as a result. Over the past few decades there has been an alarming rise in the incidence of obesity in the United States. Not everyone is destined to be as skinny

[36]Walter C. Willett and Meir J. Stampfer, "Rebuilding the Food Pyramid," *Scientific American* (January 2003).

as a rail. Nor should they be. But if you're above or below your natural weight, you may be putting extra stress on your body. The way to control that weight is by watching your calories.[37]

What are the drawbacks of butter, red meat, and refined carbohydrates?

Avoid Butter, Red Meat, and Refined Carbohydrates   Just because fats can't be entirely blamed for obesity doesn't mean that some of them don't have faults. The old pyramid treated all fats as bad in order to discourage people from eating those that are bad. The "bad fats" are saturated fats, most commonly found in butter and red meat. Its their content, not their calories, that causes trouble. Saturated fats are high in low-density lipoprotein (LDL), also known as "bad cholesterol" and associated with an increased risk of heart disease. Refined carbohydrates, such as white rice, white bread, sugar, and even potatoes, have an indirect link to cholesterol that is potentially troubling. Because these carbohydrates break down so quickly, they can spark a rapid rise in both glucose (blood sugar) and insulin, the hormone designed to keep glucose in check.[38] According to Willett and Stampfer, "High levels of glucose and insulin can have negative effects on cardiovascular health."[39] In addition, there's evidence that the sudden drop in glucose that results when insulin washes it away can make you feel hungrier faster, thus prompting you to eat more than you need.[40]

Why are healthy fats and whole grains recommended?

Emphasize Healthy Fats and Whole-Grain Foods   The big losers in the previous pyramid were probably unsaturated fats, which got unfairly swept up in the "fat is bad" barrage. As it turns out, polyunsaturated fats (found in fish and flax seeds) and monounsaturated fats (found in nuts, olive oil, and other vegetable oils) are actually quite good for you. Unlike eating their saturated siblings, consuming these fats can result in a reduced risk of heart disease.[41] Similarly, the whole grains you find in brown rice, whole-wheat flours, and a handful of other whole foods are far superior to the stripped-down, fast-acting refined version of these same foods. For one, they take longer to metabolize and thus do not trigger potentially damaging glucose and insulin spikes. In addition, they hold on to the valuable vitamins and nutrients that are normally removed when carbohydrates are refined.

[37]Ibid.
[38]Ibid.
[39]Ibid.
[40]Ibid.
[41]Ibid.

What are the advantages of fruits and vegetables?

Eat Lots of Fruits and Vegetables   Despite the heated disagreements between nutritionists on a wide variety of topics, very few have anything bad to say about fruits and vegetables. High in fiber, high in vitamins, and low in the sort of "gotchas" that seem to dog almost every other type of food, fruits and vegetables may well be the most beneficial foods to eat in abundance.

What is so important about water?

Drink Plenty of Water   Our world and our bodies are primarily made up of water. Second only to breathing as the source of our survival, water is the medium for every bodily process and the primary means by which toxins are expelled. It is absolutely essential to remain properly hydrated. Depending on your size, age, and body weight, doctors generally recommend consuming at least six to eight eight-ounce glasses of water per day.[42]

Why can't other beverages be used as a substitute for water?

Don't mistakenly assume that you are meeting your body's need for fluids by consuming liquids other than water, such as coffee, tea, alcohol, or soft drinks. Many of these beverages contain harmful ingredients that offset or undermine plain water's beneficial effect. Among these, the worst offenders are soft drinks, which have become the drink of choice in the United States. In 2001 Americans consumed more than fifty gallons of soft drinks per person per year and only forty gallons of water.[43] What's more, a typical twelve-ounce can or bottle of soda is sweetened by a whopping ten teaspoonsful of sugar,[44] empty calories that are almost certainly contributing to the epidemic of obesity in this country. If you're congratulating yourself for drinking diet soda instead, not so fast. Common artificial sweeteners can actually increase your appetite for sugar and carbohydrates and may be metabolizing into dangerous carcinogens![45] All these ominous findings reaffirm that clean, cool, fresh water is best.

Improving Your Sleep

Are most of us getting enough sleep?

If your morning starts with the sound of an alarm clock, you're probably not getting the sleep you need. According to Dr. Wilse Webb, a psychologist at the University of Florida, Gainesville, "If that's how you wake up every day, you're shortening your natural sleep pattern."[46] And yet an alarm clock is a part of

---

[42]Dr. Fereydoon Batmanghelidj, *Global Health Discoveries* 5, no. 1: 4.

[43]Wine Institute, *Wine and Other Beverage Consumption in America,* available at http://www.beekmenwine.com/prevtopat.htm.

[44]Donald S. McAlvany, *The McAlvany Health Alert,* 2, Issue 4 (April 2002).

[45]Dr. William Campbell Douglass, "NutraSweet Is Not So Sweet," *Second Opinion* VI, no. 3: 1–4.

[46]Quoted in Natalie Angier, "Cheating on Sleep: Modern Life Turns America into the Land of the Drowsy," *The New York Times* (May 15, 1990), pp. C1, C8.

most people's lives. Does that mean *all* of us are cheating ourselves on sleep? Perhaps not all, but most Americans are getting less sleep than they need. In fact, according to an article in *The New York Times*, "sleep scientists insist that there is virtually an epidemic of sleepiness in the nation."[47]

What are the dangers of sleep loss?

The image of a nation filled with semiconscious citizens may seem comical, but in reality the effects of widespread sleep deprivation are seldom humorous and sometimes deadly. The U.S. Department of Transportation estimates that up to 200,000 traffic accidents each year are sleep-related.[48] Furthermore, the worst nuclear power emergency in this country's history, at Three Mile Island, occurred at night, when workers were most susceptible to the effects of insufficient sleep.[49]

How does sleep loss affect learning?

Of course, sleep loss isn't usually deadly for students, but it can be damaging. Dr. Charles Czeisler, director of circadian (the daily rhythmic sleep/wake cycle) and sleep disorders medicine at Brigham and Women's Hospital in Boston, outlined some of the penalties that people pay for getting too little sleep: "Short term memory is impaired, the ability to make decisions is impaired, the ability to concentrate is impaired."[50] Clearly, a student who can't remember, can't make decisions, and has trouble concentrating will have a tough time surviving in an academic setting. Furthermore, the struggle to overcome the disabilities that sleep loss creates frequently leads to an even more pervasive problem: stress.

What is the connection between weariness and stress?

"Weariness corrodes civility and erases humor," reads an article in *Time* magazine. "Without sufficient sleep, tempers flare faster and hotter at the slightest offense."[51] The day-to-day challenges and inconveniences of going to school and of living in the modern world are potentially stress-inducing. Add habitual sleep loss, and you turn a chronic problem into an acute one. Dr. Ernest Hartmann's study of "variable sleepers" (patients whose sleep and wake-up times are not consistent) revealed that people under stress tend to need more sleep than do those who lead lives relatively free of anxiety and change. Yet stress often triggers insomnia, which leads to less sleep and the possibility of even more stress.[52] The results can be a vicious circle of stress and sleeplessness.

---

[47]Ibid., p. C1.

[48]Anastasia Toulexis, "Drowsy America," *Time* (December 17, 1990): 80.

[49]Angier, "Cheating on Sleep," p. C8.

[50]Quoted in ibid.

[51]Toulexis, "Drowsy America," p. 80.

[52]Lynne Lamberg, *The American Medical Association (Straight-Talk, No-Nonsense) Guide to Better Sleep*, rev. ed. (New York: Random House, 1984), p. 35.

How do you break the circle of stress and sleeplessness?

You can work to break this circle by getting the right amount of sleep, by following a regular sleep schedule, by avoiding naps, and by taking steps to improve the quality of your sleep.

Get the Right Amount of Sleep

How can you be sure that you are getting the right amount of sleep?

Are you getting enough sleep? In general, your overall alertness provides a pretty good indicator. If you are getting the right amount of sleep, you should be able to stay awake through twenty minutes of darkness at midday. Students in art history and film courses, where slides or movies are commonly shown, often complain that a darkened auditorium or classroom makes them sleepy. These situations don't *create* sleepiness. They simply reveal a problem of insufficient sleep and should serve as a warning to get more rest. Sleep behavior experts tell us that, on average, most people fall short of their needed amount of sleep by sixty to ninety minutes each night.[53] Aggravating this daily deficit is the fact that sleep loss is cumulative; it adds up. If you feel tired on Monday morning, you're apt to feel even more so when Friday rolls around.[54]

Can you make up for lost sleep on the weekends?

Although sleep loss adds up, sleep does not. You can't stash away extra hours of sleep like money in the bank. You need to get sufficient sleep seven nights a week. Just as so-called weekend athletes engage in strenuous exercise only on Saturday and Sunday and thereby jeopardize their hearts and their overall health in their effort to "stay fit," people who "sleep in" on weekends don't eliminate the effects of a week of sleep deprivation. In fact, they complicate the problem by disturbing their rhythm of sleeping and waking.

Keep to a Schedule

What effect do circadian rhythms have on sleep?

Achieving full alertness isn't simply a matter of getting enough sleep. It's equally important to do your sleeping at the right time of day. Thanks to *circadian rhythms*, the body's natural pattern of wakefulness and sleep, when morning arrives you instinctively become more alert in anticipation of the day that lies ahead. With the advent of evening, signals in your brain begin preparing you for needed sleep. You go to sleep, and when you wake up the process is repeated.

How can you take advantage of circadian rhythms?

The way to make the most of these circadian rhythms is to maintain a regular sleep/wake schedule. Sleeping late on the weekends or going to bed at widely varying times throws your circadian rhythms out of whack. You find yourself feeling drowsy when you should be alert, and wide awake when you should be fast asleep.[55] If you consistently rise at the same time regardless of when you

---

[53]Angier, "Cheating on Sleep," p. C1.

[54]Ibid., p. C8.

[55]Richard M. Coleman, *Wide Awake at 3:00 A.M.* (New York: W. H. Freeman, 1986), p. 149.

went to bed, you'll keep your circadian rhythms in tempo.[56] Furthermore, an unwavering wake-up time should help discourage you from staying up too late.

Recognize the Truth About Naps

What are the drawbacks of taking naps?

Students and others who have flexible schedules often see naps as the solution to sleep deprivation. Unfortunately, naps fall far short of their reputation and actually create a number of problems: They're impractical; they adversely affect learning; they harm both sound sleep and the sleep cycle; and they act as a convenient excuse for chronic procrastinators.

What do you lose by taking a nap?

In addition, naps generally deprive you of two of sleep's more important components: dream, or rapid eye movement (REM), sleep, the period in which all our dreaming occurs; and deep sleep (also called *delta sleep*), which many sleep experts believe recharges our batteries and increases our overall alertness.[57] Therefore, if you take a nap, you may be adding to the quantity of your sleep but you will probably be lacking the dream and deep sleep your body requires. According to Dr. William Douglass, "There is no doubt that this deep sleep is essential to health. Muramyl peptides, which are vital to tissue renewal and immune enhancement, are only released during deep, slow-wave sleep." [58]

How do naps interfere with your sleep/wake cycle?

As you might expect, naps also interfere with your sleep/wake cycle. Unless you take a nap every day at the same time and for the same duration, you will probably wind up with stay-at-home jet lag and have difficulty falling asleep at night.

What is the connection between naps and procrastination?

Finally, the temptation to misuse naps can be great. Many students give in to the urge to sleep, rationalizing that when they awaken they will feel refreshed and perform more productively. Unfortunately, few students report this happy result. The harsh reality is that if you try to escape a mountain of work by taking a nap, you will wake up to face the same amount of work, and you'll have less time in which to do it. It is far better to combat the desire to sleep, get the work done, and go to bed at your usual time with a clear conscience. You'll get the sleep you need; you'll minimize disruptions to your body's circadian rhythms; you'll feel healthier and more alert; and you'll be less susceptible to the potentially corrosive effects of stress.

Take Solid Steps for Better Sleeping

What are the advantages of optimal sleep?

Optimal sleep promotes not only a more alert, energetic, zestful life but also, according to some studies, a longer life. If you're not concentrating, if you're dozing off in class and at your desk, or if you're feeling dragged out, take steps to put yourself on the right track.

[56]Robert K. Cooper, *The Performance Edge* (Boston: Houghton Mifflin, 1991), p. 222.

[57]Dianne Hales, *The Complete Book of Sleep* (Menlo Park, CA: Addison-Wesley, 1981), p. 18.

[58]William Campbell Douglass, M.D., *Second Opinion* 4, no. 12 (December 1994): 7.

Why is sleeping in a dark room so important?

The right track means deep sleep in a dark room, which activates secretion of melatonin by the pineal gland. According to Dr. Alexander Grant's *Health Gazette*, "Melatonin not only helps us to sleep, but also may help to prevent tumors since it stimulates our tissues to destroy oxidants, chemical pollutants that produce cancer."[59] Also, under these favorable conditions, the pituitary gland releases large quantities of growth hormone into the blood. The hormone travels throughout the body to restore and rebuild body tissue. When you don't give the rebuilding process enough time, you upset the body's processes. For example, in a sleep-deprived state, the rate that the brain metabolizes glucose slows down; thus thinking slows down. Researchers calculate that a sleep-deprived person takes about one hour to do the work that could be done in forty-five minutes during the feeling-good stage.

What other steps can you take to improve sleep?

You can incorporate a few simple practices into your daily life to optimize the quality of your sleep:

Don't use caffeine after 4 P.M. Caffeine can often result in insomnia and thus throw your sleep/wake schedule off.[60] In addition, laboratory studies show that from 200 to 500 milligrams of caffeine per day may produce headaches, nervousness, and gastrointestinal disturbances, symptoms that can trigger or exacerbate stress. Keep in mind that coffee is not the only substance that contains caffeine. There's also caffeine in tea, some soft drinks, chocolate, and some nonprescription drugs.

Don't drink alcohol after 8 P.M. Although it has a reputation for making you drowsy, alcohol actually upsets your body's sleep pattern, first by reducing your REM sleep and then by triggering a "REM rebound," which can result in excessive dreaming and/or nightmares.[61]

Reserve your bed for sleeping. Eating, doing coursework, and even worrying in bed can scramble your body's contextual cues. If your bed becomes a multipurpose area, you may find it more difficult to fall asleep when the time comes.

Exercise! In addition to the benefits it provides to your heart, muscles, and self-esteem, exercise also enhances both the waking and sleeping phases of your circadian rhythms. Twenty minutes or more of vigorous aerobic exercise will boost your alertness in the daytime and improve the quality of your sleep at night. People who exercise regularly have been found to enjoy more deep sleep than people who don't.[62]

[59]*Dr. Alexander Grant's Health Gazette* 18, no. 2 (February 1995).

[60]Milton K. Erman and Merrill M. Mitler, *How to Get a Good Night's Sleep* (Phillips Publishing, 1990).

[61]Coleman, *Wide Awake at 3:00 A.M.*, p. 124.

[62]Ibid., p. 146.

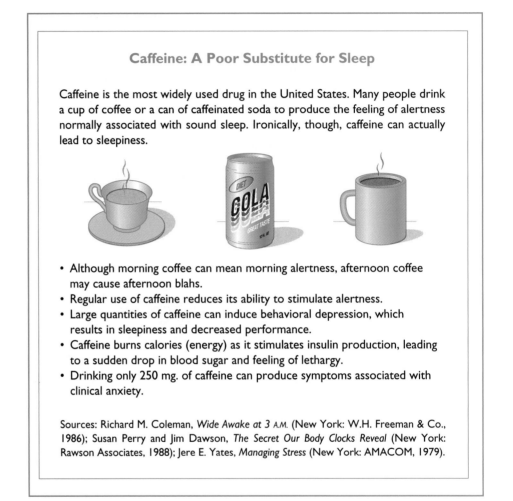

Caffeine: A Poor Substitute for Sleep

Caffeine is the most widely used drug in the United States. Many people drink a cup of coffee or a can of caffeinated soda to produce the feeling of alertness normally associated with sound sleep. Ironically, though, caffeine can actually lead to sleepiness.

- Although morning coffee can mean morning alertness, afternoon coffee may cause afternoon blahs.
- Regular use of caffeine reduces its ability to stimulate alertness.
- Large quantities of caffeine can induce behavioral depression, which results in sleepiness and decreased performance.
- Caffeine burns calories (energy) as it stimulates insulin production, leading to a sudden drop in blood sugar and feeling of lethargy.
- Drinking only 250 mg. of caffeine can produce symptoms associated with clinical anxiety.

Sources: Richard M. Coleman, *Wide Awake at 3 A.M.* (New York: W.H. Freeman & Co., 1986); Susan Perry and Jim Dawson, *The Secret Our Body Clocks Reveal* (New York: Rawson Associates, 1988); Jere E. Yates, *Managing Stress* (New York: AMACOM, 1979).

Getting Some Exercise

What does research show about the relationship between exercise and stress?

According to respected American cardiologist Dr. Paul Dudley White, "Vigorous . . . exercise is the best antidote for nervous and emotional stress that we possess."[63] In study after study, experts are corroborating the finding that exercise decreases stress and anxiety. Many other researchers report that regular exercise raises self-esteem and well-being and decreases depression. A study of forty-eight

[63]Quoted in Robert K. Cooper, *Health and Fitness Excellence* (Boston: Houghton Mifflin, 1989), p. 100.

students who had been suffering from test anxiety found that their anxiety was reduced after meditative relaxation and exercise.[64] In another study, both prisoners and prison guards took part in a carefully monitored exercise program. After a regimen of aerobic exercise, participants on both sides of the law found that they were able to sleep better, that their sense of well-being and self-esteem often improved, and that they experienced less tension and depression.[65]

What effect does exercise have on depression?

The relationship between exercise and depression, one of the most damaging emotional outgrowths of prolonged stress, led psychologist William Morgan, past president of the American Psychological Association's Division of Exercise and Sport Psychology, to suggest "that running should be viewed as a wonder drug, analogous to penicillin, morphine and the tricyclics [drugs used to treat depression]. It has a profound potential in preventing mental and physical disease and in rehabilitation after various diseases have occurred."[66] And the most effective exercise is that done regularly and aerobically.

Exercise Regularly

What are the advantages of exercising regularly?

You don't have to be an Olympic athlete to reap the benefits of exercise. Exercising three or more times per week is usually enough to improve your overall conditioning, although many students who follow an exercise routine look forward to the time away from their desks and exercise between five and seven times per week. Aside from its well-documented benefits, one of the reasons that exercise is so effective in reducing stress is a simple one. Like eating, sleeping, or any other type of recreation, it provides a welcome break from studying and recharges your mental and physical batteries.

Exercise Aerobically

Why is aerobic exercise especially important?

Although all exercise can provide relief from stress, only aerobic exercise can actually prevent the harmful effects of negative stress. Aerobic exercise is any activity that causes a steady, prolonged increase in your breathing and heart rate. A quick sprint across a football field or a dash from home plate to first base is certainly exercise, but it isn't aerobic exercise. You are inhaling lots of oxygen and speeding up your heart, but you are doing so for only a few seconds, probably not at a steady rate, and definitely not for a prolonged period of time. If, however, you swim twenty-five laps or so, pedal your bike steadily for several miles, or take a brisk thirty-minute walk, you are getting aerobic exercise.

[64]Kenneth H. Cooper, *The Aerobics Program for Total Well-Being* (New York: Bantam Books, 1982), p. 186.

[65]Ibid.

[66]Quoted in Keith W. Johnsgård, "Peace of Mind," *Runner's World* 25, no. 4 (April 1990): 81.

What is the greatest benefit of aerobic exercise?

Perhaps the greatest benefit of aerobic exercise is that it lowers your heart rate. Once your heart muscle has been strengthened through exercise, it acts more efficiently, beating fewer times to circulate the same amount of blood. And if anxiety should strike, the increase in the heart rate of an aerobically fit person is not as drastic as it is in someone who gets little or no aerobic exercise. Furthermore, if your heart rate remains comparatively low when subjected to stress, you are less likely to overreact emotionally. The result not only discourages overreaction to stress but also may save your life. A person in poor health who is subjected to unexpected stress can die from the sudden strain the excitement puts on his or her heart.[67]

What are the effects of the hormones that exercise releases?

Exercise provides a perfect example of good stress. It works as a stimulant to release the hormone *norepinephrine,* which promotes enhanced awareness, and *endorphins,* morphinelike hormones that provide the euphoric feeling commonly referred to as "runner's high." According to Dr. Kenneth Cooper, if you exercise at the end of the day when stress levels are traditionally highest, "you can continue to work or play much later into the evening than might be possible otherwise."[68] Exercise leaves you feeling simultaneously alert and relaxed, a nearly ideal state for efficient, prolonged, and stress-free study.

FINAL WORDS

Why are the stress habits you develop in college so important?

Many students are tempted to write off their college days as a time when anything goes. They eat too much (or too little), drink too much, rob themselves of sleep, and subject their bodies to an extraordinary amount of stress. As removed as college may seem to be from the "real world," the habits you develop in school may well set the tone for the rest of your life. Health doesn't take a holiday simply because you're at school. By all means, work hard and enjoy yourself. But do so in a healthy and sensible way. Keep in mind that you are gaining more than academic expertise while you're in school. You're also learning how to live your life. And in the grand scheme of things, that is the grade that truly matters.

HAVE YOU MISSED SOMETHING?

SENTENCE COMPLETION   *Complete the following sentences with one of the three words listed below each sentence.*

1. Sources of stress are called _____.

    lesions   endorphins   stressors

[67]Cooper, *The Aerobics Program for Total Well-Being,* p. 189.
[68]Ibid., p. 191.

2. Self-esteem is your personal assessment of your own _____.

   intelligence   value   finances

3. The "bad fats" are _____.

   polyunsaturated   saturated   monounsaturated

MATCHING

In each blank space in the left column, write the letter preceding the phrase in the right column that matches the left item best.

_____ 1. Timer   a. Has a silent effect on self-esteem

_____ 2. Panting   b. Developed progressive muscle relaxation

_____ 3. Jacobson   c. Working on several activities at once

_____ 4. Cortisone   d. Defined as "doing nothing with your muscles"

_____ 5. Self-talk   e. Released when body undergoes stress

_____ 6. Caloric deficit   f. Tool to counteract clock-watching

_____ 7. Relaxation   g. Has been shown to cause feelings of panic

_____ 8. Multitasking   h. Necessary for weight loss

TRUE-FALSE

Write T beside the true *statements and F beside the* false *statements.*

_____ 1. You can undergo stress when you run or walk at a brisk pace.

_____ 2. Multitasking generally makes you more productive.

_____ 3. Fear of success is one cause of procrastination.

_____ 4. Some artificial sweeteners may actually increase your appetite for sugar.

_____ 5. "Sleeping in" should eliminate the effects of sleep deprivation.

MULTIPLE CHOICE

Choose the word or phrase that completes each sentence most accurately, and circle the letter that precedes it.

1. Stress is the body's attempt to adjust to a

   a. crisis.

   b. test.

   c. demand.

   d. situation.

2. Multitasking can interfere with
   a. sound sleep.
   b. concentration.
   c. memory consolidation.
   d. all of the above.

3. The simplest way to put some sense back into your eating routine is by
   a. avoiding fats.
   b. eating breakfast.
   c. drinking water.
   d. taking vitamins.

4. A typical twelve-ounce can of soda contains
   a. a generous supply of nutrients.
   b. five grams of fat.
   c. ten teaspoons of sugar.
   d. all of the above.

5. Exercise has been shown to
   a. improve self-esteem.
   b. increase well-being.
   c. reduce depression.
   d. all of the above.

SHORT ANSWER   *Supply a brief answer for each of the following items.*

1. Explain the "two-sided potential of stress."
2. What is the James–Lange theory?
3. Discuss some methods for minimizing multitasking.
4. What makes an exercise aerobic?

WORDS IN CONTEXT

From the three choices beside each numbered item, select the one that most nearly expresses the meaning of the italicized word in the quote. Make a light check mark (✓) next to your choice.

In a political speech, we catch the phrases that are *emphasized*, and the rest becomes a *mumbo-jumbo* of political *innuendoes*.

—Louis E. Boone, author of *Quotable Business*

1. phrases . . . *emphasized*   quoted   stressed   repeated

2. *mumbo-jumbo*   recital   routine   gibberish

3. political *innuendoes*   promises   campaigns   insinuations

Perhaps no other president preferred listening over speaking more than the *taciturn* thirtieth president of the United States, Calvin Coolidge.

—Louis E. Boone, author of *Quotable Business*

4. *taciturn . . .* president   untalkative   calculating   diplomatic

Only *mediocrities* rise to the top in a system that won't tolerate wave-making.

—Laurence J. Peter (1919–1990), American author

5. *mediocrities* rise   intelligent people   average people   reliable people

Advertising has *annihilated* the power of the most powerful adjectives.

—Paul Valéry (1871–1943), French poet and philosopher

6. *annihilated* the power   exploited   enhanced   nullified

---

THE WORD HISTORY SYSTEM

Bedlam
really, a madhouse

bedlam bed'-lam *n.* A place
or situation of noisy uproar
and confusion.

In 1247 the priory of St. Mary of Bethlehem was founded in London. In the early fifteenth century it came to be used as a hospital for lunatics. Familiarly known as *Bethlehem*, the name of the asylum was contracted in popular usage to *Bethlem*, *Bedlem*, or *Bedlam*. The name came to be applied to any lunatic asylum, and consequently, in our own day, *bedlam* is used to signify any scene of uproar or confusion that is suggestive of a madhouse.

Reprinted by permission. From *Picturesque Word Origins* © 1933 by G. & C. Merriam Co. (now Merriam-Webster, Incorporated).

Enrichment Skills

6   Improving Your Reading

7   Building a Lasting Vocabulary

8   Thinking Visually

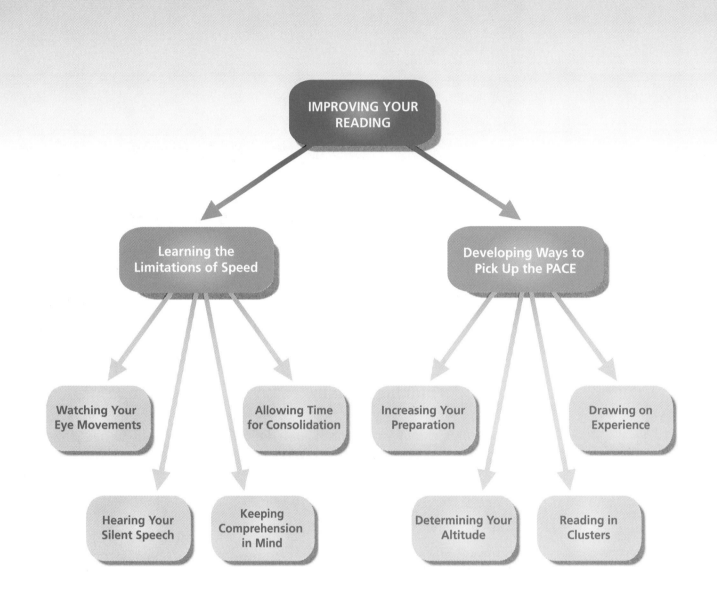

Improving Your Reading

Almost anyone who reads can read faster. The way to do so, however, is
to strengthen your natural way of reading and thinking—not to use
some artificial method. This chapter uses solid research and sound
learning principles to explain:

- **Learning the Limitations of Speed**
- **Developing Ways to Pick Up the PACE**

How can you improve your reading?

The simple question "How can I improve my reading?" does not have a simple answer. There are many different purposes in reading, many different reading techniques that can be used, and many ways in which reading can be "improved." However, when this question is asked by a student, it usually means "How can I speed up my reading so I can finish my homework in half the time with high comprehension and almost complete retention?" There is no easy way to do so, despite the numerous brochures, newspaper and magazine articles, and television programs that extol the marvels of "speed-reading." To truly improve your reading, you need to learn the limitations of speed and then, given those limitations, develop ways that you can sensibly, naturally pick up your pace.

Learning the Limitations of Speed

Why can't you read at the rates that the speed-reading advocates promise?

Many students, as well as the general public, are convinced that speed-reading is an easy-to-learn technique that can be used with any page of print. Unfortunately, speed-reading is virtually useless to anyone who desires to learn from the printed page. It's certainly possible for you to read faster. But slowed down by your eyes, by your vocal cords, and by the necessity to both comprehend and consolidate what you've read, you'll never be able to come close to some of the spectacular claims that the speed-readers make.

Watching Your Eye Movements

What does the peep-sight experiment tell us about how we read?

You can learn a lot about how the eyes work just by watching them. Here's an experiment you can conduct with the help of another person. Take a half a page of print such as the text shown in Figure 6.1, and punch a small hole in the center. Hold the page close to your own eye, with the printed side facing toward the other person, who is the reader. As the reader silently reads the printed matter, watch his or her eyes through the peephole. You will immediately notice that the reader's eyes do not flow over the lines of print in a smooth, gliding motion. Instead, they seem to jerk their way across the page, alternating fast, forward movements with momentary pauses, much like a typewriter carriage. The pauses (called fixations) are absolutely necessary, for they allow the eyes to focus on the type, to get a clear image of it. When the eyes are in motion (known as saccades), they record nothing but a blur on the retinas.

What sort of speeds do speed-readers claim?

Keep this experiment in mind as you consider the claims of speed-reading courses, some of which boast graduates who read thousands of words per minute, always making the point, "with nearly 100 percent comprehension."

What is the basic premise of speed-reading?

The basic premise of speed-reading advocates is this: The eye is able to see a vast number of words in one fixation. Some advocates say the eye can see phrases at a glance; others say entire lines; still others say paragraphs at a time;

Figure 6.1
The Peep-Sight Experiment
See the text discussion for instructions.

Source: From E. A. Tenney and R. C. Wardle, *Intelligent Reading* (New York: Crofts, 1943), preface.

A knowledge of words, what they are and how they function, is the first and last essential of all liberal education. As Carlyle says, "If we but think of it, all that a University or final highest school can do for us is still but what the first school began doing—teach us to *read.*" When a student has been trained to make the words of any page of general writing yield their full meaning, he has in his possession the primary instrument of all higher education.

●

In these days when the nation is asking that its schools produce good citizens first and specialists second, there is a marked need for a rich and wide "universal" training of the mind. This book on reading is designed to forward the process by which the whole mind, intellectual and emotional, becomes a more accurate instrument for the reception and transmission of thoughts and sensations. If our system of education does not so train the minds of its students, if it does not teach them to recognize differences, to distinguish shades of meaning, to feel as by intuition not only the hypocrisy of the demagogue and the flattery of the bootlicker but also the depth of a statesman like Lincoln and the insight of a poet like Shakespeare, it fails of its purpose.

and a few say the eye can see an entire page at a glance. Get out your calculator and let's look at the facts.

Eye-movement photography, which conducts a sophisticated version of the experiment you just tried, shows that the average college student makes about four eye fixations per second. The very same photography shows that the eye sees an average of only 1.1 words during each fixation. Seldom does any person, trained or untrained, have a usable span of recognition of more than 2.5 words.[1] Recent research using computers shows that good readers take in an average of about ten usable letters per fixation: four letters to the left of the center of fixation and five or six letters to the right of the center of fixation.[2] There is no evidence, by the way, that anyone's eyes can see a whole line of type "at a glance." So any advice to run your eyes down the middle of a page or column in order to speed-read the page is nonsense. All you'll get is a word or two from each line—a handful of scrambled words.

These facts indicate that only a most unusual person can see 10 words per second (2.5 words per fixation at four fixations per second). So, in sixty seconds it is arithmetically possible for the eye to take in 600 words. This calculation does not

What does eye-movement research conclude about reading rates?

How fast can a better-than-average reader read?

[1]Stanford E. Taylor, "Eye Movement in Reading: Facts and Fallacies," *American Educational Research Journal* 2, no. 4 (November 1965): 187–202.

[2]John M. Henderson and Fernanada Ferreira, "Effects of Foveal Processing Difficulty on the Perceptual Span in Reading: Implications for Attention and Eye Movement Control," *Journal of Experimental Psychology: Learning, Memory and Cognition* 16, no. 3 (1990): 417–429.

include the time needed to return the eyes to the beginning of each line and to turn pages. Nor does it allow time for comprehension and consolidation. After all, what's the use of reading if you can't understand or remember what you've read?

What is Cunningham's attitude toward speed-reading rates?

Anne Cunningham, a professor of education at the University of California at Berkeley, is not quite as optimistic. She points to tests that put the speed-reading ceiling at closer to 300 words per minute.[3] Then what of the claims of speed-reading entrepreneurs, who trumpet per-minute totals in the thousands or tens of thousands of words? "People who purport to read 10,000 words a minute," Cunningham explains, "are doing what we call skimming."[4]

Hearing Your Silent Speech

What is vocalization?

Another notorious impediment to faster reading is "vocalization," which is best embodied by people who move their lips as they read. Here's a case where the speed-reading advocates appear to be right. Vocalization probably *does* decrease your reading speed. No, we don't all move our lips as we read. Some of us actually whisper our words, while others move only our vocal cords or simply think the sound of each word as we read it. No matter what form our vocalization takes, it appears to be an important part of the reading process.

What is Hall's opinion on vocalization?

Robert A. Hall, Jr., an internationally known linguist, has this to say about vocalization, or silent speech:

> It is commonly thought that we can read and write in complete silence, without any speech taking place. True, many people learn to suppress the movements of their organs of speech when they read, so that no sound comes forth; but nevertheless, inside the brain, the impulses for speech are still being sent forth through the nerves, and only the actualization of these impulses is being inhibited on the muscular level, as has been shown by numerous experiments. No act of reading takes place without a certain amount of subvocalization, as this kind of "silent speech" is called, and we normally subvocalize, when we write, also. Many slow readers retain the habit of reading out loud, or at least partially moving their lips as they read; fast readers learn to skip from one key point to another, and to guess at what must lie in between. The good rapid reader knows the subject-matter well enough to guess intelligently; the poor reader does not know how to choose the high spots or guess what lies between them. As the rate of reading increases, the actual muscular movements of pronunciation are reduced; but, just as soon as the going gets difficult, the rate of reading slows down and the muscular movements of pronunciation increase again, even with skilled rapid readers.

[3]Quoted in Blair Anthony Robertson. "Speed-reading Between the Lines," *Sacramento Bee* (October 21, 1999), p. A1.

[4]Ibid.

From these considerations, it is evident that the activities of speaking and reading cannot be separated. Curiously enough, literary scholars are especially under the delusion that it is possible to study "written language" in isolation, without regard to the language as it is spoken; this is because they do not realize the extent to which, as we have just pointed out, all reading and writing necessarily involve an act of speech on the part of both writer and reader.[5]

What did Edfeldt's research conclude about "silent speech"?

Åke Edfeldt, of the University of Stockholm Institute of Reading Research, has studied vocalization with a team of medical doctors who used electrodes to detect movement in the lips, tongues, and vocal cords of volunteer readers. After exhaustive medical tests, Edfeldt concluded:

On the basis of the present experimental results, earlier theories concerning silent speech in reading may be judged. These theories often appear to have been constructed afterwards, in order to justify some already adopted form of remedial reading. In opposition to most of these theories, we wish to claim that silent speech occurs in the reading of all persons.

In any case, it seems quite clear that all kinds of training aimed at removing silent speech should be discarded.[6]

Keeping Comprehension in Mind

What did the MIT study learn about how the mind handles words?

Even if you could take in words at a phenomenal rate, would it do any good? Probably not. Remember the processing part of the reading equation. Just because you see doesn't mean you understand. Research at the Massachusetts Institute of Technology, using MIT undergraduates, gives scientific evidence that the mind can attend to only one word at a time. The researchers concluded that "even the skilled reader has considerable difficulty forming a perception of more than one word at a time."[7]

Why does it seem that we read words in rapid succession?

You often have the impression that you are seeing more than one word at a fixation because your eyes are moving rapidly from left to right, taking in words in rapid sequence. This process is almost like watching a movie. Although each film frame is a still picture, you "see" motion and action when the film is projected at a rate of twenty-four frames per second. Similarly, words projected on the brain at the rate of seven or eight words per second give the

[5]Robert A. Hall, Jr., *New Ways to Learn a Foreign Language* (New York: Bantam Books, 1966), pp. 28–29.

[6]Åke W. Edfeldt, *Silent Speech and Silent Reading* (Chicago: University of Chicago Press, 1960), p. 154.

[7]Paul A. Kolers, "Experiments in Reading," *Scientific American* 227, no. 1 (July 1972): 84–91.

impression of living, moving ideas. Nevertheless, the brain is "viewing" only one word at a time.

Allowing Time for Consolidation

What effect does speed-reading have on consolidation?

And finally there's a matter of memory. Remember the mountain climber in Chapter 4 who hit his head and was unable to recall anything that had happened to him fifteen minutes earlier? His memories had vanished because he received a blow to the head before his brain had an opportunity to transfer his recent experiences into long-term storage. That mental maneuver isn't limited to mountain climbers. In addition to seeing words and comprehending them, you also need to be consolidating that information so it doesn't quickly disappear in a fog of forgetting. Reading at astronomical speeds doesn't provide any time for consolidation.

Developing Ways to Pick Up the PACE

What is your best chance for improving your reading speed?

Given the wealth of evidence that seems to put a huge barrier between you and well-advertised, but insufficiently substantiated supersonic reading speeds, what can you realistically do to improve your reading? Your hope lies not in lengthening your saccades, shortening your fixations, or even lessening vocalization. Your best chance of success depends on the all-important processing step. If you can reduce the time it takes to extract meaning from what you're reading, you'll boost your comprehension and increase your speed, the very essence in almost everybody's book of improving your reading. You can do this—you can pick up your PACE—by increasing your <u>p</u>reparation, determining your <u>a</u>ltitude, reading by <u>c</u>lustering, and drawing on your <u>e</u>xperience.

P: Increasing Your Preparation

Why is it risky to begin reading when you aren't well prepared?

Although it might seem to save time in the short run, it's unwise in the long term to begin reading without investing some effort to warm up first. Beginning to read unprepared will often mean that you have to stop and reread a portion that was unclear, or worse that you will overlook or misunderstand crucial information because you weren't properly prepared for it. What does preparing for your reading entail? The bare-bones approach is a quick overview of the assignment. If you want to increase your preparation, you might consider adopting the distinctive regimens of two of history's great thinkers, Edward Gibbon and Daniel Webster.

Overview Your Assignment

What does overviewing an assignment involve?

At minimum, you should prepare for a reading assignment by conducting a quick overview. (Chapter 9 discusses this approach in greater detail.) In most cases, it involves understanding captions, headings, subheadings, and portions of paragraphs well enough to locate key concepts in the chapter. This kind of overview enables you to see the relative importance of each part to the whole and places you in a powerful position to organize information once you begin reading in earnest.

Use Edward Gibbon's "Great Recall"

What is Gibbon's "great recall"?

Think of the classic operating room scene that you've witnessed in countless movies and TV shows. The surgeon, face covered by a mask, eyes concentrating on the task at hand, has a nearby tray of tools, a carefully arranged array of shiny medical instruments, ready in case she should need them. The great English historian Edward Gibbon (1737–1794), author of *Decline and Fall of the Roman Empire*, took a similar approach that he called "the great recall." Before reading a new book, and before beginning to write on any subject, Gibbon would spend hours alone in his study, or he would take a long walk alone to recall everything that he knew about the subject. In a sense, like a surgeon, he was assembling his mental tools, preparing them for his intellectual operation. Gibbon's system was highly successful. His old ideas were brought to the forefront of his mind, like a tray of shiny tools that could be used to understand new ideas and new information.

Try Daniel Webster's Way

What was Daniel Webster's approach to reading preparation?

Daniel Webster (1782–1852), American statesman and orator, also placed a premium on preparation. After scanning the book's table of contents, reading the preface, and flipping through some of its pages, Webster would make lists of (1) questions that he expected to be answered in the book, (2) the knowledge he expected to gain from his reading, and (3) where the knowledge would take him. The three lists provided a strong prescription for preparation. They guided him through the book and ensured that his attention and concentration were intense.

A: Determining Your Altitude

What does *altitude* refer to when it comes to reading?

With some of the material you read, you want to be able to zero in on specific words. On other occasions that sort of attention to detail is completely unnecessary and, quite frankly, a waste of your time. There are situations in which you just need to take the 35,000-foot view of a reading assignment, to get a broad outline, a big-picture view of what a chapter or article contains. There are others in which you'll want to fly in a little closer, to clip the treetops, to go beyond the faint outline of ideas and begin to see some definition in the paragraphs and sentences of a passage. And, finally, there are occasions when you want to be right there at ground level, eyeing every word up close and in detail. These are all variations on what is commonly called skimming. To increase your speed and correctly calibrate your comprehension, it's important to set your altitude before you start skimming.

Skim at 35,000 Feet to Get the Gist

What is the purpose of skimming at 35,000 feet?

Sometimes skimming may be used to get the gist of a book or article. You can use this technique to find out whether a book pertains to the topic you are working on. To get the gist, read both introduction and summary rapidly, as well as paragraphs that have topic sentences indicating that they contain important data.

How can this method of skimming help in term paper preparation?

This skimming method can help when you have a term paper to write. After having used the computer as an aid, make a list of books that seem related to your topic, get the books, and look through them to eliminate those that are not pertinent and to keep those that are. Obviously, you would waste time and energy if you attempted to read all the books on your list. To get the main idea of each book, look at the table of contents, or select a chapter with a title related to your topic, and skim it for its outstanding ideas.

Skim at the Treetops for General Clues

What is the purpose of skimming at the treetops?

When you are seeking specific information but do not know in what words the information may appear, you must use a slower searching method. In this case, you won't be able to anticipate the exact words, so you must be alert for clues, which can appear in various forms.

How do you arrive at an answer with this sort of skimming?

In this kind of searching, you must infer the answer. For example, after reading an article about Paul Bunyan, a legendary giant lumberjack and folk hero, a student was asked a question about Paul Bunyan's birthplace. The answer was Canada, yet nowhere in the article did the word Canada appear. The answer had to be inferred from a sentence that stated that Paul Bunyan was born at the headwaters of the St. Lawrence River. Because the student discovered on a map that the headwaters are in Canada, she could answer the question.

What sort of advance guessing will help you with treetop skimming?

When you are looking for clues, try to guess the form in which the information might appear. When you believe you have found the information you want, go back and read the paragraph to make sure, from context, that it is exactly what you seek.

Skim at Ground Level for Specific Information

When does skimming at ground level come in handy?

If you want to find specific information (name, date, word, or phrase) in a textbook or article, you need to focus on individual words. Searching may be used because it is recognition, not comprehension, that will give you the answer. To ensure that your eyes do not overlook the word or fact you seek, concentrate on it, keeping it in mind as your eyes run over the pages. Concentration will trigger your mind to pick it out of the sea of words. Once you have located the specific word or fact, pause and read the sentence or paragraph surrounding it at a normal rate to make sure, through context, that you have found what you were looking for.

C: Reading in Clusters

How does clustering relate to the way in which we learn to read?

We group our letters into words without even thinking about it. Remember back to when you were first learning to read, how you sounded out a word one letter at a time until you ultimately came to recognize a growing number of words without having to break them down into their component parts? Given the size of the textbook assignments you probably face today, trying to understand what you're reading a letter at a time would be almost unimaginable. But is reading an assignment a word at a time all that much better? If you consider a ten-page assignment with an average of three hundred words per page, that's thirty thousand words to keep track of and comprehend.

How can clustering be used to help improve your comprehension?

Although, as we've learned, you can't really transcend the eye's limitations of one or two words per fixation, you can make it easier to grasp what you've read by clustering those words into larger and thus fewer groups. If instead of moving word by word, you work on understanding your assignments a phrase at a time, a paragraph at a time, and even a page at a time, you'll find that your level of comprehension improves considerably.

Use the Intonation Way

What role can intonation play in helping you read better?

Research has shown that some level of vocalization is inevitable. So rather than denying it, why not embrace it? Why not use it to improve your reading instead of interfering with it? The most efficient use of vocalization, to read faster with a high degree of comprehension, is through *intonation,* which is the rise and fall of the voice in speaking. Intonation provides a natural means for combining individual words into meaningful mental "bites" that are a little larger than the word-sized ones we're used to taking. To use this system, read silently, but with expression. In doing so, you will be replacing the important *rhythm, stress, emphasis,* and *pauses* that were taken out when the words were put into written form. This allows groups of words to hold together in clusters in a way they couldn't when the expression was removed. To make silent intonation a regular habit, start by reading aloud in the privacy of your room. Spend ten or fifteen minutes on one chapter from a novel. Read it with exaggerated expression, as if you were reading a part in a dramatic play. This will establish your own speech patterns in your mind, so that you will "hear" them more readily when you read silently.

Think in Terms of Paragraphs

How do you read when you approach an assignment in terms of paragraphs?

Intonation helps you cluster words into meaningful phrases. You can expand those clusters to paragraph size by stopping at the end of each textbook paragraph to summarize and condense it down to a single sentence. To do this, you must understand the functions of the three main types of sentences: the topic or controlling-idea sentence, the supporting sentences, and the concluding sentence. Figure 6.2 shows these three types of sentences in an actual paragraph.

Figure 6.2

The Three Elements of an Expository Paragraph

Topic sentence ⟶ Henry Ford was probably the first man to have his car stolen. Ford, as you may know, developed the automobile in the United States. Back when his motorcar was still being perfected, he would often take it out for a spin. The "horseless carriage" was sure to attract a lot of attention. This was fine with Ford, as long as he was driving. But if he parked the car he was taking a risk. As soon as the inventor was out of sight, some curious person would try to escape with his vehicle. Luckily, the car caused such a commotion that it was easy to locate the thief. Even so, Henry Ford was annoyed. Finally, he got into the habit of linking his parked car to a lamp post with a chain.

Supporting sentences

Concluding sentence ⟶

What is the purpose of the topic sentence?

The *topic* sentence announces the topic (or the portion of the topic) to be dealt with in the paragraph. Although the topic sentence may appear anywhere in the paragraph, it is usually first—and for a very good reason. This sentence provides the focus for the writer while writing and for the reader while reading.

What role do the supporting sentences play?

The bulk of an expository paragraph is made up of *supporting* sentences, which help explain or prove the main topic. These sentences present facts, reasons, examples, definitions, comparisons, contrasts, and other pertinent details. They are most important, because they sell the ideas.

What is the function of the concluding sentence?

The last sentence of a textbook paragraph is likely to be a *concluding* sentence. It is used to sum up a discussion, to emphasize a point, or to restate all or part of the topic sentence so as to bring the paragraph to a close.

How does it help to understand the three basic sentence types?

An understanding of these three sentence types leads in turn to an understanding of each paragraph as a whole. Suddenly, instead of viewing things in terms of words, phrases, or sentences, you're clustering by paragraph, improving your comprehension and even your speed as a result.

Process Your Reading a Page at a Time

What was Macaulay's weakness when it came to reading?

Thomas Babington Macaulay(1800–1859) took the clustering process to the next logical level. He sought out meaning and comprehension by the page. Macaulay was an English statesman, historian, essayist, and poet. When it was published, his greatest work, *The History of England*, outsold all other books except the Bible. Macaulay was also a prodigious reader, who began reading adult books at the age of three. But after consuming shelf after shelf of books, he suddenly came to a discouraging realization: Although he understood every word of what he read and seemed to comprehend what the writer was saying, he was often unable to summarize the ideas presented or even describe, in general terms, what the writer had written. He described his solution to this problem as follows:

> At the foot of every page I read I stopped and obliged myself to give an account of what I had read on that page. At first I had to read it three or four times before I got my mind firmly fixed. But I compelled myself to comply with the plan, until now, after I have read a book through once, I can almost recite it from the beginning to the end.

What solution did Macaulay arrive at to become a better reader?

There's something very basic, honest, and refreshing in the Macaulay way. His simple solution was to make the page his fundamental unit of meaning. There are no complicated formulas to follow. You simply stop at the bottom of a page and ask yourself, "In brief, what did the writer say on this page?" And as you'll see in Chapter 11, clustering by page is also a bedrock technique in reviewing your textbook assignments.

E: Drawing on Experience

How would lack of experience affect your reading rate?

Think how long it would take to read a chapter if you had to look up every word in the dictionary. Not just multisyllabic fifty-cent words. Every single word. Or what if a casual reference to "freedom of speech" or "Pearl Harbor" or "1984" or "Judas" sent you rushing off to the library in search of an explanation. A single assignment might take days to read and complete.

How does your experience come into play as you read?

Luckily, even difficult assignments don't normally take days to read. That's because you can count on a certain level of experience each time you begin reading. The definitions of words you might have struggled with in elementary school have long since become hard-wired in your brain. You added more in high school, and continue to add words as you go through college. You read them, unconsciously look them up in your mind's internal dictionary, and keep moving. A maneuver that might have taken minutes if you actually had to flip through the pages of a hard-copy dictionary or surf through the screens of an online one takes a fraction of a second instead.

What do authors assume about their readers' experience?

The same applies to historical or cultural references. Many of them have become part of your personal body of knowledge. Authors know this and can use these references as a kind of shorthand to efficiently express complicated ideas in just a word or two.

How can you increase your experience?

It follows that you can improve both comprehension and speed by minimizing your "lookup time" when you read. The way to do that is by drawing on experience. And the way to increase your experience is to build on your background and to boost your vocabulary.

Bolster Your Background

Why will reading good books improve your reading?

You can improve your reading tremendously by reading good books. The first reason for this is that you'll be getting a lot of practice. Even more important, you'll be storing up a stock of concepts, ideas, events, and names that will lend meaning to your later reading. This kind of information is used surprisingly often. The more good books you read, the easier reading becomes, because with an expanded background, you can more easily and quickly understand the ideas and facts in other books.

What does Ausubel point to as the most important prerequisite for learning?

Psychologist David Ausubel says that the most crucial prerequisite for learning is your already established background of knowledge.[8] Ausubel means that to understand what you read, you must interpret it in the light of knowledge (background) you already have. A background is not something you are born with. You accumulate one through both direct and vicarious experiences. The vicarious experiences, of course, are those you acquire by listening, seeing films, and reading books.

How do you begin to read the great books?

Read the great books, for it is in these books that the wisdom of the ages is passed on to posterity. Begin with the books and subjects that interest you, and don't worry about having only narrow interests. Once you begin reading, your interests will widen naturally. But remember, you are fully responsible for initiating the process and habit of reading. Always keep in mind what Mark Twain once said: "The man who *doesn't* read good books has no advantage over the man who *can't* read them."

Beef Up Your Vocabulary

What is the relationship between vocabulary and reading speed?

The fastest readers, according to Berkeley's Cunningham, have excellent "recognition vocabularies." They not only see words faster; they understand them more quickly.[9] In a precise vocabulary, every word is learned as a concept. You know its ancestry, its principal definition as well as several secondary definitions, its synonyms and the subtle differences among them, and its antonyms. Then, when you encounter the word in your reading, this vast store of knowledge flashes before you, illuminating the sentence, the paragraph, and the idea the author is trying to convey. This transfer from word to concept to understanding is quick, automatic, and powerful. For more on vocabulary building, refer to the next chapter.

FINAL WORDS

What is victory for readers?

If you're frustrated by the slow pace of your reading, that's understandable. Keep working, and you should steadily improve. We live in a world where everyone wants to get there first. Even so, it pays to remember the famous fable about the tortoise and hare. Slow and steady will often win the race. Fast readers may move through the assignment at a faster pace, but victory comes with comprehension and true understanding, not speed.

[8]D. R. Ausubel, J. D. Novak, and H. Hanesian, *Educational Psychology: A Cognitive View*, 2d ed. (New York: Holt, Rinehart & Winston, 1978).

[9]Robertson, "Speed-reading Between the Lines," p. A1.

HAVE YOU MISSED SOMETHING?

SENTENCE COMPLETION

Complete the following sentences with one of the three words listed below each sentence.

1. In a precise vocabulary, every word is learned as a _____.

   concept   synonym   noun

2. The pauses your eyes make as they read are known as _____.

   saccades   fixations   stops

3. Intonation helps you cluster words in terms of meaningful _____.

   phrases   pages   paragraphs

MATCHING

In each blank space in the left column, write the letter preceding the phrase in the right column that matches the left item best.

_____ 1. Lookup time

_____ 2. Fixation

_____ 3. Subvocalization

_____ 4. Webster

_____ 5. Gibbon

_____ 6. Background

_____ 7. Overviewing

_____ 8. Intonation

a. Drew up three lists before he started reading

b. Helps you cluster words into meaningful phrases

c. Always accompanies reading

d. Geared up for a topic by recalling all he knew about it

e. Allows the eyes to focus

f. Simplest way to prepare for an assignment

g. Most crucial prerequisite for learning

h. Slows down your overall reading speed

TRUE-FALSE

Write T beside the true statements and F beside the false statements.

_____ 1. There's only one method of skimming.

_____ 2. You will read more effectively with a background of great books.

_____ 3. Macaulay's technique is a mainstay of textbook reviewing.

_____ 4. It is possible to study "written language" in isolation.

_____ 5. One sign of a speedy reader is a good "recognition vocabulary."

MULTIPLE CHOICE

Choose the word or phrase that completes each sentence most accurately, and circle the letter that precedes it.

1. When your eyes are in motion, the words on the page

   a. are clearer.

   b. seem larger.

   c. are a blur.

   d. seem smaller.

2. Moving your lips as you read is a form of
   a. fixation.
   b. vocalization.
   c. saccade.
   d. preparation.

3. The goal when you cluster by paragraphs is to come up with a single, summarizing
   a. word.
   b. sentence.
   c. paragraph.
   d. idea.

4. Subvocalization is sometimes called
   a. silent speech.
   b. skimming.
   c. saccades.
   d. undertone.

5. The bulk of an expository paragraph is made up of
   a. topic sentences.
   b. supporting sentences.
   c. concluding sentences.
   d. prepositional phrases.

SHORT ANSWER   *Supply a brief answer for each of the following questions.*

1. Why is vocalization a necessary part of reading for comprehension?
2. Why do you think the use of intonation helps improve both speed and comprehension in reading?
3. Contrast the different altitudes for skimming an assignment.
4. Explain how the process of clustering relates to the way we read.

WORDS IN CONTEXT

From the three choices beside each numbered item, select the one that most nearly expresses the meaning of the italicized word in the quote. Make a light check mark (✓) next to your choice.

Insult: a *callous* or *contemptuous* statement or action; a verbal attack upon another person.

—dictionary definition

1. *callous* . . . statement   thoughtless   unfeeling   careless

2. *contemptuous* statement   disdainful   inconsiderate   impolite

The most important single *ingredient* in the formula of success is knowing how to get along with people.

—Theodore Roosevelt (1858–1919), twenty-sixth president of the United States

3. important . . . *ingredient*   guideline   requirement   component

Too often it's not the most creative guys or the smartest. Instead, it's the ones who are best at playing politics and soft-soaping their bosses. Boards don't like tough, *abrasive* guys.

—Carl Icahn (1936–), CEO, Trans World Airlines

4. *abrasive* guys   strict   irritating   rugged

THE WORD HISTORY SYSTEM

Bonfire
a fire of bones

bonfire   bon′-fire *n.* A large outdoor fire.

In the Middle Ages, funeral pyres for human bodies were a necessity in emergencies of war or pestilence. *Bonefires* (fires of bone), they were called. Later, when the custom of burning heretics at the stake became common, *bonefires* was the name applied to the pyres of these victims. The same term was used to designate the burning of symbols of heresy or other proscribed articles. Later, its meaning was extended to open-air fires for public celebrations or sports—but by this time in the less gruesome spelling *bonfire*, which today is a comparatively harmless word despite its grim history.

Reprinted by permission. From *Picturesque Word Origins* © 1933 by G. & C. Merriam Co. (now Merriam-Webster, Incorporated).

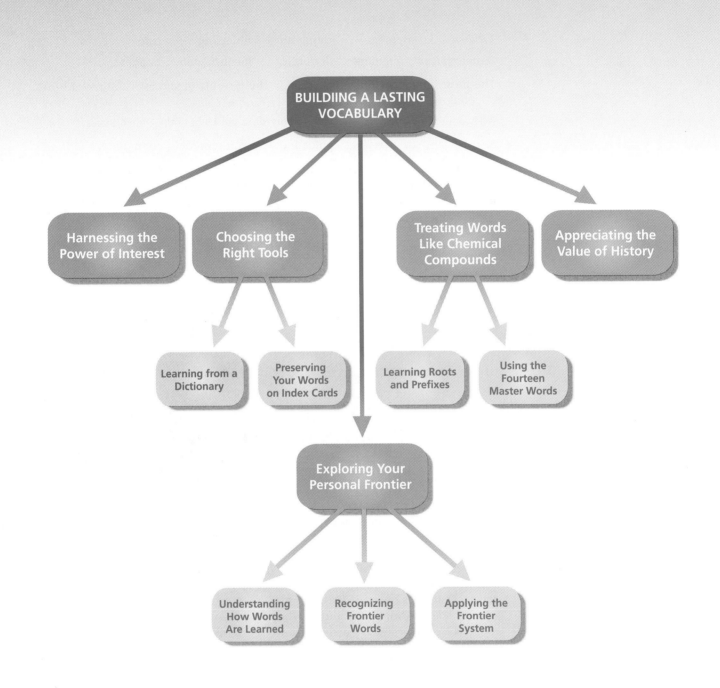

Building a Lasting Vocabulary

The difference between the almost right word and the right word is really a large matter— it's the difference between the lightning bug and the lightning.

Mark Twain (1835–1910), pen name of Samuel Clemens, American novelist

Accumulating a large and precise vocabulary can be an adventure. If you're equipped with the right tools and a sense of curiosity, you'll have an exciting journey. And as on most adventures, you'll experience the joy of serendipitous discoveries. When you discover a word you like, increase the pleasure by learning all you can about its ancestry. The territory may seem strange at first, but in time you'll be living in a community of interrelated words where you'll always be genuinely at home. This chapter discusses the value of:

- **Harnessing the Power of Interest**
- **Having the Right Tools Handy**
- **Learning from a Dictionary**
- **Preserving your Words on Index Cards**
- **Exploring Your Personal Frontier**
- **Treating Words Like Chemical Compounds**
- **Using the Fourteen Master Words**
- **Learning the History of Words**

What is the relationship between thinking and vocabulary?

The quality of our vocabulary can have a direct effect on the quality of our thought. True, some of our thoughts come in images, but we do much of our thinking in words. If we come across a person who is muttering, we're inclined to say, "He's talking to himself," when what we really should be saying is, "He's thinking out loud." Whether spoken or silent, words are the impulses sent over the electrical pathways of the mind. When you're thinking, you're probably talking. It logically follows that the more powerful and precise your vocabulary, the more powerful and precise your thoughts will be.

How can you improve the quality of your vocabulary?

To improve the quality of your vocabulary and with it the quality of your thoughts, you need to harness the power of interest, choose the right vocabulary-building tools, explore the boundaries of your existing vocabulary, learn the components for constructing a variety of words, and learn the stories that lie behind so many words in our language. These tales should make words both more meaningful and more memorable.

Harnessing the Power of Interest

What is the connection between interest and vocabulary?

What do stories of Malcolm X and the golf caddy illustrate?

Interest can be a powerful motivator when it comes to strengthening your vocabulary. Without interest, you'll be average. With it, there is no limit. Stories great and small demonstrate how people with an interest in and even a passion for words have been able to improve their vocabularies as well as their lives.

The accounts of how words dramatically changed the life of Malcolm X and improved the lot of a Depression-era caddy both can inspire anyone weighing the value of words.

Malcolm X

While in a penitentiary, Malcolm X was unable to answer letters from his brother and sister because he could not write a sentence or spell a word. He felt helpless. In his spare time, he listened to lectures by Bimbi, a self-educated black man.

> What fascinated me with him most of all was that he was the first man I had ever seen command total respect with his words.[1]

Other men commanded respect because of their strength or cunning, the number of robberies they had committed, and so forth. But Bimbi was different. Malcolm X developed a strong desire to be like Bimbi—to learn and use words. He reasoned that the best way to learn words was by studying a dictionary. So he borrowed one from the prison school and took it to his cell. He described his first encounter:

[1] Alex Haley and Malcolm X, *The Autobiography of Malcolm X* (New York: Ballantine Books, 1964), p. 428.

In my slow, painstaking, ragged handwriting, I copied into my tablet everything printed on that first page. I believe it took me a day. Then, aloud, I read back to myself, everything I'd written. Over and over, aloud, to myself, I read my own handwriting. I woke up the next morning thinking about those words.[2]

Either Malcolm X shaped his life around words, or the words took over and shaped his life. Either way, he was a winner—he became a "thinking man." He had words with which to think.

Malcolm X went on to become an outstanding leader, preacher, and public speaker. He even lectured to law students at Harvard University. With a wide and exact vocabulary, he was able to express his thoughts and ideas forcefully and intelligently. He earned and commanded respect.

A Caddy's Tale

During the Great Depression of the 1930s, jobs were hard to find. Caddying at the nearby golf course provided some income for high school boys growing up in Branford, Connecticut. Among the caddies, one fellow always got bigger tips than the others. When asked by a friend, he reluctantly divulged his secret.

On the golf course as well as on the street, one common topic of conversation is the weather. It often begins like this: The golfer would say, "Do you think it will rain this morning?" Almost all the caddies would answer "Yep!" or "Nope!" That would be the end of the conversation. But this one fellow had a better scenario. He'd say, "I'm optimistic; there's a bit of blue in the sky. It won't rain." If he were to predict rain, he'd say, "I'm pessimistic today. The clouds are gathering. It'll rain." The magic, of course, was in the words *optimistic* and *pessimistic*. These are college-type words, and they made the caddy the mental equal of the golfer. Psychologically, the golfer wouldn't degrade himself in the eyes of the caddy by tipping him the mere minimum. When his friend learned his secret, he tried it out, and it worked. The story sounds mercenary, but there's a more important dimension; that is, using college-type words creates within you a healthy self-concept—yes, self-esteem.

How do words create an interest?

The creative use of words creates interest in an audience—whatever that potential audience is. From the heights of literature and poetry to everyday life, words matter in getting us to pay attention.

The Newspaper Way

How can newspapers boost your interest in words?

If you look for it, you'll find magic in words whether you're reading your local paper or *The Wall Street Journal*. Writers strive mightily not only to report the facts but also to make their writing interesting, especially by using common words in an uncommon way. When you catch on to what writers are up to,

[2]Ibid.

your interest in words is likely to increase, and with it the desire to strengthen your vocabulary. To illustrate, the following came from a sports page:

> Mike Foligno became the 19th head hockey coach of the Bears in Hershey, Pennsylvania.[3]

The writing craft and the novelty—the interest-catcher—are in the large-lettered headline:

NEW COACH'S IMPACT BEARS WATCHING

There is nothing earthshaking in this—only the personal delight that comes when you see and appreciate what the writer is doing. You feel you're in the know. Yogi Berra said it best: "You can observe a lot by watching."[4]

Even *The Wall Street Journal*'s writers use mind-catching headlines. Here's the commentary first:

> Collectively, the continent's five major periphery nations (Ireland, Portugal, Spain, Finland and the Netherlands) make up only 17% of the market capitalization for Europe as a whole.[5]

Now, here's the large-lettered headline:

IN EUROPE, THE ALSO-RANS ARE SPRINTING

Here the writer cleverly used two words that usually are applied to runners on a track team.

Billboards

How do billboards encourage your interest in words?

Even billboards can lead you to become more interested in words, especially when you delight in their creativity and use of psychology. Here's an example.

Traveling south on Interstate 95, about thirty miles before you cross the border into South Carolina, you are bombarded with a series of large billboards featuring a tourist attraction advertised as "SOUTH OF THE BORDER." Most call it a "tourist trap," but the sayings on the billboards are alluring. Children, especially, are attracted by the words. The billboards are the Pied Piper. The words are the Piper's tune.

Most parents want to get to Myrtle Beach or Florida, and they see a stop at South of the Border as a waste of time and money. The children, however, gen-

[3]Lancaster, Pennsylvania, *Intelligencer Journal* (June 4, 1998), p. D1.

[4]Yogi Berra et al., *The Yogi Book* (New York: Workman Publishing, 1998), p. 95.

[5]*The Wall Street Journal* (January 29, 1999), p. A1.

erally want to stop. The creators of billboards know this. They counter by saying, "Keep Yelling, Kids. They'll Stop!"

No, you won't learn any new words from these billboards, but you may learn to appreciate and love the power of words, which is a lasting quality. Once you get to love words, vocabulary growth is a cinch.

Finally, this billboard line is a delight to read:

YOU NEVER SAUSAGE A THING!

It wouldn't be surprising to learn that the writer of this line looks upon it as a masterpiece.

How do you acquire an interest in words?

The question now is how to acquire an interest in words. Newspapers and billboards may work for you. Then again, they may not. There is no neat formula. You just need to keep your eyes and ears open. Different people acquire interest in different ways. Within all of us, there is a desire to lift our self-esteem; that is, we want to feel good about ourselves. And a good vocabulary is one excellent way to achieve this.

Choosing the Right Tools

What tools are needed to build your vocabulary?

Regardless of how you choose to build your vocabulary, you're going to need the right tools. One of the great things about building a lasting vocabulary is that it takes so little to do so. You don't need to take a class, use computer software, or purchase some other special book or device. All you really need is a decent dictionary and a generous stack of file cards.

Learning from a Dictionary

What's the best way to learn new words?

The best way to learn new words is to keep a good dictionary close to your elbow and use it. Gliding over a word that you don't quite know can be costly. Consider this sentence: "The mayor gave *fulsome* praise to the budget committee." What does *fulsome* mean? If you think it means "full of praise," you're mistaken. Look it up.

What are the limitations of learning words from context?

Sometimes, you can get some idea of the meaning of a new word from its context—how it is used in your reading material. Use context when you can, but be aware that it has limitations. Lee C. Deighton of Columbia University points out three: (1) Context provides only the meaning that fits that particular situation. (2) You often end up with a synonym, which is not quite the same as a definition. (3) When you have to infer the meaning of a word, you can be slightly (or greatly) in error.[6] Your safest bet is to avoid all the guesswork and go straight to your dictionary.

What should you do when you come across a word you don't understand?

As you study, consult your dictionary whenever you come to a word that you don't know precisely. Find the exact meaning you need; then go back to your textbook and reread the paragraph, with the meaning substituted for the word. If you become interested in a particular word, write it along with the sentence it occurred in on an index card. Later, go back to the dictionary and investigate the word. But don't break into your studying for a long session with the dictionary; save that for later.

Carry a Pocket Dictionary

Why are pocket dictionaries so popular with some people?

Many scholars and businesspeople rely on pocket dictionaries. The main attraction of a pocket dictionary is its portability. A typical one is less than an inch thick and slightly longer and wider than a standard index card. It is a cinch to stash in a handbag or knapsack and fairly easy to put in a pocket. As a result, it can travel with you wherever you go.

When does a pocket dictionary come in handy?

Follow the example of thousands of successful people. Get yourself a pocket dictionary such as *Webster's II New Riverside Pocket Dictionary,* and always carry it with you. Instead of reading the print on cereal boxes, or looking at advertising placards on buses and subways, or staring into space, take out your dictionary and *read* it. Its definitions will be terse, consisting mainly of synonyms, but its value lies in its ability to spark a lifelong interest in words as well as increase your vocabulary. Of course, a pocket dictionary is no substitute for a larger desk dictionary, but as a portable learning tool, the pocket dictionary is worth its weight in gold.

How do you read a dictionary?

If the idea of simply reading a dictionary sounds boring or difficult, it's neither. To illustrate how a dictionary is read, let's study Figure 7.1, which is a page from a pocket dictionary.[7] When you open to page 1 and your eyes drift down the column of words, an internal conversation takes place: You think about what you already know about the word and you think about the other aspects of the word, such as the syllable that must be accented, the precise definition, and how you could use the word in your writing and speaking.

What are the pros and cons of pocket electronic dictionaries?

A number of dictionaries are available for personal digital assistants (PDAs), such as the Palm Pilot or the PocketPC. If you're already carrying one of these electronic devices, adding a dictionary may make sense. But don't buy a hand-held computer just for the dictionary. Also, be aware that some electronic dictionaries do not include all the regular elements that you find in a standard

[6]Lee C. Deighton, *Vocabulary Development in the Classroom* (New York: Teachers College Press, 1959), pp. 2–3.

[7]*Webster's II New Riverside Pocket Dictionary* (Boston: Houghton Mifflin, 1991), p. 1.

Figure 7.1

How to Read a Dictionary

Source: Copyright © 1991 by Houghton Mifflin Company. Reproduced by permission from *Webster's II New Riverside Pocket Dictionary,* Revised Edition.

A

abroad

a, A (ā) *n.* The 1st letter of the English alphabet.

a (ə; *emphatic* ā) *indef. art.* One; any.

a•back (ə-băk´) *adv.* **—take aback.** To startle; confuse.

The Chinese used this device from ancient times → **ab•a•cus** (ăb´ə-kəs) *n., pl.* **-cuses** or **-ci.** A manual computing device with rows of moveable beads.

a•ban•don (əbăn´dən) *v.* **1.** To give up; forsake. **2.** To desert. **—***n.* A complete surrender of inhibitions. **—a•ban´-doned** *adj.* **—a•ban´don•ment** *n.*

Strong, simple word → **a•base** (ə-bās´) *v.* **abased, abasing.** To humble; humiliate. **—a•base´ment** *n.*

Somewhat similar to abridge → **a•bate** (ə-bāt´) *v.* **abated, abating.** To reduce; lessen. **—a•bate´ment** *n.*

ab•bey (ăb´e) *n., pl.* **-beys.** A monastery or convent.

ab•bre•viate (ə-brē´vē-āt´) *v.* **-ated, -ating.** To make shorter. **—ab•bre´vi•a´tion** *n.*

King Edward VIII Throne of England → **ab•di•cate** (ăb´dǐ-kāt´) *v.* **-cated, -cating.** To relinquish (power or responsibility) formally. **—ab´di•ca´tion** *n.*

Preferred accent on 1st syllable → **ab•do•men** (ăb´də-mən, ăb-dō´mən) *n.* The part of the body between the thorax and the pelvis. **—ab•dom´i•nal** *adj.*

ab•duct (ăb-dŭkt´) *v.* To kidnap. **—ab•duc´tion** *n.* **—ab•duc´tor** *n.*

"Exception" to the rule → **ab•er•ra•tion** (ăb´ə-rā´shən) *n.* Deviation or depature from the normal, typical, or expected. **—ab•er´rance, —ab•er´ran•cy** *n.* **—ab•er´rant** *adj.*

In law: to "aid & abet" → **a•bet** (ə-bĕt´) *v.* **abetted, abetting.** **1.** To encourage; incite. **2.** To assist. **—a•bet´tor, a•bet´ter** *n.*

a•bey•ance (ə-bā´əns) *n.* Temporary suspension.

ab•hor (ăb-hôr´) *v.* **-horred, -horring.** To dislike intensely; loathe. **—ab•hor´rence** *n.* **—ab•hor´rent** *adj.*

a•bide (ə-bīd´) *v.* **abode** or **abided, abiding.** **1.** To wait. **2.** To tolerate; bear. **3.** To remain; last. **—abide by.** To conform to; comply with. **—a•bide´ing** *adj.*

a•bil•i•ty (ə-bĭl´ĭ-tē) *n. pl.* **-ties. 1.** The power to perform. **2.** A skill or talent.

ab•ject (ăb´jĕkt´, ăb-jĕkt´) *adj.* **1.** Contemptible; base. **2.** Miserable; wretched. **—ab•jec´tion** *n.* **—ab•ject´ly** *adv.*

{ Looks like object but far off

ab•jure (ăb-jŏŏr´) *v.* **-jured, -juring.** To renounce under oath; forswear.

{ In unabridged dictionary: "He abjured all titles, preferring 'Mr.'"

a•ble (ā´bəl) *adj.* **abler, ablest. 1.** Having sufficient ability. **2.** Capable or talented. **—a´bly** *adv.*

ab•ne•gate (ăb´nǐ-gāt´) *v.* **-gated, -gating.** To deny to oneself; renounce. **—ab´ne•ga´tion** *n.*

{ Personal rights. Abdicate – national power

ab•nor•mal (ăb-nôr´məl) *adj.* Not normal; deviant. **—ab´nor•mal´i•ty** *adv.*

a•bode (ə-bōd´) *v.* p.t. & p.p. of **abide.** **—***n.* A home.

a•bol•ish (ə-bŏl´ĭsh) *v.* To put an end to; annul. **—ab´o•li´tion** *n.* **—ab´o•li´tion•ist.** *n.*

a•bom•i•na•ble (ə-bŏm´ə-nə-bəl) *adj.* Detestable; loathsome. **—a•bom´i•na•bly** *adv.* **—a•bom´i•nate´** *v.* **—a•bom´i•na´tion** *n.*

{ Usually connected to Snowmen of the Himalayas

ab•o•rig•i•ne (ăb´ə-rĭj´ə-nē) *n.* An original inhabitant of a region. **—ab´o•rig´i•nal** *adj. & n.*

{ Usually applied to original people of Australia

a•bort (ə-bôrt´) *v.* To terminate pregnancy or full development prematurely. **—***n.* Premature termination of a rocket launch or space mission. **—a•bor´tive** *adj.*

a•bor•tion (ə-bôr´shən) *n.* **1.** Induced premature termination of pregnancy or development. **2.** Something malformed. **—a•bor´tion•ist** *n.*

a•bound (ə-bound´) *v.* To be great in number or amount; teem.

{ "The mosquitoes abound in swamps"

a•bout (ə-bout´) *adv.* **1.** Approximately. **2.** Toward a reverse direction. **3.** In the vicinity. **—***prep.* **1.** On all sides of. **2.** Near to. **3.** In or on. **4.** Concerning. **5.** Ready. **—***adj.* Astir.

a•bove (ə-bŭv´) *adv.* **1.** Overhead. **2.** In a higher place, rank, or position. **—***prep.* **1.** Over. **2.** Superior to. **3.** In preference to. **—***n.* Something that is above. **—***adj.* Appearing or stated earlier.

a•bove•board (ə-bŭv´bôrd´, -bōrd´) *adv.* Without deceit. **—a•bove´board´** *adj.*

ab•ra•sion (ə-brā´zhən) *n.* **1.** A wearing away by friction. **2.** A scraped or worn area. **—a•brade´** *v.* **—a•bra´sive** *adj. & n.*

{ Rubbing, scraping as in friction

a•bridge (ə-brĭj´) *v.* **abridged, abridging.** To condense; shorten. **—a•bridg´ment, a•bridge´ment** *n.*

{ Big dictionary – unabridged

a•broad (ə-brôd´) *adv.* **1.** Out of one's own country. **2.** Out of doors. **3.** Broadly; widely.

pocket dictionary, such as detailed information on pronunciation. The convenience you gain from storing your dictionary on a hand-held computer can be offset if the information is incomplete or inadequate. Also, depending on the sophistication of the application and the resolution of your screen, you may lose some of the helpful elements—such as boldface, italics, type size, and color—that can make a printed pocket dictionary so easy to consult.

Keep an Abridged Dictionary at Your Desk

What advantages does an abridged dictionary provide over a pocket dictionary?

Unless you're really strapped for cash, don't settle for one of those paperback abridged dictionaries, as they are only slightly better than most pocket dictionaries and are too bulky to easily carry around. If you know you're going to stay put, a full-sized abridged dictionary is your best bet. Rather than simply providing pronunciation and bare-bones definitions, good abridged dictionaries tell you far more about the words you are investigating. With an abridged dictionary you usually get more definitions, more information on a word's derivation, and in some instances information about a word's synonyms, usage, and history. Buy and use the best abridged dictionary that you can afford, but be aware that no word is ever fully defined, even by a good abridged dictionary. Words have multiple shades of meaning that add richness to our language. These various shades will become apparent to you as you keep reading, listening, and trying to use words in a variety of contexts.

Good abridged desk dictionaries include the following:

The American Heritage Dictionary (Houghton Mifflin Company)
Webster's New Collegiate Dictionary (Merriam-Webster, Inc.)
Webster's New World College Dictionary, 4th ed. (Webster's New World)

What are some of the features of the *American Heritage Dictionary*?

Of these three, the *American Heritage Dictionary* has some distinct advantages. Unlike most abridged dictionaries, it offers many of the special features—such as synonyms, usage notes, and word histories—that you normally would expect to find only in unabridged dictionaries. (See Figure 7.2.)

How do synonyms help you understand a word's meaning?

Synonyms   Synonyms not only help clarify the meaning and usage of the word you initially looked up, but also provide an opportunity to weave more strands into your background. Finding a cluster of synonyms is like finding a cache of gold nuggets. But watch out. Not all words in a cluster are interchangeable. Each word has a color, flavor, and niche of its own. It fits perfectly in a specific context where its meaning, feeling, and tone are just right.

Take, for example, this cluster of common synonyms: *eat, consume, devour, ingest.* The central meaning shared by these verbs is "to take food into the body by mouth." Now, notice the appropriate contexts:

Figure 7.2

A Page from *The American Heritage Dictionary*

Source: Copyright © 2000 by Houghton Mifflin Company. Reproduced by permission from *The American Heritage Dictionary of the English Language, Fourth Edition.*

pol•i•ti•cian (pŏl′ĭ-tĭsh′ən) *n.* **1a.** One who is actively involved in politics, especially party politics. **b.** One who holds or seeks a political office. **2.** One who seeks personal or partisan gain, often by scheming and maneuvering: "*Mothers may still want their favorite sons to grow up to be President, but . . . they do not want them to become politicians in the process*" (John F. Kennedy). **3.** One who is skilled or experienced in the science or administration of government.

po•lit•i•cize (pə-lĭt′ĭ-sīz′) *v.* **-cized, -ciz•ing, -ciz•es** *—intr.* To engage in or discuss politics. *—tr.* To make political: "*The mayor was given authority to appoint police commissioners and by virtue of that power was able to politicize the department*" (Connie Paige). **—po•lit′i•ci•za′tion** (-sĭ-zā′shən) *n.*

pol•i•tick (pŏl′ĭ-tĭk) *intr.v.* **-ticked, -tick•ing, -ticks** To engage in or discuss politics. [Back-formation from *politicking*, engaging in partisan political activity, from POLITIC.] **—pol′i•tick′er** *n.*

po•lit•i•co (pə-lĭt′ĭ-kō′) *n., pl.* **-cos** A politician. [From Italian or from Spanish *político*, both from Latin *polīticus*, political. See POLITIC.]

pol•i•tics (pŏl′ĭ-tĭks) *n.* **1.** *(used with a sing. verb)* **a.** The art or science of government or governing, especially the governing of a political entity, such as a nation, and the administration and control of its internal and external affairs. **b.** Political science. **2.** *(used with a sing. or pl. verb)* **a.** The activities or affairs engaged in by a government, politician, or political party: "*All politics is local*" (Thomas P. O'Neill, Jr.). "*Politics have appealed to me since I was at Oxford because they are exciting morning, noon, and night*" (Jeffrey Archer). **b.** The methods or tactics involved in managing a state or government: *The politics of the former regime were rejected by the new government leadership. If the politics of the conservative government now borders on the repressive, what can be expected when the economy falters?* **3.** *(used with a sing. or pl. verb)* Political life: *studied law with a view to going into politics; felt that politics was a worthwhile career.* **4.** *(used with a sing. or pl. verb)* Intrigue or maneuvering within a political unit or group in order to gain control or power: *Partisan politics is often an obstruction to good government. Office politics are often debilitating and counterproductive.* **5.** *(used with a sing. or pl. verb)* Political attitudes and positions: *His politics on that issue is his own business. Your politics are clearly more liberal than mine.* **6.** *(used with a sing. or pl. verb)* The often internally conflicting interrelationships among people in a society.

Usage Note *Politics,* although plural in form, takes a singular verb when used to refer to the art or science of governing or to political science: *Politics has been a concern of philosophers since Plato.* But in its other senses *politics* can take either a singular or plural verb. Many other nouns that end in *–ics* behave similarly, and the user is advised to consult specific entries for precise information.

pol•i•ty (pŏl′ĭ-tē) *n., pl.* **-ties 1.** The form of government of a nation, state, church, or organization. **2.** An organized society, such as a nation, having a specific form of government: "*His alien philosophy found no roots in the American polity*" (New York Times). [Obsolete French *politie*, from Old French, from Late Latin *polītīa*, the Roman government. See POLICE.]

Polk (pōk), **James Knox** 1795–1849. The 11th President of the United States (1845–1849), whose term was marked by the establishment of the 49th parallel as the country's northern border (1846).

pol•ka (pōl′kə, pō′kə) *n.* **1.** A lively dance originating in Bohemia and performed by couples. **2.** Music for this dance, having duple meter. *—intr.* **-kaed, -ka•ing, -kas** To dance the polka. [Czech, probably from Polish, from *Polka*, Polish woman, feminine of *Polak*, Pole. See **pelə-²** in Appendix I.]

polka dot *n.* **1.** One of a number of dots or round spots forming a pattern, as on cloth. **2.** A pattern or fabric with such dots.

poll (pōl) *n.* **1.** The casting and registering of votes in an election. **2.** The number of votes cast or recorded. **3.** The place where votes are cast and registered. Often used in the plural with *the.* **4.** A survey of the public or of a sample of public opinion to acquire information. **5.** The head, especially the top of the head where hair grows. **6.** The blunt or broad end of a tool such as a hammer or ax. ❖ *v.* **polled, poll•ing, polls** *—tr.* **1.** To receive (a given number of votes). **2.** To receive or record the votes of: *polling a jury.* **3.** To cast (a vote or ballot). **4.** To question in a survey; canvass. **5.** To cut off or trim (hair, horns, or wool, for example); clip. **6.** To trim or cut off the hair, wool, branches, or horns of: *polled the sheep; polled the trees.* *—intr.* To vote at the polls in an election. [Middle English *pol*, head, from Middle Low German or Middle Dutch.] **—poll′er** *n.*

pol•lack also **pol•lock** (pŏl′ək) *n., pl.* **pollack** or **-lacks** also **pollock** or **-locks** A marine food fish *(Pollachius virens)* of northern Atlantic waters, related to the cod. [Alteration of Scots *podlok.*]

pol•lard (pŏl′ərd) *n.* **1.** A tree whose top branches have been cut back to the trunk so that it may produce a dense growth of new shoots. **2.** An animal, such as an ox, goat, or sheep, that no longer has its horns. ❖ *tr.v.* **-lard•ed, -lard•ing, -lards** To convert or make into a pollard. [From POLL.]

polled (pōld) *adj.* Having no horns; hornless.

pol•len (pŏl′ən) *n.* The fine powderlike material consisting of pollen grains that is produced by the anthers of seed plants. [Latin, fine flour.]

pol•len•ate (pŏl′ə-nāt′) *v.* Variant of **pollinate.**

pollen count *n.* The average number of pollen grains, usually of ragweed, in a cubic yard or other standard volume of air over a 24-hour period at a specified time and place.

pollen grain *n.* A microspore of seed plants, containing a male gametophyte.

pol•len•if•er•ous (pŏl′ə-nĭf′ər-əs) *adj.* Variant of **polliniferous.**

pollen mother cell *n.* The microsporocyte of a seed plant.

pol•len•o•sis (pŏl′ə-nō′sĭs) *n.* Variant of **pollinosis.**

pollen sac *n.* The microsporangium of a seed plant in which pollen is produced.

pollen tube *n.* The slender tube formed by the pollen grain that penetrates an ovule and releases the male gametes.

pol•lex (pŏl′ĕks′) *n., pl.* **pol•li•ces** (pŏl′ĭ-sēz′) See **thumb** (sense 1). [Latin, thumb, big toe.]

pollin– *pref.* Variant of **pollini–.**

pol•li•nate also **pol•len•ate** (pŏl′ə-nāt′) *tr.v.* **-li•nat•ed, -li•nat•ing, -li•nates** also **-len•at•ed, -len•at•ing, -len•ates** To transfer pollen from an anther to the stigma of (a flower). [New Latin *pollen, pollin-*, pollen (from Latin, fine flour) + –ATE¹.] **—pol′li•na′tion** *n.* **—pol′li•na′tor** *n.*

pollini– or **pollin–** *pref.* Pollen: *polliniferous.* [From New Latin *pollen, pollin-*, pollen. See POLLINATE.]

pol•li•nif•er•ous also **pol•len•if•er•ous** (pŏl′ə-nĭf′ər-əs) *adj.* **1.** Producing or yielding pollen. **2.** Adapted for carrying pollen.

pol•lin•i•um (pŏ-lĭn′ē-əm) *n., pl.* **-i•a** (-ē-ə) A mass of coherent pollen grains, found in the flowers of orchids and milkweeds. [New Latin, from *pollen, pollin-*, pollen. See POLLINATE.]

pol•li•nize (pŏl′ə-nīz′) *tr.v.* **-nized, -niz•ing, -niz•es** To pollinate. **—pol′li•ni•za′tion** (-nĭ-zā′shən) *n.* **—pol′li•niz′er** *n.*

pol•li•no•sis also **pol•len•o•sis** (pŏl′ə-nō′sĭs) *n.* See **hay fever.**

pol•li•wog also **pol•ly•wog** (pŏl′ē-wŏg′, -wôg′) *n.* See **tadpole.** [Variant of *polliwig*, from Middle English *polwigle* : *pol*, head; see POLL + *wiglen*, to wiggle; see WIGGLE.]

pol•lock (pŏl′ək) *n.* Variant of **pollack.**

Pol•lock (pŏl′ək), **Jackson** 1912–1956. American artist. Using his drip technique of painting, he became a leader of abstract expressionism.

poll•ster (pōl′stər) *n.* One that takes public-opinion surveys. Also called *polltaker.*

Word History The suffix *–ster* is nowadays most familiar in words like *pollster, jokester, huckster,* where it forms agent nouns that typically denote males. Originally in Old English, however, the suffix (then spelled *–estre*) was used to form feminine agent nouns. *Hoppestre,* for example, meant "female dancer." It was occasionally applied to men, but mostly to translate Latin masculine nouns denoting occupations that were usually held by women in Anglo-Saxon society. An example is *bæcester,* "baker," glossing Latin *pistor;* it survives as the Modern English name *Baxter.* In Middle English its use as a masculine suffix became more common in northern England, while in the south it remained limited to feminines. In time the masculine usage became dominant throughout the country, and old feminines in *–ster* were refashioned by adding the newer feminine suffix *–ess* (borrowed from French) to them, such as *seamstress* remade from *seamster.* In Modern English, the only noun ending in *–ster* with a feminine referent is *spinster,* which originally meant "a woman who spins thread."

poll•tak•er (pōl′tā′kər) *n.* See **pollster.**

poll tax *n.* A tax levied on people rather than on property, often as a requirement for voting.

pol•lut•ant (pə-lo͞ot′nt) *n.* Something that pollutes, especially a waste material that contaminates air, soil, or water.

pol•lute (pə-lo͞ot′) *tr.v.* **-lut•ed, -lut•ing, -lutes 1.** To make unfit for or harmful to living things, especially by the addition of waste matter. See synonyms at **contaminate. 2.** To make less suitable for an activity, especially by the introduction of unwanted factors: *The stadium lights polluted the sky around the observatory.* **3.** To render impure or morally harmful; corrupt. **4.** To make ceremonially impure; profane: "*Churches and altars were polluted by atrocious murders*" (Edward Gibbon). [Middle English *polluten*, from Latin *polluere, poll t-.*] **—pol•lut′er** *n.*

pol•lu•tion (pə-lo͞o′shən) *n.* **1.** The act or process of polluting or the state of being polluted, especially the contamination of soil, water, or the atmosphere by the discharge of harmful substances. **2.** Something that pollutes; a pollutant or a group of pollutants: *Pollution in the air reduced the visibility near the airport.*

Pol•lux (pŏl′əks) *n.* *Greek Mythology* **1.** One of the Dioscuri. **2.** A bright star in the constellation Gemini. [Latin *Poll x*, from Greek *Poludeukēs.*]

Pol•ly•an•na (pŏl′ē-ăn′ə) *n.* A person regarded as being foolishly or blindly optimistic. [After the heroine of the novel *Pollyanna*, by Eleanor Hodgman Porter (1868–1920), American writer.]

pol•ly•wog (pŏl′ē-wŏg′, -wôg′) *n.* Variant of **polliwog.**

po•lo (pō′lō) *n.* **1.** A game played by two teams of three or four players on horseback who are equipped with long-handled mallets for driving a small wooden ball through the opponents' goal. **2.** Water polo. [Balti (Tibeto-Burman language of Pakistan), ball.] **—po′lo•ist** *n.*

Po•lo (pō′lō), **Marco** 1254–1324. Venetian traveler who explored Asia from 1271 to 1295. His *Travels of Marco Polo* was the only account of the Far East available to Europeans until the 17th century.

polo coat *n.* A loose-fitting, tailored overcoat made from camel's hair or a similar material.

pol•o•naise (pŏl′ə-nāz′, pō′lə-) *n.* **1.** A stately, marchlike Polish dance, primarily a promenade by couples. **2.** Music for or based on the traditional rhythm of this dance, having triple meter. **3.** A woman's dress of the 18th century, having a fitted bodice and draped cutaway skirt, worn over an elaborate underskirt. [French, from feminine of *polonais*, Polish, from Medieval Latin *Polōnia*, Poland.]

po•lo•ni•um (pə-lō′nē-əm) *n.* *Symbol* **Po** A naturally radioactive metallic element, occurring in minute quantities as a product of radium

ă pat	oi boy
ā pay	ou out
âr care	o͝o took
ä father	o͞o boot
ĕ pet	ŭ cut
ē be	ûr urge
ĭ pit	th thin
ī pie	*th* this
îr pier	hw which
ŏ pot	zh vision
ō toe	ə about, item
ô paw	♦ regionalism

Stress marks: ′ (primary); ′ (secondary), as in **dictionary** (dĭk′shə-nĕr′ē)

ate a hearty dinner; greedily consumed the sandwiches; hyenas devouring their prey; whales ingesting krill[8]

Nothing can give greater precision to your words than knowing the fine differences among synonyms.

What is the purpose of usage notes?

Usage Notes   It's possible to learn a word's definition and still use it incorrectly. For example, a student who learned that the word *incite* means "to stir up" wrote: "The cook incited the soup." Usage notes provide clarification that goes beyond standard definitions. A form of this category is found in almost all unabridged dictionaries, but rarely in abridged dictionaries. Such notes are interesting and instructive. Here is an example:

> USAGE NOTE: In nautical usage knot is a unit of speed, not of distance, and has a built-in meaning of "per hour." Therefore, a ship would strictly be said to travel at ten knots (not ten knots per hour).[9]

Usage notes impart information in an easy-to-read, nontechnical, nonobfuscating manner.

What is the value of knowing a word's history?

Word History   The story of a word's origin adds dimension and life to something we might otherwise view as flat and inert. The end of each chapter in this book contains an excerpt from *Picturesque Word Origins*, which describes the background and evolution of some commonly used words. *Picturesque Word Origins* was published more than seventy years ago and may not be readily available, but the word history items you can find in the *American Heritage Dictionary* as well as in most unabridged dictionaries can serve as very good substitutes. A plus factor is that these histories are written in an easy-to-read narrative manner. Here's a sample:

> The identity of the Pueblo peoples is undeniably connected to the stone and adobe dwellings they have occupied for more than 700 years—especially from an etymological point of view. Originally coming from the Latin word populus, "people, nation," the Spanish word pueblo, meaning "town, village," as well as "nation, people," was naturally applied by 16th-century Spanish explorers to villages they discovered or founded in the Southwest.[10]

What are the pros and cons of electronic abridged dictionaries?

By the way, with many of the newer dictionaries you often get a CD-ROM along with the traditional print version. This enables you to load an electronic

---

[8]*The American Heritage Dictionary of the English Language,* 4th ed. (Boston: Houghton Mifflin, 2000), p. 564.

[9]Ibid., p. 970.

[10]Ibid., p. 1417.

version of the dictionary onto your personal computer. Unlike hand-held electronic dictionaries, the dictionaries designed for desktop computers can be fairly sophisticated in their presentation, navigation, resolution, and design. For example, instead of having to flip through paper pages, you can often go directly to the word you're looking for and jump to the definition of a synonym just by clicking on a link. Some of the dictionaries allow you not only to read a word's pronunciation, but also to hear it pronounced correctly. On the other hand, each dictionary may have a slightly different (and often copyrighted) system for navigating its words. Some are better than others, and very few are immediately intuitive. And, of course, you lose some of the tactile experience of turning pages and the serendipity of stumbling upon one fascinating word while looking up another. Ultimately, it's a question of personal taste and, in some cases, a matter of a few dollars more.

Dig Deeper with an Unabridged Dictionary

What is the advantage of an unabridged dictionary?

Although abridged dictionaries occasionally provide interesting and important details about words, for intensive word study, there is no substitute for an unabridged dictionary. Locate the unabridged dictionaries in your library—usually they are in the reference room—and use them to supplement your abridged desk dictionary. An unabridged dictionary provides more definitions, more about the derivations of words, and more on usage. Good one-volume unabridged dictionaries include *Webster's Third New International Dictionary of the English Language* and the *Random House Dictionary of the English Language. The Oxford English Dictionary*, in twenty volumes plus supplements, is indispensable for the historical study of words but is more detailed than you will need for most purposes.

How do the definitions in an unabridged dictionary differ from those in an abridged dictionary?

Whereas synonyms, usage notes, and word histories are considered extras in abridged dictionaries, they are standard in most unabridged dictionaries. In addition, for words that have multiple meanings, an unabridged dictionary will include all the definitions instead of just the most common ones.

That fact came in handy when a friend wrote a letter about attending a seminar on Vladimir Nabokov, the Russian-born American writer who was best known for the satirical novel *Lolita*. "All the experts were there," he explained in his letter. "Lots of discussion, but it was too precious for me." Too precious? The sentence was startling. After all, *precious* is commonly used to refer to something valuable. But a quick look at the word's definitions helped clear up the mystery. Here they are:

1. Of high cost or worth; valuable
2. Highly esteemed; cherished
3. Dear; beloved
4. Affectedly dainty or overrefined: *precious mannerisms*[11]

[11]*The American Heritage Dictionary of the English Language,* 4th ed. (Boston: Houghton Mifflin, 2000), p. 1381.

The fourth definition was the one that slid into the context of the letter perfectly. "Overrefined" was the answer. By reading all the definitions of a word, we weave more strands into the background of each word we look up. This will enable us to later use and understand such words with greater correctness and precision.

What makes the *Oxford English Dictionary* special?

The *Oxford English Dictionary*   When it comes to unabridged dictionaries, the *Oxford English Dictionary* (popularly known as the OED) is in a class by itself. It presents the words that have formed the English vocabulary from the time of the earliest records to the present day. Five million excerpts from English literature were amassed during preparation of the work; about 1,800,000 quotations were actually printed.

Work began on the OED in 1878, and the last page was delivered to the press on April 19, 1928. It took fifty years to produce all the volumes. On its completion in 1928, it was presented to King George V, and a copy was also officially provided to Calvin Coolidge, the president of the United States.

Here is a brief sample of information gleaned from the *Oxford English Dictionary.* The word is *acre.*

> a. The historical spellings of *acre* are: acer, aker, & akre.
> b. The historical meanings of *acre,* in order of time, are:
>   1. a piece of tilled land.
>   2. as much as a yoke of oxen could plow in a day.
>   3. consists of 32 furrows of the plow, a furlong in length.
>   [A furlong is about 220 yards.][12]

The ruling king had the power to stipulate weights and measures. For example, under Henry VIII, an acre was forty poles long and four poles wide. The measures, though varied, were somewhat similar throughout history.

Over the years, with each printing, the *OED* has increased in size. The latest edition, printed in 1989, consists of twenty volumes, made up of 22,000 pages. Use this prodigious dictionary with gratitude and respect.

Should you use the electronic versions of unabridged dictionaries?

As it has with pocket and abridged dictionaries, computer software has attempted to increase access to unabridged dictionaries. Oxford University Press sells a CD-ROM version of the OED that you can run on your PC. Some of the better-known unabridged dictionaries also offer unabridged versions, either as CD-ROMs or as Web sites that you can subscribe to. These may be viable options for serious scholars of words, but for most of us the library dictionaries are probably more than adequate.

[12]*The Oxford English Dictionary,* vol. 1, 2nd ed. (Oxford: Clarendon Press, 1989), pp. 117–118.

Preserving Your Words on Index Cards

How do you make new words a permanent part of your vocabulary?

Once you find the words you need or that interest you, you'll want to hold onto them. Using the word in a sentence is a common suggestion, and it's good as far as it goes. But if you want to make sure that each new word becomes a permanent part of your vocabulary, you have to go a little further. The only sure way to master words is to *overlearn* them by using the undisputedly best memory-enhancing technique of *recitation*.

Write One Word per Card

What should you write on each vocabulary card?

To get started, all you need is a dictionary and a stack of index cards (see Figure 7.3). On the cards, write the difficult words that you find in your textbooks and hear in the classroom. These are words you need to know to understand your coursework. Here are the steps to make the system work for you:

1. **Consider its context.** When you select a word, write it on the front of an index card. But don't just write it in isolation. To provide a meaningful context, write the complete sentence in which the word occurs and underline the word so that it stands out.

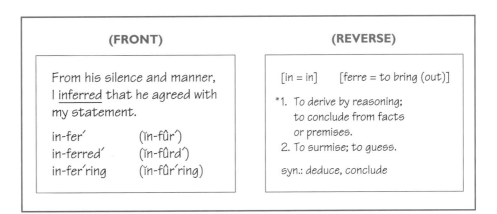

(FRONT)	(REVERSE)

From his silence and manner, I <u>inferred</u> that he agreed with my statement.
 	
in-fer′   (ĭn-fûr′)
in-ferred′   (ĭn-fûrd′)
in-fer′ring (ĭn-fûr′rĭng)
	[in = in] [ferre = to bring (out)]
	
	*1. To derive by reasoning;
	    to conclude from facts
	    or premises.
	2. To surmise; to guess.
	
	syn.: deduce, conclude

Figure 7.3
Index Card System
The front and back of this vocabulary card for the word *inferred* demonstrates the format of the index card system. Notice that the front of the card shows the new word underlined in a complete sentence. It also shows how to pronounce the word. The reverse of the card defines prefixes and roots and gives important dictionary definitions of the word. An asterisk is placed beside the definition that most nearly matches the use of the word on the front of the card. Synonyms are also given.

2. **Sound it out.** Look the word up in a dictionary and, on the front of the card, write the word out in syllables, including accent and diacritical marks, so that you can pronounce it correctly. If you can't pronounce it and spell it correctly, you won't use it later.

3. **Break it down.** On the back of the card, write the prefix and root that make up your word. The prefix and root will help you remember the word by showing you its logical linguistic structure.

4. **Find its meaning.** Still on the back of the card, write the several pertinent definitions of the word. You might as well extract the maximum in meanings while you're at it! Then put an asterisk beside the definition that best fits the meaning of your word in its specific context.

How should you handle vocabulary cards for technical terms?

Technical terms can be handled in almost the same way. However, for these words you may want to rely on the definitions in your textbook. Special terms are usually defined when first introduced or in a glossary. Even for a special term, on the reverse side record any information you find about its derivation. Often, you'll have to consult an unabridged dictionary.

Master Each Word

How do you master the words you've collected on index cards?

In the above four steps we've covered how to construct cards for the index system. Now, we'll present the steps for using the cards efficiently and effectively. You've put in a lot of work. Get the maximum learning from it. To master the words on the cards, do the following:

1. **Start with the front.** Always look first at the front of the card. First, pronounce the word aloud and correctly. Then read the sentence aloud and think about it momentarily. Next, define the word—not necessarily in a dictionary's language, but meaningfully in your own words. Read the sentence aloud. All this should be done before you look at the definition on the back. Reading and speaking aloud forces you to think alertly, and hearing the word brings your auditory memory into play. Thus, seeing, saying, hearing, and thinking are all working for you.

2. **Check your work.** After you have defined the word to the best of your ability, turn the card over to check the accuracy of your definition.

3. **Say it again.** If you are not satisfied with your definition, keep reciting until your definition is correct. For memory's sake, you must, in order to extract it later, enter into your mind a correct, crisp, concise meaning for the word. This is pure logic.

4. **Mark the difficult ones.** When you fail to define the word correctly on your first try, place a dot in the upper-right-hand corner of the front of the card. The next time you go through your cards, the dot will remind you that you missed the word on a previous try. When a card has three dots, it is time

to give that word extra attention by determining why you keep getting it wrong.

5. **Try another stack.** After a small stack of cards has been mastered, place them in a shoebox and put together another small stack for studying.

6. **Conduct a review.** From time to time, review the words that you have mastered. Reviewing mastered words will take much less time than learning unmastered ones. Remember, the erosive power of forgetting is working day and night. A quick periodic review will foil this relentless force.

What is the advantage of putting vocabulary words on index cards?

The advantage of index cards is that they are convenient to carry around for study at odd moments. At all times, carry a few blank cards on which to record interesting words. Learning words that intrigue you will be immeasurably more valuable than memorizing a list made up by someone else. Finally, as you master the precise meaning of each word, there will be a corresponding advance in your reading, writing, speaking, and thinking. The index card system doesn't exhaust its usefulness when your college education ends. Successful people, including company presidents, frequently carry around a small stack of vocabulary cards.

Exploring Your Personal Frontier

How can you increase your vocabulary systematically?

Consulting the dictionary whenever you encounter a word you don't know can help increase your vocabulary a word at a time. But it can be an inconsistent and unpredictable process. One highly effective way to increase your vocabulary more systematically is by using the Frontier Vocabulary System developed by Johnson O'Connor. The Frontier Vocabulary System is based on natural learning processes.[13] We know that a baby must crawl before it can walk and walk before it can run. We know, too, that a child can pronounce the sound *p* at about age three-and-a-half but usually does not master the sound *r* until about age seven-and-a-half. Many other skills develop along with physical growth and general maturation. All learning processes have four characteristics:

1. Skills progress from the simple to the complex.
2. Each skill is developed in an orderly sequence of steps.
3. Each step is at a different level of difficulty.
4. No significant step may be skipped. Each step seems to develop the muscle or brain pattern that makes the next step possible.

[13]Much of this discussion is based on Dean Trembly, "Intellectual Abilities as Motivating Factors," *Japanese Psychological Research* 10, no. 2 (July 1968): 104–108.

What did Johnson O'Connor conclude about how we learn words?

From his analytical research, O'Connor concluded that learning new words is much like learning any other skill. We progress from simple words to more difficult ones in an orderly sequence. The difficulty or ease of learning a word does not depend on the length of the word, its frequency of use, its geographic origin, or its pronunciation—or on teachers, books, or parents. Instead, difficulty in learning a word depends on the complexity of the *idea* that the word stands for. Defining words with simple synonyms does not provide the learner with a background sufficient to think with the words. Because words stand for ideas, the ideas behind them must also be learned.

What was Hayakawa's view on vocabulary building?

S. I. Hayakawa, the noted semanticist, shared this view. He questioned the old-fashioned notion that the way to study words is to concentrate exclusively on words. Hayakawa suggested that words should be understood in relationship to other words—not only other words on the same level but also words at a higher (more abstract) level and words at a lower (more concrete) level.

Understanding How Words Are Learned

What principles underlie the Frontier Vocabulary System?

The following findings by O'Connor form the basis of the Frontier Vocabulary System:

1. The easiest words are learned first; then the harder ones are learned.
2. At the forward edge of the mass of all the words that have been mastered is the individual's *frontier*. Only a very few words *beyond the frontier* have already been mastered.
3. The greatest learning takes place in the frontier area, which lies between the zone of known words and the zone of totally unknown words (see Figure 7.4).
4. The most significant characteristic of the words in the frontier area is that they are, to some extent, familiar. The maximum advancement in a person's mastery of words takes place in the frontier area, where hundreds of almost-known words need only a slight straightening out to make them familiar.
5. Learning becomes extremely inefficient and may actually break down when a person skips the frontier area and tries to learn totally unknown words.

What is the value of being familiar with words in the frontier area?

Familiarity with a word in the frontier area means that you already know something about the word or its definition. You may, for example, know its general meaning and how to pronounce it. Or you may know one of its several meanings. The important point is this: By singling out a frontier word and learning its specific meaning, or its several definitions, you can master the word with minimal time and effort.

What happens as you learn more frontier words?

By working continually in the frontier area, you can rapidly master words. At the same time, you will continually be discovering new frontier words to con-

Figure 7.4
The Concept of Frontier Words

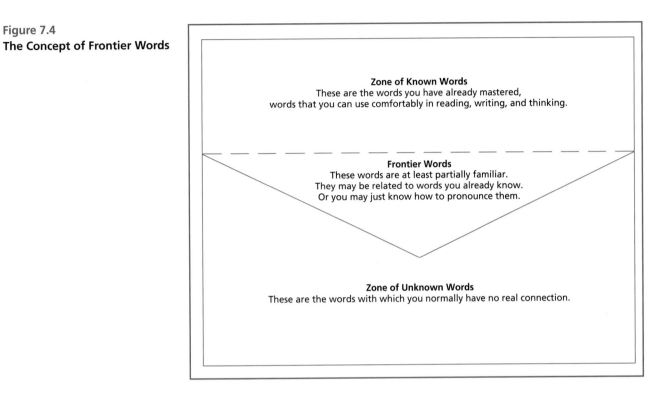

Zone of Known Words
These are the words you have already mastered,
words that you can use comfortably in reading, writing, and thinking.

Frontier Words
These words are at least partially familiar.
They may be related to words you already know.
Or you may just know how to pronounce them.

Zone of Unknown Words
These are the words with which you normally have no real connection.

quer. As the process continues, the frontier area will push farther into the zone of what were once totally unknown words.

Recognizing Frontier Words

How can you find your own frontier words?

To find your own frontier words, first become aware of your daily speech, and make a list of the unusual words you use. Next, be on the lookout for words that you recognize in reading but do not use in speaking and writing. From this source choose *only* the words that appeal to you. Listen attentively while other people speak. The chances are great that you will recognize and know the general meaning of all the words you hear. From this stream of speech, choose the words that appeal to you—words that you would like to incorporate into your own speech.

What is the value of learning a word's antonym?

Later, after writing out the definition for each of your frontier words, look for its antonym (opposite). If it interests you, learn that word, too. Learning pairs of contrasting words creates the strong force of spontaneous suggestion—either word suggests the other.

Applying the Frontier System

How do you master your frontier words?

After you have selected words from your own frontier, you must have a system for memorizing them. Luckily, you already have one. There is no better system than the one already explained in detail: the index card system (see Figure 7.3 on page 143). As you master the precise meaning of each frontier word, there will be a corresponding advance in your reading, writing, speaking, and thinking.

Treating Words Like Chemical Compounds

How is a typical word similar to a chemical compound?

The Frontier System paints a picture of realms or regions of words. But what about the individual words themselves? It's not unusual to think of a word as being indivisible, like an atom, the smallest part of a sentence. In some cases this is true. In English, words such as *who, what, where, when,* and *why* can't be broken down any further. But many other words in our language—most of them in fact—are products of smaller components that, when pieced together in different combinations, can provide a variety of different words. In that sense, a word can be compared to a chemical compound: Although a word may hold together as a single unit, in reality it is made up of individual atoms or elements. With words, these elements are known as roots, prefixes, and suffixes.

Learning Roots and Prefixes

How can you learn whole clusters of words?

It has been estimated that 60 percent of the English words in common use are made up partly or entirely of prefixes or roots derived from Latin and Greek. If you would like to learn whole clusters of words in one stroke, you should get to know the most common roots, prefixes, and suffixes. A word *root* is the core of a word, the part that holds the basic meaning. A *prefix* is a word beginning that modifies the root. A suffix is an element tacked on to the end of a word that alters or refines its meaning. Table 7.1 lists some common word roots, and Table 7.2 lists some common prefixes.

What is the value of learning prefixes and roots?

The value of learning prefixes and roots is that they illustrate the way much of our language is constructed. Once learned, they can help you recognize and understand many words without resorting to a dictionary. With one well-understood root word as the center, an entire "constellation" of words can be built up. Figure 7.5 shows such a constellation, based on the root *duct*, from the Latin *ducere* ("to lead"). Notice that it makes use of some of the most common prefixes and of other prefixes and combining words as well as various word endings. This does not exhaust all the possibilities either; you should be able to think of several other words growing out of "duct."

Table 7.1
Common Word Roots

Root	Meaning	Example	Definition
agri	field	agronomy	*Field*—crop production and soil management
anthropo	man	anthropology	The study of *humans*
astro	star	astronaut	One who travels in interplanetary space (*stars*)
bio	life	biology	The study of *life*
cardio	heart	cardiac	Pertaining to the *heart*
chromo	color	chromatology	The science of *colors*
demos	people	democracy	Government by the *people*
derma	skin	epidermis	The outer layer of *skin*
dyna	power	dynamic	Characterized by *power* and energy
geo	earth	geology	The study of the *earth*
helio	sun	heliotrope	Any plant that turns toward the *sun*
hydro	water	hydroponics	Growing of plants in *water* reinforced with nutrients
hypno	sleep	hypnosis	A state of *sleep* induced by suggestion
magni	great, big	magnify	To enlarge, to make *bigger*
man(u)	hand	manuscript	Written by *hand*
mono	one	monoplane	Airplane with *one* wing
ortho	straight	orthodox	Right, true, *straight* opinion
pod	foot	pseudopod	False *foot*
psycho	mind	psychology	Study of the *mind* in any of its aspects
pyro	fire	pyrometer	An instrument for measuring high temperatures
terra	earth	terrace	A raised platform of *earth*
thermo	heat	thermometer	Instrument for measuring *heat*
zoo	animal	zoology	The study of *animals*

Can you memorize prefixes and roots instead of consulting the dictionary?

Although knowing the meanings of prefixes and roots can unlock the meanings of unfamiliar words, this knowledge should supplement, not replace, dictionary use. Over the centuries many prefixes have changed in both meaning and spelling. According to Lee Deighton, "Of the 68 prominent and commonly used prefixes there are only 11 which have a single and fairly invariant meaning."[14] The other 57 prefixes have more than one meaning each.

For example, the prefix *de-* means "of" or "from"; yet the dictionary lists four different meanings for it:

1. It means "down" as in *descend,* which means to pass from a higher to a lower place.
2. It indicates separation as in *dehumidify,* which means to separate moisture from air, or in *decapitate,* which means to behead—that is, to separate the head from the rest of the body.

[14]Deighton, *Vocabulary Development in the Classroom,* p. 26.

Table 7.2
Common Prefixes

Prefix	Meaning	Example	Definition
ante-	before	antebellum	*Before* the war; especially in the U.S., before the Civil War
anti-	against	antifreeze	Liquid used to guard *against* freezing
auto-	self	automatic	*Self*-acting or *self*-regulating
bene-	good	benefit	An act of *kindness;* a gift
circum-	around	circumscribe	To draw a line *around;* to encircle
contra-	against	contradict	To speak *against*
de-	reverse, remove	defoliate	*Remove* the leaves from a tree
ecto-	outside	ectoparasite	Parasite living on the *exterior* of animals
endo-	within	endogamy	Marriage *within* the tribe
hyper-	over	hypertension	*High* blood pressure
hypo-	under	hypotension	*Low* blood pressure
inter-	between	intervene	Come *between*
intra-	within	intramural	*Within* bounds of a school
intro-	in, into	introspect	To look *within,* as one's own mind
macro-	large	macroscopic	*Large* enough to be observed by the naked eye
mal-	bad	maladjusted	*Badly* adjusted
micro-	small	microscopic	So *small* that one needs a microscope to observe
multi-	many	multimillionaire	One having *two* or *more* million dollars
neo-	new	neolithic	*New* stone age
non-	not	nonconformist	One who does *not* conform
pan-	all	pantheon	A temple dedicated to *all* gods
poly-	many	polygonal	Having *many* sides
post-	after	postgraduate	*After* graduating
pre-	before	precede	To go *before*
proto-	first	prototype	*First* or original model
pseudo-	false	pseudonym	*False* name; esp., an author's pen-name
retro-	backward	retrospect	A looking *back* on things
semi-	half	semicircle	*Half* a circle
sub-	under	submerge	To put *under* water
super-	above	superfine	*Extra* fine
tele-	far	telescope	Seeing or viewing *afar*
trans-	across	transalpine	*Across* the Alps

3. It indicates reversal as in *decode,* which means to convert from code into ordinary language, or in *depreciate,* which means to lessen in value.

4. It may be used to intensify as in *demonstrate,* which means to show or prove publicly, or in *declare,* which means to announce.

Where do suffixes come in?

In some ways, suffixes can be more helpful than prefixes in understanding words. And—the best part—learning and remembering a handful of suffixes is relatively easy.

For example, we come across many medical words, such as *laryngitis* and *tonsillitis.* Once we know that the suffix *-itis* means "inflammation or disease of,"

Figure 7.5
A Constellation of Words from One Root

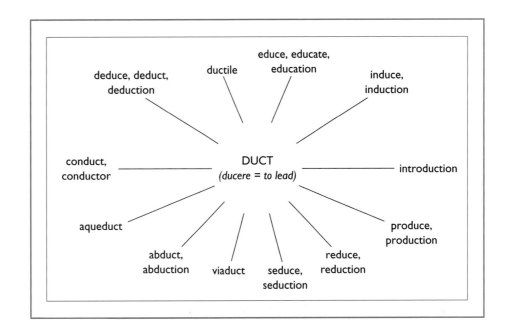

we see how logically the words were put together, and their meanings become obvious—with hardly any work at all.

Once we know that the suffix -*ectomy* means "surgical removal," the words *laryngectomy* and *tonsillectomy* and *appendectomy* are no longer the sole possession of doctors. We, too, know and can use them.

Take the suffix -*cide*, which means "killer." Now the words *insecticide* and *germicide* become fully understandable.

What is the key benefit of learning prefixes, roots, and suffixes?

Learn as many of the common prefixes, roots, and suffixes as you can, but learn them for better and more precise understanding of words you already know and words that you have yet to look up in the dictionary. The key benefit of learning these components comes from the precision they provide. When you go to the dictionary, make sure to spend some time on the prefixes and roots that make up each word. You will soon become convinced that a word is not an assemblage of letters put together like an anagram, but the true and natural outcome of evolution.

Using the Fourteen Master Words

What are the Fourteen Master Words?

Recognizing our reliance on Latin and Greek for the components of many English words, Professor James I. Brown of the University of Minnesota decided to find out which prefixes appear most frequently in English. To do so, he recorded the number of times certain word-elements appeared in an

Table 7.3

Fourteen Master Words: Key to Meanings of More Than 14,000 Words

Words	Prefix	Common Meaning	Root	Common Meaning
precept	pre-	(before)	*capere*	(take, seize)
detain	de-	(away, from)	*tenere*	(hold, have)
intermittent	inter-	(between)	*mittere*	(send)
offer	ob-	(against)	*ferre*	(bear, carry)
insist	in-	(into)	*stare*	(stand)
monograph	mono-	(alone, one)	*graphein*	(write)
epilogue	epi-	(after)	*logos*	(say, word)
aspect	ad-	(to, toward)	*specere*	(see)
uncomplicated	un-	(not)	*plicare*	(fold)
	com-	(together with)		
nonextended	non-	(not)	*tendere*	(stretch)
	ex-	(out of)		
reproduction	re-	(back, again)	*ducere*	(lead)
	pro-	(forward)		
indisposed	in-	(not)	*ponere*	(put, place)
	dis-	(apart from)		
oversufficient	over-	(above)	*facere*	(make, do)
	sub-	(under)		
mistranscribe	mis-	(wrong)	*scribere*	(write)
	trans-	(across, beyond)		

James I. Brown "A Master-Word Approach to Vocabulary" by James I. Brown. Reprinted by permission from the May 1949 issue of WORD STUDY © 1949 by Merriam-Webster, Inc. Publishers of the Merriam-Webster ® Dictionaries.

unabridged dictionary. He found that twenty prefixes and fourteen roots were part of 14,000 relatively common English words and of an estimated 100,000 words in that dictionary. He then compiled a list of common English words that contained the twenty prefixes and fourteen roots. These words he called the *Fourteen Master Words* (see Table 7.3).[15]

What is the value of the Fourteen Master Words?

The value of this list is that it illustrates the way much of our language is constructed. If learned, it can help you recognize and understand many words without resorting to a dictionary. With one well-understood root word as the center, an entire "constellation" of words can be built up, as was shown in Figure 7.5.

Appreciating the Value of History

What does learning words through their components overlook?

Breaking down words into their component parts and reassembling them in different combinations can be an extremely efficient way to learn huge num-

[15]Professor Brown's findings are described in detail in "Reading and Vocabulary: 14 Master Words," which appeared in the May 1949 issue of *Word Study*, published by G. & C. Merriam Co., Springfield, MA.

bers of words. But this process, as helpful as it can be, tends to overlook one important aspect of words: their history.

What are some of the benefits of learning a word's history?

Many of the words we use didn't simply materialize when someone mixed a prefix, a root, and a suffix together like chemicals in a laboratory. Words are vibrant, dynamic things, each with a history, a story of its own. Learn the story, and you'll remember the word. Better yet, if you learn the life history of a word, the chances are great that you'll grow to *like* the word, not simply *learn* it. Learning words in this fashion may not be as efficient as finding them with the Frontier System or arriving at long lists based on commonly used prefixes and roots. But if you learn a word by learning its history, the connection you establish is almost certain to make that learning last. To help you in this endeavor, at the end of each chapter are both a picture and the story of a word, taken from *Picturesque Word Origins,* one of the best books of its kind. Each story not only provides a definition of the word; it also establishes a bond.

The stories behind two common words in a college context—*scholar* and *sophomore*—are entertaining examples of how histories can strengthen your understanding and appreciation of the words around you.

What is the connection between the word *scholar* and leisure?

Scholar.   Although we generally think of a scholar as a hard-working, serious student, the word has a surprisingly different history. *Scholar* comes from the ancient Greek word for leisure. That's because the only people who had the luxury of learning were the children of the privileged classes. Everyone else was expected to work. In time the connection with leisure was lost, and most scholars would bristle at any suggestion that they are simply taking it easy.

How does the origin of *sophomore* convey the status of a second-year student?

Sophomore.   The word *sophomore* may be viewed as a rather harmless label for a second-year student, but its derivation provides a fascinating insight into how students partway through their education are viewed. The word originates from the Greek word *sophos* for "wise," but also from *moros,* which means stupid! So, although sophomores may feel as though they know it all, the people who coined the word *sophomore* must have felt these students still needed a little humility.

Finding Books That Tell the Stories of Words

How can you locate books that discuss the histories of words?

There are dozens of books that relate the often-fascinating histories of words. Of these, *Picturesque Word Origins* is one of the best, but because it has been out of print for quite some time you may have difficulty locating a copy. Ask your librarian or visit any of a number of Web sites, such as http://www.alibris.com, devoted to rare or used books. In the meantime, here's a list of books both in and out of print that tell the stories behind some well-known words. You should be able to find many of the books in library catalogs. The books still in print should also be available for purchase in bookstores or online.

Books still in print

Almond, Jordan. *Dictionary of Word Origins: A History of the Words, Expressions and Clichés We Use.* Citadel Press, 1995.

American Heritage Dictionary Editors and Barry Moser. *Word Mysteries and Histories: From Quiche to Humble Pie.* Houghton Mifflin, 1987.

Ayto, John. *Dictionary of Word Origins.* Arcade, 1993.

Flavell, Linda, and Roger Flavell. *Dictionary of Word Origins.* Trafalgar Square, 2001.

Funk, Charles Earle. *Thereby Hangs a Tale: Stories of Curious Word Origins.* HarperResource, 2002.

Funk, Wilfred. *Word Origins: An Exploration and History of Words and Language.* Outlet, 1992.

Hendrickson, Robert. *The Facts on File Encyclopedia of Word and Phrase Origins.* Facts on File, 2000.

Hunt, Cecil. *Word Origins: The Romance of Language.* Citadel Press, 1991.

Isil, Olivia A. *When a Loose Cannon Flogs a Dead Horse There's the Devil to Pay: Seafaring Words in Everyday Speech.* International Marine/Ragged Mountain Press, 1996.

Morris, William, and Mary Morris. *Morris Dictionary of Word and Phrase Origins*, 2nd edition. HarperCollins, 1988.

Popkin, David. *Vocabulary Energizers II: Stories of Word Origins.* Hada Publications, 1990.

————. *Vocabulary Energizers: Stories of Word Origins.* Hada Publications, 1988.

Rees, Nigel. *Cassell's Dictionary of Word and Phrase Origins.* Cassell Academic, 2002.

Verma, Dhirendra. *Encyclopaedia of Word Origins.* New Dawn Books, 1999.

Out-of-print books

Ernst, Margaret S. *In a Word.* Alfred A. Knopf, 1939.

Picturesque Word Origins. G. & C. Merriam, 1933.

FINAL WORDS

How does vocabulary building relate to learning career skills?

Thus far in this book, you've seen how words shaped the life of Malcolm X and improved the lot of a golf caddy. Words can shape your life and career as well. It's natural to focus most of your academic energy on preparing for your future career and employment. But let the success stories at the beginning of this chapter be a constant reminder of the importance of a lasting vocabulary. Once you are established in your career, professional progress will depend, of course, on your work skills; but your ability to use words—to express yourself clearly and convincingly—may be the real propellant in climbing the ladder. So, let building a vocabulary go hand in hand with building your career skills.

HAVE YOU MISSED SOMETHING?

SENTENCE COMPLETION   *Complete the following sentences with one of the three words listed below each sentence.*

1. Building your vocabulary can increase your _____.

   self-esteem   self-consciousness   self-promotion

2. A chief advantage of vocabulary cards is their _____.

   completeness   convenience   complexity

3. The most significant characteristic of a frontier word is its _____.

   difficulty   familiarity   pronunciation

MATCHING   *In each blank space in the left column, write the letter preceding the phrase in the right column that matches the left item best.*

_____ 1. Interest

_____ 2. 60

_____ 3. Constellation

_____ 4. 20

_____ 5. Context

_____ 6. Usage

_____ 7. Serendipity

_____ 8. Frontier area

a. Has limitations as a means of learning new words

b. Provides clarification that goes beyond a word's definition

c. Percentage of English words derived from Latin or Greek

d. Can be a powerful motivator for strengthening vocabulary

e. Greatest learning takes place here

f. Number of volumes in the current *Oxford English Dictionary*

g. A group of words with a common root

h. Can be lost when you use an electronic dictionary

TRUE-FALSE   *Write* T *beside the* true *statements and* F *beside the* false *statements.*

_____ 1. Quality of vocabulary can have a direct effect on quality of thought.

_____ 2. The creative use of words can generate interest in an audience.

_____ 3. Not all electronic dictionaries contain the features you find in a pocket dictionary.

_____ 4. No word is ever fully defined in an abridged dictionary.

_____ 5. Unabridged dictionaries normally include only the most common definition for each word.

MULTIPLE CHOICE

Choose the word or phrase that completes each sentence most accurately, and circle the letter that precedes it.

1. After he left prison, Malcolm X went on to become an outstanding
   a. leader.
   b. preacher.
   c. public speaker.
   d. all of the above.

2. Frontier words are
   a. inexhaustible in their supply.
   b. the easiest words to master.
   c. familiar in one way or another.
   d. all of the above.

3. From his analytical research, Johnson O'Connor determined that learning new words
   a. requires an above-average memory.
   b. is much like learning any other skill.
   c. interferes with your ability to concentrate.
   d. enables you to clarify your career goals.

4. With some electronic dictionaries, a word's pronunciation can actually be
   a. incorrect.
   b. heard.
   c. abridged.
   d. none of the above.

5. Three dots on a vocabulary card indicate that the word
   a. has three different definitions.
   b. may require extra attention.
   c. has been properly mastered.
   d. consists of a common prefix and root.

SHORT ANSWER

Supply a brief answer for each of the following questions.

1. Suggest at least two reasons why index cards are an effective tool for building your vocabulary.

2. Using what you know about memory, explain why it's effective to learn words in relation to other words, as Hayakawa recommended.

3. Compare and contrast building your vocabulary by learning word histories and by memorizing prefixes and roots.

4. Discuss places and situations in which you would be likely to encounter frontier words.

WORDS IN CONTEXT

From the three choices beside each numbered item, select the one that most nearly expresses the meaning of the italicized word in the quote. Make a light check mark (✓) next to your choice.

When strangers start acting like neighbors, communities are *reinvigorated.*

—Ralph Nader (1934–), American lawyer, presidential candidate, and consumer advocate

1. are *reinvigorated*   given new leaders   given old standards   given new life

If you help others, you will be helped, perhaps tomorrow, perhaps in one hundred years, but you will be helped. Nature must pay off the debt. It is a *mathematical* law and all life is mathematics.

—George Ivanovitch Gurdjieff (1872–1949), Armenian mystic and philosopher

2. a *mathematical* law   probable   improbable   absolute

It is one of the most beautiful *compensations* of life that no man can sincerely try to help another without helping himself.

—Ralph Waldo Emerson (1803–1882), American writer and philosopher

3. *compensations* of life   thoughts   acts   rewards

THE WORD HISTORY SYSTEM

Neighbor
once a nearby farmer

neighbor   neigh'-bor *n.*
1. One who lives near or next to another. 2. A person, place, or thing adjacent to or located near another. 3. A fellow human being.

Neighbor is one of those interesting words that carry us back to Anglo-Saxon days. In Anglo-Saxon, néah meant "nigh," and gebūr meant "dweller," "farmer." These two words were combined into néahgebūr, meaning, literally, "a nearby farmer." Its meaning, changing with the evolution of civilization, no longer applies particularly to neighboring farmers, but refers to persons living near each other. Even nations in the modern world are called "neighbors"—an interesting development of a word that means, literally, "nearby farmers."

Reprinted by permission. From *Picturesque Word Origins* © 1933 by G. & C. Merriam Co. (now Merriam-Webster, Incorporated).

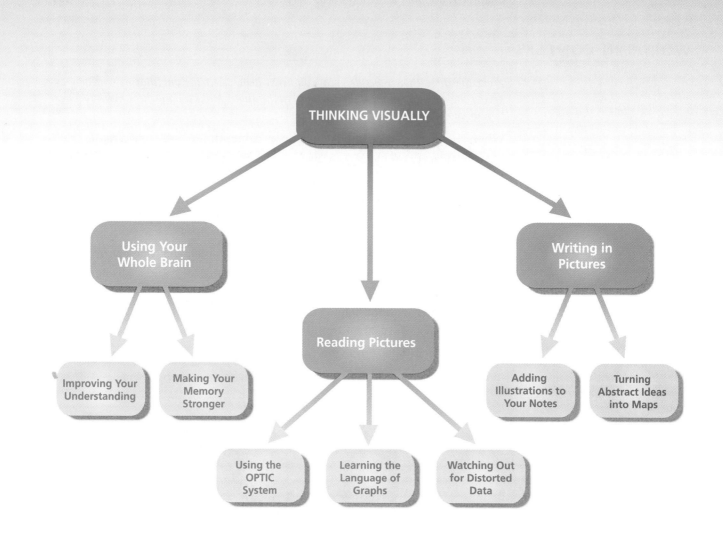

THINKING VISUALLY

Using Your Whole Brain
- Improving Your Understanding
- Making Your Memory Stronger

Reading Pictures
- Using the OPTIC System
- Learning the Language of Graphs
- Watching Out for Distorted Data

Writing in Pictures
- Adding Illustrations to Your Notes
- Turning Abstract Ideas into Maps

Thinking Visually

Man's body is faulty, his mind untrustworthy, but his imagination has made him remarkable.

John Masefield (1878–1967), English author and poet laureate

Most of us are comfortable with reading and writing in words. But the same usually doesn't hold true for pictures. This means that the entire right half of our brains, the half that processes pictures, is largely ignored or underused during a typical school day. If you can learn to read and write in pictures as comfortably as you do in words, you will be adding a visual dimension to your studying that could dramatically affect your learning and remembering. To aid you in thinking visually, this chapter deals with:

- **Using Your Whole Brain**
- **Making Your Memory Stronger**
- **Using the OPTIC System**
- **Learning the Language of Graphs**
- **Watching Out for Distorted Data**
- **Adding Illustrations to Your Notes**
- **Turning Abstract Ideas into Maps**

Why is thinking visually important?

We live in a world of words, where reading and writing are crucial not only to our success but also to our survival. But words are not our only form of communication (see Figure 8.1). Thinking visually is important because we just as commonly communicate in pictures as in words—if not more so. Consider the millions of pictures that flash on your TV screen, or the signs that use only pictures and shapes to convey their meaning. Although there's little danger that words will become extinct, the role of visual images appears to be increasing. Learning to think visually will broaden your mind. With your whole brain engaged, you'll be able to extract messages from pictures and use visuals to expand your understanding.

Using Your Whole Brain

What are the functions of the brain's two sides?

Although each of us has only one brain, that brain is divided into two distinct sides, or hemispheres, each with a separate set of functions. The chief function of the left side of the brain is to process written and spoken information. As you might expect, that side of the brain gets quite a workout. One of the main functions of the brain's right side is to analyze and interpret visual information.

Figure 8.1
Words Are Not Our Only Form of Communication

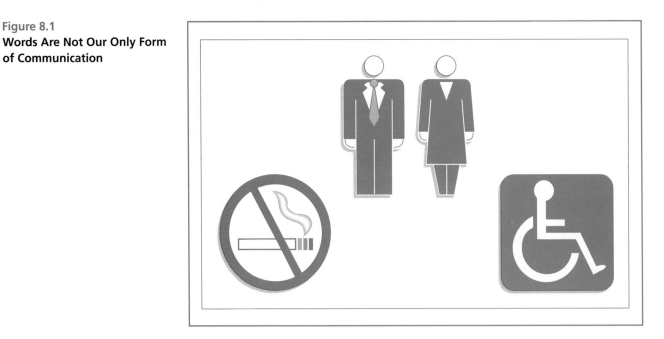

Thinking in pictures puts the right side to work. Suddenly, instead of relying primarily on the left side of the brain, you're using both hemispheres. Your analysis of information becomes broader and more balanced, allowing you to more easily understand and remember information than you could when you did the bulk of your thinking with only the left half of your brain.

Improving Your Understanding

How can using the right side of your brain improve your understanding?

There is some information that the left side of the brain may be unable to understand without help. Take, for example, an elaborate set of street directions. Written out, they become the responsibility of the left side of the brain. And yet you can read and reread all the directions and still wind up scratching your head and getting lost. But if you put this same information into visual form—in this case, onto a map—you give your right brain a chance to interpret the data. With the two sides of the brain working in concert, information that would have taken time to untangle using one-sided thinking can often be grasped in an instant.

Making Your Memory Stronger

How does using both sides of your brain improve memory?

Thinking with your whole brain virtually doubles the odds of remembering what you've just learned. Memories that would normally be stored in only the left side of the brain are now filed in the right side as well. Indeed, Allan Paivio from the University of Western Ontario, using what he calls "dual coding," has concluded that pictures are easier to remember than words and that information is more readily recalled when it is learned as both pictures and words.[1] Thus, if you make both a verbal and a visual effort to recall something you've learned, your memory will have two places in which to search for the information instead of just one.

Reading Pictures

What does "reading a picture" mean?

When you read a paragraph, you're cracking a code. That code is the English language, and its message is the meaning you extract from words, sentences, and paragraphs. Although we spend a great deal of time decoding language, most of the codes around us are visual. We can decode a smile, for example,

[1]Allan Paivio, Mary Walsh, and Trudy Bons, "Concreteness Effects or Memory: When and Why?" *Journal of Experimental Psychology: Learning, Memory and Cognition* 20, no. 5 (1994): 1196–1204.

and know how its meaning differs from that of a frown. Visual materials in textbooks use codes as well to supply messages that are often as important as the meanings contained in sentences and paragraphs. For that reason, they must be read every bit as carefully. Like reading a paragraph, reading a picture simply means extracting its message.

Using the OPTIC System

What is the purpose of the OPTIC system?

Many students mistakenly give visuals only a quick glance or even skip over them entirely. But these graphic materials should be scrutinized as carefully and as systematically as paragraphs. The OPTIC system will help you take an organized approach to this task.

What do the five letters in OPTIC stand for?

The five letters in the word *OPTIC* (which means "pertaining to the eye") provide you with a simple system for remembering the five elements of analyzing a visual:

O is for *overview.*
P is for *parts.*
T is for *title.*
I is for *interrelationships.*
C is for *conclusion.*

What are the five steps of the OPTIC system?

Using these five elements as cues, you can conduct a meaningful analysis of almost any diagram, graph, or illustration by following these steps:

1. Begin by conducting a brief *overview* of the visual.
2. Then zero in on the *parts* of the visual. Read all labels, and note any elements or details that seem important.
3. Now read the *title* of the visual so you're clear on the subject it is covering.
4. Next use the title as your theory and the parts of the visual as clues to detect and specify the *interrelationships* in the graphic.
5. Finally, try to reach a *conclusion* about the visual as a whole. What does it mean? Why was it included in the text? Sum up the message of the visual in just a sentence or two.

Learning the Language of Graphs

What are the most common types of graphs?

You are most likely to encounter three general types of graphs: circle graphs, bar graphs, and line graphs. The purpose of a circle graph is unique, whereas bar and line graphs perform the same basic function.

Decode Circle Graphs

What is the purpose of the circle graph?

The purpose of a circle graph, also known as a pie chart, is to proportionally show the relationship of parts (slices) to a whole (the pie). Although these graphs are relatively rare in highly technical books, they regularly appear in newspapers as well as in textbooks on topics other than mathematics and science. The popularity of the circle graph is mainly due to its simplicity. In most cases, you can tell at a glance the proportions the graph illustrates—that is, the various-sized slices of the pie. For example, in Figure 8.2, the circle graph gives you a clear picture of the population distribution of the United States.

Decode Bar and Line Graphs

What is the purpose of a bar or line graph?

The purpose of a bar or line graph is to illustrate the relationship of a set of dependent variables to a set of independent variables. Variables are numbers that can change. For example, the number we use to refer to the year is a variable. It increases by one every twelve months. Population is another variable. It changes when someone is born or dies, when someone becomes a citizen, or when someone leaves the country. Years and dates in general are called independent variables because they change on their own. The population of the United States does not influence the fact that a new year begins every 365 or 366 days. Quantities such as population are called dependent variables because

Figure 8.2
U.S. Population by Region
Circle graphs (pie charts) show the relationship of several parts to a whole.
Source: U.S. Census Bureau, Census 2000.

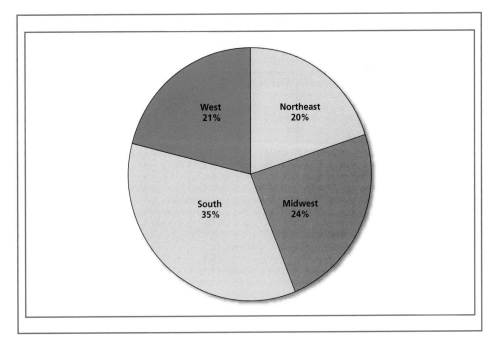

How do bar and line graphs differ?

their change occurs in relation to another variable, such as the year. For example, we measure the changes of U.S. population every ten years when the census is taken.

Although bar and line graphs both show how a dependent variable such as population increases or decreases in relation to an independent variable such as the year, each takes a slightly different approach. Bar graphs (see Figure 8.3) focus on specific changes; line graphs (see Figure 8.4) illustrate long-term trends. One way to visualize this distinction is to think of bar graphs as snapshots and line graphs as movies. If you were to take successive snapshots of a long jumper, you would have a series of photographs showing successive stages of the jump. If you were to film the same jump with a movie camera, you'd have a continuous record of the entire jump. Figure 8.5 illustrates this idea.

What are the relative strengths and weaknesses of bar and line graphs?

Like snapshots and movies, each type of graph has strengths. Bar graphs are good for comparing the individual sizes or amounts of items, and they provide clear comparisons of several sets of data at once. Line graphs are useful for showing changes in data over long periods of time. For instance, if you wanted to examine the country's population increase over a brief period of time or if you wanted to compare it with the population of another country, you would probably use a bar graph. Figure 8.3 shows that the growth in U.S. population was relatively steady from 1950 through 2000, whereas Canada's population growth surged during the 1950s and 1960s and then again at the end of the twentieth century. But if you wanted to show the percentage increase in U.S.

Figure 8.3

Population Growth in the United States and Canada, 1950–2000

Bar graphs show sizes of individual items and illustrate comparisons.

Sources: U.S. Census Bureau; Statistics Canada.

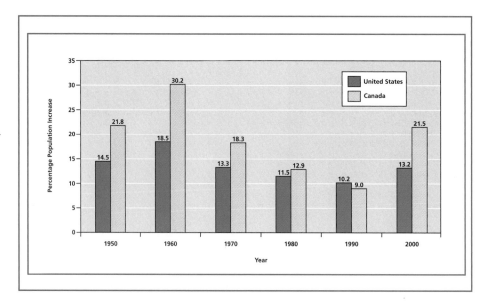

Figure 8.4

Percentage Increase in U.S. Population, 1800–2000
Line graphs show long-term trends in data.

Source: U.S. Census Bureau.

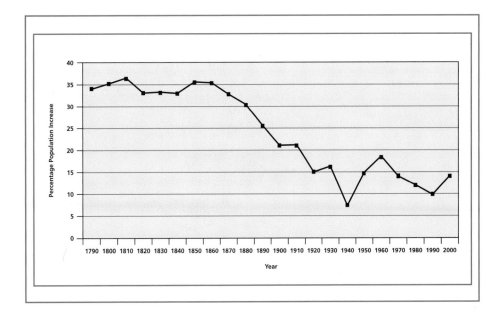

Figure 8.5

Snapshots Versus Movies: Bar Graphs and Line Graphs
A bar graph can be compared to a set of snapshots, whereas a line graph is more like a movie.

Source: Track and Field Omnibook, Fourth Ed., 1985, by Ken Doherty, Tafnews Press (Track and Field News), Mountain View, Calif. Reprinted with permission.

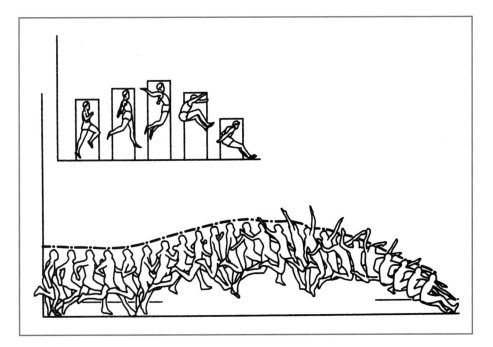

Figure 8.6
Using the OPTIC System to Analyze a Graph

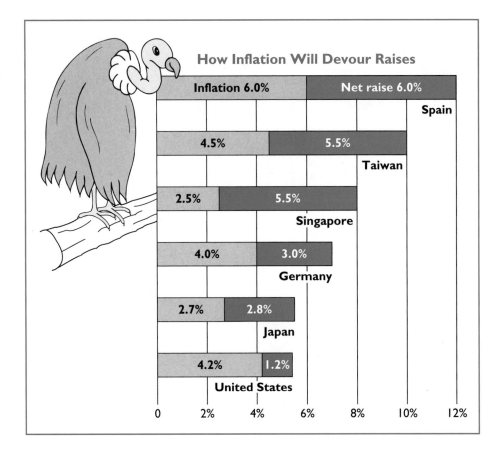

How Inflation Will Devour Raises

population since the eighteenth century, a line graph would be a better visual. Figure 8.4 shows that the growth in U.S. population has generally slowed since 1850.

What should you do once you understand the language of graphs?

Regardless of whether the graphic is a circle, bar, or line graph, once you understand the language of the particular graph, you can methodically extract its meaning in the same way you would with a picture or diagram—by using the OPTIC system. Figure 8.6 analyzes a graph using this system.

Watching Out for Distorted Data

How can you avoid being misled by pictures?

Pictures, like words, can occasionally be misleading. Whereas many readers have learned to detect deceptive phrases or sentences, not everyone is quite as sophisticated about detecting distortions in pictures or other kinds of graphic materials.

Figure 8.6.
Using the OPTIC System to Analyze a Graph—_continued_

OVERVIEW
A bar graph with a vulture in the corner and six bars moving from longest to shortest with each bar divided into plain and hatched lined sections and marked with percentages.

PARTS
- The six bars represent six countries: Spain, Taiwan, Singapore, Germany, Japan, and the United States.
- Percentages run horizontally at the bottom of the graph—from 0% to 12%—and represent percentage increases in salaries.
- The total length of each bar represents raises, the shaded section stands for the rate of inflation, the colored part of the bar is the net raise—the raise that remains after inflation.

TITLE
* "How Inflation Will Devour Raises"
The word _devour_ seems to imply that inflation has a major impact on raises. The vulture is being used to make the point more dramatic and perhaps make the graph more interesting.

INTERRELATIONSHIPS
- Spain appears due for the largest raises, while the United States will be receiving the smallest.
- Half of the raises in Spain will be "devoured" by inflation, while roughly four-fifths of American raises will be lost to inflation.
- Of those countries listed, Spain has the highest rate of inflation (6%), while Singapore (2.5%) has the lowest rate.
- The net raises in Taiwan and Singapore are identical (5.5%), even though their rates of inflation are very different (4.5% and 2.5%).

CONCLUSION
With the exception of Singapore, inflation will devour a large portion—close to half and more—of anticipated raises. The United States is the hardest hit of all the countries represented in the graph, retaining only 1.2% of a 5.4% raise after inflation.

When you consider a graph, illustration, or chart, it helps to do so with a critical eye, paying particular attention to the format, the scale, and the overall context.

Format

How does the way that data are formatted affect their meaning?

Factual data—especially statistics—can be placed in graphic formats that distort the information. The book _How to Lie with Statistics_ exposes some of the devious tricks that are used and is also fun to read.[2] For example, you should be wary of

[2]Darrell Huff, _How to Lie with Statistics_ (New York: W. W. Norton, 1993).

the word *average*, and you should try to find the highest and lowest figures that went into each average. Two companies may have an average salary of $29,000. But if the range of salaries in one company is from $6,000 to $90,000, and the range in the other company is from $20,000 to $35,000, the salary policies of the two companies are quite different.

Scale

What effect does scale have on a graphic?

Don't be overly impressed by the steepness of the lines in graphs. Look at the side of every graph to find the scale—the value of each increment. Units of $100 can make a line much steeper than units of $1,000. Always convert what you see into words; otherwise you'll remember the steepness or flatness but not the real information that is being presented.

Context

How does context affect the meaning of a graphic?

Remember that visual relationships can be tricky. The frame around a diagram can actually change the way you see the diagram. For example, this is a diamond-shaped figure:

But notice that when the same figure is placed in a frame,

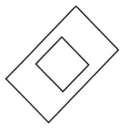

it looks like a square. The size and shape of a chart or graph can also affect what you see. Data that may be quite neutral or ordinary can be made to appear startling by the form and scale of the graphic. If you read graphics carefully, you'll see them properly, rather than as someone else may expect—or want—you to see them.

Writing in Pictures

How do you write in pictures?

We now know that reading a visual means studying a diagram or a graph and turning its message into a sentence or two. When you write in pictures, you simply reverse the process. You convert the sentences you've read or heard into a diagram or graph.

If the information you encounter is concrete, your task is fairly simple. For instance, you can turn a description of a computer modem into a diagram by using that description as directions for your sketch (see Figure 8.7). If, however, the ideas you read or hear are more abstract, such as information about the characteristics of amphibians, your approach needs to be a bit more involved. Instead of drawing sketches of the animals, which doesn't tell you much about their characteristics, you need to create a concept map. Although your approach to abstract ideas is different from your approach to concrete ones, your goal is the same: to turn something you can read into something you can see (see Figure 8.8).

Adding Illustrations to Your Notes

When should you add illustrations to your notes?

As you read your textbook or go over your lecture notes, don't just jot down the key ideas in words; sketch some of them as well. In some subjects this sketching will come naturally. Science courses, for example, are full of information that can be drawn. The parts of a one-celled organism or the connections in a computer network are much easier to understand if you put little diagrams of them in your notes. Sometimes the drawing is done for you. If the instructor puts a sketch on the board or the textbook author includes diagrams in the chapter, add these pictures to your notes in the same way that you would jot down important examples. When a drawing doesn't exist, make one of your own.

What should you do in subjects where elements aren't easily drawn?

A history course may not feature easily drawn elements, but it does include plenty of concrete data that can be translated into picture form. A series of important dates, for example, can be turned into a timeline, and individual historical facts can be visualized almost as easily.

Here is an example of how words can be converted into a picture. The following paragraph describes an experiment conducted by the English physicist and chemist Michael Faraday (1791–1867):

In 1831, Michael Faraday, one of Britain's greatest scientists, did the experiments which completely demonstrated the close relationship between electricity and magnetism. One of his famous experiments was to take a coil of wire and connect the

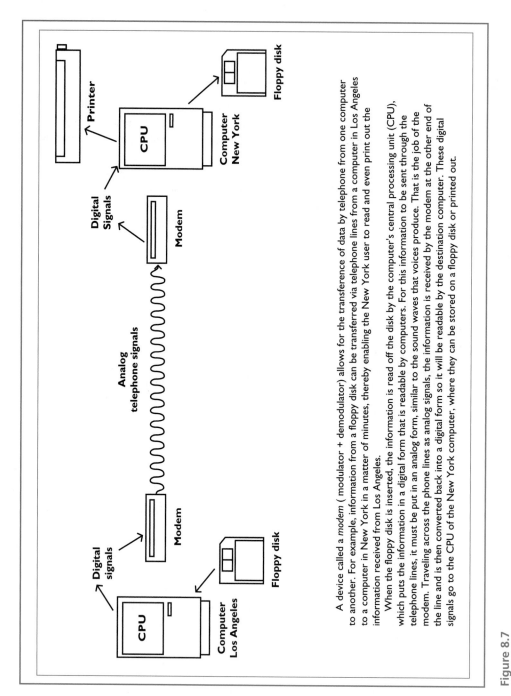

A device called a *modem* (modulator + demodulator) allows for the transference of data by telephone from one computer to another. For example, information from a floppy disk can be transferred via telephone lines from a computer in Los Angeles to a computer in New York in a matter of minutes, thereby enabling the New York user to read and even print out the information received from Los Angeles.

When the floppy disk is inserted, the information is read off the disk by the computer's central processing unit (CPU), which puts the information in a digital form that is readable by computers. For this information to be sent through the telephone lines, it must be put in an analog form, similar to the sound waves that voices produce. That is the job of the modem. Traveling across the phone lines as analog signals, the information is received by the modem at the other end of the line and is then converted back into a digital form so it will be readable by the destination computer. These digital signals go to the CPU of the New York computer, where they can be stored on a floppy disk or printed out.

Figure 8.7

A Diagram Based on Text Information

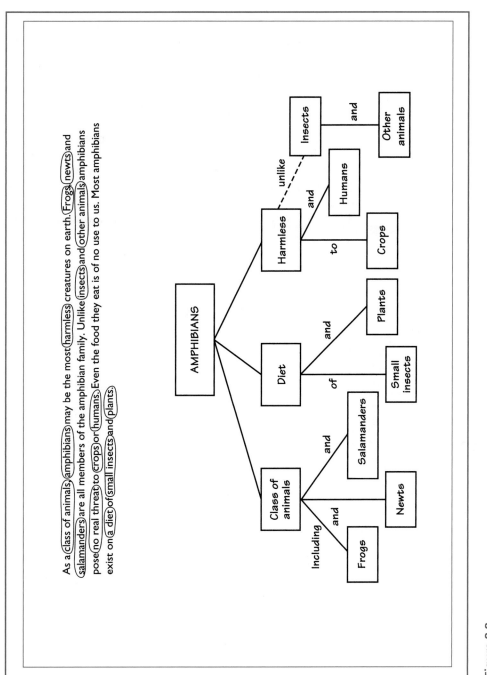

As a class of animals, amphibians may be the most harmless creatures on earth. Frogs, newts and salamanders are all members of the amphibian family. Unlike insects and other animals amphibians pose no real threat to crops or humans. Even the food they eat is of no use to us. Most amphibians exist on a diet of small insects and plants.

AMPHIBIANS

Harmless — unlike — Insects — and — Other animals

Harmless — and — Humans

Harmless — to — Crops

Diet — and — Plants

Diet — of — Small insects

Class of animals — and — Salamanders

Class of animals — Including — and — Frogs

Newts

Figure 8.8
A Concept Map of Text Information

ends across an instrument capable of measuring tiny currents. By quickly pushing a bar magnet through the coil he was able to produce a small current in the coil and to measure that current. What he was really doing was to change the strength of the magnetic field in the coil by inserting and removing the magnet. The more rapidly he changed the field the more current he could generate.[3]

Figure 8.9 is an example of how one student converted this descriptive paragraph into a diagram, which helped the student not only to understand the described process but to visualize and remember it as well. If a question about Faraday's experiment appeared on a test, it is not hard to imagine how well a student with this picture in mind would do.

You don't have to be Michelangelo or Leonardo da Vinci to draw diagrams in your notes. The important point is to tap into the right side of your brain. With your full mind at work, you will increase your brain power, regardless of whether your drawing looks like doodling or a priceless work of art.

Why is it helpful to add diagrams to your notes?

Turning Abstract Ideas into Maps

What are concept maps used for?

Abstract ideas don't lend themselves quite as easily to diagrams as do concrete ideas. For example, you can draw a rough sketch of farmland, a field worker, and a tractor, but how would you diagram economic production, a procedure that involves all three? That's where a concept map comes in. Concept maps

Figure 8.9
A Descriptive Paragraph Made Visual

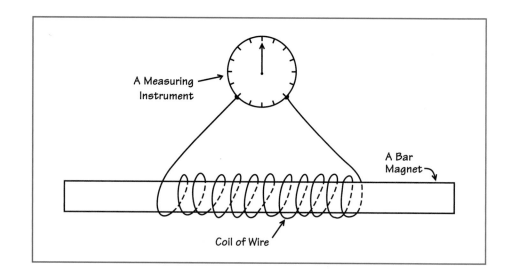

[3]J. D. Jukes, *Man-Made Sun* (New York: Abelard-Schuman, 1959), p. 33.

are used to diagram abstract processes and relationships. Drawing a concept map based on a set of abstract ideas is similar to drawing a road map based on a set of hard-to-follow directions. In both cases, the map will make the idea easier to visualize, understand, and remember.

Here are the steps for mapping a textbook passage:

1. Determine the topic of the passage you are planning to map. Put the topic at the top of a sheet of paper, and circle it.
2. Go back to the passage and circle or list the concepts involved.
3. Find the two to five most important concepts on your list. These are the key concepts. List them on your map in a row beneath the circled topic. Circle these key concepts as well.
4. Cluster the remaining concepts under the key concepts to which they relate. After adding them to your map beneath the key concepts they support, circle these new concepts.
5. Draw lines connecting related concepts. Along each line, you may want to specify the relationship that connects the concepts.

Master the Map

Drawing a concept map, like taking notes, does a great deal to help cement important ideas and concepts in your memory. And like your notes, your maps can be mastered. Although there are several systems for mastering your map, the simplest and most effective is to look it over carefully and then, without peeking at the original passage, write a short summarizing paragraph explaining the key concepts and how they relate. The result is like writing your own textbook. You start out with the same concepts the textbook uses, but the words are your own instead of the author's. Figure 8.10 shows a map and its summary paragraph.

Concept maps are flexible study aids. They don't lock you into a single method or approach. Here are some additional ways you can use a concept map to improve your studying:

Use the concepts for recitation. Take one circled concept from your map and explain out loud and without looking at the rest of the map how it relates to the map as a whole.

Add to your map. New ideas frequently connect with old information. Take a moment to think about how the concepts in your map relate to ideas you already know. Add the appropriate old ideas to your map, and connect them to what you've just learned.

Redraw your map. There's no right or wrong way to draw a concept map. The same information can be mapped in a number of ways. Look over your original

What is the simplest way to master a map?

What are some other ways to use a concept map?

Figure 8.10
Mastering a Concept Map

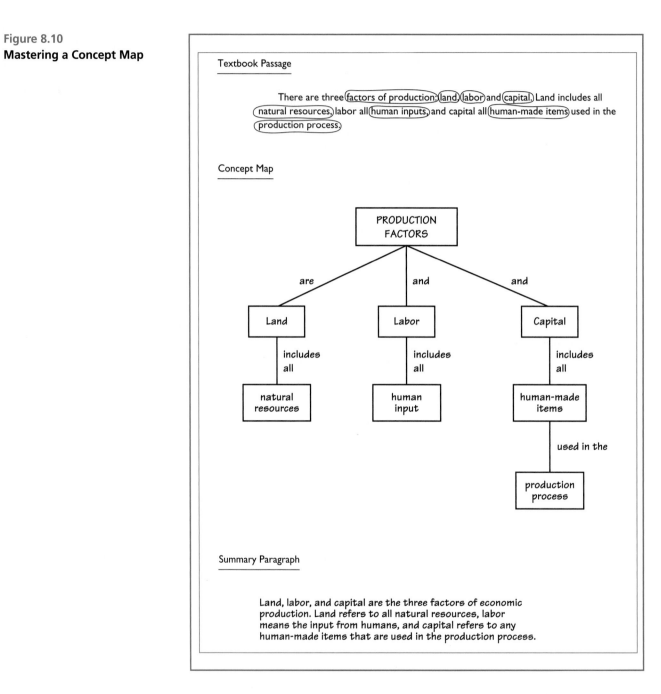

Textbook Passage

There are three factors of production: land, labor and capital. Land includes all natural resources, labor all human inputs, and capital all human-made items used in the production process.

Concept Map

PRODUCTION FACTORS

are — Land
and — Labor
and — Capital

Land: includes all — natural resources
Labor: includes all — human input
Capital: includes all — human-made items

human-made items: used in the — production process

Summary Paragraph

Land, labor, and capital are the three factors of economic production. Land refers to all natural resources, labor means the input from humans, and capital refers to any human-made items that are used in the production process.

map, and see if you can organize the concepts a little differently. Looking at the information from a different angle often makes some of the concepts clearer. Also, creating a second map of the same information means that the concepts will be stored in your memory an additional time.

Use Maps for Summaries

How can you use a concept map to summarize key concepts?

Although a map of every concept in a chapter would be huge, and a concept map for even a small book would likely be about the size of a billboard, you can use mapping to summarize the key concepts from chapters, articles, and books. The procedure for summarizing information with a concept map is identical to the one you just followed for mapping a single paragraph from your textbook or section from your notes, except that you cover more ground. Instead of containing information from one paragraph, a summary map may draw from dozens of paragraphs. For this reason, summary maps do not contain as much detail as maps created for more specific sections. The maps at the beginning of each chapter in this book are good examples of summary maps. Notice how they include the most important concepts from the chapters they illustrate.

Use Maps as Planning Strategies

How can you use concept maps to help plan a paper or report?

Concept maps can be used to plan a paper or an oral report. First, write the topic you've chosen at the top of a blank sheet of paper. Then, after you have done a bit of preliminary research and have come up with several main concepts, add these to your map, and connect them to your topic with lines. Finally, fill out your map with any supporting ideas you've acquired, making sure to cluster them under the main concepts to which they refer. Once again, draw connecting lines to show how each piece fits into the puzzle. Here is the step-by-step procedure for mapping a paper or an oral report:

1. Do some preliminary research on your subject.
2. Write your topic at the top of a blank sheet of paper.
3. Add two to five main ideas that you plan to cover, and link them to the topic on your map.
4. Cluster subideas under the main ideas that they support. Link them with lines.
5. Survey your map in order to decide whether its branches are evenly developed.
6. If your map seems lopsided, rearrange it or add information so that all its branches are balanced.
7. Use your map as a guide to do in-depth research on the concepts you plan to cover. Add to your map if necessary.

How do concept maps differ
from conventional outlines?

At the very least, your finished concept map can function as an outline, supplying you with all the main ideas and subideas you plan to include in your paper or oral report. In addition, the map can be used as a guide to help you do your more detailed research as systematically as possible.

Unlike a conventional outline, a map enables you to *see* your structure instead of just reading it. In general, a well-organized report looks fairly symmetrical when you map it. If your map has a lopsided appearance, your report may need to be more evenly balanced. Adding some concepts or clustering your existing topics in a different arrangement should do the trick. Once you're happy with the look of your map, it can serve as a plan for further research.

FINAL WORDS

For a great many people, visual analysis is an untapped resource. Oh, we certainly do plenty of visual thinking, as we've seen. But few of us devote the time and attention to developing sophisticated skills in reading and writing pictures that we do almost instinctively with words. If you think about it, reading and writing words have been a mandatory element of your education. But other than art classes, which place an emphasis on aesthetics, not meaning, there are no real visual equivalents to the elementary school reading group or to those early lessons in penmanship. It's true that we've had a head start with words, but that doesn't mean we shouldn't build up our visual abilities. Like boosting your vocabulary, honing your visual skills will strengthen your thinking. And as someone who thinks both in words and in pictures, you're bound to be a better balanced, more successful student.

HAVE YOU MISSED SOMETHING?

SENTENCE COMPLETION   *Complete the following sentences with one of the three words listed below each sentence*

1. The left side of the brain tends to be _____.

   ethical   creative   analytical

2. Words and pictures both can be seen as _____.

   text   codes   challenging

3. When presented as a map, a well-organized report is usually _____.

   detailed   unbalanced   symmetrical

MATCHING

In each blank space in the left column, write the letter preceding the phrase in the right column that matches the left item best.

_____ 1. Circle graphs

_____ 2. Words

_____ 3. Pictures

_____ 4. OPTIC

_____ 5. Dual coding

_____ 6. Snapshots

_____ 7. Movies

_____ 8. Concept maps

a. Idea of storing information as both words and pictures

b. Used to diagram abstract relationships and processes

c. Illustrate the relationship of parts to a whole

d. One way to think of the function of line graphs

e. Normally fall under the jurisdiction of the brain's right side

f. Usually fall under the jurisdiction of the brain's left side

g. One way to think of the function of bar graphs

h. Method for systematically analyzing graphic materials

TRUE-FALSE

Write T *beside the* true *statements and* F *beside the* false *statements.*

_____ 1. Although we may think visually, all of our communication is done with words.

_____ 2. Line graphs can provide an effective illustration of long-term trends.

_____ 3. The OPTIC system can be used for analyzing both pictures and graphs.

_____ 4. Artistic ability isn't necessary for drawing pictures to help you study.

_____ 5. History courses don't contain information that can be translated into picture form.

MULTIPLE CHOICE

Choose the word or phrase that completes each sentence most accurately, and circle the letter that precedes it.

1. Using both sides of the brain
   a. results in conflicting information.
   b. can improve comprehension and memory.
   c. requires artistic training or ability.
   d. none of the above.

2. A circle graph is also known as a
   a. Venn diagram.
   b. color wheel.
   c. pie chart.
   d. lookup table.

3. The simplest way to master a concept map is by
   a. erasing it.
   b. summarizing it.
   c. highlighting it.
   d. redrawing it.

4. Summary maps should be drawn with
   a. less detail than standard maps.
   b. black marking pen.
   c. independent variables.
   d. concrete concepts.

5. When used with a paper or an oral report, a map can function as
   a. a guide for research.
   b. a visual outline.
   c. a taking-off point.
   d. all of the above.

SHORT ANSWER   *Supply a brief answer for each of the following items.*

1. Contrast the functions of the left and right sides of the brain.
2. Outline the steps involved in the OPTIC system.
3. Explain the effect that scale can have on a line graph.
4. Discuss methods for mastering a concept map.

WORDS IN CONTEXT

From the three choices beside each numbered item, select the one that most nearly expresses the meaning of the italicized word in the quote. Make a light check mark (✔) next to your choice.

We have lived through the age of big industry and the age of the giant corporation. But I believe that this is the age of the *entrepreneur.*

—Ronald Reagan (1911–), fortieth president of the United States

1. *entrepreneur*   entertainer   computer whiz   impresario

The executive's chief business is to organize, *deputize,* and supervise.
—George Ripley (1802–1880), American literary critic

2. *deputize*   enforce   delegate   regulate

Those who make the worst use of their time are the first to complain of its *brevity.*
—Jean de La Bruyère (1645–1696), French writer and moralist

3. *brevity*   briefness   dullness   wastefulness

Nothing is given so *profusely* as advice.
—François, Duc de La Rochefoucauld (1613–1680), French writer

4. *profusely*   expertly   belatedly   abundantly

THE WORD HISTORY SYSTEM

Congregation
a flock

congregation con'-gre-ga'-tion *n.* 1. A body of assembled people or things; a gathering. 2. Those who regularly worship at a specific church or synagogue.

The symbolism so beautifully expressed in David's twenty-third Psalm is fully justified by the origins of our words *congregation* and *pastor.* Latin *grex, gregis,* means "flock" or "herd" and is the basis for the word *congregare,* meaning "to gather into a flock." Derived from this is the Latin *congregatio,* which is taken into English as *congregation.* The word *pastor* carries out the same symbolism. Latin *pascere* means "to pasture," "to feed." The past participle *pastum* gives Latin *pastor,* "a shepherd" or "one who has the care of flocks." Later, the figurative meaning developed, "a keeper of souls" or "minister of the church." The two words, therefore, preserve the symbolism of the shepherd and his flock as applied to the *pastor* and his *congregation.*

Reprinted by permission. From *Picturesque Word Origins* © 1933 by G. & C. Merriam Co. (now Merriam-Webster, Incorporated).

PART

III

Note-Taking Skills

9   Adopting a Note-Taking Mindset

10   Taking Effective Notes

11   Mastering Your Notes

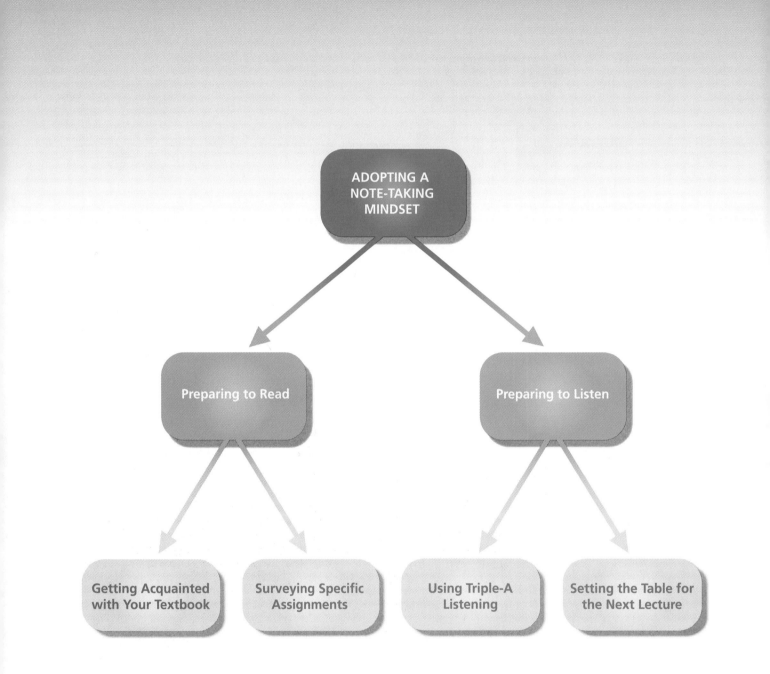

Adopting a Note-Taking Mindset

Begin a match or run a race without warming up first, and you won't be doing yourself much good. You may even be doing some harm. It makes sense to warm up, psych up, and just plain be ready before you undertake anything of importance. Note taking is certainly no exception. This chapter talks about:

- **Preparing to Read**
- **Preparing to Listen**
- **Surveying Specific Assignments**
- **Setting the Table for the Next Lecture**

How do you give your note taking real value?

Note taking doesn't work in isolation. You need to build a background and create a context in order for the sentences you jot down or the paragraphs you mark up to have real value. If you don't speak the language of your textbook or know the way to listen effectively to a lecture, it's unlikely that you'll be in a position to take meaningful notes. And even if you do, you still need to take your preparations one step further by previewing each textbook assignment before you begin reading or by setting the table for an upcoming lecture. The time you invest at the beginning will strengthen your memories throughout and make you a much better student in the end.

Preparing to Read

What's the best way to prepare for reading?

Because you and your textbooks are going to spend a quarter or a semester together, you'd better become friends. How? By getting acquainted with the textbook as a whole and by surveying specific assignments as they arise.

Getting Acquainted with Your Textbook

What's the first thing you should do when you get a new textbook?

What steps can you take to become acquainted with a textbook?

Not all textbooks are alike. Most have distinct styles of organizing their ideas and communicating their information. It's important to learn a textbook's language before you begin trying to understand what it has to say.

Give yourself enough time to understand how each of your textbooks works by buying them as soon as you've registered. This is a wise policy even if your school allows a period in which you can attend many courses before deciding on a final few. Don't wait until the first day of class. Get a head start by reading the tables of contents, prefaces, introductions, and other up-front material in all your books. Underline important words and sentences, and make notes in the margins. Look at the pictures, tables, and diagrams; read the captions. Read chapter titles, headings, and subheadings that interest you. This will give you a good idea of what the book is like and where you will be going during the semester. Later, you'll be glad you did, for you'll be able to see how the various parts of the course fit together.

Read the Prefatory Material

How does a book's prefatory material differ from the rest of its pages?

Although most textbooks are written in a serious, scholarly tone, in the prefatory material—which may be called "Preface," "To the Student," or something similar—the authors often take a more personal approach to their subjects and their readers than they do in the body of the text. This provides an opportunity to meet the authors as people and to get comfortable with them. Once you do, you'll find that you can converse and even argue with them as you read the text. Now and then, you'll find yourself saying, "No, I don't agree with that statement," or "What do you mean by that?"

In the prefatory material you can also find valuable information about the concepts and content of the book. For instance, if you began this book by reading the "To The Student" section, you know the purpose and use of the questions that appear in the margins of every chapter. If, on the other hand, you skipped over this part, you may have squandered a valuable component of the book. In prefaces you can find valuable information such as (1) what the author's objective is and is not, (2) the organizational plan of the book, (3) how and why the book is different from other books about the same subject, (4) the author's qualifications for writing the book, and often (5) an explanation of any supplementary learning aids. As a practical exercise, you might find it interesting to read the preface of this book, if you have not already done so. See how much you can gain toward understanding not only the book but also the authors.

What sort of valuable information does a preface typically contain?

The Author's Objective　Learning the author's objective—the purpose or goal he or she meant to achieve—enables you to read and interpret the text appropriately. For instance, the authors of *American Government* state their objective succinctly:

How does learning the author's objective help?

> In preparing every edition of *American Government*, including this new sixth edition, we have committed ourselves to two major goals: (1) to write a concise yet comprehensive textbook that (2) helps students think critically about the U.S. political system.[1]

In a single sentence, they tell you straight off what to expect and what particular philosophy they will be following.

The Organizational Plan of the Book　Knowing the book's organizational plan is like having a road map. You know not only what the authors are doing but also where they are going. In the following example, you learn of the carefully organized introduction of topics as well as the self-contained, flexible nature of the individual chapters:

Why is it helpful to know a book's organizational plan?

> The contents have been arranged so that as each new topic is introduced, it is fully explained and its fundamentals are thoroughly examined before commencing further study. For example, Chapter 13, Investment Fundamentals and Portfolio Management, precedes chapters on specific types of investments. In addition, not only does each chapter follow an overall logical sequence, but each is also a complete

[1]Alan R. Gitelson, Robert L. Dudley, and Melvin J. Dubnick, *American Government*, 6th ed. (Boston: Houghton Mifflin, 2001), p. xv.

entity. The chapters can therefore be rearranged to follow any instructor's developmental sequence without losing students' comprehension.[2]

What is the advantage of knowing why a book is unique?

How and Why the Book Is Different   Recognizing what makes the textbook unique enables you to read with greater awareness and comprehension and to avoid the trap of thinking the book is "more of the same old stuff." In this case, the author chooses to reinforce the unique nature of his textbook by placing this paragraph in boldface:

The text you are holding in your hands is literally the product of the research program undertaken in our laboratory. I have had opportunities to present these data at professional conferences and am encouraged by the responses I have received from course instructors. As one reviewer of the book put it, "Finally there is a text that uses psychology to teach psychology."[3]

Why do writers want you to know they are experts?

The Author's Qualifications   Writers usually try in some subtle way to let the reader know that their book is written by an expert on the subject and that therefore the information is trustworthy and credible. Note in the following example how the authors allude to their "considerable experience" while explaining their book's philosophy:

It is our conviction, based on considerable experience in introducing large numbers of students to the broad sweep of civilization, that a book reflecting current trends can excite readers and inspire a renewed interest in history and the human experience.[4]

What does the prefatory material tell you about learning aids?

Supplementary Learning Aids   Today's textbook is often one component of a larger package of learning aids. The prefatory material generally names these aids and tells how they'll benefit you. In addition to in-text features, supplementary materials such as workbooks, study guides, software, Web sites, and videos are often available. Reading the introductory material will alert you to the presence of these features and ancillary materials, as you can see from the following example:

[2]E. Thomas Garman and Raymond E. Forgue, *Personal Finance*, 7th ed. (Boston: Houghton Mifflin, 2003), p. xxviii.

[3]Jeffrey S. Nevid, *Psychology: Concepts and Applications* (Boston: Houghton Mifflin, 2003), p. xviii.

[4]John P. McKay, Bennett D. Hill, John Buckler, and Patricia Buckley Ebrey, *A History of World Societies*, 5th ed. (Boston: Houghton Mifflin, 2000), p. xxvii.

The teaching package for the fifth edition includes the *Instructor's Resource Manual with Test Questions, Case Teaching Guide*, a computerized test bank, a videotape with instructor's guide, PowerPoint slides, and student and instructor web sites, which are new to this edition.[5]

Read the Introduction

What is the role of a book's introduction?

While the prefatory material often supplies a glimpse of the author's personality, the introduction provides a preview of the book itself. The introduction is the book's showcase. It is designed not only to introduce a book, but also to sell it. Authors and publishers both know that this is the place prospective customers often go to decide whether a book is worth reading and worth buying. As a result, the introduction is often especially well written and inviting.

Figure 9.1 is a densely packed introduction containing information of great and immediate value for the sharper reading of textbooks. It is from a book titled *Six-Way Paragraphs.*[6] The book's sole purpose is to teach students how to spot main ideas. One hundred paragraphs are provided for practice. To prepare students for such practice, the introduction strives to explain the ins and outs of the paragraphs found in textbooks. As you read it, be aware not only of *what* the writer says but also of *how* he says it and his *purpose* for saying it.

Preview from Front to Back

What can you learn from a book's table of contents?

After you've read the introductory material, survey the rest of the book. Begin by scanning the table of contents (TOC). It lists the parts, the chapters, and sometimes the major headings within each chapter. Some books, such as this one, actually have two TOCs, an abbreviated one that supplies the part and chapter names and a more detailed table of contents that lists the names and page references of sections and subsections in addition to those for the chapters and parts. General or detailed, the TOC is designed to show the overall organization of the book and how the chapter topics relate to one another. It also indicates whether the book contains extra material: appendixes, glossaries, bibliographies or references, and indexes.

What sort of valuable information can you glean from a book's extra sections?

Now turn to the back of the book and look at these extra sections. Appendixes contain additional information such as tables and graphs, documents, or details about specific aspects of a subject. Glossaries are specialized dictionaries of terms common to the subject the book discusses. Bibliographies and references list the sources the authors consulted in writing the book and can point you in the direction of further reading. Indexes—alphabetical listings of

[5]Jean-Pierre Jeannet and H. David Hennessey, *Global Marketing Strategies,* 5th ed. (Boston: Houghton Mifflin, 2001), p. xviii.

[6]Walter Pauk, *Six-Way Paragraphs* (Providence, RI: Jamestown Publishers, 1974).

Figure 9.1
The Content of an Introduction
Source: Walter Pauk, *Six-Way Paragraphs* (Providence, RI: Jamestown Publishers, 1974), pp. 7–8. Reprinted by permission.

what: wants you to focus on the paragraph – unit

how: brings you and the writer together

purpose: wants you to look at the paragraph through the eyes of the writer

The paragraph! That's the working-unit of both writer and reader. The writer works hard to put meaning into the paragraph; the reader works hard to take meaning out of it. Though they work at opposite tasks, the work of each is closely related. Actually, to understand better the job of the reader, one must first understand better the job of the writer. So, let us look briefly at the writer's job.

what: each paragraph has but one main idea

how: shows you how a writer thinks

purpose: to convince you to look for only one idea per paragraph because writers follow this rule

To make his meaning clear, a writer knows that he must follow certain basic principles. First, he knows that he must develop only one main idea per paragraph. This principle is so important that he knows it backward, too. He knows that he must not try to develop two main ideas in the same, single paragraph.

what: the topic of the main idea is in the topic sentence, which is usually the first one

how: the writer needs to state a topic sentence to keep his own writing clear and under control

purpose: to instill confidence in you that the topic sentence is an important tool in a writer's kit and convince you it is there, so, look for it!

The next important principle he knows is that the topic of each main idea must be stated in a topic sentence and that such a sentence best serves its function by coming at or near the beginning of its paragraph. He knows, too, that the more clearly he can state the topic of his paragraph in an opening sentence, the more effective he will be in developing a meaningful, well-organized paragraph.

what: developing main ideas through supporting material

how: "more to a writer's job," still keeps you in the writer's shoes

purpose: to announce and advance the new step of supporting materials

Now, there is more to a writer's job than just writing paragraphs consisting of only bare topic sentences and main ideas. The balance of his job deals with *developing* each main idea through the use of supporting material that amplifies and clarifies the main idea and many times makes it more vivid and memorable.

Figure 9.1
The Content of an Introduction—*continued*

what: (a) main ideas are often
          supported by examples,
          (b) other supporting
          devices listed

how: still through the
          writer's eyes

purpose: to develop the new idea
          of supporting materals

To support his main ideas, a writer may use a variety of forms. One of the most common forms to support a main idea is the *example*. Examples help to illustrate the main idea more vividly. Other supporting materials are anecdotes, incidents, jokes, allusions, comparisons, contrasts, analogies, definitions, exceptions, logic, and so forth.

what: paragraph contains (a)
          topic sentence, (b) main
          idea, and (c) supporting
          material

how: transfer the knowledge
          from the writer to you,
          the reader

purpose: to summarize all the
          three steps

To summarize, the reader should have learned from the writer that a textbook-type paragraph usually contains these three elements: a topic sentence, a main idea, and supporting material. Knowing this, the reader should use the topic sentence to lead him to the main idea. Once he grasps the main idea, then everything else is supporting material used to illustrate, amplify, and qualify the main idea. So, in the final analysis, the reader must be able to separate the main idea from the supporting material yet see the relationship between them.

significant topics, ideas, and names along with page references that appear at the end of texts—give you a sense of the scope of the book and help you locate specific material quickly.

By familiarizing yourself with your textbook, you not only bolster your background knowledge about the subject; you also become aware of the features of the book you can use throughout the term. As a result, future assignments will be easier and less time consuming, and you'll have a greater chance to master the material.

What is the general advantage of getting to know your textbook?

Surveying Specific Assignments

What is the value of surveying a reading assignment?

Moving systematically through your textbook at the beginning of the semester will give you a strong context and a solid foundation that you can strengthen and further build on by briefly surveying your assignment before you begin reading it.

Why Surveying Is Important

How important is it to survey your assignment first?

A good scholar would no more begin reading a chapter without first skimming it than an automotive engineer would run a car without first greasing it. The grease does not supply the power, but without it the gasoline would not be of much use. If you try to cut corners by skipping the skimming, you will lose time, not save it. If you burrow directly into one paragraph after another, you'll be unearthing one compartmentalized fact after another, but you won't see how those facts relate to each other. Psychologists call this not-seeing-the-big-picture condition *tunnel vision.*

How does surveying make a difference in your reading?

There are three practical ways that surveying can make a real and immediate difference in your reading: by creating a background, by limbering your mind, and by overcoming inertia.

How does surveying create a background?

1. Surveying creates a background.   When you don't have some prior knowledge about the subject matter of an assigned chapter, you read slowly and have difficulty understanding the material. When you come to something that you recognize, your reading speed quickens and your comprehension grows. The difference is your prior knowledge. Surveying counteracts tunnel vision and prepares you for reading by giving you some background information about a chapter.

What are advanced organizers?

According to David P. Ausubel, a learning-theory psychologist, previewing the general content of a chapter creates advance organizers, which help students learn and remember material they later study closely.[7] These familiar landmarks act as topics or categories under which ideas, facts, and details may be clustered. John Livingston Lowes, a professor of literature at Princeton University, characterized such familiar landmarks as *magnetic centers* around which ideas, facts, and details cluster like iron filings around a magnet.

What did Katona's test find about advance organizers?

George Katona, a psychologist, tested the effectiveness of advance organizers with two groups of students. One group was asked to read a selection in which a general principle of economics was stated in the first sentence. The second group was given the same selection, but with the first sentence deleted. When the students in the first group were tested, they not only remembered the specific content of the paragraph better than the second group, but they were able to apply the general principle to all the examples in the selection. Without the first sentence, which was an advance organizer, students in the second group viewed the

[7]John F. Wakefield, *Educational Psychology* (Boston: Houghton Mifflin, 1996), p. 368.

examples as separate, unrelated entities and were unable to see that they could be clustered under the umbrella of a common principle in economics.

What are some examples of the way in which surveying creates a background?

When you skim a chapter, you spot and pick up topics by reading headings and subheadings. You pick up ideas by reading the first and last sentences of paragraphs. You become familiar with the names of people and places by skimming these names. You grasp the general objective of the chapter by reading the introductory paragraph, and you get an overview by reading the summarizing paragraph at the end of the chapter. All of these elements combine to provide the background you need for strengthening your memory and serve as a foundation for learning that lasts. Of course, it's unlikely that you'll know any of these facts and ideas cold after the first go-round. But when you encounter them again during your careful reading, you will recognize them, and this familiarity will give you confidence and understanding.

How does surveying compare to an athlete's pregame warm-up?

2. Surveying limbers the mind.   For an athlete, a pregame warm-up limbers the muscles as well as the psyche and brain. An athlete knows that success comes from the coordination of smoothly gliding muscles, a positive attitude, and a concentrating mind. The prestudy survey of a textbook achieves for the scholar what the pregame warm-up achieves for the athlete.

How does surveying overcome inertia?

3. Surveying overcomes mental inertia.   How often have you said, with impatience and exasperation, "C'mon. Let's get started!" Getting started is hard. According to Newton's First Law of Motion (also known as the Law of Inertia), "A body in motion tends to remain in motion; a body at rest tends to remain at rest." Many students find it difficult to open a textbook and begin to study. If you are one of them, use surveying to ease yourself into studying. Surveying does the job: It gets you started.

Do you need to survey the entire chapter before you begin reading?

Although surveying is essential in successfully completing a textbook assignment, you need not always survey an entire chapter as the first step. You may begin by surveying the first part before you read it. Later, as you work your way through the chapter, you may want to skim further ahead, page by page, as you read and study to understand. Whether you survey your assignment all at once or in chunks, it's a step you don't want to skip.

How to Survey an Assignment

What is the advantage of previewing your assignments?

Surveying specific assignments allows you to overcome inertia, delve into the text, and get a sense of the larger picture into which you can fit specific ideas and facts. When previewing, you can use any or all of the following techniques.

How should you think about a chapter's title?

Think About the Title   Take a few moments to reflect on the chapter's title. Is its meaning obvious? If not, can you guess what the chapter will discuss?

What is the value of reading the introduction and summary first?

Read the Introduction and the Summary   Although they may not be marked as such, textbook chapters frequently include an introductory paragraph, a brief summary at the end, or both. Reading these sections provides advance organizers, which create a framework on which you can build the information in the chapter.

What role do headings and subheadings play in previewing?

Look Over Headings and Subheadings   Flip through the pages and read the headings and subheadings. Notice their hierarchy and sequence. This will provide a big-picture view of where the chapter will take you.

Why should you pay attention to information set apart from the rest of the text?

Note Any Information Set Apart from the Rest of the Text   In general, information that is boxed, boldfaced, bulleted (preceded with dots or squares), screened (printed on a gray or colored background), or otherwise set apart is information that you don't want to miss. Take a moment to look it over now so you will already be familiar with it when you go back to read the chapter completely.

How do visuals help your understanding of a chapter assignment?

Glance at the Visuals   Pictures and graphic materials can provide a distillation of an entire chapter's ideas in less than a page. They can sometimes succinctly express in a small space what may take several paragraphs to explain in words. The concept maps at the start of each chapter in this book, for example, show the chapter at a glance. Other visuals supply vivid and easy-to-understand examples of key points.

Is there a downside to previewing a textbook assignment?

As important and helpful as it is to preview a specific reading assignment, you may still want to limit the amount of time you spend surveying the chapter. After all, your primary purpose is to read and understand the assignment. If you spend too much time preparing to read, you'll run out of time and energy for the actual reading. Or as an old Chinese proverb warns, "Keep sharpening your knife and it will grow dull."

Preparing to Listen

How do you develop good listening habits?

Of the many skills a person needs to learn in this complex world, listening is just about the easiest to acquire. And yet it is a skill that is often overlooked. Figure 9.2 presents a short quiz to help you learn where you stand as a listener. All you need to do is recognize the habits of a poor listener as well as the techniques used by a good listener. Then, knowing the good techniques, apply them without exception in all your daily activities. You can make a fresh and immediate start today by referring to Figure 9.3, which lists the ten most important keys to effective listening.

Figure 9.2

Listening Habits

Source: Adapted from Ralph G. Nichols and Thomas R. Lewis, *Listening and Speaking*, p. 166. Originally published by Wm. C. Brown Group, 1954. Reprinted by permission of the authors.

How often do you find yourself engaging in these ten bad habits of listening? Check the appropriate columns.

How often do you ...	Frequency					
	Almost always	Usually	Sometimes	Seldom	Almost never	Score
Decide that the topic is boring?						
Criticize the speaker?						
Overreact by disagreeing?						
Listen only for bare facts?						
Outline everything?						
Fake attention?						
Yield to distractions?						
Avoid listening to tough technical information?						
Let emotion-laden words arouse personal antagonism?						
Waste thought speed by daydreaming?						
Total score						

Tally your score as follows:

Almost always	2
Usually	4
Sometimes	6
Seldom	8
Almost never	10

Interpret your score as follows:

Below 70	Need training in listening
70 to 90	You listen well
Above 90	Extraordinarily good listener

Figure 9.3
Ten Keys to Effective Listening
Source: Reprinted by permission of Unisys Corporation.

Keys to Effective Listening	The Poor Listener	The Good Listener
1. Find areas of interest	Tunes out dry topics.	Seizes opportunities: "What's in it for me?"
2. Judge content, not delivery	Tunes out if delivery is poor.	Judges content, skips over delivery errors.
3. Hold your fire	Tends to enter into argument.	Doesn't judge until comprehension is complete.
4. Listen for ideas	Listens for facts.	Listens for central themes.
5. Be a flexible note taker	Is busy with form, misses content.	Adjusts to topic and organizational pattern.
6. Work at listening	Shows no energy output, fakes attention.	Works hard; exhibits alertness.
7. Resist distractions	Is distracted easily.	Fights or avoids distractions; tolerates bad habits in others; knows how to concentrate.
8. Exercise your mind	Resists difficult expository material; seeks light, recreational material.	Uses heavier material as exercise for the mind.
9. Keep your mind open	Reacts to emotional words.	Interprets emotional words; does not get hung up on them.
10. Thought is faster than speech; use it	Tends to daydream with slow speakers.	Challenges, anticipates, mentally summarizes, weighs the evidence, listens between the lines to tone of voice.

Using Triple-A Listening

What are the three basic skills of good listening?

Listening is the first step in lecture note taking. Being a good listener means being an active listener. But listening is not the same as hearing. Listening isn't simply a matter of acting as a human microphone and picking up the sound of the lecturer's voice. It is a conscious activity based on three basic skills: *a*ttitude, *a*ttention, and *a*djustment. These skills are known collectively as *triple-A listening*.

A₁: Maintain a Positive Attitude

Why do you need a positive attitude to listen effectively?

You can take many steps to improve your listening, but the primary prerequisite to effective listening is a positive mental attitude. A positive attitude sets the stage for the open-mindedness that is essential to learning and comprehension. As businessman and author Kevin J. Murphy says in *Effective Listening,* "Minds are like parachutes; they only function when open."[8] You must walk into the classroom convinced that the lecturer has something useful to say. If you have any doubts, take a moment to think about the kind of preparation that goes into a typical lecture. The lecturer had to do the searching, reading, selecting, discarding, and organizing of information from dozens of books and other sources—a task that can take hundreds of hours. You can reap the benefits of all that effort in a single lecture.

What can you do to help cultivate a positive attitude?

Cultivating a positive attitude isn't always easy. But it is worth the effort. If you're struggling to give the speaker the benefit of the doubt, try finding areas of interest in what he or she has to say, judge the content of the lecture instead of the delivery, and hold your fire if you're inclined to lash out at those things you don't agree with.

How can you find areas of interest in a "boring" lecture?

Finding Areas of Interest   It doesn't take any talent to tune out a lecture or to brand it as "boring." Anyone can do that. Most speakers work hard to make their lectures informative and interesting. But they can't do it alone. It requires some effort on your part as well. Don't waste your time by ignoring the instructor or by reading your textbook when you should be giving the speaker your full attention. You can usually find an element or an aspect of the lecture topic that appeals to your personal interests. For example, a student who played basketball developed a greater interest in physics when he realized the instructor's discussions of trajectory and momentum could be applied to his foul shots.

What if you can't find anything in the lecture that interests you?

Even if you can't immediately find something about the lecture that interests you, it still makes sense to listen intently, take notes vigorously, and show interest by your facial expression. These outward manifestations of interest will help generate genuine internal interest.

What is the most important aspect of a lecture?

Judging Content, Not Delivery   Listeners are sometimes terribly rude or downright cruel when a lecturer's delivery fails to measure up to some preconceived standard. Keep in mind that great thinkers aren't always excellent orators. Try to approach each lecture with a humane attitude, and concentrate on what the lecturer is saying, not on how it's being said. If you do, you'll emerge from the lecture with a positive self-image. You will also learn something.

[8]Kevin J. Murphy, *Effective Listening: Hearing What People Say and Making It Work for You* (New York: Bantam Books, 1987), p. 28.

What should you do if the lec-
turer says something you don't
agree with?

Holding Your Fire   In college you're bound to hear ideas that are different from or even contrary to those you hold. When this happens, your knee-jerk reaction may be to speak up immediately to defend your position. Hold your fire! Try to listen intently to thoroughly understand the viewpoint expressed by the lecturer. If you shift all your focus to rebutting a point you don't agree with, you'll be unable to concentrate on the rest of the lecture. In a war of words of this type, understanding is often the first casualty.

A_2: Strive to Pay Attention

Why is attention important?

Attention is the path that will lead you into the wonderful state of concentration. Without concentration there is no focus, and without focus there is almost no learning. If you pay attention and concentrate, you will become an active listener able to synthesize new information with facts and ideas you've already known.

How can you build
anticipation?

Attention often thrives on anticipation. Before class, look over your notes from the last lecture, and take a minute to speculate about what your instructor is going to talk about today. If the lectures follow your textbook, peek ahead to see what's coming. Once the lecture starts, let your mind dart ahead (during pauses) to anticipate what's coming next. You'll be alert, engrossed in the material, and concentrating 100 percent.

What should your attention be
focused on?

Of course, as we learned in Chapter 3, you cannot attain concentration by concentrating on concentration. Your attention must focus on the lecture, not on the act of concentration itself. Deep cognition, or deep thinking, is vital. When you hear a lecture, the words enter your short-term memory, where they have to be swiftly processed into ideas. Active listening sets that process in motion. If your instructor's words are not processed through the kind of active listening that attention sets in motion, they will be dumped from short-term memory and gone for good. If you process the words into ideas, in a flash the ideas will be stored in your long-term memory.

How can you foster the kind
of attention that leads to
concentration?

You can foster the kind of attention that leads to concentration and in turn to active listening by focusing on ideas instead of facts, by working to stay fully engaged, by tuning out distractions, and by using the natural lag between speech and thought to forge ahead in your mind in order to consider a speaker's current point and anticipate the next one.

What's the drawback of listen-
ing for facts instead of ideas?

Listening for Ideas   Don't imitate the detective who says, "The facts, ma'am, just stick to the facts." Sure, facts are important. And it's true that they're often what you'll be tested on. But facts in isolation don't hold together well. In order to organize a lecture's information in both your notes and your memory, look to the ideas that lie behind the facts. Strive to uncover the principle or idea that each fact is supporting. Try to see how the pieces of the puzzle fit into the big picture.

How do you work at listening?

Working at Listening   Listening isn't a passive activity; it requires true participation. Good listeners are fully engaged, outwardly calm, but inwardly dynamic; and they sit toward the front of the classroom. While taking notes, the listener may nod in agreement or look quizzical when the presentation becomes unclear. These sorts of gestures aren't just for effect. Such activity actually promotes comprehension and learning by the listener and provides encouragement to the speaker.

What's the best way to resist distractions?

Resisting Distractions   There are distractions aplenty in the classroom: antics of other students, whispering, the speaker's dress and mannerisms, outside noise, and outside views. In some classes, students may actually be browsing the Web or sending instant messages while the lecturer is speaking! The best way to resist distractions and maintain your concentration is to rivet your eyes on the speaker when you have a chance and focus on taking notes the rest of the time. You may also want to consider sitting close to the front. The level of distraction tends to increase as you move farther away from the instructor, especially in large lecture halls.

How can you take advantage of thought speed?

Using Your Thought Speed   In a race of ideas, thought is speedier than speech. Most of us can grasp a point faster than a lecturer can deliver it. This "thought speed" leaves a bit of a lag during which your mind is apt to wander. Rather than using this time to daydream or to dart off on mental side trips, devote it to thinking more deeply about what the lecturer is saying. Mentally enumerate the ideas that have been expressed and summarize them until it's time to shift your focus back to what's being said. Keep alternating in this fashion throughout the lecture.

A_3: Cultivate a Capacity for Adjustment

Why is adjustment so important to active listening?

Even though most speakers try to indicate what they intend to cover in their lectures, you still need to be mentally limber enough to follow a lecture regardless of the direction it may take. Sometimes a speaker says, "This event had three important results," but then discusses four or five. Other times a question from the audience suddenly shifts the speaker's focus. In such cases, you can't simply tune out the parts of the lecture that don't fit with your expectations. You have to be able to "roll with the punches." That's why adjustment is such an important component of active listening. You can cultivate your capacity for adjustment by remaining flexible while taking notes, by exercising your mind by sitting in on subjects that you are unfamiliar with, and by keeping your mind open to ideas and information that you may initially want to tune out.

What is the key to being a flexible note taker?

Being a Flexible Note Taker   Flexibility in note taking depends on informed listening. Informed listening means being able to identify the organizational patterns used by the speaker. Organizational patterns are easily recognizable if you know their basic structures in advance. (A number of the most common organizational patterns are described in Chapter 10.) Once you have detected a pattern, you'll have a framework you can use to anticipate the form of the message and adjust the way you record your notes. Similarly, when the speaker shifts gears and adopts a different pattern, a flexibile note taker should be able to adjust accordingly.

How can you exercise your mind to become a better listener?

Exercising Your Mind   From time to time, try to sit in on lectures in fields that you know very little about. When you do, make a serious effort to follow the lecturer's chain of thoughts and ideas. True, some parts of the lecture may be unintelligible to you, but you're bound to understand other parts of it. Such listening can be hard work, but in the same way that hard work at a gym can strengthen your muscles, the hard work of listening will strengthen your will to concentrate and your power to persist.

How can you prevent highly charged words from interfering with your ability to listen?

Keeping Your Mind Open   It is hard to believe that a single word or phrase can cause an emotional eruption. Among poor listeners, however, that is frequently the case, and even among very good listeners fireworks occasionally go off. Words that are red flags for some listeners include *activist, liberal, conservative, evolution, creationism, feminist, abortion, pro-life,* and *free market.* Dealing with highly charged language is similar to dealing with a fear or phobia. Often, the emotional impact of the words can be decreased through a frank and open discussion. Don't be so inflexible as to totally shut out opposing ideas, as incendiary as they may seem at first. Genuinely listen to the other point of view. You might learn something that you didn't know before.

Setting the Table for the Next Lecture

What information can you use to help prepare for an upcoming lecture?

Once you've cultivated listening skills to build an effective base for comprehending any lecture, you can zero in on the upcoming lecture by marshalling the available information to provide a context for what the speaker is going to talk about. Of course, lectures aren't like textbook chapters; unless they've been written down or recorded already, you can't survey them in advance. But in most courses, there is enough available information supporting the lecture that it should enable you to effectively prepare for it. Each lecture can be viewed as a piece of a puzzle. The more pieces you have in place, the more you know about the shape and size of the pieces that remain. The course syllabus, the notes from your last lecture, and related reading assignments can all function as these puzzle pieces as you prepare for a lecture.

Look Over the Syllabus

How can you use your course syllabus to prepare for an up-coming lecture?

Assuming that your instructor is sticking to the syllabus, you should be able to read the list of lecture topics to get a big-picture sense of where this latest lecture will fit in. Pay especially close attention to the title and description of the previous lecture, the upcoming lecture, and the one that will follow. Encourage active thinking about the lecture topics by transforming each title into a question and then answering your question in cases where the lecture has already been deliv-ered or by speculating on the answer in cases where the lecture is still to come.

Review Your Notes from the Previous Lecture

Why is it helpful to prepare for an upcoming lecture by reviewing your notes from the previous lecture?

Each lecture will normally build on the concepts from the lectures that came before it. Most instructors will assume that you attended, understood, and can remember the previous lecture. After all, time will rarely permit a rehash of ideas that have already been fully explained. Although the upcoming lecture will often have some ties to all the lectures that came before it, the bond will usually be strongest with the most recent one. In fact, depending on the course, the current lecture may simply be a continuation of the previous lecture. In some courses, each lecture is like the next episode of a continuing story. To un-derstand what's going on in Chapter 2 in a novel, you must understand and re-member Chapter 1. Lectures often work in a similar way.

Do the Assigned Reading

How do reading assignments relate to the upcoming lecture?

A course syllabus will often include related reading assignments as well as lec-ture topics. Some instructors will assign readings as background for an upcom-ing lecture. Others will give you readings designed to follow up on what you've just heard and learned in a lecture. In either case, these readings can help pro-vide advance organizers that will make it easier to understand and remember an upcoming lecture.

How can you prepare by using readings assigned before the lecture?

If a reading assignment precedes the lecture.   Skipping the assigned reading can be as bad as skipping the previous lecture. You run the risk of sitting through an hour of discussion on topics that you are unfamiliar with or don't understand. If this happens, the time you spend in the classroom will largely be wasted. If the instructor assigns readings, make sure you do them. And once you've read your assignment, refresh your memory of what you've read by conducting a quick review shortly before the lecture begins. The concepts from the reading will provide advance organizers that will enable you to arrange and better re-member what you learn in the lecture.

How can you prepare by using readings assigned after the lecture?

If a reading assignment follows the lecture.   Most students are too busy to read ahead and complete assignments that aren't due. That's understandable.

Furthermore, future reading assignments may deal with concepts that won't be clear until after you've attended the lecture. Even so, you should be able to skim an upcoming reading assignment without the knowledge and perspective you need to fully understand it. A quick survey of the assignment may prompt more questions than answers, but it will enable you to walk into a lecture with a pretty good idea of the sort of topics the speaker will be covering as well as a broader sense of where the course is heading.

FINAL WORDS

Why should you invest your time in preparing to take notes?

In a sense, note-taking preparation is a kind of investment. It requires you to do some work up-front that seems to take up time, yet yields few or no immediate results. But very few long-term benefits come without initial and sometimes costly investments. As a student, you understand this better than most. You appreciate the fact that the time and tuition you are devoting to your education will pay off in the long run. Apply this same sort of thinking to the preparations you make for taking notes. You'll be glad you did.

HAVE YOU MISSED SOMETHING?

SENTENCE COMPLETION   *Complete the following sentences with one of the three words listed below each sentence.*

1. Effective note taking requires building a background and creating a
   _____.

   context   summary   memory

2. A good listener places great emphasis on the speaker's _____.
   delivery   appearance   ideas

3. In listening to a lecture, attention often thrives on _____.
   appearance   anticipation   agreement

MATCHING   *In each blank space in the left column, write the letter preceding the phrase in the right column that matches the left item best.*

_____ 1. Surveying   a. May distract some listeners from the content of a lecture

_____ 2. Attention   b. Often reveals a textbook's overall organizational plan

_____ 3. Preface

    c. Serves as a preview of what's to come in a textbook

_____ 4. Background

    d. Can express a chapter's worth of ideas in a single page

_____ 5. Visuals

    e. Sometimes faked by a poor listener

_____ 6. Delivery

    f. Helps provide context for an upcoming lecture

_____ 7. Thought

    g. Developed when you survey a textbook before reading it

_____ 8. Syllabus

    h. Moves at a faster rate of speed than speech

TRUE-FALSE

Write T _beside the_ true _statements and_ F _beside the_ false _statements._

_____ 1. It is helpful to acquire your course textbooks as early as possible.

_____ 2. The first few pages of a textbook should usually be skipped.

_____ 3. Surveying a chapter provides advance organizers.

_____ 4. The terms _listening_ and _hearing_ are synonymous.

_____ 5. One way to exercise your mind is by sitting in on lectures in fields you know little about.

MULTIPLE CHOICE

Choose the word or phrase that completes each sentence most accurately, and circle the letter that precedes it.

1. A textbook's prefatory material is likely to discuss
   a. the author's objective.
   b. the book's organizational plan.
   c. supplementary materials.
   d. all of the above.

2. The prefatory material in a textbook does not include
   a. the book's purpose.
   b. the author's credentials.
   c. the book's organization.
   d. the course's objective.

3. The primary prerequisite to effective listening is
   a. a positive mental attitude.
   b. systematic note-taking skills.
   c. a thorough hearing examination.
   d. all of the above.

4. Listening is
   a. strictly mechanical.
   b. the same as hearing.
   c. not automatic.
   d. all of the above.

5. When you disagree with a lecturer's statement,
   a. begin rehearsing your rebuttal.
   b. automatically decide he or she is misinformed.
   c. take his or her stand as a bias.
   d. make a note of it, but keep on taking notes.

SHORT ANSWER   *Supply a brief answer for each of the following items.*

1. What are the advantages of buying your textbooks well before classes begin?
2. Outline some of the things you can expect to learn from a textbook's preface.
3. Which listening skill is the most important? Why?
4. Explain the greatest impediment to listening.

WORDS IN CONTEXT

From the three choices beside each numbered item, select the one that most nearly expresses the meaning of the italicized word in the quote. Make a light check mark (✓) next to your choice.

Failure! There is no such word in all the bright *lexicon* of speech, unless you yourself have written it there! There is no such thing as failure except to those who accept and believe in failure.

—Orison Swett Marden (1906–1975), American lawyer

1. *lexicon* of speech   expressions   idioms   dictionary

In the depth of winter, I finally learned that within me there lay an *invincible* summer.

—Albert Camus (1913–1960), French novelist, essayist, and dramatist

2. an *invincible* summer   fiery hot   unbeatable   intense

The gambling known as business looks with *austere* disfavor upon the business known as gambling.

—Ambrose Bierce (1842–1914), American author

3. with *austere* disfavor   stern   enormous   particular

THE WORD HISTORY SYSTEM

Calculate
from the counting stones of Romans

calculate   cal'-cu-late' *v.*
1. To ascertain by computation; reckon. 2. To make an estimate of; evaluate.

The Romans had no adding machines. Even the art of writing was known to comparatively few persons. So they did their adding and subtracting with the aid of little stones used as counters. The Latin word for the little stone used in this way was *calculus*, diminutive of *calx*, meaning "limestone." From *calculus* the verb *calculare*, "to calculate," was formed, and its past participle, *calculatus*, is the immediate origin of English *calculate*.

Reprinted by permission. From *Picturesque Word Origins* © 1933 by G. & C. Merriam Co. (now Merriam-Webster, Incorporated).

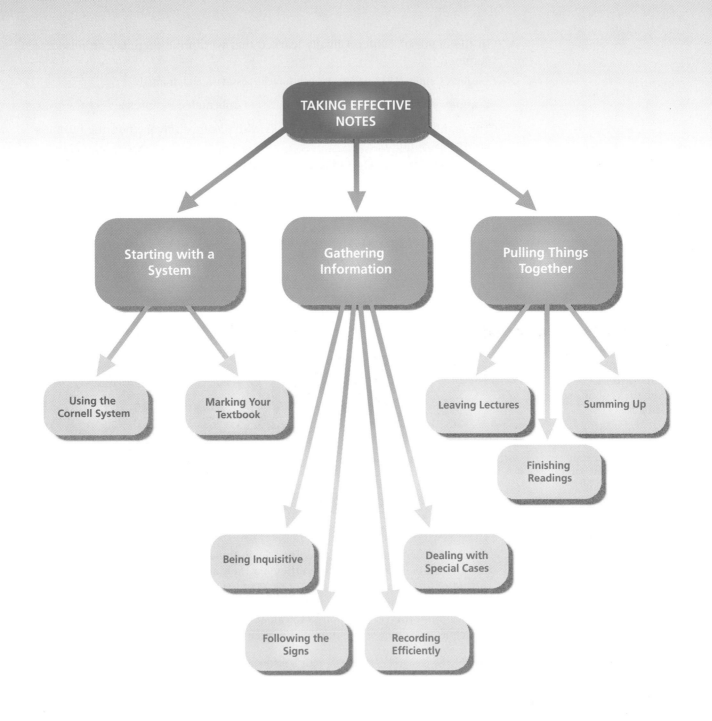

Taking Effective Notes

*Learn, compare, collect
the facts!*

Ivan Petrovich Pavlov
(1849–1936), Russian
physiologist

The lectures you hear and the assignments you read are a potential gold mine. Both include valuable nuggets of knowledge. Because you spend so much of your academic life accumulating information, it's unwise to do so haphazardly. After all, anybody can take notes, just as anyone can doodle. But it's crucial for your notes to go beyond mere busywork. The key is to take notes effectively. This chapter maps out a strategy for effective note taking:

- **Starting with a System**
- **Gathering Information**
- **Pulling Things Together**

How do you build on the framework of preparing for lectures and assignments?

What is the primary purpose of note taking?

What does research tell us about the fragility of memory?

Although it's obviously very important to have the right mindset before reading a textbook assignment or listening to a lecture, the efforts you make to prepare and foster a good frame of mind will be wasted if you don't build on this foundation. The way to do this is by taking notes.

The primary purpose of note taking is to provide a written record of what you've read or heard. You can't depend on short-term memory to retain all the ideas in a typical lecture or textbook chapter. Forgetting can be instantaneous and complete. For example, who hasn't forgotten a name only minutes after an introduction? Or had to reread a telephone number after getting a busy signal?

Given these experiences, it would be folly to rely solely on memory for something as important as an academic course. Carefully controlled research further points out the fragility of our memories. Experiments have shown that unrehearsed information is sometimes forgotten in as little as twenty seconds.[1] In a classical experiment, Hermann Ebbinghaus found that almost half of what is learned is forgotten within an hour.[2] Recently, psychologists carrying out experiments similar to Ebbinghaus's affirmed his findings.

The following true story further confirms the rapidity and scope of forgetting. Three professors eating lunch in the faculty lounge had this conversation:

CLYDE: Did you hear last night's lecture?
WALTER: No, I was busy.
CLYDE: Well, you missed one of the best lectures in recent years.
LEON: I agree. The four points that he developed were gems.
CLYDE: I never heard anyone make his points so clearly.
WALTER: I don't want you to repeat the lecture, but what were those four points?
LEON: (Long silence) Clyde? (Passage of two or three minutes; seems like an hour.)
LEON: Well, I'd better get back to the office.
CLYDE: Me, too!
WALTER: Me, too!

What can we learn from the Leon-Clyde story?

Both Leon and Clyde were brilliant men, yet neither was able to recall even a fragment of any point made in the previous night's lecture. Each had forgotten the four points because neither had transferred the points from short-term memory to long-term memory by silently reciting them. Instead, both had recited that the speaker was clear, forceful, and wise and that he had made four points—and they remembered only what they had recited. As you can surmise

[1] Douglas A. Bernstein, Edward J. Roy, Thomas K. Srull, and Christopher D. Wickens, *Psychology* (Boston: Houghton Mifflin, 1988), p. 293.

[2] Alan J. Parkin, *Memory: Phenomena, Experiment and Theory* (Cambridge, MA: Blackwell, 1993); Hermann Ebbinghaus, *Memory* (New York: Dover, 1964), p. 76.

from the anecdote, the only sure way to overcome forgetting is by taking notes and then studying and reciting them.

But taking notes doesn't simply mean scribbling down or marking up the things that strike your fancy. It means starting with some sort of system and then gathering information quickly and efficiently before pulling things together.

What are the elements of successful note taking?

Starting with a System

What can you do to make your notes more meaningful?

Too many students rely on a seat-of-the-pants method of taking notes. Whether you're taking notes for a lecture or for a reading assignment, it pays to have a system in place. If you're taking notes in a lecture or separate notes for a textbook assignment, the Cornell System is your best bet. If you're actually marking up your textbook pages, it's unwise to star, underline, and highlight in a haphazard fashion. You need to follow some consistent guidelines to ensure that your markings are meaningful.

Using the Cornell System

In what sense are notes more valuable than a textbook?

The notes you jot down can become a handwritten textbook. In fact, in many instances they are more practical, meaningful, and up-to-date than a textbook. If you keep your notes neat, complete, and well organized, they will serve you splendidly.

What is the Cornell System?

The best way to ensure that the notes you take will be useful is by adopting the Cornell System, which was developed at Cornell University almost fifty years ago. Over the years, the Cornell System has been embraced by countless colleges and universities in the United States and throughout the world. Although the system is far-reaching, its secret is simple: Wide margins on the outside and the bottom of each page are the key.

What are the principal components of Cornell-style note paper?

Many office and school supply stores now sell Cornell-style note paper, but you can easily use a pen and ruler to adapt standard loose-leaf paper to the task. First draw a vertical line down the left side of each page two-and-one-half inches from the edge of the paper; end the line two inches from the bottom of the sheet. This creates the *cue column.* Next draw a horizontal line two inches up from the bottom of the page. This is the border for your *summary area.* The large space to the right of the cue column and above the summary area is where you write your notes. Figure 10.1 shows a Cornell note sheet.

What are the cue column and summary area used for?

As you're taking notes, the cue column should remain empty, as should the summary area. But when the time comes to review and recite what you've jotted down, you'll use the cue column for questions to help clarify meanings,

Figure 10.1
The Cornell Note Sheet

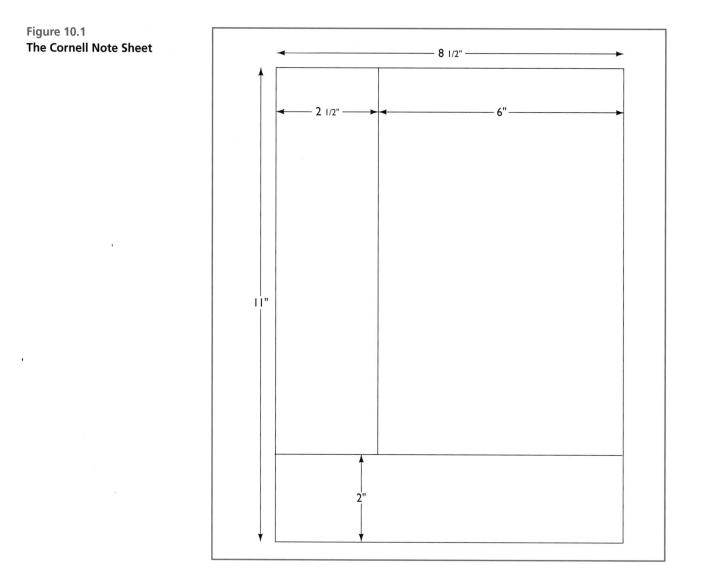

reveal relationships, establish continuity, and strengthen memory. The summary area will be used to distill a page's worth of notes down to a sentence or two.

The information that goes in the largest space on the page varies from class to class and from student to student. Different courses come with different demands. The format you choose for taking your notes and the ideas you jot down are almost entirely up to you. If you have a special way of jotting down your notes, you should be able to use it with the Cornell note sheet.

How does the Cornell System adjust to the demands of different courses?

Why is the outline format discouraged?

About the only format you should be wary of is the outline. As crisp and neat as they may look at a glance, outlines have a way of tying your hands and forcing you to squeeze information into an unforgiving framework. When you're taking notes—especially in a lecture—the last thing you want to be worrying about is Roman numerals.

What was Professor Fox's objection to outlines?

Edward W. Fox, Cornell University's great teacher, lecturer, and historian, was skeptical about the value of outlines and other rigid setups in note taking:

> Elaborate arrangements tend to confuse, and the traditional topical form, the use of Roman numerals, capital letters, Arabic numerals, and small letters, etc., with much indentation, has a fatal tendency to imply a logical analysis rather than elicit one.[3]

What should be your primary focus in all note-taking formats?

In short, you should be concentrating on the information itself, not on its numbering scheme. Here are a few formats that should work well with either lectures or textbook readings.

How do sentences in your notes differ from traditional sentences?

Sentences.   Take key ideas from a lecture or reading and jot them down in your own words. If you're taking notes in a lecture, you probably won't have time to write out complete sentences. Instead, write telegraphically, leaving out articles such as *a*, *an*, and *the*, and abbreviating words you use often. Figure 10.2 provides an example.

Figure 10.2
Sentence Notes

	Oct. 10 (Mon.) – Soc. 102 – Prof. Oxford
What's animism?	A. Animism
	1. Object has supernatural power
	2. Power called mana (not limited to objects)
Describe mana!	a. Objects accumulate mana
	Ex. Good canoe – more mana than poor one.
	b. Objects can lose mana
How to gain mana?	c. People collect objects w/lots of mana
	d. Good person's objects collect mana
	e. People, animals, plants have mana, too.
	Ex. Expert canoe builder has mana –
	imparts mana to canoe
Who has mana?	f. Chief has lots of mana – dangerous to
	get too close to chief – mana around head.

[3]Edward W. Fox, *Syllabus for History* (Ithaca, NY: Cornell University Press, 1959). Reprinted by permission of the author.

Figure 10.3
Paragraph Notes

	Nov. 6 (Mon.) — World Lit. 106 — Prof. Warnek
What is the Greek concept of a well-rounded person?	<u>Greece</u> 1. Unity = well rounded Early Greeks vigorous. Goal was to be well rounded: unity of knowledge & activity. No separate specializations as law, literature, philosophy, etc. Believed one person should master all things equally well; not only knowledge, but be an athlete, soldier, & statesman, too.

How do note-taking paragraphs compare to traditional paragraphs?

Paragraphs.   Cluster related sentences in a block of text, often under a heading or label that serves to tie them together. As you see in Figure 10.3, these are not traditional paragraphs where one complete sentence flows smoothly to the next. Your sentences in paragraph-style notes will usually be telegraphic, and smooth transitions are not important. However, these paragraphs share one important thing with traditional paragraphs: All the sentences should relate to the same main idea.

What do definition-style notes look like?

Definitions.   Write a name or term, add a dash or colon, and then provide a succinct explanation or elaboration. Figure 10.4 provides an example.

How do you make items stand out in list-style notes?

Lists.   Start with a topic, name, term, or process, and then list phrases or telegraphic sentences that relate. Avoid numbering the items unless the numbers are relevant to the list. If you want to make the items stand out in your notes, consider beginning each with a bullet point. Figure 10.5 shows what these lists are apt to look like.

What is the advantage of using drawings in your notes?

Drawings.   Drawings and diagrams can succinctly sum up information that may be difficult to explain in words alone. A sketch can often convey locations or relationships more effectively than a sentence or two. Figure 10.6 shows the sort of diagram that a biology student might include in her notes.

Figure 10.4
Definition Notes

	Mar. 14 (Fri.) – Ed. 103 – Prof. Pauk
What are main types of note-taking formats?	<u>Types of note-taking formats</u> <u>sentence</u> - Notes written in sentences, but telegraphically: w/ abbrevs. for common wds. Articles ("a", "an", etc.) left out. <u>paragraph</u> - Like real paragraphs, clustered around main idea, but sentences telegraphic & transitions left off <u>definition</u> - name or term, followed by dash or colon and explanation <u>list</u> - word or phrase heading, followed by series of items. No numbers unless relevant. Use bullet pts. instead. <u>combination</u> - mix of other formats

Figure 10.5
List Notes

	Mar. 14 (Fri.) – Ed. 103 – Prof. Pauk
How do texts show intonation?	Intonation in textbooks * boldface signals heading, subhead. May also indicate key word, phrase * italics place emphasis * underline like boldface or italics. Depends on format of book * bullets (circles, dots, squares, etc.) set off items in lists

Figure 10.6
Diagramming as a Study Aid

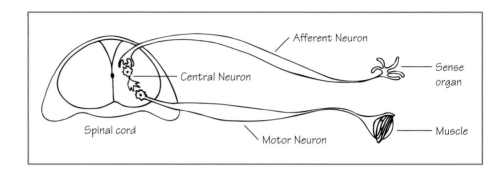

When will you need a combi-
nation of formats for your
notes?

Combination.   Some chapters and a few lectures may fit into a single note-
taking format, but it's unlikely that most will. Good note takers must remain
flexible, shifting quickly from one format to another to capture key information
as efficiently and meaningfully as possible. It's important to choose the right
tool for the job. Figure 10.7 shows notes that combine several formats.

Marking Your Textbook

What is your other option
when taking textbook notes?

Although the Cornell System can work as well with readings as it does with lec-
tures, when you're taking notes for a textbook assignment, you also have the
option of putting those notes directly on the pages of your book instead of jot-
ting them down on Cornell note paper.

What happens to the key Cor-
nell components when you
choose to mark your text in-
stead of taking separate notes?

When you choose to take notes directly in your textbook, the outside margin
of the textbook page becomes the substitute for the cue column, and the spaces
at the bottom and top of each page serve the same purpose as the summary
area in your Cornell note paper. The big difference, of course, between a Cor-
nell note sheet and a textbook page is the large note-taking area itself. Because
a textbook page is already filled with text, you obviously can't put traditional
notes where the text already is. What may at first seem like a disadvantage can
actually be a great boon. Rather than jotting down your notes from scratch,
you can mark the words or phrases in your textbook that make up the most
important ideas.

Figure 10.8 contains twelve suggestions for marking textbooks. Notice espe-
cially the use of single and double underlines; the use of asterisks, circling, and
boxing for important items; and the use of the top and bottom margins for long
notations or summaries. If some of these ideas appeal to you, work them into
your marking system. Be sure to use them consistently so that you will in-
stantly remember what they mean.

What is the risk of marking up
your textbook?

Textbook marking can be a useful aid to study and review, but it must be
done sparingly and with some self-discipline. If you overmark your book, you

CHAPTER
10

Figure 10.7
Notes That Use a Combination of Formats

Mar. 14 (Fri.) – Ed. 103 – Prof. Pauk

Organizational patterns

How do org. patterns help make books, lectures easier to follow?	Where is this going? Org. patterns provide guidance in lectures & texts. Tell you where author, speaker is headed. Learning common patterns can make it easier to follow both. Also, <u>signposts</u> (next, finally, thus) can provide clues about path.
What are movement patterns?	<u>Movement patterns</u> systematically travel through time, space, process. Can be easiest pattern to follow. Several types:
Examples?	* time or chronological pattern - events presented in order.
	* place or spatial pattern - info presented based on location or arrangement. Ex: descrip. of geog. features of U.S., outline of company setup
	* process pattern - steps or events lead to desired situation or product. Ex: recipe.

will defeat your purpose: quick identification of important points. When the time comes to master your notes, instead of reviewing ideas you may find yourself trying to decipher a code. Also, bear in mind that the "you" who reviews the marked book will not be quite the same "you" who did the marking. As the term progresses, your knowledge will grow. By the end of the term, you will be accepting as commonplace many things that seemed so important to underscore, box, circle, star, question, comment on, or disagree with at the beginning of the term. Your early marks may hamper your review. So use the help that marking can give you, but don't go overboard. Think ahead.

What advantage does textbook marking have over separate notes?

If you can manage to keep your marking under control, you'll wind up with a valuable study tool. One advantage of marking up your textbook directly is that your notes and your textbook travel together as a unit. Whenever you need clarification for a sentence or phrase you have marked, you have an

Figure 10.8

A System for Marking Your Textbooks

EXPLANATION AND DESCRIPTION	SYMBOLS, MARKINGS, AND NOTATIONS
1. Use double lines under words or phrases to signify main ideas.	Radiation can produce mutations. . .
2. Use single lines under words or phrases to signify supporting material.	comes from cosmic rays. . .
3. Mark small circled numbers near the initial word of an underlined group of words to indicate a series of arguments, facts, ideas—either main or supporting.	Conditions change. . . ① rocks rise. . . ② some sink. . . ③ the sea dashes. . . ④ strong winds. . .
4. Rather than underlining a group of three or more important lines, use a vertical bracket in the margin.	had known. . . who gave. . . the time. . . of time. . .
5. Use one asterisk in the margin to indicate ideas of special importance, and two for ideas of unusual importance. Reserve three asterisks for principles and high-level generalizations.	* When a nuclear blast is. . . ** People quite close to the. . . ***The main cause of mutations. . .
6. Circle keywords and key terms.	The genes are the. . .
7. Box words of enumeration and transition.	fourth, the lack of supplies. . . furthermore, the shortage. . .
8. Place a question mark in the margin, opposite lines you do not understand, as a reminder to ask the instructor for clarification.	The lastest. . . cold period. . . ? about 1,000,000. . . Even today. . . Life became. . . on land only. . . 340 million years. . .
9. If you disagree with a statement, indicate that in the margin.	Disagree
10. Use the top and bottom margins of a page to record ideas of your own that are prompted by what you read.	Why not use carbon dating? Check on reference of fossils found in Tennessee stone quarry.
11. On sheets of paper that are smaller than the pages of the book, write longer thoughts or summaries; then insert them between the pages.	Fossils Plants = 500,000,000 years old Insects = 260,000,000 " " Bees = 100,000,000 " " True Fish = 330,000,000 " " Amphibians = 300,000,000 " " Reptiles = 300,000,000 " " Birds = 150,000,000 " "
12. Even though you have underlined the important ideas and supporting materials, still jot brief cues in the side margins.	Adapt – fossil – layer –

entire book's worth of supporting material, including a table of contents, an index, and often a glossary, at your fingertips.

What is a potential disadvantage of textbook marking?

Of course, a potential disadvantage of textbook marking is that it doesn't require your complete concentration. When you read a paragraph in your textbook and write down a summarizing sentence on a separate Cornell note sheet, you have already initiated the process of taking the textbook information and making it your own. Contrast this to textbook marking, where it's possible to thoroughly annotate your textbook without truly understanding what you've marked. Drawing lines and boxes and inserting symbols and question marks can give you a false sense of accomplishment if you're not thinking deeply about what you read.

How can you make sure you understand what you've marked?

Luckily, there is a simple but powerful way to solve this problem: recitation. Rather than marking each paragraph as you go, read it through completely and then recite its main idea in your own words. Then and only then should you return to the paragraph and mark the words or phrases that express or support the answer you've just recited. This step will move you out of the realm of simple recognition and into recall. Recalling your notes is the way to help make information your own.

On the following pages are examples of appropriately marked textbook pages. Figure 10.9 shows how to organize a page using enumeration, that is, encircling words such as *first* and *second*. Write in numbers to identify salient points. The underlinings should be sparse and form the answers to the questions in the margins. This type of organization not only aids in comprehending and remembering the main points of the page, but also helps immensely when you're studying for an examination and time is short.

Gathering Information

What can you do to be fully engaged as you take notes?

Whether you are taking notes on sheets of paper or making marks in your textbook, you need to be fully engaged. To avoid drifting into the sort of robotic routine that adds little to learning, it is important to remain inquisitive as you take your notes, to keep alert for signs that will tip you off to the meaning of what you're reading or learning, to record things efficiently, and, as always, to stay flexible for the inevitable exceptions and special cases.

Being Inquisitive

What is the secret to being an active participant?

You can't really expect to do a good job of gleaning the most important information from a lecture or reading unless you are paying attention. And while getting enough sleep and sitting up straight can help promote alertness, the real

Figure 10.9
Use of Enumeration in Textbooks

Source: John P. McKay, Bennett D. Hill, and John Buckler, *A History of World Societies.* Copyright © 2000 by Houghton Mifflin Company, Boston. Reprinted by permission.

MARITIME EXPANSION

Ming period Naval expeditions When? Who?	Another dramatic development of the Ming period was the series of naval expeditions sent out between 1405 and 1433 under Hong Wu's son Yong Lu and Yong Lu's successor. China had a
Naval history	strong maritime history stretching back to the eleventh century, and these early fifteenth-century voyages were a continuation of that tradition. The
Relative power?	Ming expeditions established China as the greatest maritime power in the world—considerably ahead
Portugal power when?	of Portugal, whose major seafaring reconnaissances began a half-century later.
Purpose of expeditions? Tribute system?? 2 motives? Contender – who?	In contrast to Hong Wu, Yong Lu broadened ①diplomatic and ②commercial contacts within the tribute system. Yong Lu had two basic motives for launching overseas voyages. First, he sent them in search of Jian Wen, a serious contender for the throne whom he had defeated but who, rumor claimed, had escaped to Southeast Asia. Second, he launched the expeditions to explore, to expand trade, and to provide the imperial court with luxury objects. Led by the Muslim eunuch admiral
Admiral? 1st expedition	Zheng He and navigating by compass, seven fleets sailed to East and South Asia. The first expedition (which carried 27,800 men) involved 62 major
Ship's size?	ships, the largest of which was 440 feet in length and 180 feet in the beam and had 9 masts. The
Sea route?	expeditions crossed the Indian Ocean to Ceylon, the Persian Gulf, and the east coast of Africa.
3 consequences?	These voyages had important consequences. They extended the prestige of the Ming Dynasty throughout Asia. ①Trade, in the form of tribute from as far as the west coast of southern India, greatly increased. ②Diplomatic contacts with the distant Middle East led to the arrival in Nanjing of embassies from Egypt. ③The maritime expeditions also led to the publication of geographical works.

secret to being an active participant is to maintain an inquisitive mindset. Formulating questions, whether silently or aloud, will unlock the meaning of information in a way that listening or reading passively just can't approach.

Use Questions to Unlock Meaning

How does Eddie Rickenbacker's story illustrate the effect of questions on understanding?

Why are questions so important? The story of Eddie Rickenbacker provides a dramatic illustration of their effect on understanding. Rickenbacker was a highly decorated World War I flying ace who went on to become chairman of Eastern Airlines. Brought up in humble circumstances, he was forced to leave school at the age of twelve so he could find work and support his widowed mother.

Although Eddie couldn't attend school regularly, he still appreciated the value of an education and later decided to take a correspondence course in mechanical engineering. Here's part of his story:

> The first lesson, I do not mind admitting, nearly finished my correspondence-school education before it began. It was tough. . . . As there was no teacher of whom I could ask a question, I had to work out the answers myself. Once I reached the answer through my own individual reasoning, my understanding was permanent and unforgettable.[4]

Perhaps you can picture young Eddie Rickenbacker with paper and book spread out on a kitchen table, struggling to gain meaning from a paragraph. Doubts began to mount. Plain grit wasn't enough. He felt overwhelmed. Then, in desperation, he probably said to himself, "All right, Eddie, try it once more: What's this fellow trying to tell me?"

Why did questions provide such a breakthrough in Rickenbacker's learning?

Right then, he created a miniature miracle. How? He asked a question! Armed with this questioning technique, he became his own teacher. Previously, his eyes touched the words on the page and, in touching, expected that meaning would somehow, like a jack-in-the-box, pop up. Unfortunately, it didn't (and it doesn't). But with a question ringing in his ears, Rickenbacker was able to focus on hearing an answer. He heard it and understood it. You can too.

How did Socrates use questions?

We shouldn't be surprised that questions are packed with so much power. Human beings have known this for more than twenty-four hundred years. Socrates (469–399 B.C.), the greatest of the Greek philosophers, developed what is known as the Socratic method, *the questioning method*. By employing a series of carefully directed questions, Socrates would lead another person, through his own step-by-step answers, to arrive at the understanding or conclusion himself.

[4]Edward V. Rickenbacker, *Rickenbacker* (Englewood Cliffs, NJ: Prentice-Hall, 1967), pp. 31–32.

Why are questions so powerful?

What is it that makes a question so powerful? Maybe, as the psychologists say, questions promote concentration. If true, what a sure and easy way to gain concentration with a technique that is available to all of us!

Ask Questions Both Silently and Out Loud During a Lecture

What are the roles of the speaker and listener in a lecture?

Although the communication may seem one-sided, both the speaker and the listener play important roles in a classroom lecture. The speaker's responsibility is to make points clearly. The listener's responsibility is to understand what the speaker says. If a speaker's message is not clear and the listener asks a clarifying question, both the speaker and the listener benefit. The speaker is encouraged and gratified to know that the audience is interested. The listener can concentrate on what the speaker has to say and feel good about raising a question that other, more timid members of the audience might have been hesitant to ask.

What did the University of Virginia survey reveal about questions?

As vital as questions can be to comprehension, they often go unasked. A professor at the University of Virginia who conducted a survey found that 94 percent of her students had failed to understand something in at least one class lecture during the semester. Seventy percent of the students had not asked clarifying questions even though they knew they could. When she asked them why they had remained silent, they answered with such statements as "I was afraid I'd look stupid," "I didn't want to make myself conspicuous," "I was too proud to ask," and "I was too confused to know what question to ask."

How do you overcome the fear of asking questions?

The way to dispel the fear of asking is to remember that the only dumb question is the one that is never asked. The way to dispel confusion is to acknowledge it by saying, "I'm confused about the last point you made" or "I'm confused about how the example pertains to your main point." In this situation, as in most, honesty is the best policy.

Formulate Questions as You Read

How do you ask questions when you're reading a book that can't talk back?

It's easy to see how questions can help clarify important points in a classroom lecture. After all, you usually have an expert right there who can sense your confusion and respond to the questions. Not so with a textbook assignment, where all you have are silent words on a printed page. Instead of approaching a textbook as a passive recipient of its information, build on the relationship you formed with the author or authors when you first surveyed the book and read over its prefatory material by constantly formulating questions as you read, by wondering out loud about issues or aspects that concern you, and by writing out questions that help you pinpoint and remember the most important information. The latter really serves as the foundation for taking notes and mastering them.

What's a good way to start asking questions as you read?

If asking questions as you read doesn't seem to come naturally at first, a good way to start is by reading the headings and subheadings in your assignment and turning them into questions. This is an important ice-breaker in a number of textbook reading systems, including the well-known SQ3R system (see Figure 10.10).

It doesn't take much to transform a typical textbook heading or subheading into an attention-getting question. For example, the main heading "Basic Aspects of Memory" could be turned into the question "What are the basic aspects of memory?" The technique is simple, but it works. Here are some additional examples.

Subtopic Heading	Question Formulated
The Memory Trace	What is a memory trace?
Rate of Forgetting	How fast do we forget?
Organization of Recall	How is recall organized?
Decay Theory	What is the decay theory?

What do you do once you've turned a heading into a question?

Once you have turned a heading into a question, you read the material under the heading to answer your question. Suddenly you are reading with a purpose instead of just passively taking in information. If the question is answered early in the discussion, ask another, based on what you have read.

Following the Signs

What signs help improve comprehension of lectures or readings?

Whether information is delivered in the form of a lecture or a textbook chapter, there are usually signs that help direct you down the road to comprehension. Both the intonation of the words and the way they are organized provide clues about the author or speaker's purpose and approach.

Pay Attention to Intonation

How does intonation affect the meaning of words?

Consider the dramatic effect that intonation can have on the meaning of even a simple phrase, such as "Excuse me." Depending on the tone of voice, these two words can sound polite, tentative, argumentative, or downright resentful. In each case, the words are identical, but the delivery is different. If you pay attention only to the words when you're listening to a lecture or reading a textbook, but ignore their delivery, you may be missing a critical component of their meaning.

What are the three components of intonation?

Intonation in Lectures　　Most college lecturers speak about 120 words per minute, which means that in a fifty-minute lecture you hear roughly 6,000 words. Listening for signals in a lecture is especially helpful because, unlike in reading, you don't have the luxury of retracing your steps if you discover that you're lost. In addition to words, intonation—variations in the lecturer's voice—is the most significant signal in spoken language. Intonation has three components: volume, pauses, and cadence.

Figure 10.10

The SQ3R System

Source: Adaptation of "Steps in the SQ3R Method" (pp. 32–33) from *Effective Study,* 4th Edition, by Francis P. Robinson. Copyright 1941, 1946 by Harper & Row Publishers Inc. Copyright © 1961, 1970 by Francis P. Robinson. Reprinted by permission of the publisher.

THE SQ3R SYSTEM

S   SURVEY   *Glance through all the headings in the chapter, and read the final summary paragraph (if the chapter has one). This survey should not take more than a minute, and it will show you the three to six core ideas on which the discussion will be based. This orientation will help you organize the ideas as you read them later.*

Q   QUESTION   *Now begin to work. Turn the first heading into a question. This will arouse your curiosity and thereby increase comprehension. It will bring to mind information you already know, thus helping you understand that section more quickly. The question also will make important points stand out from explanatory details. You can turn a heading into a question as you read the heading, but it demands conscious effort on your part.*

R₁   READ   *Read the paragraph or section to answer the question. Read actively.*

R₂   RECITE   *After you finish reading the paragraph or section, stop, look away from the book, and try to recite the answer to your formed question. If you cannot recite the answer correctly or fully, reread the section and try again.*

R₃   REVIEW   *When you have finished reading and reciting page after page, go back to the beginning of the chapter, glance at the headings and subheadings, and think briefly about the answers that you have already recited. Work your way in this manner to the end of the chapter. Now you should have ended with an integrated bird's-eye view of the entire chapter.*

Volume.   In general, the introduction of a crucial idea is preceded by a change in volume; the speaker raises or lowers his or her voice.

Pauses.   Pausing before and after main ideas sets these ideas apart from the rest of the lecture. Pauses achieve a dramatic effect and, on a practical level, provide note takers with extra writing time.

Cadence.   The rhythm of a lecturer's speaking patterns can be particularly helpful. Often, like the bulleted lists you find in textbooks, the speaker lists a series of important ideas by using a steady speaking rhythm, sometimes even beginning each idea with the same words or phrase. Whenever you detect these oral signals, your pencil should be moving steadily, adding these important points to your notes.

Intonation in Textbooks   Reading with intonation can make the words on your textbook page come alive. This doesn't mean reading out loud, but it does mean reading with expression. Intonation helps you combine individual words into meaningful mental "bites."

What does reading with intonation involve?

As your eyes move rapidly across the page, let your mind swing along each line with an intonational rhythm that can be heard by your "inner ear." Read the line expressively. In doing so, you will be supplying the important rhythm, stress, emphasis, and pauses that were taken out when the words were turned into written form. This will put the meaning of the words more quickly within your grasp.

How does reading expressively help?

To make silent intonation a regular habit, take a few minutes to read aloud in the privacy of your room. This will establish your own speech patterns in your mind so you will "hear" them more readily when you read silently.

How do you develop the habit of reading with intonation?

Adding your own intonation in this way can help impart meaning and expression to words that may otherwise seem to lack pizzaz. In addition, books provide another form of intonation that mimics the volume, pauses, and cadence of speech.

How do type styles mimic the volume, pauses, and cadence of speech?

Open any textbook and you'll quickly discover that the words aren't all printed in the same size or the same style. The format may differ from text to text, but in general each book takes advantage of a variety of type sizes and styles to convey information. By noting these typographical differences, you can pick up on signals for organization and emphasis.

Boldface (thick, dark type) often signals a textbook heading or subheading. It may also be used to draw your attention to a specific principle, definition, or keyword within the text.

Italics (type that slopes to the right) places emphasis on a word or a phrase.

<u>Underlining</u> often performs the same functions as boldface and italics, depending on the format of the particular textbook.

• Bullets (small markers, often circular or square) set off the items in lists.

Size, color, and placement of type often call attention to headings and subheadings. Take note of words printed in larger type, in color, or on lines by themselves.

You can usually crack a book's particular typographical code by skimming through it before you start reading. In addition, look for an explanation of format—especially if it is unconventional—in the book's introductory material.

Recognize Organizational Patterns

Where are we going? And how are we going to get there? Those are both reasonable questions to ask when you're heading off on a journey. They're equally reasonable when you're reading an assignment or listening to a lecture. Luckily, both authors and speakers normally tell you where you're headed and how you're going to get there by using common organizational patterns to help arrange their information. Familiarize yourself with these patterns, and you should find things easier to follow. In addition, you can often navigate through information by noticing certain verbal signposts that commonly line the route. Simple words such as *next, thus,* or *finally* can provide valuable clues to the path that a chapter or lecture is taking.

Movement Patterns   Authors or speakers will frequently move you systematically through time, through space, or through a process. Once you catch on, these patterns can be among the easiest to follow.

With the **time or chronological pattern,** events are presented in the order in which they occurred. This pattern can be recognized quickly from the author's or lecturer's use of dates and such phrases as *in previous years, the next day,* and *two years later,* which denote the passage of time.

Items in a **place or spatial pattern** are presented or discussed on the basis of their locations or their arrangement relative to one another. For example, an author might use a spatial pattern to describe the geographical features of the United States from the West Coast to the East Coast. This is often called a *geographical pattern.* It is also called a *topical pattern* when it is used to describe the organization of a corporation along the lines of purchasing, manufacturing, sales, and so forth. The progression from item to item is usually orderly and easy to follow: from left to right, from high to low, from north to south, and so on.

Steps or events in a **process pattern** are presented in an orderly sequence that leads to a desired situation or product. A recipe and the instructions for assembling a bicycle are examples of process patterns. They often include words such as *first, after this, then, next,* and *finally.* You'll often encounter this pattern in computer courses and the sciences, where the steps in a process are described in the order in which they must occur to put something together, run an application, or blend ingredients.

Importance Patterns   A common way of organizing facts or information is by arranging them in terms of their relative importance.

How can you learn the meaning of a book's typographical intonation?

What role do organizational patterns play in lectures and textbooks?

What are movement patterns?

How are importance patterns organized?

In the **increasing importance pattern,** the most important or most dramatic item in a series is placed at the end. Each succeeding item is more important than the previous one, so a crescendo effect is created. Thus, this pattern is also called the *climactic-order pattern.*

In the **decreasing importance pattern,** the most important or most dramatic item in a series is placed at the very beginning. Such an organization grabs your interest immediately, so there is a good chance that you will stay with the writer or speaker all the way through. This pattern is commonly used in newspaper articles and is known by journalists as the *inverted pyramid pattern.*

What do causal patterns all share in common?

Causal Patterns   One thing leads to another in a number of patterns, most of which are variations on the well-known idea of cause and effect.

In the **problem–effect–solution pattern,** the writer or speaker outlines a problem (cause), explains its effect, and then often (though not always) maps out a solution.

The **problem–cause–solution pattern** inverts this approach. A predicament (effect) is introduced, followed by its antecedents (cause) and eventually by remedies. In short, the effect comes first this time, followed by the cause.

Of course, not all cause–effect patterns involve problems. In technical subjects, the generic **cause–effect pattern** is quite common. In this case, variables are defined and their result (effect) is explained. Meanwhile, in the social sciences, you'll often run into the **action–impact pattern,** where some sort of initiative is outlined, such as increased funding for education, followed by a result, such as a higher average income for employees who received a college education.

Regardless of the variation, phrases such as *as a result* or *consequently* will usually alert you to a causal pattern.

When do writers and speakers use comparison patterns?

Comparison Patterns   Writers and speakers compare things, events, or people when they emphasize similarities, and contrast them when they emphasize differences. Individual characteristics may be compared or contrasted one at a time, or several characteristics may be discussed as a group. In either case, the pattern can be recognized from the various similarities or differences and from the use of words such as *similarly, likewise, conversely,* and *on the other hand.*

What do logical patterns have in common?

Logical Patterns   In these patterns, a conclusion is either drawn or stated at the outset and then supported.

With the **inductive pattern,** a number of incidents are cited, then a conclusion is arrived at. The main point will be something like this: "So, on the basis of all these facts, we come to this overriding principle, which is so-and-so."

With the **deductive pattern,** the reverse is true. Here, the principle or general statement is given first, then the events or proofs are enumerated.

Table 10.1
Signposts

Categories and Examples	When you come across these words, immediately think . . .

Example Words
   specifically
   to illustrate
   for example
   for instance
   that is
	"Here comes an example. Must be double-checking to make sure I understood the point just made."

Cause-and-Effect Words
   consequently
   therefore
   as a result
   if . . . then
   accordingly
   thus, so
   hence
	"There's an effect word. Better check back when I have a chance to make sure I can find the cause now that I know what the effect is."

Enumeration Words
   the four steps . . .
   first, second, third
   next, finally
	"That's a lot of steps. I'd better be sure I'm keeping track of all of them and getting them in the right order."

Addition Words
   furthermore
   as well as
   along with
   in addition
   moreover
   also
   not only . . . but also
	"Seems there's always something else to be added. Must be worth remembering."

Contrast Words
   on the other hand
   in contrast
   conversely
   although
   however, despite
   whereas
	"Here comes the other side of the coin. Let's see how it differs from what's been said already."

Comparison Words
   likewise
   similarly
   comparatively
   identical
	"Lots of similar things, it seems."

Swivel Words
   however
   nevertheless
   yet
   but
   still
	"Looks like there's going to be a little bit of doubt or 'give back' on the point just made. Better pay attention to this qualifying remark."

(continued)

Table 10.1

Continued

Categories and Examples	When you come across these words, immediately think . . .
Concession Words to be sure indeed though, although granted of course	"Okay! Here comes an argument or two from the opposing point of view."
Emphasis Words more important above all remember in other words finally	"Looks as though what's coming up is going to be important."
Repeat Words in other words it simply means that is briefly in essence as we've seen	"Here comes another explanation. Maybe I'll understand this one a little better."
Time Words before, after formerly, soon subsequently prior, during meanwhile	"Hmm! A time relationship is being established. Let's see: What came first, what came last, and what came in-between?"
Place Words above below beyond adjacent to	"Okay! I'll put these ideas and facts not only in their proper places, but also in their proper relationship."
Summary Words for these reasons on the whole in conclusion in a nutshell to sum up in short finally	"Good. Now I'll get a simple wrap-up of the points that have been made. It's almost sure to be full of key ideas."
Test Words (lectures) This is important. Remember this. You'll see this again. Here's a pitfall.	"Sounds like a potential test item. Better be sure to pay close attention to it."

What should you do if you can't identify a precise organizational pattern?

Signposts   Although identifying the precise organizational pattern can be extremely helpful, it isn't always easy or even possible. Some textbook chapters may defy easy organization, and some lectures can be rambling. In these cases, all is not lost. Keep in mind that your key goal while taking notes is to use cues and patterns to help arrange your thoughts and aid your search for meaning. Luckily, the signposts that often tip you off to a particular organizational pattern can still be helpful even if you have a tough time nailing down the overall arrangement. Table 10.1 lists some common signposts and the directions they're likely to point you in.

Recording Efficiently

What are the key factors in taking notes efficiently?

Depending on whether you're taking lecture notes or textbook notes, you may find that you are short on space, short on time, or both. There are ways that you can take notes more efficiently to avoid any and all of these problems.

How do you make your notes both legible and speedy?

Strive to make your note taking both speedy and sparing. Of course, if you scribble down information too quickly, your notes may be illegible. And if you're too choosy about what you record, you could be left with costly gaps in your information. The way to circumvent these problems and record legible, useful notes at a reasonable speed is to adopt the modified printing style, use telegraphic sentences, and record selectively.

Use Modified Printing

What is modified printing?

Poor handwriting need not keep you from taking legible notes. The *modified printing style* combines the rapidity of writing with the legibility of printing. Letters are formed smoothly, as with cursive or longhand writing, but are punctuated with the sort of stops and starts characteristic of printing. Your words take on a cursive look, and the periodic breaks between letters prevent your writing from eroding into an unreadable blur.

Why is modified printing so effective?

What makes the modified printing style so effective and easy to learn is that it combines your style of printing with your style of cursive in a mixture that brings out the best elements of both. Here's how:

$$a\ b\ c\ d\ e\ f\ g\ h\ i\ j\ k\ l\ m\ n\ o\ p\ q\ r\ s\ t\ u\ v\ w\ x\ y\ z$$

Figure 10.11 shows how modified printing looks in a typical paragraph.

Take Notes Telegraphically

What does it mean to take notes telegraphically?

The best way to take notes is telegraphically. Long before e-mail and the fax machine were invented, important business and personal messages were sent by telegraph. The sender paid by the word; the fewer the words, the lower the

Figure 10.11
Modified Printing Style

> There are four advantages to using this modified printing style. First, it is faster than cursive writing; second, it is neater, permitting easy and direct comprehension; third, it saves time by precluding rewriting or typing; and fourth, it permits easy and clear re-forming of letters that are ill-formed due to haste.

cost. A three-word message such as "Arriving three pm" was much less expensive than an eleven-word message: "I will arrive home promptly at three o'clock in the afternoon." Of course, taking notes doesn't cost money, but it does cost time.

How do you take telegraphic notes?

To save valuable time when you're taking notes, leave out unnecessary words such as articles *(a, an, the)*, abbreviate words you use often (see Figures 10.12 and 10.13), and streamline definitions by using a colon (:) or a dash (—). Two examples of this telegraphic style are shown in Figure 10.14.

Take Notes Selectively

How do you take notes selectively?

Of course, you can't and shouldn't jot down every word. With textbook note taking it's impractical. In lectures it's an impossibility. Taking thorough notes, regardless of the format you choose, should not mean writing down everything you hear. Your emphasis should be on the ideas, not the words. And you don't want all the ideas, either, just the key ones (as Figure 10.15 shows), along with any details or examples you need to make those ideas easier to understand.

Dealing with Special Cases

What should you do in special cases?

Not all note-taking scenarios are ideal. If you can't make it to a lecture or have difficulty taking notes when you do, you need an alternate plan. In the same way, there are factors that can throw a wrench into traditional textbook note taking.

Figure 10.12

Examples of Technical Symbols

Symbol	Meaning	Symbol	Meaning
+	plus, positive, and	↕	vibration, motion
−	minus, negative	log	common logarithm
×	algebraic x, or multiplied by	ln	natural logarithm
÷	divided by	∈	base of natural logarithms
≠	does not equal	π	pi
≈	equals approximately, approximates	∠	angle
>	greater than, greatly, increased, increasing	⊥	perpendicular to
<	less than, reduced, decreasing	‖	parallel to
~	sine curve, cosine curve	$a°$	a degrees (angle)
→	approaches as a limit, approaches	a'	a minutes (angle)
≧	greater than or equal to	a''	a seconds (angle)
≦	less than or equal to	∫	integral, integral of, integration
≡	identical to	f	frequency
μ	varies directly as	f_n	natural frequency
∴	therefore	cps	cycles per second
$()^{1/2}$	square root	m	mass
$()^{n}$	nth root	Φ	phase
vs	versus, against	F	force
⏚	ground	/	ratio, the ratio of
↔	varied, variation	⊤⊤	base, support, mount, foundation
□	area	(	curve, curvilinear

Figure 10.13

Typical Technical Abbreviations

Reprinted by permission from G. H. Logan, "Speed Notes for Engineers," *Product Engineering,* September 30, 1963. Copyright © 1963 by Morgan-Grampian, Inc.

Abbr.	Word	Abbr.	Word
anlys	analysis	*pltg*	plotting
ampltd	amplitude	*reman*	remain
asmg	assuming	*rsnc*	resonance
cald	called	*rltnshp*	relationship
cnst	constant	*smpl*	simple
dmpg	damping	*smpfd*	simplified
dmnsls	dimensionless	*stfns*	stiffness
dfln	deflection	*systm*	system
dfnd	defined	*sgnft*	significant
dstrbg	disturbing	*ths*	this
eftvns	effectiveness	*trnsmsblty*	transmissibility
frdm	freedom	*thrtly*	theoretically
frcg	forcing	*valu*	value
gvs	gives	*wth*	with
hrmc	harmonic	*whn*	when
isltr	isolator	*xprsd*	expressed
isltn	isolation		

Figure 10.14
Examples of Telegraphic Sentences

<u>Lecture's words</u>

In marketing, we try to understand customers' needs and then respond to them with the right products and services. In the past, firms often produced goods first and tried to fit the customer's needs to the goods. Today's world-class marketers pride themselves on their customer orientation. We begin with the customer and build the product or service from there. A good example is McDonald's, the fast-food chain, which tailors its menus to local tastes and customs when it opens fast-food outlets in Moscow and other international locations.

<u>Student's telegraphic sentences</u>

Marketing understands customers' needs first.
- In past, firms produced goods first, then fit them to customers.
- World-class = having customer orientation.
- Ex. McDonald's in Moscow

<u>Lecture's words</u>

The US Patent Office has granted numerous patents for perpetual motion machines based upon applications with complete detailed drawings. Some years ago, though, the patent office began requiring working models of such a machine before a patent would be granted. Result: No patents granted for perpetual motion machines since that time.

<u>Student's telegraphic sentences</u>

Perpetual motion machine (drawings) = many patents.
Required working model = no patents since.

Figure 10.15
Selective Note Taking

What's sympathetic magic?
 	
Describe contagious magic.
	Oct. 10 (Mon.) — Soc. 102 — Prof. Oxford
	
	A. Two kinds of magic
	 1. Sympathetic — make model or form of a person from clay, etc. — then stick pins into object to hurt symbolized person.
	 2. Contagious magic
	  a. Need to possess an article belonging to another person.
	  b. Ex. Fingernail clippings. By doing harm to these objects, feel that harm can be transmitted.

Have a Backup Plan When You Can't Attend the Lecture

What's the best strategy if you have to miss a lecture?

If you know you'll be missing a class, supply a friend with a cassette or tape recorder and ask him or her to tape the lecture for you. Then you'll be able to take your own notes when you play the tape back.

Use the Two-Page System for Fast-Moving Lectures

How can you cope with a lecturer who speaks too rapidly?

When you need to scramble to keep up with a fast-talking lecturer, you may find this two-page system helpful. Here's how it works: Lay your binder or notebook flat on the desk. On the left-hand page, record main ideas only. This is your primary page. On the right-hand page, record as many details as you have time for. Place the details opposite the main ideas they support. After the lecture, remain in your seat for a few minutes and fill in any gaps in your notes while the lecture is still relatively fresh in your mind.

Take a Different Approach for Supplemental Readings

Why do instructors assign outside reading?

In many undergraduate courses, assignments and lectures focus on a single textbook, but instructors often assign outside reading in other publications. Reasons for assigning the extra work include the following:

1. To amplify topics treated in the textbook or mentioned in class lectures
2. To go into greater detail—for example, by assigning original documents or primary sources

3. To expose students to other points of view or different philosophies
4. To bring background material into discussions

What's the best approach to supplemental readings?

Instructors generally do not expect you to master such supplementary material as thoroughly as you master your textbook. Nevertheless, once the assignment has been made, you must cope with it. Clearly, you cannot spend an inordinate amount of time, but you must learn something from your supplemental reading. Here are some suggestions for doing so:

1. Try to figure out why the book was assigned. You might ask the instructor. If you find out, then you can skim the book, looking for pertinent material and disregarding the rest.
2. Read the preface. As you already know from the previous chapter, the preface provides inside information. It may tell you how this book is different from your textbook.
3. Study the table of contents. Notice especially the chapter titles to see whether they are like those in your textbook. If the chapters with similar titles contain the same information as the chapters in your textbook, read the chapters that do not duplicate your textbook's coverage. (Do this with topics covered in classroom lectures, too.)
4. If you have not yet found an "angle," read the summarizing paragraph at the end of each chapter. Make brief notes on each chapter from the information thus gained. With these notes spread out before you, try to see the overall pattern. From the overall pattern, come up with the author's central thesis, principle, problem, or solution.
5. Don't put the book away with only a vague notion of what it is about. You must come up with something so definite that you can talk about it the next day or write about it two weeks later. Do not waste time on details, but be ready to answer general questions: What was the author's central approach? How was it different from that of your textbook? How was it the same? Look for the central issues around which everything else is organized.
6. Have the courage to think big. If you lack courage, you'll waste time on minor details that you won't remember. Select the big issues and concentrate on them.

When a highly condensed summary of a book or of a long selection is required, you need a special approach. The introduction–thesis–body–conclusion sequence is useful in forcing you to understand the material and the way the author develops and supports it. Furthermore, a summary that follows this sequence can be highly condensed; you may be able to capture the main ideas of a collateral book in only a page or two of notes. Figure 10.16 is an example.

Figure 10.16
Notes in the Form of a Highly Condensed Summary

I. <u>Introduction</u>

Experiment in living close to nature.

Thoreau voluntarily withdrew from civilization which he felt was getting too complicated. He spent 2 yrs., 2 mos., and 2 days living at Walden Pond to regain the simplicity of life that comes when one lives close to the soil.

II. <u>Thesis</u>

Each man and woman should pause to decide just how they should spend their lives. Are they paying too dearly for unessentials?

In a complex civilization, the fast flowing current of unessentials stemming from custom, tradition, advertising, etc., somehow sweeps a person away from the genuine goals in life.

Only by temporarily cutting oneself off from civilization, could people realize that their lives need not be so complex. By getting back to nature to rethink the basic issues of life people can chart their course, and attempt to steer their lives in accordance with these standards (not expediences set up by the pressures of complex civilization).

III. <u>Body</u>

People should awaken and become aware of real life.

Thoreau did not wish to hold up progress or civilization; rather, he wished that people would be more contemplative and selective in their actions.

Thoreau chronicled his experiences at Walden Pond. He wanted to become familiar with nature.

a. He built his own hut.

b. Average cost of living a week was 27 cents.

c. He observed nature: trees, birds, animals, etc.

Live simply & you will live more fully.

He believed that every person ought to measure up to the best they could do. What the best is, depends upon the individual. To have a standard to measure up does not mean that all must have the same, but every one should measure up to a standard in the best way she or he is able to.

IV. <u>Summary</u>

Urged people to reject unessentials, and get back to fundamentals.

Thoreau wanted to demonstrate that many so-called necessities were not necessary at all. He wanted people to observe, appreciate, and evaluate what was important in life. Once people set their sights upon the good life, they should follow their sights without compromising.

Pulling Things Together

Why is it a mistake to end your
note taking abruptly?

As a lecture draws to a close or a chapter comes to an end, there's a great temptation to just pack up and move on. That may be understandable, but it can prove to be a great waste of an especially valuable time.

Leaving Lectures

What should you do at the end
of a lecture?

The closing minutes can sometimes prove to be the most important part of an entire lecture. Speakers who do not pace themselves well may have to cram half the lecture into the last five or ten minutes. Record such packed finales as rapidly as you can. After class, stay in your seat for a few extra minutes to write down as much as you can remember.

What should you do once
you've left the lecture room?

As soon as you leave the lecture room, while walking to your next class, mentally recall the lecture from beginning to end. Visualize the classroom, the lecturer, and any chalkboard work. After mentally recalling the lecture, ask yourself some questions: What was the lecturer getting at? What was the central point? What did I learn? How does what I learned fit with what I already know? If you discover anything you don't quite understand, no matter how small, make a note of it and ask the instructor to explain it before the next class.

Finishing Readings

How do you conduct a quick
overview of a reading
assignment?

After you've completed a reading assignment, step back and quickly overview what you've just read. Here are two ways to do so:

1. *Reread the abstract, introduction, or summary.* Any of these three common elements provides a brief overview of what you've just read and puts the ideas you've picked up in an appropriate context.
2. *Reread the title and headings.* If the text doesn't include an obvious overview, create one yourself by rereading the title, headings, and subheadings. In combination, these elements can help you mentally organize the information you've just learned. Don't spend a great deal of time doing this rereading. The primary purpose is to refresh your memory of the important points so that you'll be able to focus more carefully on them later. If you find you have questions, jot them down so you can ask them in class.

Summing Up

What are the basic steps in taking lecture and textbook notes?

Despite some obvious differences, the core concepts that underlie taking lecture notes, taking textbook notes, and marking up your textbook are remarkably similar. If you are careful to devise a system and stick with it, to gather information actively, efficiently, and flexibly, and to pull things together conscientiously at the end of a note-taking session, the handful of steps below should put you in a powerful position to master your notes and make them your own.

How to Take Lectures Notes

Figure 10.17 is a flow chart of this process.

1. **Record.** Put the lecturer's ideas and facts (along with any relevant diagrams) in the six-inch column of your Cornell System note sheet.
2. **Remember.** As soon as class is over, take a moment to mentally recall the entire lecture from start to finish.
3. **Refine.** Looking over your note sheets, add words, phrases, and facts you may have skipped or missed, and fix any difficult-to-decipher jottings.

Figure 10.17
Taking Lecture Notes

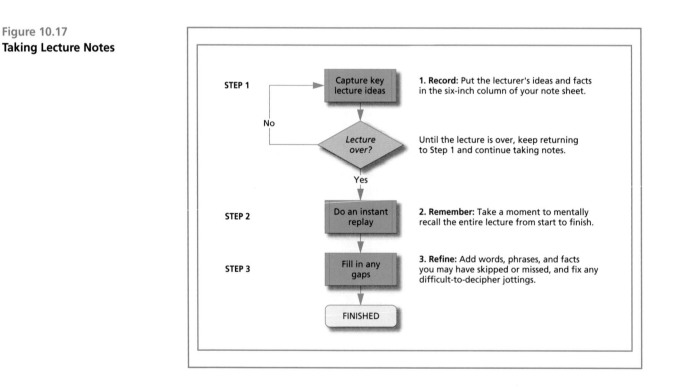

STEP 1 — Capture key lecture ideas

1. Record: Put the lecturer's ideas and facts in the six-inch column of your note sheet.

No — Lecture over?

Until the lecture is over, keep returning to Step 1 and continue taking notes.

Yes

STEP 2 — Do an instant replay

2. Remember: Take a moment to mentally recall the entire lecture from start to finish.

STEP 3 — Fill in any gaps

3. Refine: Add words, phrases, and facts you may have skipped or missed, and fix any difficult-to-decipher jottings.

FINISHED

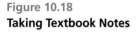

Figure 10.18
Taking Textbook Notes

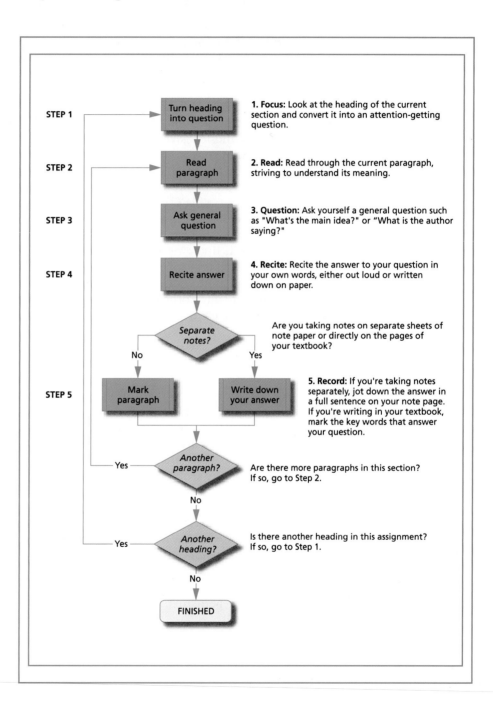

How to Take Textbook Notes

Figure 10.18 shows how this process works for textbook marking and separate notes.

1. **Focus.** As you read through each section, turn the headings and subheadings into attention-getting questions that help stimulate your thinking and your curiosity as you read on.
2. **Read.** Move through the assignment a paragraph at a time, striving to understand the meaning of the current paragraph.
3. **Question.** Before you move on to the next paragraph, take a moment to ask yourself, "What's the main idea?" or "What is the author saying?"
4. **Recite.** Recite the answer to the question you just asked, in your own words and preferably out loud.
5. **Record.** If you're marking your textbook, find the words or phrases in the paragraph that support your recited answer and mark them. If you're taking separate notes, jot down the answer you've just recited in the six-inch column of your Cornell System note sheet. Then repeat the entire process until you have completed the assignment.

FINAL WORDS

What does taking effective notes require?

Despite indisputable benefits, taking effective notes can be difficult for many students. Of course, most students take some sort of notes when they attend lectures; and a smaller number do so when they're reading. But in each case, the students who take notes often come close but don't reach the point where their notes are truly effective. Taking effective notes requires work; it requires time; and it forces you to be actively engaged in what you're reading or listening to. This can be a little daunting, especially when you may already have a false sense of accomplishment from half-baked notes or markings. Take that final step. Cross that threshold and make your note taking truly effective. You'll be working harder initially, it's true. All new skills require a little extra effort at the outset. But the benefits you derive will materialize almost immediately when you begin to master the notes that you have taken and make your new knowledge permanent instead of just fleeting.

HAVE YOU MISSED SOMETHING?

SENTENCE COMPLETION

Complete the following sentences with one of the three words listed below each sentence.

1. The Leon-Clyde story illustrates the rapidity and scope of
   _____.

   note taking   concentration   forgetting

2. Words such as *next, thus,* and *finally* often function as _____.

   signposts   diversions   intonation

3. The margin area at the outside of each page should be reserved for
   _____.

   reminders   questions   definitions

MATCHING

In each blank space in the left column, write the letter preceding the phrase in the right column that matches the left item best.

_____ 1. Socratic

_____ 2. Drawings

_____ 3. Summary area

_____ 4. Telegraphic

_____ 5. Two-page

_____ 6. Outline

_____ 7. Signposts

_____ 8. Cornell

a. Time-tested system for recording and mastering your notes

b. Ancient method that uses questions and answers to promote understanding

c. Provide clues for the organization of a chapter or lecture

d. Used for distilling a page's worth of notes down to a few sentences

e. The only note-taking format that is explicitly discouraged

f. Can succinctly describe ideas that are difficult to put in words

g. System for taking notes in especially fast-paced lectures

h. Note-taking style that employs only the most essential words

TRUE-FALSE

Write T *beside the* true *statements and* F *beside the* false *statements.*

_____ 1. Memory alone is sufficient for holding on to key ideas from text-books and lectures.

_____ 2. It's unlikely that a chapter or lecture will fit into a single note-taking format.

_____ 3. A sketch can rarely convey locations or relationships as clearly as a few sentences.

_____ 4. The "you" who took your notes may not be the same "you" who reviews them.

_____ 5. You're seldom expected to read supplemental materials as thoroughly as your textbook.

MULTIPLE CHOICE

Choose the word or phrase that completes each sentence most accurately, and circle the letter that precedes it.

1. To take notes effectively, you need
   a. a loose-leaf notebook.
   b. a system.
   c. sheets of unlined paper.
   d. several fundamental questions.

2. As you're taking notes, the cue column should
   a. remind you.
   b. get wider.
   c. remain empty.
   d. be filled.

3. One advantage of taking notes directly in your textbook is that
   a. your book is more valuable when you sell it at the end of the semester.
   b. your notes and your textbook can travel together as a unit.
   c. you can use a highlighter to single out important ideas and concepts.
   d. as the term progresses, your knowledge is likely to grow.

4. The story of Eddie Rickenbacker underscores the importance of
   a. airlines.
   b. correspondence courses.
   c. questions.
   d. textbook note taking.

5. Modified printing is
   a. speedy, like writing.
   b. neat, like printing.
   c. easy to learn.
   d. all of the above.

SHORT ANSWER   *Supply a brief answer for each of the following items.*

1. Discuss the principal components of the Cornell System.
2. Explain the various formats for taking notes.
3. Explain how organizational patterns can help increase understanding of lectures and readings.
4. Contrast the process of taking lecture notes with that of taking textbook notes.

WORDS IN CONTEXT

From the three choices beside each numbered item, select the one that most nearly expresses the meaning of the italicized word in the quote. Make a light check mark (✓) next to your choice.

No amount of *sophistication* is going to *allay* the fact that all your knowledge is about the past and all your decisions are about the future.

—Ian E. Wilson (1941–), chairman, General Electric Corporation

1. *sophistication*   argument   refinement   discussion

2. *allay* the fact   change   resolve   relieve

There is always an easy solution to every human problem—neat, *plausible* and wrong.

—H. L. Mencken (1880–1956), American editor and critic

3. *plausible*   reasonable   smart   advantageous

A committee is a *cul-de-sac* down which ideas are lured and then quietly strangled.

—Sir Barnett Cocks (1907–), English scientist

4. a *cul-de-sac*   trap   net   dead end

THE WORD HISTORY SYSTEM

Anecdote
unpublished notes

anecdote   an'-ec-dote' *n.* 1. A short account of an interesting or humorous incident. 2. Secret or hitherto undivulged particulars of history or biography.

Even among the ancient Greeks there were two kinds of stories—those given out publicly and those known only privately. The latter kind was called *anekdotos*, "not published." The word was formed by combining *a, an,* "not," and *ekdotos,* "given out." From this source comes French *anecdote* and thence English *anecdote,* which originally retained the Greek significance of "unpublished narratives." But an "unpublished narrative" especially about interesting things and famous people, has a ready market; so *anecdotes* are eagerly brought out on every occasion, and the word loses its original sense, coming to mean simply "a story," "an incident."

Reprinted by permission. From *Picturesque Word Origins* © 1933 by G. & C. Merriam Co. (now Merriam-Webster, Incorporated).

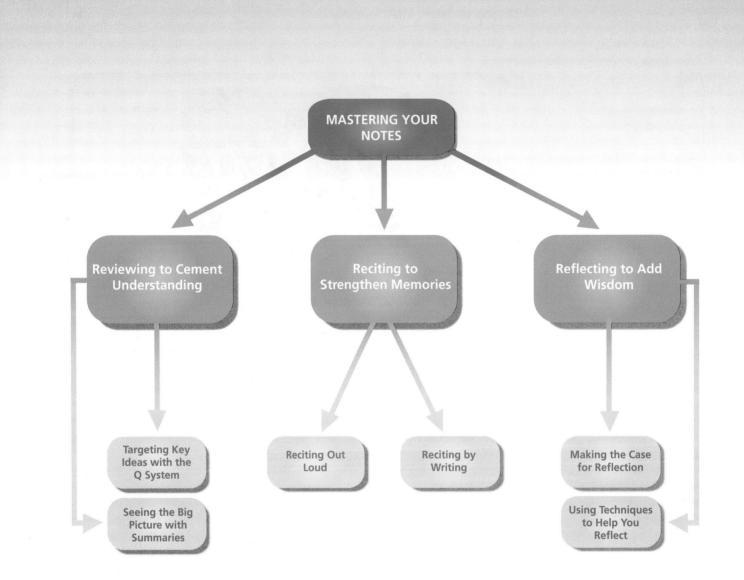

Mastering Your Notes

Order and simplification are the first steps toward the mastery of a subject— the actual enemy is the unknown.

Thomas Mann (1875–1955), German-American author

You've reached a crossroads. Now that you've conscientiously taken notes, you can let all that work go out the window and surrender to the unforgiving power of forgetting. Or you can put in extra effort and make what you've read and heard a permanent part of your knowledge. Congratulations. You've made the right choice. This chapter tells you how to take those notes and make them last by:

- **Reviewing to Cement Understanding**
- **Reciting to Strengthen Memories**
- **Reflecting to Add Wisdom**

How do you master your notes?

If you've taken notes thoroughly and conscientiously, you have every right to feel good about your efforts. But taking notes is not an end in itself. In fact, it is only the beginning. Far too many students jot down their notes and then forget about them until exam time rolls around. They leave them neglected in a desk drawer or repeatedly pass over their detailed textbook markings as they move on to subsequent chapters. This a tragic mistake and a great waste of time and effort. The only way to take advantage of all the information you've jotted down or marked up and highlighted—to master information that you've worked so hard to understand—is to review it carefully, recite it regularly, and reflect on it deeply until it becomes a permanent part of your knowledge.

Reviewing to Cement Understanding

What's wrong with reviewing your notes just by looking them over?

Most students review their notes by reading them over and perhaps by asking themselves a question or two to see what they remember. This spot-check approach may be common, but it's also haphazard. A systematic approach not only makes your review worthwhile, but also enables you to gain a clear sense of how you're doing.

What do you gain by conducting an immediate review?

The purpose of the immediate review is to cement your understanding of what you've just read or heard. As you learned in Chapter 4, memory can be fleeting; Chances are that when you were taking notes, especially in a lecture, you were taking in information an idea at a time. You probably didn't have the opportunity to make sure you truly understood everything you'd marked or written down, and you almost certainly didn't have the chance to step back and see how things all fit together. That's where the immediate review comes in. By targeting key ideas with the Q System, you are able to verify that you understand your notes. And by pulling things together in summary, you gain a valuable big-picture perspective.

Targeting Key Ideas with the Q System

What is the Q System?

The left-hand margins of your Cornell System paper or the outside margins of your textbook assignment should have remained blank up to this point. Here's your chance to put them to good use. At your earliest opportunity, move systematically through the notes you've just taken or the assignment you've just marked up, and come up with a question for each important idea. This is known as the Q System. Each question you write will provide a cue for the answer it addresses. Figure 11.1 provides a diagram of the Q System process.

How do you arrive at Q System questions for each important idea?

When using the Q System, try to avoid formulating a question that can be answered with a simple yes or no. Aim instead for questions that prompt you

Figure 11.1

Using the Q System to Review Your Notes

Whether you're reviewing text-book notes, lecture notes, or markings you've made directly in your textbook, the Q System is your best bet.

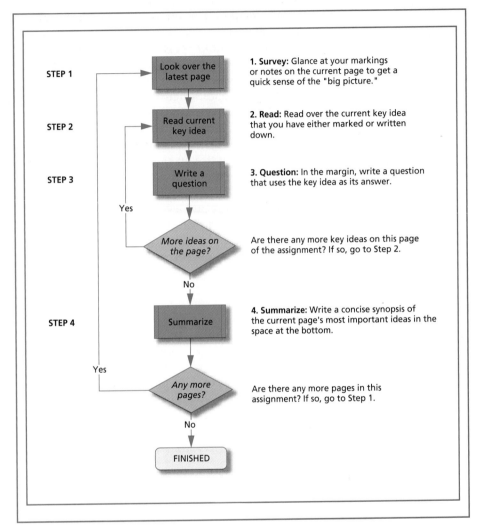

STEP 1 — Look over the latest page

1. Survey: Glance at your markings or notes on the current page to get a quick sense of the "big picture."

STEP 2 — Read current key idea

2. Read: Read over the current key idea that you have either marked or written down.

STEP 3 — Write a question

3. Question: In the margin, write a question that uses the key idea as its answer.

More ideas on the page? — Yes

Are there any more key ideas on this page of the assignment? If so, go to Step 2.

No

STEP 4 — Summarize

4. Summarize: Write a concise synopsis of the current page's most important ideas in the space at the bottom.

Any more pages? — Yes

Are there any more pages in this assignment? If so, go to Step 1.

No

FINISHED

to recall key information. Arriving at a suitable question is a little like playing the popular TV game show where contestants are given the answers and asked to supply the questions. And it's almost identical to the process you went through as you were reading an assignment and converting the headings into questions. The only real difference is that this time you're using ideas from your notes or the lines you underlined in your textbook as the starting point. The goal is to pose a question whose answer most effectively sums up the entire key idea or paragraph. Jot the question down in the margin alongside the information it refers to. Figure 11.2 shows some marginal questions for a textbook passage.

Repeat the process of formulating questions and jotting them in the margin as you systematically move through all the paragraphs in your text or notes from your note paper. It's OK to abbreviate your question, especially if you are short on space. (Figure 11.3 shows an excerpt from some classroom notes with abbreviated questions in the margins.) But be certain there's nothing ambiguous about what you've written down. After all, you'll want to be able to read these jottings throughout the semester. A badly abbreviated question may make sense to you now, but it could leave you scratching your head later on. The same applies to your handwriting. Make sure you can read it. You may want to use the modified printing style (explained in Chapter 10) to help you write quickly and legibly.

Properly ruled Cornell System note paper should provide plenty of room for your Q System questions. But if you've marked up your textbook and it has skinny margins, you have a handful of options to adjust for the limited space.

What form should your marginal questions take?

What should you do if there's no space for your questions?

Figure 11.2
Using the Q System with a Textbook Assignment

WRITING GOOD PAPERS IN COLLEGE

What 2 aspects lead to success?

The techniques of writing a good paper are easy to follow. You should remember two important aspects that lead to success. First, start work early on the paper. Second, if you have a choice, choose a subject that you are interested in or that you can develop an interest in.

What 3 elements might make up a paper?

Much of your work in college involves absorbing knowledge; when it comes to writing papers, you have the opportunity to put down on paper what you've ① learned about a subject, and perhaps ② your opinions and ③ conclusions on the subject.

What's the key in choosing a topic?

Writing is an important form of communication. To communicate well you must have something you really want to say. So if you have a choice of topics, choose one that intrigues you. If it isn't one that everyone else is writing on, all the better.

If not sure of a topic, do what?

If you're not sure about your choice of topic, do a little preliminary research to see what's involved in several topics before you make a final decision. Remember the caution about allowing yourself enough time? Here's where it comes into play. Take enough time to choose a topic carefully.

Figure 11.3
Using the Q System with Classroom Notes

Sept. 10, 2001 (Mon.) – History 101 –
Prof. A. Newhall

A. Some facts about Alaska

Who purchased Alaska? When? Cost?	1. William H. Seward, Sec. of State – fr. Russia in 1867 – $7,200,000.
Rough dimensions of mainland?	2. Size – mainland: length = 1,500 mi. – width = 1,200 mi.
How long is the Yukon River?	3. Yukon River – 1,979 mi. long
Name kinds of minerals?	4. Minerals – oil, gold, silver, coal, chrome, iron, etc.
How are the forests?	5. Forests – commercial timber = 85 billion board feet
Two most numerous fish?	6. Fish – world's richest in salmon and halibut
Name several kinds of fur?	7. Furs – seal, mink, otter, beaver, fox, etc.
What's the highest mt. in No. America?	8. Mt. McKinley – 20,320 ft. – highest in No. America
When admitted as state?	9. Statehood – Jan. 3, 1959 – 49th State
Who designed the state flag?	10. State flag – designed by 13-year-old Benjamin Benson

Try the Sticky Note Method

How does the sticky note method work?

Jot down the same sort of question that you would have written in the margin, but put it on a "sticky note" instead (use one sticky note per question). When you've finished writing the question, affix it near the paragraph it refers to. Because your sticky notes may come unstuck, it's often a good idea to put a circled number in the margin of your textbook next to the paragraph your question is intended for and to number your sticky note to match, adding the page number as well in case you renumber with each new page.

Use the Bookmark Method

What does the bookmark method involve?

One method that many students swear by is to jot their questions on slips of scrap paper that resemble extra-wide bookmarks (about two-and-a-half inches wide, the same dimension as the margin in Cornell System paper). Use one bookmark for each pair of facing pages, keeping a running list of the questions for the left-hand page on one side and putting the questions for the right-hand page on the other. Just as you did with the sticky note system, number each question and put a corresponding number in the margin alongside the paragraph it refers to. When you've written all of the questions for the two pages, you can lodge the slip in the book at just the right spot, the same way you would an ordinary bookmark.

Take Separate Notes

What is the advantage of using separate notes?

Of course, if your textbook doesn't offer an accommodating set of margins, it might be simpler to take separate notes. You'll miss some of the advantages of taking notes directly in your book (see Chapter 10), but you'll be able to carry the notes for your assignment (even stash them in a pocket or purse) without having to lug around the book.

What do you accomplish by writing marginal questions?

Regardless of the method you choose when using the Q System, you will be accomplishing something vital. The straightforward process of formulating questions should provide you with a thorough and immediate review of your material. Although it's possible to do so, it's unnecessarily difficult (not to mention pointless) to "fake" questions for each idea. Ask questions that truly get to the heart of the information. To be able to turn an idea into a meaningful question, you need to have a genuine grasp of that idea.

Seeing the Big Picture with Summaries

What role do summaries play in your notes?

In the same way that questions from the Q System provide you with a better grasp of the important ideas from your notes, summaries help supply the context. It's surprisingly easy to get caught up in the details of your notes and lose the grand scheme of things in the process. Writing a summary is a sure-fire way to force yourself to think about and come to grips with the broader ideas, trends, lessons, and themes that run through notes like a thread. Summaries supply a straightforward answer to the question, "What is this page about?" This cut-to-the-chase aspect of summaries should be especially handy when you're studying for an exam or doing research for a paper and want to go straight to the key information in your notes without having to read through every note on every page to find it.

The Standard Summary

What is the standard system for writing summaries?

The standard system for summaries is to write one at the bottom of every page. Figure 11.4 shows an example. If you're taking notes directly in your textbook, you may find that there's more room to write at the top of each page than at the bottom. Either place is fine. Regardless of whether you're taking notes in your textbook or on separate sheets, don't pen an epic; you probably don't have the time, and you definitely don't have the room. Just come up with a concentrated

Figure 11.4
Summarizing a Page of Lecture Notes in Two Sentences

Psych. 105 – Prof. Martin – Sept. 14 (Mon.)

MEMORY

Memory tricky – Can recall instantly many trivial things of childhood, yet forget things recently worked hard to learn & retain.

How do psychologists account for remembering?

Memory Trace
— Fact that we retain information means that some change was made in the brain.
— Change called "memory trace."
— "Trace" probably a molecular arrangement similar to molecular changes in a magnetic recording tape.

What's a "memory trace"?

Three memory systems: sensory, short term, long term.
— Sensory (lasts one second)
   Ex. Words or numbers sent to brain by sight (visual image) start to disintegrate within a few tenths of a second & gone in one full second, unless quickly transferred to S-T memory by verbal repetition.
— Short-term memory [STM] (lasts 30 seconds)
   • Experiments show: a syllable of 3 letters remembered 50% of the time after 3 seconds.
     Totally forgotten end of 30 seconds.
   • S-T memory — limited capacity — holds average of 7 items.
   • More than 7 items — jettisons some to make room.
   • To hold items in STM, must rehearse — must hear sound of words internally or externally.
— Long-term memory [LTM] (lasts a lifetime or short time).
   • Transfer fact or idea by
     (1) Associating w/information already in LTM.
     (2) Organizing information into meaningful units.
     (3) Understanding by comparing & making relationships.
     (4) Frameworking – fit pieces in like in a jigsaw puzzle.
     (5) Reorganizing – combining new & old into a new unit.
     (6) Rehearsing – aloud to keep memory trace strong.

What are the three memory systems?

How long does sensory memory retain information?

How is information transferred to STM?

What are the retention times of STM?

What's the capacity of the STM?

How to hold information in STM?

What are the retention times of LTM?

What are the six ways to transfer infomation from STM to LTM?

Three kinds of memory systems are sensory, which retains information for about 1 second; short-term, which retains for a maximum of 30 seconds; and long-term, which varies from a lifetime of retention to a relatively short time.
   The six ways (activities) to transfer information to the long-term memory are associating, organizing, understanding, frameworking, reorganizing, and rehearsing.

sentence or two that efficiently pulls together the key information on the page. If space permits, it's a good idea to use complete sentences for your summaries. This reinforces your goal of articulately expressing what's important on the page. It can be a little too easy to disguise your confusion in an abbreviated sentence. Now is the time to make sure you grasp what you've written down or read. If you don't understand things at this stage, there's a good chance that they will grow murkier with time. Make the effort right now to see clearly. If you still don't understand, you have time to get help from a tutor or instructor. If you wait, it may be too late.

The Wrap-Up Summary

What is the approach for the wrap-up summary?

Rather than summarizing each page, you may choose to write a longer summary at the very end of your lecture notes or textbook assignment. Depending on the length or importance of the assignment, this method may be enough, but in general it's not recommended, at least not in isolation. Even if you write several paragraphs for your wrap-up summary, you probably can't expect to approach the level of insight and detail that you gain from summarizing each page. However, if the lecture is especially brief or the reading assignment is a supplemental one that doesn't require a great deal of attention (see Chapter 10), a wrap-up summary may suffice.

The Split-Level Summary

Why is the split-level approach best for summarizing your notes?

The best way to review and summarize your notes is to combine the standard summary with the wrap-up summary. Start with the standard summary, summarizing each page with a sentence or two. Then, rather than rereading all of your notes to arrive at a wrap-up summary, simply reread the summaries you've written for each page and come up with a summary of your summaries. This two-level approach makes your notes extremely useful and flexible. If you just need a reminder of what a single assignment or lecture was about, you can read the wrap-up summary. If you need more detail, you can go to the next level and read the summary on a particular page.

What else do questions and summaries provide besides an immediate review?

Formulating questions for each important idea in your notes and then coming up with summaries not only provides an extremely directed and effective means of review, but it also sets the stage for recitation, the most valuable technique you can use to help commit your notes to memory.

Reciting to Strengthen Memories

What is the role of reciting?

Now that you've added Q System questions (and brief summaries) to each page and conducted a thorough review in the process, how are you going to hold onto all that valuable information? After all, forgetting never lets up. It works continuously to expel from memory what you worked so hard to put there. You can bring forgetting almost to a standstill by using the power of recitation.

How does reciting work?

Reciting forces you to think, and this thinking leaves a neural trace in your memory. Reciting promotes concentration, forms a sound basis for understanding the next paragraph or the next chapter, provides time for consolidation, ensures that facts and ideas are remembered accurately, and supplies immediate feedback on how you're doing. Moreover, experiments have shown that the greater the proportion of reciting time to reading time, the greater the learning. Students who spent 20 percent of their time reading and 80 percent reciting did much better than students who spent less time reciting and more time reading.

What is the process for reciting?

The process of reciting is relatively straightforward. Go back to the first page and cover it with a blank sheet of paper, exposing only your Q System questions. (If you used the sticky note method, you should still be able to obscure the text while reading your questions. If you chose the bookmark method, you can use your marker to cover the text.) Read the first question, and answer it in your own words. Slide the blank sheet down to check your answer. If your answer is wrong or incomplete, try again. Do this until you get the answer right. Go through the entire assignment this way. (See Figure 11.5 for a diagram of the entire process.) Your aim is to establish an accurate, crystal-clear impression in your memory, because that's what you want to return to during an exam. If the impression in your memory is fuzzy at this time, it will be even fuzzier three or four weeks later (see Chapter 4).

Reciting Out Loud

How do you recite out loud?

The traditional way to recite is out loud and in your own words. When you recite aloud, speak clearly so there's no mistake about what you are saying. Express the ideas in complete sentences, using the proper signal words. For example, when you are reciting a list of ideas or facts, enumerate them by saying *first, second,* and so on. Insert words such as *furthermore, however,* and *finally.* When you do so in oral practice, you will do so more naturally in writing during an exam.

Reciting by Writing

How do you recite by writing?

If you are reluctant or unable to recite aloud, you can recite by writing out (or typing) your answers instead. This method is slower than traditional reciting, but it provides added benefits. Even more than reciting aloud, reciting by writing supplies solid proof that you can answer your questions. After all, you have a written record. And it provides excellent practice for essay and short-answer tests. To recite by writing, move through your notes a question at a time just as you would normally. But instead of speaking your answer, write it down on a sheet of paper. Then uncover the page and compare the answer you've just written with the one in your notes.

Figure 11.5
The Process of Reciting Your Notes

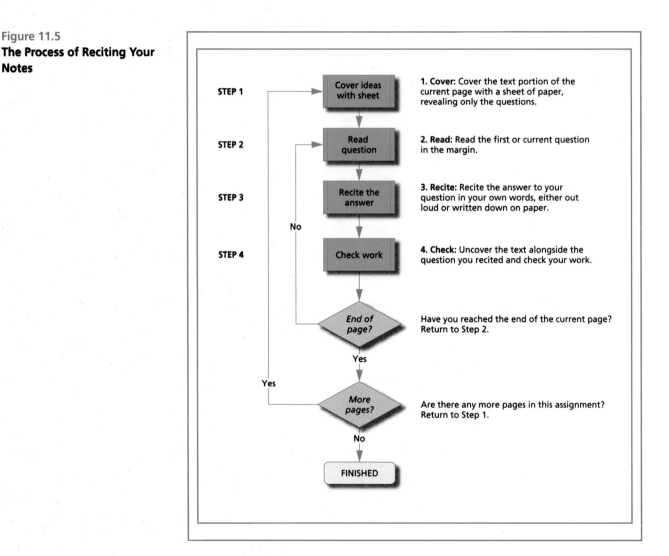

STEP 1 — Cover ideas with sheet — **1. Cover:** Cover the text portion of the current page with a sheet of paper, revealing only the questions.

STEP 2 — Read question — **2. Read:** Read the first or current question in the margin.

STEP 3 — Recite the answer — **3. Recite:** Recite the answer to your question in your own words, either out loud or written down on paper.

STEP 4 — Check work — **4. Check:** Uncover the text alongside the question you recited and check your work.

No

End of page? — Have you reached the end of the current page? Return to Step 2.

Yes

Yes

More pages? — Are there any more pages in this assignment? Return to Step 1.

No

FINISHED

Reflecting to Add Wisdom

What is reflection?

After you learn facts and ideas through reviewing and reciting, take some time to mull them over. Use your innate sense of curiosity to speculate or play with the knowledge you've acquired. This is called reflection. To engage in reflection is to bring creativity to your learning. Ask yourself such questions as these:

What is the significance of these facts and ideas? What principle or principles are they based on? What else could they be applied to? How do they fit in with what I already know? From these facts and ideas, what else can I learn? When you reflect, you weave new facts and ideas into your existing knowledge and create a fabric of genuine wisdom. History's greatest thinkers have relied on reflection for their breakthroughs. They make a strong case for reflection as a vital skill. With a technique or two to get you started, you can begin using reflection on your own to master your notes and gain lasting learning and genuine insight.

Making the Case for Reflection

What did Bethe say about reflection?

Professor Hans Bethe, Cornell University's famous nuclear physicist and Nobel Prize winner, talked about reflection as used by a scientist:

> To become a good scientist one must live with the problem he's working on. The problem must follow the scientist wherever he goes. You can't be a good scientist working only eight hours a day. Science must be the consuming interest of your life. You must want to know. Nothing matters more than finding the answer to the question or the problem you are engaged in.[1]

What is the connection between reflection and creativity?

Professor Bethe went on to say that students who go only as far as their textbooks and lectures take them can become proficient, but never creative. Creativity comes only with reflection. That is, seeing new material in the light of what you already know is the only road to original ideas, for having an idea is nothing more than discovering a relationship not seen before. And it is impossible to have ideas without reflecting.

What was Whitehead's position on reflection?

Alfred North Whitehead, famous British philosopher and mathematician, strongly advocated reflection. He, too, spoke about the knowledge that grows out of throwing ideas "into fresh combinations." He viewed reflection as taking what one already knows and projecting one's thought beyond familiar experience—considering new knowledge and ideas in the light of the old, and the old in the light of the new.

What was Schopenhauer's point about reflection?

The famous German philosopher Arthur Schopenhauer had exceptionally strong views on the importance of reflection.

> A library may be very large, but if it is in disorder, it is not so useful as one that is small but well arranged. In the same way, a man may have a great mass of knowledge, but if he has not worked it up by thinking it over for himself, it has much less value than a far smaller amount which he has thoroughly pondered. For it is only

[1] Interview with Professor Hans Bethe, May 19, 1960.

when a man looks at his knowledge from all sides, and combines the things he knows by comparing truth with truth, that he obtains a complete hold over it and gets it into his power.

Reflections should not be left vague. Pursue the problem until ideas take definite shape. If you need more information, an encyclopedia or a standard book on the subject will often give you what you need to bring fuzzy ideas into focus.[2]

What is the connection between reflection and the subconscious?

The subconscious plays an important role in creative thinking and discovery. We have all had an exciting idea or even the solution to a problem suddenly flash upon us when we weren't consciously thinking about it. The great Hungarian physicist Leo Szilard came up with the solution to the nuclear chain reaction while crossing a London street. Archimedes arrived at the principle of displacement while sitting in his bathtub. The mind continues to work on concepts even when you aren't aware of it. The process that initiates much of this deep thinking is reflection.

Using Techniques to Help You Reflect

What is a big advantage of reflection?

A great advantage of reflection is its flexibility. It can be molded to fit your imagination. You can take it with you wherever you go and make use of it in spare moments. You can reflect while walking from one building to another, standing in line, waiting for a friend, or riding a bus.

What is a drawback of reflection?

But reflection's flexibility can also be a disadvantage if you're unsure of how to get started. This uncertainty prompts some students to skip over the reflection step completely. Although there are no specific reflection steps like those you might find for reviewing or reciting, there are a number of strategies you can use to ease into a reflective mindset.

Use the Silver Dollar System

How does the Silver Dollar System work?

You can reflect on the information from your notes and make it more manageable by using the Silver Dollar System:

Read through your notes and make an *S* in the margin next to any idea that seems important. Depending on the number of pages of notes you read, you'll probably wind up with several dozen *S*'s.

Now read only the notes you have flagged with an *S*. As you go through these flagged notes for a second time, select the ideas that seem particularly important, and draw a vertical line through the *S*'s that are next to them. Your symbol will look like this: $.

[2]*Essays of Arthur Schopenhauer,* selected and translated by T. Bailey Saunders (New York: A. L. Burt, 1892), p. 321.

Make a third and final pass through your notes, reading only those ideas that have been marked $. Out of these notes, mark the truly outstanding ideas—there will be only a handful of them—with another vertical line so your markings look like dollar signs: **$**

How does the Silver Dollar System stimulate reflection?

The Silver Dollar System stimulates reflection by helping you compare the relative weights of the ideas you have noted. It shows you at a glance which ideas are crucial to remember and which are not. The **$** sign alerts you to the truly important ideas, the "Silver Dollar" ideas that should receive most of your attention. Next come the $ ideas; they are worthy but shouldn't clutter up your memory if you have a lot to remember in a limited amount of time. Finally, the *S* ideas can be ignored. Although you flagged these as potentially important ideas, since then you've twice marked ideas that were even more important.

Rearrange Your Information

How is rearranging your information helpful?

You almost always gain insight when you look at information from a different perspective. If, for example, you've been studying countries geographically, you might want to consider grouping them by their systems of government or comparing them chronologically. You may want to group existing information under categories such as "pros" and "cons" or "before" and "after," depending on the nature of the information you are mastering.

Put It in Context

Why is context an important factor in reflection?

Few ideas are meaningful when viewed in isolation. They need context to establish them in a realm that you can truly understand. For example, if you read about a scientific discovery from a certain time period, consider examining other events from the year the discovery was made or the place where the discovery occurred. Was this before or after the Civil War, the Second World War, the Vietnam War? Had the telephone, the radio, or the computer been invented? Were people traveling by horse, by car, or by jet? These investigations supply a basic background (see Chapter 4) that will often yield a deeper understanding.

Ask More Questions

Why is it helpful to ask additional questions?

In press conferences, the follow-up question is sometimes more insightful than the original question. If you've been using the Q System, each idea in your notes or paragraph in your reading assignment has an accompanying question. Come up with a follow-up to the original question and see if your notes or your text can provide the answer. If not, you might want to dig deeper for clues.

Think Visually

How can concept maps be used as a reflection tool?

Chapter 8 explains how concept maps can be used to work out problems, explore possibilities, and establish connections. These are exactly the sorts of issues that reflection addresses. Take the key concepts from your notes or from a chapter assignment, put them in ovals on a plain sheet of paper, and try numerous ways of arranging and connecting them. If you do, you will almost certainly learn something that wasn't clear to you when they were merely isolated words on a page.

Combine Textbook and Lecture Notes

How do you combine textbook and lecture notes?

Although the classroom lectures you attend should presumably relate to your reading assignments, you won't always see the connections clearly until you can actually place notes from both side by side. Using the format shown in Figure 11.6, jot down the most important information from a textbook assignment in the middle column of the three-column note sheet. Then add any lecture notes that deal with the same topic in the right column, alongside the textbook notes they pertain to. Finally, just as you did with your original notes, use the Q System to arrive at a question for which the textbook note *and* any related information from the lecture is the answer. It's impossible to predict in advance what you'll learn from this experience, but by combining two sets of notes you'll almost certainly arrive at an answer that is greater than the sum of the parts. This is the essence of reflection.

FINAL WORDS

How do a scholar and a student differ?

There's a huge difference between proficiency and creativity. You can become proficient by studying your textbooks and lecture notes, but you will never be creative until you try to see beyond the facts, to leap mentally beyond the given. If your object is simply to tackle tests, pass your courses, and emerge from college with a degree and reasonably good prospects for employment, this book should serve you well. But if your aspirations aim higher, this book will serve you even better. The things that distinguish a scholar from a mere student are perpetual curiosity and an unquenchable thirst for learning. Reviewing and reciting should help you reach your modest goals. Reflection will enable you to reach for the stars.

Figure 11.6

Cornell System Format for Combining Lecture and Textbook Notes

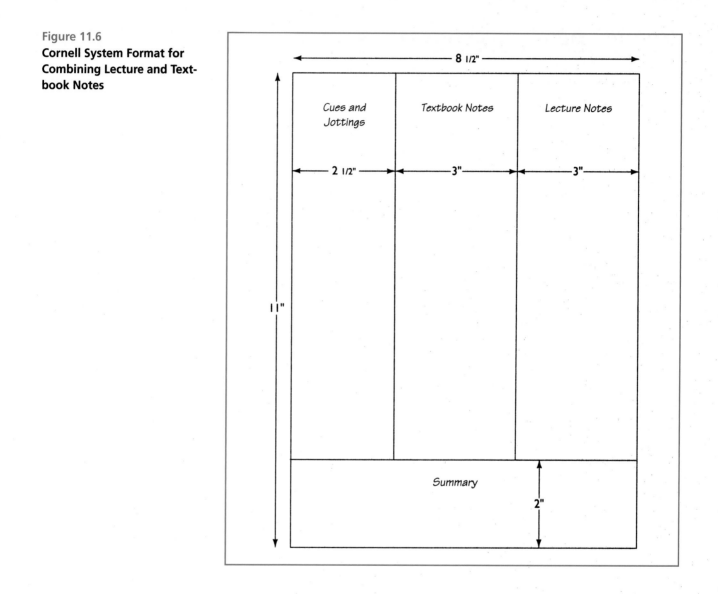

HAVE YOU MISSED SOMETHING?

SENTENCE COMPLETION   *Complete the following sentences with one of the three words listed below each sentence.*

1. You can bring forgetting almost to a standstill with _____.

   summaries   recitation   questions

2. Creativity comes only with _____.

   practice   reflection   summaries

3. Ideas in your notes that you have marked with an *S* can be _____.

   saved   difficult   ignored

MATCHING   *In each blank space in the left column, write the letter preceding the phrase in the right column that matches the left item best.*

_____ 1. Reflection	a.	Method that summarizes an entire assignment as well as each page
_____ 2. Recitation	b.	System that allows you to reduce and reflect on your note sheets
_____ 3. Split-level	c.	Used as an alternative to the traditional method of reciting your notes
_____ 4. Bookmark	d.	Using your innate curiosity to mull over ideas
_____ 5. Rereading	e.	Alternate Q System method when your textbook margins are too narrow
_____ 6. Silver Dollar	f.	Provided when you add questions and summaries to your notes
_____ 7. Review	g.	Mistakenly thought to be an effective method of reviewing
_____ 8. Writing	h.	Repeating key information from memory and in your own words

TRUE-FALSE   *Write* T *beside the* true *statements and* F *beside the* false *statements.*

_____ 1. Most students review their notes by reading them over.

_____ 2. When using the Q System, try to come up with yes-or-no questions.

_____ 3. It's OK to abbreviate your Q System questions.

_____ 4. Cornell System paper should provide plenty of room for your Q System questions.

_____ 5. Although reciting by writing is slower than traditional reciting, it provides added benefits.

MULTIPLE CHOICE

Choose the word or phrase that completes each sentence most accurately, and circle the letter that precedes it.

1. The primary purpose of an immediate review is to
   a. cement your understanding.
   b. spot-check your notes.
   c. look up words or terms you don't know.
   d. make sure your notes are legible.

2. If your textbook's margins are too narrow for Q System questions, you can use
   a. the sticky note method.
   b. the bookmark method.
   c. separate notes.
   d. all of the above.

3. Adding summaries to your notes helps you
   a. zero in on key ideas.
   b. gain a broader perspective.
   c. anticipate multiple-choice questions.
   d. include questions you couldn't fit in the margins.

4. The traditional way to recite is
   a. out loud.
   b. in your own words.
   c. from memory.
   d. all of the above.

5. One strength and weakness of reflection is its
   a. cost.
   b. repetitiveness.
   c. flexibility.
   d. imagination.

SHORT ANSWER   *Supply a brief answer for each of the following items.*

1. Elaborate on the role that questions play in the review process.
2. Explain the steps in the Silver Dollar System.
3. Discuss how reflection is important and why it is often overlooked.
4. Compare the differing approaches to summarizing your notes.

WORDS IN CONTEXT

From the three choices beside each numbered item, select the one that most nearly expresses the meaning of the italicized word in the quote. Make a light check mark (✔) next to your choice.

It is a *capital* mistake to theorize before one has data.

—Sir Arthur Conan Doyle (1859–1930), British physician and novelist, author of Sherlock Holmes series

1. *capital* mistake   federal   criminal   major

A theory has only the alternative of being right or wrong. A model has a third possibility—it may be right but *irrelevant.*

—Manfred Eigen (1927–), German chemist

2. but *irrelevant*   unreliable   unrelated   dangerous

Economics is a subject *profoundly conducive* to *cliché, resonant* with boredom. On few topics is an American audience so practiced in turning off its ears and minds. And none can say that the response is ill advised.

—John Kenneth Galbraith (1908–), American economist

3. *profoundly*   completely   academically   abundantly

4. *conducive*   impartial   favorable   difficult

5. *cliché*   grasp   ridicule   trite phrase

6. *resonant*   complete   filled   echoing

THE WORD HISTORY SYSTEM

Arrive
to come to shore

arrive ar-rive' *v.* 1. To reach a destination. 2. To achieve success or recognition.

Latin *ad* means "to" and *ripa* means "shore" or "sloping bank of a river." These two words combined are found in the Late Latin *arripare,* "to come to shore." Old French in the course of centuries changed the word into the form *ariver,* and Medieval (Middle) English borrowed it as *ariven,* meaning "to land." The meaning broadened from "going ashore" to mean reaching a point in any way. Today, when we *arrive* by automobile or airplane, it is interesting to think of the original meaning, "to come to shore."

Reprinted by permission. From *Picturesque Word Origins* © 1933 by G. & C. Merriam Co. (now Merriam-Webster, Incorporated).

PART

IV

Test-Taking Skills

12   Managing Test Anxiety

13   Answering Objective Tests

14   Tackling Essay Tests

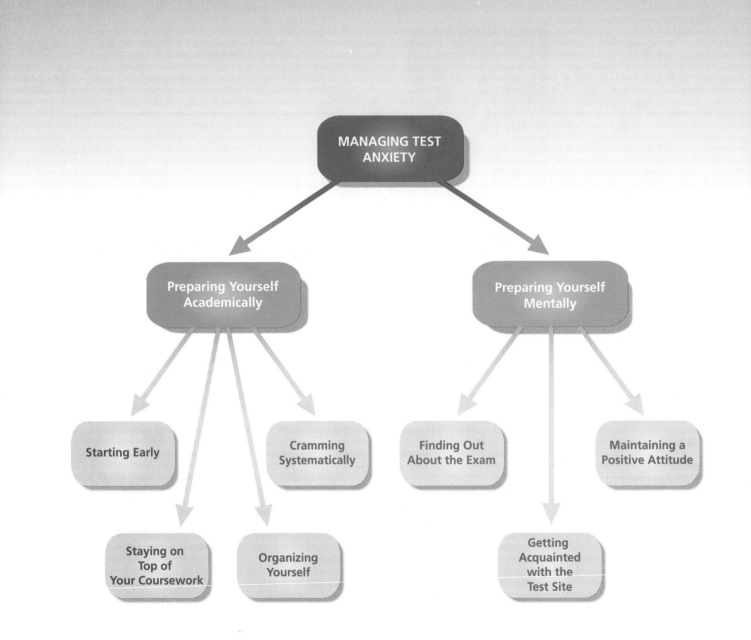

Managing Test Anxiety

The will to win is nothing without the will to prepare.

Juma Ikangaa, marathoner

Walking into an exam room can be a frightening journey into the unknown. But if you're prepared before you sit down to take a test, any fear you initially feel will evaporate, and anxiety will subside. This chapter explains how to manage test anxiety by:

- **Preparing Yourself Academically**
- **Preparing Yourself Mentally**

What is the simple cure for test anxiety?

The cure for test anxiety is simple but powerful: preparation. Advance preparation is like a fire drill: It teaches you what to do and how to proceed, even in a high-stress situation, because you've been through the procedure so many times that you know it by heart. To manage the anxiety that often arises at test time, you can prepare yourself both academically and mentally.

Preparing Yourself Academically

How do you prepare yourself academically?

To be prepared academically, start early, stay on top of your coursework, and organize yourself and your studying plan. Even if you're forced to cram for a test, do so as sensibly and methodically as you would if there were no time constraints.

Starting Early

How can you get a head start on a course?

The pressure is almost nonexistent at the start of a new term. Take advantage of this calm before the storm. Get a head start in a course by picking up your textbooks, looking over your syllabus, and learning where and how to get academic help.

Get Your Textbooks Right Away

What's the advantage of getting your textbooks early?

Many students wait until the last minute, sometimes even until after the first assignment, before they get their textbooks. This is a common mistake. There's no reason to wait this long and every reason to buy your books as soon as you are registered for a course. Obtaining your books in advance allows you to look through the text in a leisurely manner and get a sense of where the book and the course will be headed. With this early start, you will be able to build a foundation of understanding.

Read Your Syllabus

How does reading your syllabus help you prepare?

One of the most frequently wasted resources in a college-level course is the syllabus, or course plan, usually handed out by the instructor during the first week of class. In the same way that surveying your textbook gives you a sense of the book as a whole, reading the syllabus from start to finish at the earliest opportunity provides a valuable overview of the course and makes preparing for tests much easier.

Other than a course plan, what information may the syllabus contain?

At times a syllabus can be an unexpected source of information. A few years ago, a student complained to the instructor that a paragraph-long essay question on the final exam was unreasonably difficult and totally unexpected. The instructor calmly pulled out a copy of the syllabus and pointed to the bottom of the page as the student's jaw dropped. The "unexpected" question had been printed on the last page of the syllabus and had been handed out at the beginning of the semester! The student hadn't bothered to read it.

Get Help If You Need It

When should you look for help in a course?

As soon as you realize you're going to have trouble with one of your courses, get help. Don't struggle through a course and wait until the last minute before seeking tutoring help. By then, the tutors may all have been taken.

What can you do to make getting a tutor a little easier?

Before the semester even begins, find out where your campus tutoring service is located and how to arrange for a tutor. New students can usually pick up this information during orientation. Keep it handy; if you find that you are struggling with a course, you can arrange for a tutor without delay.

Staying on Top of Your Coursework

How do you stay on top of your coursework?

When the time comes to start focusing on an exam, you can seriously endanger your performance if you have to spend valuable time getting caught up. If you stay on top of your assignments throughout the semester—by taking notes as you read or listen and by mastering those notes at the earliest possible opportunity—they won't come back to haunt you when it's time to study for finals.

Take Notes

Why is note taking so important?

If you make a regular habit of taking notes in the Cornell format for both lectures and textbook assignments and of singling out the key ideas from the notes you have taken, you'll accumulate a valuable storehouse of knowledge, and you'll have an excellent start in your preparation for upcoming exams. The next step is to master the notes you have taken.

Master Your Material

What is the key to mastering your material?

The key to mastery is recitation (see Chapter 4), which is the most powerful method known to psychologists for embedding facts and ideas in your memory. If you took notes using the Q System (see Chapter 11), writing the questions in the left margin enabled you to recite the information you had jotted down on your note sheet. Not only do these questions prompt you to recall information instead of simply recognizing it, but they also provide an opportunity to study in a way that closely matches the format of your exams. Remember, if you can't answer the questions now, you haven't learned the material, and you won't be able to recall it during an exam.

Organizing Yourself

How can you organize yourself?

The work you put into preparing yourself academically by starting early and by keeping up with your classes and assignments can be best used if you make it a point to organize both your time and your notes.

Organize Your Time with Schedules

What kinds of schedules help prepare you for exams?

Scheduling is important throughout the term. Three-part scheduling plans (explained in Chapter 2) allow you to set aside time for reviewing material so that you won't get caught off-guard by a quiz or test.

How should you deal with scheduling a week or two before test time?

As you near the end of a term or semester, scheduling your time becomes even more crucial. If you haven't been using schedules, now's a good time to start. If you have been, you probably feel on top of things already. In either case, it's a good idea to organize your time with a homestretch schedule especially designed to help you tie up loose ends and get you through that all-important last week before exams begin. When exam week arrives, devise another schedule that specifies when each of your tests takes place and that includes time for meals, sleep, and recreation, which are particularly crucial during exam week.

What sort of things belong in a homestretch schedule?

Make up a homestretch schedule.   Use the format in Figure 12.1 for your homestretch schedule. (This schedule uses the grid discussed in Chapter 2.) Start by filling in the time blocks that will be taken up by meals, sleep, job, and recreation. Next fill in your classes. Do not miss classes for any reason; you will want to hear the instructors' answers to students' questions about exams. Finally, fill in the time you will need to complete term papers and other assignments. Make sure you get them done before exam week. You don't want unfinished business to interfere with your studying or distract your thinking during exams.

What should you do with the available time at the end of the week?

Even after you've scheduled time for all your pre-exam obligations, you will likely find that some time is available toward the end of the week. Use it to study for your exams. Fill in the exact study times and subjects. Instead of writing "Study" in the time blocks, write exactly what you plan to study: "Study economics, chaps 1 to 10" or "Summarize sociology notes." Make a schedule that you'll be able to follow, and then be sure to follow it.

What sort of things belong in an exam-week schedule?

Use an exam-week schedule.   Toward the end of the week before finals, make up a schedule for exam week. Fill in the times for your exams and for meals, rest, and recreation. Remember that you must be in tiptop mental, emotional, and physical shape to do your best on the exams. Eating the right food, getting the right amount of sleep, and exercising regularly are important tools not only for maintaining good health but also for managing the sort of stress all too common around exam time. Therefore, don't skip meals, sleep, or recreation in an effort to squeeze in more studying time.

When should you schedule your final reviews?

By finals' week, the bulk of your preparation should be completed. Leave a block of time immediately before each exam to review important information. The less time you allow between this last review and the exam, the less forgetting will take place. Review calmly and thoughtfully, and carry this calm, thoughtful behavior right into the exam room.

Figure 12.1
Format for the Homestretch Schedule

	M	Tu	W	Th	F	Sat	Sun
7:00							
8:00							
9:00							
10:00							
11:00							
12:00							
1:00							
2:00							
3:00							
4:00							
5:00							
6:00							
7:00							
8:00							
9:00							
10:00							

What is the best way to organize your notes?

Organize your notes with summary sheets. The best way to organize your notes before an exam is by consolidating them into a set of summary sheets (a highly concentrated version of the notes), then reciting those sheets as you would your regular notes.

How do you pare down a semester's worth of notes to a handful of sheets?

How can you reduce your notes so dramatically? You can do it by being selective. Although you may have been able to master the main ideas and subideas after each lecture or reading assignment, combining all this information and remembering it are not easy tasks. To recall all the lectures and readings without overloading your memory, you should limit your notes to a handful of truly important ideas from each lecture and reading.

Why bother distilling your notes down to summary sheets?

Why go through the process of making up summary sheets? First, it enables you to review and add to the notes you took throughout the semester and thereby increase the information you have retained. Second, it produces a superconcentrated set of notes that you can use as a refresher immediately before the exam. Finally, it helps you categorize your information under specific headings and thus improve your ability to retrieve it from your memory during the exam.

What are regular summary
sheets?

Make regular summary sheets.   If you have used the Silver Dollar System to pick out the main ideas and subideas from your notes, reducing those notes one step further should be relatively simple. Include only notes marked with a **$** in your summary sheets. If you haven't used the Silver Dollar System, you can narrow your notes all at once by employing it now, although the process will be time consuming.

Figure 12.2 is an example of a standard summary sheet. It is indistinguishable from a regular Cornell note sheet except that it contains the most important ideas from several lectures, rather than just one, compressed into the same amount of space.

How do advanced summary
sheets differ from regular ones?

Devise advanced summary sheets.   Although making up summary sheets of any kind gives you a chance to review your notes, devising advanced summary sheets also enables you to reflect on the information you have learned thus far. Reflection involves thinking about and applying the facts and ideas you've learned. By rearranging your notes into categories that you've chosen yourself, you are doing just that.

How does creating advanced
summary sheets help
reflection?

Remember that "creativity comes only with reflection" (see Chapter 11). That's because reflection leads to *advantageous learning*—learning propelled by a burning desire to know something. What distinguishes advantageous learning from regular learning and advanced summary sheets from ordinary summary sheets is your mental attitude. You can't help being curious about your notes when you reorganize them for your summary sheets. The knowledge you gain from doing so not only provides excellent preparation for an exam but also remains with you long after the test is over.

Figure 12.3 shows an advanced summary sheet that represents more than ten pages of notes taken during two lectures. Notice how the points are categorized by century and are placed side by side for ease of comparison. The questions in the margin are appropriately brief; they hint at, but do not supply, each comparison.

Figure 12.4 shows an advanced summary sheet derived from textbook markings. The subcategories "Advantages" and "Disadvantages" were supplied by the student who took the notes. The material in each subcategory was originally scattered throughout the chapter.

Figure 12.2
A Standard Summary Sheet

<u>Steps in Writing</u>

What are four
elements of college
writing?

<u>Writing must have:</u> basic premise, logical
development of ideas, support in paragraphs,
good word choice

<u>Prewriting</u>

What are steps in
prewriting?

Brainstorm about a subject - generate ideas
Narrow to a topic - use list or concept map
Focus on a basic premise - ask a meaningful
   question that makes a point
Plot a pattern - organize points into a
   framework

<u>Writing</u>

What is the basic
structure?

Structure - use introduction, body
   paragraphs, and conclusion
   - write body first

What should a body
paragraph contain?

Body Paragraphs - begin each with
   topic sentence that supports basic
   premise (controlling idea)
   - support points with good examples
   and detail

What is the purpose of
introduction?
What does it reveal?

Introduction - 1st paragraph-states
   basic premise
Reveals: - topic of essay
   - opinion about topic
   - organization pattern
   you'll use

How do you conclude?

Conclusion - should leave reader with
   a feeling of completion
Either: summarize basic premise
   or main points
   - state your opinion

<u>Revising</u>

What are the two
main facets of
revising?

Strengthen support - data, examples, etc.
Edit for transitions, spelling, and
grammar errors.

Figure 12.3
An Advanced Summary Sheet for Classroom Lecture Notes: Cornell System

Sociology 103--Dr. Lund

	19th CENTURY	20th CENTURY
How is family governed?	1. Patriarchal, Father head of family.	1. Now, individualistic & democratic
Difference in stability?	2. Family stable	2. Family less stable
Status of extended family?	3. Many children and relatives under one roof--extended family	3. Smaller in size. Only two generations (parents& children)
Changes in mobility?	4. Non-mobile. Rarely moved "Old family homestead"	4. Mobility increased & residences changed often
Relationship between women & work?	5. Women: housework and children	5. Women: work outside & care for children after hours.
Attitude toward sex?	6. Puritanical on sex	6. Increasingly liberal
Variance in family types?	7. Family types in community alike	7. Greater variability in family type
Family's function?	8. Family had many functions: political, religious, economic	8. Now: function -- procreation and socialization

Cramming Systematically

If you're forced to cram, how do you cram systematically?

Academic preparation usually eliminates the need for cramming. But if you find yourself unprepared for an exam, cramming is an unfortunate necessity. To cram systematically, limit the information that you attempt to commit to memory, and devote the bulk of your time to reciting what you've chosen to remember instead of trying to learn even more.

Limit What You Try to Learn

What is the keyword in limiting what you try to learn?

If your only chance to pass a course is to cram, the one word to remember is *selectivity*. You must avoid falling into the trap of trying to learn too much. It will be extremely difficult to resist picking up important-looking bits of information along the way, but that is what you must do. Concentrate on essential facts, and use as much of your time as possible for remembering them. Each textbook

Figure 12.4
**An Advanced Summary Sheet
from a Textbook Chapter**

Economics 102 – Professor Maxwell

I. Single
Adv:
  1. freehand
  2. profits—his
Disadv:
  1. liable
  2. "venture capital"

II. Partner—
Adv:
  1. common pool
  2. "vertical
     integration"
  3. "horizontal
     integration"
Disadv:
  1. death & change
  2. liable

III. Corporation
Adv:
  1. legally formed
  2. stock—capital
  3. limited liability
  4. perpetual—board
Adv. to society:
  1. production—eff.
  2. continuation
  3. creates capital
  4. pays taxes

I. Single proprietorship
         ADVANTAGES
  1. Can do what desires
  2. All profit goes to owner
       DISADVANTAGES
  1. All losses hurt owner (unlimited liability)
  2. Commerical banks ordinarily will not provide
     "venture capital"

II. Partnership
         ADVANTAGES
  1. Pool wealth, profits, losses
  2. "Vertical integration" = gain control of resources,
     become own wholesaler
  3. "Horizontal integration" = buy out competitors;
     add products; improve products
       DISADVANTAGES
  1. Each time a member dies or leaves, a new
     partnership needs to be formed
  2. Unlimited liability, even if own a small share

III. Corporation
         ADVANTAGES
  1. Easy to form (legal permission needed)
  2. Issue stock to raise capital; banker underwrites
     stock issue and sells to public
  3. Limited liability – Corp., distinct from its owners;
     can sue and be sued
  4. "Perpetual succession," or existence. Board of
     directors
     ADVANTAGES TO SOCIETY
  1. Technical efficiency – production of goods & services
  2. Pool business risks – continuation of production
  3. Creates further capital for expansion or finance new
  4. It is taxed

chapter has to be skimmed and searched, and the main ideas and pertinent supporting materials must be ferreted out and written in your own words on summary shets ruled in the Cornell format. The same must be done with your lecture notes.

Recite Instead of Reread

What should you do after you've gleaned the most important ideas from your notes?

Once you've extracted the most important ideas from both your textbook and lecture notes, push aside the books and notebooks. Resist the temptation to read even more in search of important information you may have missed. It's time to admit that it's too late to learn everything. Limit yourself to only ten or so sheets of notes from your textbook and ten sheets of notes from your classroom notes. Your hope of passing the upcoming test lies not in force-feeding yourself more and more information at the last minute but in mastering the few facts you have in front of you.

Why is reciting so important when you're cramming?

Now recite, recite, and recite. The notes you have selected will do you no good unless you embed them in your mind so that you can mentally carry them into the examination room. To make these notes your own, read each fact you've chosen, and devise a question you can jot down in the margin of your summary sheet for which that fact is the answer. Formulating these questions will act as written recitation. Then, once you have a question for every idea, cover up the answers and test yourself by reading each question and reciting the answer from memory, again and again, until you know the information cold.

By judiciously selecting the very top ideas and by using your own set of questions to help memorize them, you will have a chance of passing the exam. You may not remember much once the test is over, but for now the objective is to survive the battle so that you can come back next term and continue the war.

Next time, through organized note taking, regular recitation, and systematic review, you can avoid the pressure and anxiety of cramming. A few days spent with your summary sheets will organize vast amounts of material in your mind—far more than you could ever learn by cramming. Moreover, you will be rested, confident, and ready for exams.

Preparing Yourself Mentally

What role should mental preparation play in getting ready for an exam?

When it comes to getting ready for an upcoming exam, there's no substitute for academic preparation. But even if you know your material inside out, there's still an advantage to be gained from putting yourself in the proper mindset. Some students who experience test anxiety claim that even when they've studied hard, they freeze when the test is placed in front of them. Although academic preparation is essential, a little mental preparation can help take the sting out of an exam. If you take time to find out all you can about the exam, get yourself acquainted with the test site or a similar site, and work at maintaining a positive attitude, you're more likely to escape the test-taking anxiety that plagues unprepared students.

Finding Out About the Exam

How can you lessen the fear of the unknown that contributes to test anxiety?

Fear of the unknown can be a great contributor to test anxiety. If you walk into a test without knowing what to expect, you are likely to feel anxious. Except in those rare cases in which the instructor provides you with a copy of the test in advance, you can't be expected to know exactly what the exam will contain. Does this mean that anxiety is inevitable? Not at all. By asking the instructor directly and by looking at previous exams, you should be able to "guesstimate" what might be on the exam and in the process dispel some unnecessary anxiety.

Ask the Instructor Directly

What can you learn from the instructor about an upcoming exam?

Many students overlook the most obvious method for finding out about the content of an upcoming exam: asking the instructor directly. In many cases, instructors are not at all hesitant to discuss what the test will involve. Ask your instructor about the types of questions (objective, essay, or both) that will be asked. Find out whether your instructor will allow partial credit, how long the exam will take, and whether textbooks, notes, calculators, or other equipment will be allowed in the exam room. When you do finally sit down to take the exam, you're less apt to be knocked off balance by surprises.

Use Past Exams

How can past exams help you prepare for the upcoming exam?

Instructors frequently take the same approach to their exams semester after semester. Therefore, a look at an old exam can often tell you something helpful about the exam you're studying for. Try to get a copy of last semester's exam to see what kinds of questions were asked and to make sure you know the meanings of the words used in the directions. Use all this information to direct your study effort and to make sure you have the background you need to take the exam.

Getting Acquainted with the Test Site

How can you get acquainted with the site where your exam will be held?

Exams may be held in auditoriums, large lecture halls, or ordinary classrooms. To be mentally prepared for an exam, get acquainted with the site where the test will take place or with a similar location. A week or two before the exam, study for a few hours each evening at the site where you will be taking the test. Your familiarity with the room and the sense of control you feel while studying will help establish a link between working in this room and succeeding on the exam. If you can't study at the site of the test, you can still prepare yourself for the atmosphere of the test.

Study in quiet.   Some students who become anxious during tests are unnerved by the silence that is a normal part of an exam. If you take time to study in silence, the quiet of the exam should be less disconcerting.

Practice at a chairdesk.   If you can't study at the actual test site, find an empty classroom that has a similar seating arrangement, and make an effort to adjust to the feel of the slightly uncomfortable accommodations.

Use a time limit.   So that you are not waiting until the last minute to discover how well you perform under a deadline, spend some of your study time working under artificial time limits not only to get a sense of how efficiently you work but also to grow accustomed to the inevitable pressure of time.

Maintaining a Positive Attitude

How do you cultivate a positive attitude about an upcoming exam?

Of course, the ideas and strategies for managing stress in Chapter 5 can be helpful throughout the semester. But often it's not until exam time that these techniques are truly put through their paces. It is essential to address the stress of a test with a can-do approach. Exam-anxious students often sabotage their own efforts by preparing themselves for failure. To counteract this inclination and cultivate an optimistic attitude, you need to relax, use self-talk, and visualize success.

Learn to Relax

What can you do to help yourself relax?

To relax, systematically tense and release your major muscle groups using progressive muscle relaxation (see Chapter 5), or breathe deeply to help shift your mental state out of the realm of anxiety and into a feeling of ease. One deep breathing technique that seems especially well suited for exam time is "belly breathing," which involves inhaling deeply from the abdomen, instead of up in the chest, where anxiety often resides. Here's how:

1. Push out your stomach. That creates a pocket where the air can go.
2. With your stomach slightly puffed out, inhale slowly through your nose— one, two—filling up your abdomen with air.
3. Continue inhaling—three, four—this time sending air up into your lungs.
4. Exhale through your mouth, and reverse the process, counting—one, two— as you empty the air from your chest and then—three, four, five, six, seven, eight—as the air leaves your abdomen and your stomach deflates.
5. Repeat Steps 1–4 three or four times until you're feeling relaxed.

Use Self-Talk

How can self-talk affect your attitude?

Often when you're feeling the burden of an approaching exam, the most derogatory voice you hear is your own. This is the self-talk discussed in detail in Chapter 5. It helps to prepare for an upcoming exam by listening carefully to what this inner voice is saying. If the message is self-destructive, now is the time to rewrite the script. Psychologist S. C. Kobasa says that when you are facing a stressful situation, you can prevent overreaction and aggravation simply by *believing that you are in control and that you can find a solution to any problem or crisis.*[1] If your inner voice is preaching doom and gloom, talk back to it, not necessarily out loud, but in your mind. Here are some examples of transforming negative self-talk into positive encouragement.

Negative—Don't Think This	Positive—Think This
Three exams in two days are more than I can handle.	I've survived worse than this. I'll just do the best I can.
This time there's no escape.	I'll just hang in there. There's always a way out.
I can't do these math problems.	I'll work on them as far as I can and see the TA first thing in the morning.
I don't know how to start this research paper. I never could write.	I'll make a list of ten titles or topics and see the instructor in the morning for ideas.
I can't make heads or tails out of this chapter. I'll just forget it.	I'll go as far as I can, identify what it is I don't understand, and see the TA or instructor immediately.

Visualize Success

How is visualization used to improve your attitude about an exam?

In the same way that changing your inner voice can promote relaxation, so can changing your inner view. The technique of visualization, also discussed in Chapter 5, can be used not only to promote relaxation but also to help you anticipate a positive outcome in a test or exam. The more vivid the picture you paint in your mind, the more effective it's likely to be. After all, if you visualize eating a lemon, your body will often respond by salivating the same way it would if you actually tasted the fruit. Similarly, if you visualize taking an exam and succeeding at it, when the time comes to take the test you will have already charted a course for success.

---

[1]S. C. Kobasa, "Stressful Life Events, Personality, and Health: An Inquiry into Hardiness," *Journal of Personality and Social Psychology* 37 (1979): 1–11.

FINAL WORDS

Exams don't have to be situations of stress. They can actually be times of great triumph. Know your material, know your test site, and know as much as you ethically can about the content of the upcoming test. But above all, know yourself. Learn to distinguish a natural sense of excitement from a damaging feeling of doom. Keep in mind that some of the world's greatest actors still feel nervous when they first walk on stage. But these actors quickly settle down when they realize the obvious: They know their lines and they know their abilities. Like an accomplished actor, with preparation and confidence you can overcome your initial hesitation and be a star.

HAVE YOU MISSED SOMETHING?

SENTENCE COMPLETION

Complete the following sentences with one of the three words listed below each sentence.

1. The cure for test anxiety is _____.

   preparation   relaxation   intelligence

2. Academic preparation usually eliminates the need for _____.

   studying   cramming   testing

3. One of the most obvious but overlooked sources of information on an upcoming exam is your _____.

   instructor   textbook   intuition

MATCHING

In each blank space in the left column, write the letter preceding the phrase in the right column that matches the left item best.

_____ 1. Selectivity

_____ 2. Recitation

_____ 3. Homestretch

_____ 4. Textbooks

_____ 5. Summary sheets

_____ 6. Reflection

a. Should be obtained as soon as you've registered for the course

b. A frequently wasted resource in a college-level course

c. Good time for new students to get information about tutoring

d. The key to effectively mastering your notes

e. Schedule that ties up loose ends as exam week approaches

f. A highly consolidated version of your notes

_____ 7. Syllabus

g. Helps distill your notes down to a handful of summary sheets

_____ 8. Orientation

h. Added benefit that comes from creating advanced summary sheets

TRUE-FALSE

Write T _beside the_ true _statements and_ F _beside the_ false _statements._

_____ 1. When it comes to preparing for exams, mental preparation eliminates the need for academic preparation.

_____ 2. If you've been using the Silver Dollar System, creating summary sheets should be relatively easy.

_____ 3. By finals' week, the bulk of your exam preparation should be completed.

_____ 4. The homestretch schedule should be used during the week of your exams.

_____ 5. Instructors frequently take the same approach to their exams semester after semester.

MULTIPLE CHOICE

Choose the word or phrase that completes each sentence most accurately, and circle the letter that precedes it.

1. During exam week, it is OK to skip
   a. meals.
   b. sleep.
   c. recreation.
   d. none of the above.

2. The advantage of creating summary sheets is that it
   a. allows you to annotate existing notes.
   b. provides a super-concentrated version of your notes.
   c. helps you to conveniently categorize your information.
   d. all of the above.

3. Reflection
   a. leads to advantageous learning.
   b. is a prerequisite to creativity.
   c. is enhanced by advanced summary sheets.
   d. all of the above.

4. You can avoid cramming through
   a. organized note taking.
   b. regular recitation.
   c. systematic review.
   d. all of the above.

5. Deep breathing has been shown to produce feelings of
   a. relaxation.
   b. fatigue.
   c. anxiety.
   d. resentment.

SHORT ANSWER   *Supply a brief answer for each of the following items.*

1. Outline ways you can prepare for the atmosphere of an upcoming exam.
2. Explain how you can be your own worst enemy when preparing for an exam.
3. Point out the difference between regular and advanced summary sheets.
4. Elaborate on the use of progressive muscle relaxation in exam preparation.

WORDS IN CONTEXT

From the three choices beside each numbered item, select the one that most nearly expresses the meaning of the italicized word in the quote. Make a light check mark (✓) next to your choice.

No one wants advice—only *corroboration.*
—John Steinbeck (1902–1968), American novelist

1. only *corroboration*   cooperation   agreement   confirmation

Incomprehensible jargon is the *hallmark* of a profession.
—Kingman Brewster Jr. (1919–1988), president of Yale University and U.S. ambassador
   to Britain

2. *incomprehensible*   self-evident   unfathomable   foreign

3. *jargon*   lingo   shorthand   writing

4. the *hallmark*   direction   identification   standard

If you do good, people will accuse you of selfish *ulterior motives*. Do good anyway.
—Dr. Robert Schuller (1926–), American evangelist

5. *ulterior*   monetary   hidden   self-serving

6. *motives*   advantages   profits   reasons

A team should be an *extension* of the coach's personality. My teams were *arrogant* and *obnoxious*.
—Al McGuire (1928–), American basketball coach

7. *extension*   mirror-image   counterpart   continuation

8. *arrogant*   haughty   excitable   high-spirited

9. *obnoxious*   tough   noisy   nasty

THE WORD HISTORY SYSTEM

Curfew
cover the fire for the night

curfew cur'-few *n.* A regulation requiring certain or all people to leave the streets or be at home at a prescribed hour.

In the Middle Ages, peasants were required to cover or to extinguish their fires at a fixed hour in the evening announced by the ringing of a bell called the "cover-fire," French *couvre-feu*. The Norman French used the word in England, where it was adopted as *curfu*, modern *curfew*, meaning the hour and the signal for citizens to retire to their homes, or, as now, for the closing of a public place or the cessation of an activity for the night.

Reprinted by permission. From *Picturesque Word Origins* © 1933 by G. & C. Merriam Co. (now Merriam-Webster, Incorporated).

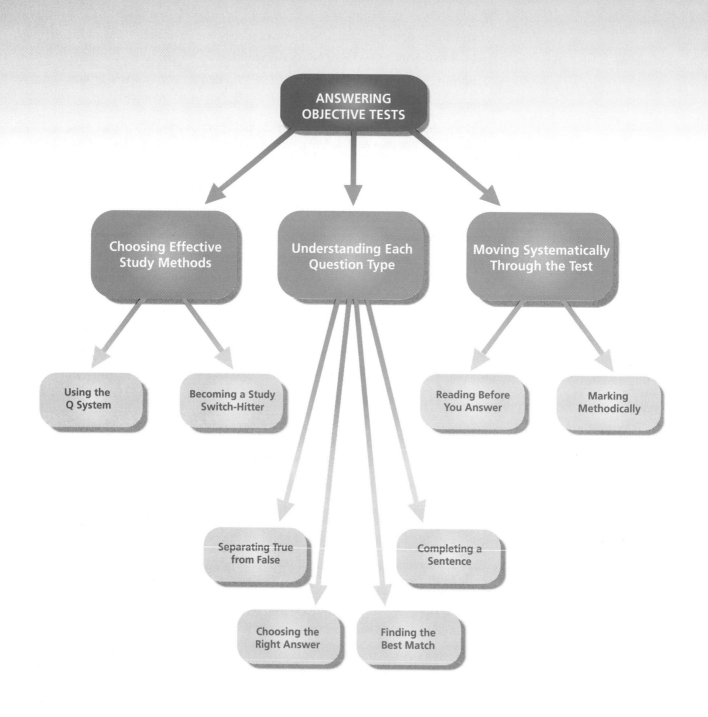

Answering Objective Tests

The real purpose of objective tests is to test your knowledge, not to try your patience. Yet when faced with the prospect of answering true-false, multiple-choice, matching, or sentence-completion questions, many students would prefer to choose "none of the above." What they may not realize is that becoming an objective-test expert is easy. To show you how, this chapter looks at:

- **Choosing Effective Study Methods**
- **Understanding Each Question Type**
- **Moving Systematically Through the Test**

What are the two basic categories of test questions?

Most of the test questions you'll be expected to answer in college fall into one of two categories: essay questions and objective questions. Essay questions take a broader view of a subject and generally emphasize your ability to recall and organize what you've learned and to write about it. Objective questions focus more on details and on your ability to recognize, rather than recall, them.

What does mastering an objective test involve?

Mastering an objective test involves choosing an effective study method for committing material to memory, understanding each question type, and moving systematically through the test.

Choosing Effective Study Methods

What are the best study methods to prepare you for an objective test?

As we've already discovered, your success on a test is directly related to how effectively you've studied for that test. You must master your material as efficiently as possible but in a way that will prepare you for any type of test question. The best way to prepare for an objective test is to use the Q System and to be able to recall your material from multiple directions instead of just one.

Using the Q System

How can you tackle an objective question with confidence?

The safest way of preparing yourself for an objective test is the safest way of preparing yourself for any kind of test—by studying to the point of recall. Although objective exams and quizzes generally test your ability to recognize, rather than recall, information, learning your notes to the point of recall gives you far greater control over what you've learned. You can tackle a question with confidence when you arrive at the answer independently of the cues that the rest of the question offers.

Why is the Q System such a logical way to study for objective tests?

For that reason, the best way of studying for an objective test is by mastering your notes with the Q System (see Chapter 11). This system of adding a question alongside each important fact or idea provides your notes with a built-in method for mastery. With the Q System, each question becomes a cue that compels you to recall the idea it refers to. You'd be hard-pressed to find a more logical way of preparing for a test filled with questions than by mastering your notes using questions as cues.

Becoming a Study "Switch Hitter"

What is a study "switch hitter"?

Baseball players who bat from both sides of home plate are more flexible than those who can hit only right-handed or left-handed. In the same way, you can often improve your test-taking average when you master the material in your notes from both directions instead of from just one. Use the Q System as you normally would to recall each important idea, but reverse the process from time to time by covering your questions, reading your notes, and then seeing whether you can remember the questions you wrote to accompany each important idea.

What helps you master your material regardless of its order?

If you have time and want to make absolutely certain you know your material, write each important idea from your notes on the front of a separate index card, and jot your cue on the back. A stack of cards, instead of a few sheets of paper, enables you to constantly rearrange your notes, ensuring that you will be able to recall important information regardless of the order in which it's presented.

Understanding Each Question Type

What is the "trick" to taking objective tests?

In the strictest sense, there are no tricks for taking objective tests. The requirement for taking any test is basically the same: Know your material. Even so, it helps to be acquainted with the quirks and characteristics of each basic question type so you can feel equally at ease whether your test consists of true-false, multiple-choice, matching, sentence-completion, or a mix of all four types of questions.

Separating True from False

What makes a true-false question's simple premise more difficult?

The basic idea behind a true-false question is simple: Faced with a single statement; your job is to decide whether it's true. What makes the choice more difficult is that to be true, the statement must be 100 percent true, not 50 percent or even 99 percent true. One word can be all it takes to turn a true statement into a false one. Consider, for example, the impact of a word like *always* on a true-false statement or how words like *no* and *not* can radically change a statement's meaning. You have to be especially careful about reading each statement thoroughly before you answer it. Look at the following example:

T F In 1787, the year the United States ratified the Constitution, Washington, D.C., became our nation's capital.

The statement is false. Although the Constitution was ratified in 1787 and the nation's capital is Washington, D.C., the United States had no federal capital until 1790, when Congress chose Philadelphia. Washington didn't officially become the capital until June 10, 1800.

What are your chances of guessing correctly in a true-false test?

Although you have a fifty-fifty chance of answering a single true-false statement correctly, the odds are not that high for the entire test. In fact, your chances of guessing correctly on every statement decrease geometrically with every question. In a ten-question test, the odds on guessing are against you by more than a thousand to one. If you're unsure whether to mark "True" or "False," and you're forced to guess, adopt the following two strategies to influence your decision and improve your odds.

Mark "True" If You're Stumped

Why should you mark "True" as your answer if you are stumped?

Because instructors would rather leave true information in your mind, they tend to stack true-false tests with more true statements than false ones. You shouldn't guess right away on a true-false question, but if you're stumped and pressed for time, the odds are in your favor if you choose true over false.

Be Suspicious of Longer Statements

Why are longer statements more likely to be false?

Remember the importance of context, and remember that true-false statements must be 100 percent true. Each word added to a true-false statement increases its chances of being false. All it takes is one incorrect word to make the statement false.

Choosing the Right Answer

What is the basic setup for a multiple-choice question?

A multiple-choice question normally begins with an incomplete sentence known as a stem, followed by a series of choices, known as options, for completing that sentence. In most cases, your job is to find the option that best completes the stem. Here is an example:

> In 1787, the year the United States ratified the Constitution,
> a. George Washington became the country's first president.
> b. Washington, D.C., became the nation's capital.
> c. New Mexico was admitted to the Union.
> d. the country had no official capital.

In this question, connecting option (d) to the stem results in a true statement. Linking the stem to any other option results in a false statement.

Answering multiple-choice questions entails problems you won't encounter when you're taking a true-false test:

How can directions complicate things in a multiple-choice test?

Varying directions.   Some multiple-choice directions tell you to pick more than one correct option; others ask you to mark the one option that is incorrect. Be sure to read the directions carefully and go over all the options before you mark your selection.

What does divided context do to make multiple-choice harder?

Divided context. Because each choice in a multiple-choice question is usually divided into stem and option, you have to mentally connect the two components to determine whether an option is correct. Correct answers aren't always obvious, even when you know your material.

What is the effect of a differing format in multiple-choice questions?

Differing format. Most multiple-choice questions follow the incomplete stem and option format. In some cases, however, the stem may be made up of an entire sentence. A setup of this sort can take you by surprise if you're expecting a standard multiple-choice question, but in general this variation is easier because you don't have to work with a divided context.

You can use several more strategies to cope with multiple-choice questions.

Pick "All of the Above" If You're in Doubt

Why is "all of the above" a good guess?

Most multiple-choice questions present just a single fact, the option that correctly completes the stem. But with "all of the above," the test maker can include several options instead of just one. As the purpose behind a quiz or exam is not only to test but also to teach, "all of the above" becomes an attractive choice for the test maker.

Here's an example of a question that uses "all of the above":

Until the first half of the second millennium B.C., an army laying siege to a city could use
a. scaling ladders.
b. siege towers.
c. archery fire.
d. all of the above.

The correct answer is (d).

What's one way to confirm that "all of the above" is correct?

One way to confirm the choice "all of the above" is to pick out two correct answers in the options. For instance, in the last example, suppose you are sure that ladders and towers were used, but aren't certain about archery fire. Unless the directions permit you to mark more than one option, you already have all the information you need to choose the correct answer. If option (a) is correct and option (b) is correct, option (d) is the only logical answer.

Should you always choose "all of the above"?

It would be a mistake to mark every "all of the above" you run into before reading the question and carefully considering the options. But if you can't seem to come up with an answer and you're running out of time, choosing "all of the above" is usually a pretty safe bet.

Use the True-False Technique to Change Perspective

What is the idea behind the true-false technique?

If you know your material but have a mental block about the multiple-choice format, you can gain a new perspective on a difficult question by using the true-false technique. Almost any multiple-choice question can be thought of as a series of true-false statements. Here's an example:

Before becoming president in 1857, James Buchanan was
a. married and divorced.
b. secretary of defense.
c. prime minister of Canada.
d. secretary of state.

This question and its options can be thought of as four true-false statements:

T (F) Before becoming president in 1857, James Buchanan was married and divorced.
T (F) Before becoming president in 1857, James Buchanan was secretary of defense.
T (F) Before becoming president in 1857, James Buchanan was prime minister of Canada.
(T) F Before becoming president in 1857, James Buchanan was secretary of state.

Viewing the question this way can sometimes make it easier to spot the correct answer. The true statement you find in the true-false statements you create usually contains the correct multiple-choice option.

Discard Foolish Options

What are distracters?

Some multiple-choice options are *distracters*. Whatever the reason for their inclusion, these foolish options are almost always good news for students. Exactly what the foolish option says is irrelevant. The important point is that you can eliminate it right away and pick the correct answer from the options that remain. Look at this example:

According to British tradition, the queen of England is not permitted to enter
a. West London.
b. Westminster Abbey.
c. the House of Commons.
d. the Indianapolis 500.

Option (d) is so silly that you can immediately cross it out. (Option [c] is correct.)

Choose the Middle Number from a Range of Numbers

Why is a middle number more likely to be the correct option?

Questions that use numbers as choices can be easily answered if you've memorized the correct number. But if you haven't really mastered your material or if you have a tough time with numbers in general, this kind of question can be a nightmare. If you have no other information to go on, you can increase your chances of guessing correctly by eliminating the highest and lowest numbers. Test writers usually include at least one number lower than the correct answer and one number higher. Using this "rule," you can eliminate half the options in a four-option question. For instance:

A water polo team has _____ players.
a. three
b. ten
c. seven
d. five

Even if you know nothing about water polo, you can use the midrange rule to eliminate two options and improve your odds from one out of four to one out of two. (The correct option in this case is [c].)

Finding the Best Match

What is the basic idea of a matching question?

Items in a matching test are usually divided into two columns and arranged in random order. Using a relationship that is normally explained in the directions, you systematically match the items in one column with the items in the other. (Consider the test shown on the following page.)

How are matching questions similar to multiple-choice questions?

What sort of complications does this extra dimension add?

Matching tests work like multiple-choice questions with an added dimension. You're faced with a *multiple* multiple choice. Instead of one stem and several options, you have several stems and several options.

This extra dimension adds extra complications as well. Matching carelessly or guessing prematurely can sometimes lead to a chain reaction of mistakes. If you make an incorrect match, you will deprive another item of its rightful match. This can aggravate your error by increasing the chances of another bad connection, which in turn can lead to another wrong match. Avoid this potential pitfall by making your matches carefully and by pairing up the items you are sure of before you begin guessing on items you're uncertain about. Answering matching questions effectively is mainly a matter of staying organized and saving time. A few strategies can increase your efficiency and reduce your confusion.

Mark Off Matches to Avoid Redundancy

How does marking used items help?

This idea is so simple that it's often overlooked: Each time you match two items in a matching test, cross them off or mark them with a circle or an X. That way, when you move on to the next match, you'll have fewer items to read, and you won't be confused about which items you've chosen and which ones you haven't.

Groundbreaking Women of Science

Directions: Match the name of the scientist in the left-hand column with her discovery or distinction in the right-hand column by writing the proper letter in the space provided alongside each scientist's name. Use each item from the right-hand column only once.

Scientist	Discovery or Distinction
_____ **1.** Rachel Carson	a. Created the first programming language
_____ **2.** Mary Leakey	b. Devised the system for classifying stars by brightness
_____ **3.** Marie Curie	c. Garnered a Nobel Prize for her groundbreaking work in genetics
_____ **4.** Margaret Mead	d. Earned fame for children's books but gained respect as a mycologist
_____ **5.** Jane Goodall	e. First female physics instructor at Princeton University
_____ **6.** Grace Hopper	f. Invented the pie chart, although she is best known as a nurse
_____ **7.** Georgia Dwelle Rooks	g. First woman elected to the National Academy of Sciences
_____ **8.** Caroline Herschel	h. First American woman in space
_____ **9.** Florence Sabin	i. Founded the first hospital for African American women
_____ **10.** Florence Nightingale	j. Invented the compiler, a critical element in most computer programs
_____ **11.** Chien-Shiung Wu	k. Studied chimpanzees as a means of understanding human evolution
_____ **12.** Beatrix Potter	l. Popularized anthropology with her book *Coming of Age in Samoa*
_____ **13.** Barbara McClintock	m. Received two Nobel prizes for her work on radioactivity
_____ **14.** Annie Jump Cannon	n. Uncovered fossils that helped unlock the origins of humankind.
_____ **15.** Sally Ride	o. Founded the contemporary environmental movement
_____ **16.** Ada Byron King	p. Teamed up with her brother to discover the planet Uranus

Answers: 1. o   2. n   3. m   4. l   5. k   6. j   7. i   8. p
9. g   10. f   11. e   12. d   13. c   14. b   15. h   16. a

Match Shorter Items to Longer Ones

What's the benefit of matching shorter items to longer ones?

In most matching tests, the items in one column are longer than the items in the other. For example, a typical matching test might contain a column of terms and a column of definitions. In cases like these, you can save yourself some time if you set out in search of matches for the longer items instead of the reverse. In other words, the column you keep reading and rereading contains the shorter items. That way you need to read each long item only once. It's a case of the dog wagging the tail instead of the other way around.

Completing a Sentence

How are sentence-completion questions like multiple-choice questions?

Sentence-completion questions work like multiple-choice questions without the choice. A typical sentence-completion question consists of a partial sentence and one or more blanks. Your job is to read the sentences and to use both context and recall to determine what words belong in the blanks.

How do sentence-completion questions differ from multiple-choice questions?

Unlike multiple-choice questions, sentence-completion questions can't actually be considered objective questions, but because the sentence is incomplete and because the answer is seldom vague or ambiguous, most sentence-completion questions can be answered following the same basic procedure you use for answering bona fide objective questions. For example:

> Sentence-completion questions work like multiple-choice questions without the _____.

Why are there no real tricks for answering a sentence-completion question?

Because with a sentence-completion question the answer isn't there for you to choose, there are no real tricks to help you pick out the correct answer. But there are methods that enable you to clearly define the specific context of the question. When you do this, you zero in on the answer that will fill in the blank.

Clarify Ambiguity with a Specific Question

What is the best strategy for coping with ambiguous test questions?

Sometimes a question seems to have two or more reasonable answers. In these cases, you may need to clarify the kind of answer the question is seeking. The best strategy for coping with ambiguous questions is to raise your hand and ask a well-formulated, unambiguous question of your own to clear up the confusion. Consider this item:

> In 1901, at the age of forty-two, Republican Theodore Roosevelt became the country's _____ president.

In this example, both "youngest" and "twenty-sixth" would be reasonable answers, but it's unlikely the instructor would be looking for both. If you raised your hand and said, "I don't understand this question," you would probably get a response like "Do your best." But a well-thought-out, more specific question would probably be rewarded with a more helpful response. For example, if you asked, "Are you looking for a number?" the instructor's response would enable you to decide which of your two answers is expected.

Disregard the Length of the Blank

What effect does the length of the blank have on the desired answer?

Sometimes the length of the empty line equals the length of the answer expected. But in general there's no connection between the two. Pay attention to the words that are present, rather than to those that are missing, to come up with your answer for a sentence-completion question. Don't let the blank line distract you.

Treat Some Sentences as Two Separate Questions

What effect should two blanks have on your question-answering strategy?

Even students who aren't influenced by the size of one blank when answering a sentence-completion question may become flustered by a question that has two blanks. If the blanks are side by side, the question may be calling for a person's name or a place name. Paying attention to the question's context should help you confirm whether this is the case. But if the blanks in a sentence-completion question are widely separated instead of side by side, a different strategy is called for.

How do you treat two blanks that are widely separated?

The best way to treat two blanks that are widely separated is as if each occurred in a separate sentence. There may or may not be a direct relationship between the missing words, so make sure that each filled-in word makes sense in its own part of the statement. Here's an example:

> Although corn is second only to _____ as the most widely grown crop in the world, no one in Europe had even heard about corn until _____ returned from the New World.

In the first portion of the sentence, the word *corn* indicates that you're dealing with a grain. If you had read your textbook carefully (or if you used your common sense), you'd know the answer is wheat. The second blank demands a person's name: Columbus.

Moving Systematically Through the Test

How can you move systematically through an objective test?

Good students—those who understand what different objective questions require and have employed the most effective study methods—may still run into trouble unless they apply the same reasoned, organized approach they used in preparation to the process of taking the test. The only way to put what you know to good use is to move through the test systematically by reading carefully before you answer, by marking methodically, by paying attention to grammar, and by choosing the best answer instead of simply the first one that springs to mind. If you approach the test in this orderly fashion, you have an excellent chance of making the most of what you've learned.

Reading Before You Answer

What causes some students to skip over the obvious step of reading?

It may sound silly to suggest reading through the test before you begin answering. After all, the advice seems obvious. But because of anxiety and time pressure, common sense is often a casualty, and many students skip the directions and even rush through the questions without paying attention to what they say. In the long run, cutting corners on these crucial elements of a test could cost you time and points. Take a few moments to read the directions before you make a single mark on your test and to read each question carefully as well.

Read the Directions First

Why should you read the directions first?

It takes just a minute or two to read a test's directions, yet the little time you invest can often make a drastic difference in your score. Carelessness may do as much to torpedo a test as genuine ignorance. If, for example, the directions for a multiple-choice test say, "Mark the two best answers," but you pass over the directions and mark only one option, most of your efforts will have been in vain. Although simply reading the directions won't guarantee that you will pass, it will protect you from needless mistakes.

Read Questions Carefully

Why is it important to read each test question carefully?

Objective questions, no matter the type, are usually filled with information. Each word in the question is likely to be far more important than a word in an ordinary sentence. Nuances in phrasing, such as qualifiers and negatives, can have a huge impact on a question's meaning. For that reason, you must read each question carefully and thoroughly to pick up important details and the complete context.

How do qualifiers complicate a test question?

Cope with qualifiers.   The English language has more than a dozen common qualifiers—including *always, most, equal, good,* and *bad.* We use such words regularly in writing and conversation, and test makers often deliberately insert them into objective test questions, especially true-false and multiple-choice questions. Qualifiers do precisely what their name implies: They complicate a simple statement or option by adding a qualification. The following two statements

It *often* rains in Seattle, Washington.
It *always* rains in Seattle, Washington.

are nearly identical. Yet the first one is true, while the second one is false. In this case, the only thing that differentiates the two statements is their qualifiers: *often* and *always*. If you read through these statements too quickly, you may overlook their qualifiers.

Now look at a multiple-choice example:

The head of a kettledrum is
a. struck only with wooden mallets.
b. always made of sheepskin.
c. often made of calfskin.
d. tightened once a day.

In this example, option (d) is just plain incorrect. Qualifiers indicate which of the three remaining options is correct. Without the qualifiers, all three options would be correct: Kettledrum heads *are* struck with wooden mallets; they *are* made of sheepskin; and they *are* made of calfskin. But because the qualifiers *only* and *always* overstate the case, options (a) and (b) are incorrect; while *often*, the qualifier in option (c), takes a more moderate stance and is therefore correct.

The qualifiers *only* and *always* in the first two options are good examples of 100 percent words. They imply that the statements are true 100 percent of the time. Such qualifiers almost always make a statement false; very few things in this world are 100 percent one way or the other. Although it is wise to watch out for these words, don't automatically consider a statement wrong because it contains one of them. To keep you honest and alert, some instructors occasionally use 100 percent words in true statements:

All stars are surrounded by space.
All human beings need food to survive.
No human being can live without air.

A simple and effective strategy for coping with qualifiers is to keep careful track of them by circling each one that appears in a test question. Circling the qualifiers helps ensure that you don't ignore them.

With the qualifiers circled, you can mentally substitute other words that will change the meaning of the question. This method is sometimes referred to as the Goldilocks Technique because you try out several qualifiers until you find the one that's "just right." Most qualifiers are clustered in groups, or "families." If you can find another family member that does a better job of completing the sentence, the original question is probably false or, in a multiple-choice question, is probably an incorrect option. The qualifiers in the families that follow may overstate a true-false statement, understate it, or make it just right. Memo-

What are 100 percent words?

What is a good strategy for keeping tabs on qualifiers?

What is the Goldilocks Technique?

rize the six families. They will help you answer true-false questions and make the right choice among multiple-choice options.

All—most—some—none (no)
Always—usually—sometimes—never
Great—much—little—no
More—equal—less
Good—bad
Is—is not

What should you do when you recognize a word from a qualifier family?

Whenever one qualifier from a set is used in a true-false statement or a multiple-choice option, substitute each of the others for it in turn. In this way, determine which of the qualifiers from the family fits best (makes the statement just right). If that is the given qualifier, the answer is true; otherwise, the answer is false.

For example, suppose you are given this question:

T   F   All birds can fly.

Substituting the other qualifiers in the *all* family gives you these four statements:

Original Statement
All birds can fly.

Related Statements
Most birds can fly.

Some birds can fly.

No birds can fly.

The statement that begins with *most* is just right, but that is not the statement you were originally given. Therefore, the original answer is false.

What words are considered negatives in test questions?

Notice negatives.   Negatives can be words such as *no, not, none,* and *never* or prefixes such as *il-*, as in illogical; *un-*, as in uninterested; and *im-*, as in impatient. Negatives are common in everyday speech and writing and almost as common in objective tests.

Why are negatives a problem?

Negatives cause problems in objective questions because, like qualifiers, they can easily be overlooked. This is particularly the case with negative prefixes, which have a way of blending in with the words they modify. For example:

Because it is liquid at room temperature, mercury is indistinguishable from other metals.

If you read this sentence quickly, you may miss the letters *i-n* and mark the statement true. But if you read the statement carefully, you will realize that just the opposite is true.

What about sentences with more than one negative?

Objective questions that contain two or more negatives can be even more troublesome. Each additional negative shifts the meaning of the sentence in the opposite direction. For example, you would probably be able to mark this statement true without much difficulty:

> It is logical to assume that Thomas Edison's fame was due to his many practical inventions.

Yet you might have trouble with the sentence

> It is illogical to assume that Thomas Edison's fame was not due to his many practical inventions.

even though it is also true.

What should you do when you encounter negatives in a test question?

When you find negatives in objective questions, circle them. Then disregard them for a moment and try to gain the meaning of the question that remains. Finally, reread the sentence with the negatives included. Each negative you add reverses the meaning of the question. With two negatives, for example, the question's meaning should be the same as it was with none.

Hold Out for the Best Response

How can you tell a good response from the best response?

Some objective questions supply more than one good response, but in most cases there is only one best response. It's difficult to tell a good response from a best response unless you have read through the question completely. If you grow impatient and mark the first answer that sounds right, you risk missing the best answer.

Here's a multiple-choice example:

> You would expect to find an aglet
> a. on your foot.
> b. in a nest.
> c. in a small farming community.
> d. at the tip of a shoelace.

An aglet is the cap, often made of plastic, at the end of a shoelace. If you read only part of this question, you might be tempted to pick option (a). That's a good choice, but if you read the whole question, you can easily see that it's not the best choice. Only with the question's entire context can you tell which option is a good answer and which is even better. (The best option is [d].)

Pay Attention to Grammatical Clues

How can grammar make test taking easier?

Although formats vary, all questions should follow the rules of grammar. This fact can help you narrow your choices by eliminating those possible answers that don't produce grammatically correct sentences. The only way to determine whether the rules of grammar are being followed or broken is by reading the entire question so you are able to get its total context. Consider this question:

> The people of Iceland
> a. a country located just outside the Arctic Circle.
> b. are the world's most avid readers.
> c. claim to be descendants of the Aztecs.
> d. the capital, Reykjavik, where arms talks have been held.

If you race through this example, you might be tempted to mark either (a) or (d) as the correct response. Indeed, Iceland is a country located just outside the Arctic Circle, and Reykjavik, the capital, has been the site of important arms negotiations. But if you take the time to read the entire question, you can see that these two responses do not complete the stem grammatically. Response (a) is missing a verb, and response (d) is missing any grammatical connection to "The people of Iceland." That leaves (b) and (c) as the only legitimate options. (The correct answer is [b].)

Grammatical clues are even more helpful in sentence-completion questions, where your response must be recalled instead of chosen from a list of possible answers. For example, you don't have to be an expert in astronomy to complete this sentence:

> Although about 75 million meteors enter our atmosphere each day, on the average only _____ of them ever reaches the ground.

Because *reaches* is a singular verb, the only correct answer is *one*. (Otherwise the question would have read *reach*, the plural form.)

Marking Methodically

How do you move methodically through an objective test?

As with many things, a key to successfully answering objective questions is to move through the test methodically. Don't tackle the questions in a slapdash fashion. Instead, cycle through each section from start to finish, marking only the "sure things" at first and making an intelligent guess if you're still stymied by a question the third time around.

Mark Only the "Sure Things" at First

Why should you mark only the "sure things" at first?

On your initial pass through the test, mark only those answers you are sure of. This is especially crucial in matching questions, where one mistake can set off a chain reaction of incorrect answers. If a question has you stumped at first, don't feel compelled to answer it right away. And don't pick a temporary answer with the thought that you can come back and change it later. You may not have time, and even if you do, you may not be able to distinguish your uncertain answers from your certain ones.

What should you do if the correct answer doesn't immediately come to mind?

If an answer doesn't come to mind right away, circle any qualifiers or negatives, eliminate any choices you know are incorrect, and then move on to the next questions. These markings will provide you with a head start on your second pass.

Guess the Third Time Around

Is there any benefit to guessing?

Except when there's an extra penalty for incorrect answers, guessing is always better than simply leaving a question blank. A question unanswered guarantees a zero, whereas a guess may score some points. Furthermore, if you know something about the material and have given it some genuine thought, you should be able to make an intelligent guess. Intelligent guesses are always superior to random ones. Consider this particular sentence-completion item:

> You can travel by ship from New England to Florida without ever entering the usually rough open seas by using a system of rivers and canals called the _____.

If you don't know the official name for the system, this sentence is long enough and descriptive enough to help you come up with a good guess. You might call it the "Inland Waterway." That's not the exact name, but it is very close, and you would likely receive partial credit for it. (The answer is Intracoastal Waterway.)

FINAL WORDS

How are objective tests like pasta?

If you're like many students, you have a favorite type of objective question as well as a type that you dread. To some extent, that's only natural. But as you prepare for your next objective test, keep this in mind. Objective tests are really a lot like pasta. Some people love rigatoni, some like capellini, and others would rather stick with plain old macaroni. Yet despite their differences, most pastas share the same basic ingredients. It's only the shapes that separate one from the other. If you have the dough to make macaroni, you can always make rigatoni or capellini instead. In the same way, if you feel confident and well prepared for a true-false test, you're probably in a better position to take a matching or multiple-choice test than you realize. Learn to appreciate the shared ingredients of all objective questions, and there's a good chance that your next test will be a little less traumatic.

HAVE YOU MISSED SOMETHING?

SENTENCE COMPLETION

Complete the following sentences with one of the three words listed below each sentence.

1. Negatives and qualifiers should be _____.

   avoided   circled   defined

2. In matching questions, the fewer the remaining choices, the better your chances of being _____.

   incorrect   correct   alert

3. The greatest threat of negatives is that they can be easily _____.

   replaced   overlooked   dismissed

MATCHING

In each blank space in the left column, write the letter preceding the phrase in the right column that matches the left item best.

_____ 1. Negative	a. Statement that starts off a multiple-choice question
_____ 2. Guessing	b. One of the choices that make up a multiple-choice question
_____ 3. Context	c. Mastering possible test material from both sides
_____ 4. Stem	d. Is almost always better than leaving a question blank
_____ 5. "Sure thing"	e. Should be marked on the first pass through the test
_____ 6. "Switch hitting"	f. Best choice when stumped by a true-false question
_____ 7. True	g. Usually reverses the meaning of a true-false statement
_____ 8. Option	h. Is provided when you read the entire question

TRUE-FALSE

Write T *beside the* true *statements and* F *beside the* false *statements.*

_____ 1. For a statement to be marked true, it must be entirely true.

_____ 2. Some multiple-choice questions ask you to pick more than one answer.

_____ 3. The stem of a multiple-choice question is always an incomplete statement.

_____ 4. True-false tests generally contain more true statements than false ones.

_____ 5. The length of the blank dictates the size of the answer in a sentence-completion question.

MULTIPLE CHOICE

Choose the word or phrase that completes each sentence most accurately, and circle the letter that precedes it.

1. A multiple-choice question can be viewed as a series of
   a. stems.
   b. qualifiers.
   c. true-false statements.
   d. decoys or distracters.

2. One way to think of a matching question is as
   a. a multiple-choice question without the choice.
   b. a true-false question in two dimensions.
   c. a multiple multiple-choice question.
   d. none of the above.

3. Reading the entire question should help you
   a. detect grammatical clues.
   b. take advantage of context.
   c. select the best response.
   d. all of the above.

4. If at first a question has you stumped, you should

   a. move on to another question.

   b. ask a clarifying question.

   c. pick a temporary answer.

   d. cross out any negatives or qualifiers.

5. A sentence-completion question with two widely separated blanks should be treated as

   a. a true-false question.

   b. two questions.

   c. a decoy or distracter.

   d. an essay question.

SHORT ANSWER   *Supply a brief answer for each of the following items.*

1. Compare and contrast the four basic types of objective questions.
2. Explain the Goldilocks Technique.
3. What is the chain reaction associated with matching tests?
4. What is the purpose of the true-false technique?

WORDS IN CONTEXT

From the three choices beside each numbered item, select the one that most nearly expresses the meaning of the italicized word in the quote. Make a light check mark (✓) next to your choice.

Nations are not ruined by one act of *violence,* but gradually and in an almost *imperceptible* manner by the *depreciation* of their circulating currency, through its *excessive* quantity.

—Nicolaus Copernicus (1473–1543), Polish astronomer

1. act of *violence*	damaging force	enormous effect	gigantic power
2. almost *imperceptible*	unknown	controlled	unseen
3. the *depreciation*	stable value	decreased value	increased value
4. *excessive* quantity	commercial	inordinate	required

Another advantage of being rich is that all your faults are called *eccentricities.*
—Anonymous

5. called *eccentricities*	creative	peculiarities	inventive

No man can be *conservative* until he has something to lose.
—James P. Warburg (1896–1969), American publicist

6. *conservative*	objective	cautious	judicious

When a subject becomes totally *obsolete* we make it a required course.
—Peter Drucker (1909–), American business philosopher and author

7. totally *obsolete*	indispensable	outdated	necessary

THE WORD HISTORY SYSTEM

Enthrall
literally, to enslave

enthrall en-thrall' *v.* 1. To hold spellbound; captivate. 2. To enslave.

Enthrall presents another case of a word the original and literal sense of which is cruel, but the modern, figurative use of which is much more pleasant. When we say that we are *enthralled* by a song, or a book, or something else with captivating charm, it is interesting to remember that the original meaning of the word was "to enslave." *Thrall* is Anglo-Saxon for "slave." To *enthrall* meant, therefore, "to enslave," "to reduce to the condition of a thrall." The literal sense of "enslave," "make captive," easily yields a figurative sense, "captivate the senses," "hold spellbound," "charm," as with a song or a story.

Reprinted by permission. From *Picturesque Word Origins* © 1933 by G. & C. Merriam Co. (now Merriam-Webster, Incorporated).

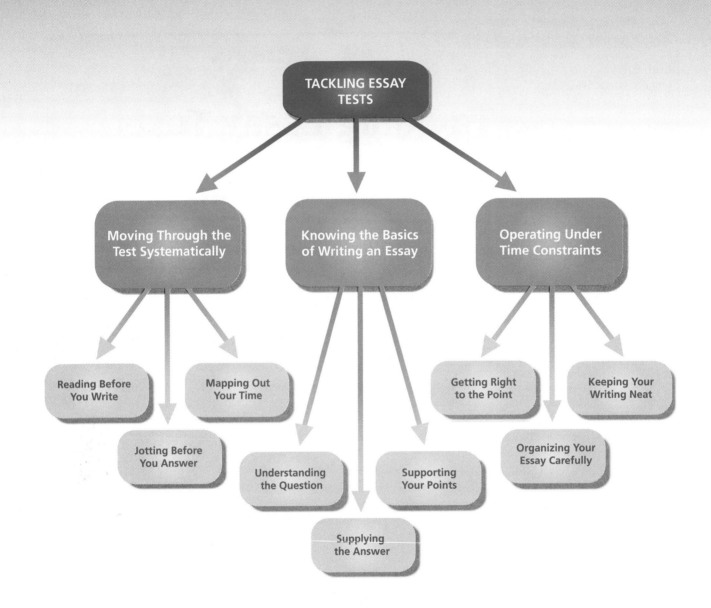

Tackling Essay Tests

Omit needless words. Vigorous writing is concise.

William Strunk, Jr.
(1869–1946), professor of English, coauthor of *The Elements of Style*

For many students, the thought of taking an essay test, of actually writing words "from scratch" instead of marking *T* or *F* or circling an option, is terrifying. Yet what these students don't realize is that writing an essay puts them in control; they are not compelled to choose from among answers someone else has devised. With a solid strategy, any student can take the dread out of the essay test and put his or her knowledge into it. To help take the sting out of essay tests, this chapter provides advice on:

- **Moving Through the Test Systematically**
- **Knowing the Basics of Writing an Essay Exam**
- **Operating Under Time Constraints**

How do essay tests differ from objective tests?

Taking an essay test requires writing anywhere from a few paragraphs to several pages on each question. Unlike objective questions, which ask you to simply recognize correct information, essay tests require you to recall ideas and facts accurately and to organize them into thoughtful, forceful responses. You do so by moving through the test calmly and systematically, by knowing the basics of writing an essay exam, by writing effectively under time constraints, and by adequately supporting your points.

Moving Through the Test Systematically

Why are students tempted to rush through essay exams?

When an essay test is handed out, some students have difficulty resisting the temptation to jump right in and start writing. Confident students are often anxious to "get down to business" and show what they know; apprehensive test takers want to get the whole thing over with as quickly as possible. At first glance, these behaviors seem reasonable because time is limited. But if you take a few moments to plan a systematic response to the test, you'll be a lot more efficient as a result. A little preparation saves you a lot more time than it uses. You can make the most of your test-taking experience if you read before you write, jot before you answer, and manage your time wisely.

Reading Before You Write

What should you read before you begin writing?

True, time is short. But resist the temptation to write down any answers until you're crystal clear on what is being asked. Read the directions carefully for a broad sense of what's expected. And read all the questions to get a quick overview of the topics your test will cover.

Read the Directions Carefully

What sort of information do essay test directions contain?

Exam directions often contain specific instructions for answering the questions. They may establish the length of your answers (one paragraph, three hundred words, five pages), the approach you should take (explain, compare, contrast), the number of questions to be answered (say, four of the six presented), or time requirements (say, spend no more than fifteen minutes per question). If you miss such instructions, you will not only do a lot of needless writing and waste a great deal of time, but you may also invite criticism for carelessness.

Read All the Questions First

Why should you read all the essay questions first?

Before you write anything, read all the questions. If you have a choice among questions, select those for which you are best prepared. If you have to answer every question, you'll know in advance which ones will require the most attention. And if several questions tackle different aspects of the same topic or issue, you'll be able to avoid including information on one answer that should have been saved for another.

Jotting Before You Answer

Although it's unwise to begin answering an essay question before you've read everything carefully, you may have important ideas that you want to get down on paper before they slip your mind. Feel free to do this, but not by abruptly beginning one of your essays. Instead, use the back of your exam sheet to jot general thoughts and the area on your test paper around each question to record cues or observations that pertain to specific essays.

Make Notes on the Back of Your Exam Sheet

What sort of notes should you jot on the back of your exam?

As you walk into the exam room, your brain may be buzzing with information you want to include in your essays. Before you begin reading the test, unburden your mind by quickly jotting on the back of the exam sheet the ideas, facts, and details you think you may forget. Almost like a summary of your summary sheets, these jottings act as cues for the Silver Dollar ideas you gleaned from your lectures and readings (see Chapter 11). Furthermore, the action of writing these notes involves you in the exam immediately. But remember: You are graded for what you write on the *front* of the exam, so don't spend more than a minute or so jotting down reminders on the *back*.

Jot a Cue Beside Each Question

What sort of cue should you add to each question?

As you read through each question, underline or circle important words that provide clues for answering that question. Also, keep track of any keywords or key phrases that come to mind by jotting them in the margin. Later, when you begin writing, use these jottings and those on the back of the exam sheet to help organize your answer.

Mapping Out Your Time

Once you've carefully read over the directions and questions and jotted down any thoughts you may have, you should be able to get a realistic sense of how much time remains for answering the questions. Using this as a starting point, divide the time you have left by the number of questions to figure out roughly how much time you can spend on each question in order to complete the test. Stick as close to your time plan as you can, but don't become overly anxious or rigid about doing so.

Answer the Easiest Question First

Why should you answer the easiest question first?

A good way to get a head start is by tackling the easiest question first. Nothing inspires confidence and clear thinking more than answering one question right away. If the first question has you stumped, don't let it deflate your morale and throw off your time plan. Just pick an easier question, number your answer correctly, and begin writing.

Keep Your Schedule Flexible

How do you keep your schedule flexible?

What approach should you take if time is short?

What should you do if you finish early?

Of course, even with an easy question under your belt, your time schedule still may not go exactly as planned. It's important to keep your schedule flexible by developing strategies to deal both with a time shortage and a time surplus.

If time is running out, outline the key points you were trying to make in any unfinished questions. Instructors sometimes award partial credit when you can demonstrate that you know the material.

If you finish early, use the surplus time to your advantage by going over your exam, double-checking your spelling and grammar, and, if necessary, inserting words, phrases, and examples that may make your essays clearer.

Knowing the Basics of Writing an Essay

How do you write an effective essay?

To write an effective essay, you need to be able to understand each question with precision, answer that question correctly, and provide your answer with suitable support.

Understanding Each Question with Precision

Why is it important to understand the questions precisely?

A precise question requires a precise answer. Read each question carefully so you understand exactly what it is asking. A good essay question is never vague or ambiguous. As you can see from Figure 14.1, words such as *criticize, interpret,* and *describe* have specific definitions. Therefore, if you have even the slightest uncertainty about what's being asked, don't hesitate to check with the instructor for clarification.

Supplying the Correct Answer

How are essay questions similar to other test questions?

Although they may require some specialized skills, essays are basically no different from other types of questions. To answer any exam question, you must have mastered the material. That means attending all lectures, reading all assignments, taking thoughtful notes, and then reviewing and reciting what

Figure 14.1

Keywords in Essay Questions
This alphabetical list contains keywords encountered in the directions for essay questions, along with brief explanations of what each word means.

Key Word	Explanation
Apply a principle	Show how a principle works, through an example.
Comment	Discuss briefly.
Compare	Emphasize similarities, but also present differences.
Contrast	Give differences only.
Criticize	Give your judgment of good points and limitations, with evidence.
Define	Give meanings but no details.
Demonstrate	Show or prove an opinion, evaluation, or judgment.
Describe	State the particulars in detail.
Diagram	Show a drawing with labels.
Differentiate	Show how two things are different.
Discuss	Give reasons pro and con, with details.
Distinguish	Show main differences between two things.
Enumerate	List the points.
Evaluate	Discuss advantages and disadvantages with your opinion.
Explain	Give reasons for happenings or situations.
Give cause and effect	Describe the steps that lead to an event or a situation.
Give an example	Give a concrete example from the textbook or from your experience.
Identify	List and describe.
Illustrate	Give an example.
Interpret	State the meaning in simpler terms, using your judgment.
Justify	Prove or give reasons.
List	List without details.
Outline	Make a short summary with headings and subheadings.
Prove	Give evidence and reasons.
Relate	Show how things interconnect.
Review	Show main points or events in summary form.
Show	List your evidence in order of time, importance, logic.
Solve	Come up with a solution based on given facts or your knowledge.
State	List main points briefly without details.
Summarize	Organize and bring together the main points only.
Support	Back up a statement with facts and proof.
Trace	Give main points from beginning to end of an event.

you've written down until you know the information cold. Students who think they can "snow" their instructors with long but fundamentally flawed essays are sadly mistaken. If your essay is missing the correct answer, this will be obvious to even the most inexperienced teacher.

What aspects of your essay are likely to affect your grade?

A correct answer is often a correctly phrased answer. The tone you use or the approach you take in constructing the essay can have a strong influence on the grade you receive. Most instructors have favorite approaches and ways of looking at questions and are naturally, if not unconsciously, disposed to favor essays that correspond to their ways of thinking. Theoretically, you shouldn't have to worry about this—the accuracy and thoroughness of your answer should be sufficient—but practically, an essay that incorporates some of the instructor's "pet ideas" is more likely to be viewed in a better light. According to respected educator Hugo Hartig, author of *The Idea of Composition:*

> An alert student can easily identify these "pet ideas" and work them out carefully in his own words. The student who does this is prepared not only to see through the instructor's questions quite readily, but he also knows exactly how to answer them, using the teacher's own methods of problem solving! Perhaps this is the very essence of grade-getting in any course that depends heavily on essay exams.[1]

Supporting Your Points

How does a well-supported essay affect your grade?

A well-supported essay goes a long way in convincing graders that they are reading the work of a superior student. You can ensure that your essay is well supported by backing up your answer with solid evidence, by supporting general opinions, and by avoiding personal opinions.

Using Solid Evidence

What should most of your essay consist of?

Obviously, whether you answer an essay question correctly is important. But because a well-written essay usually contains the answer in the first sentence (or, in a longer essay, the first paragraph), the bulk of your essay should be devoted to the evidence that supports your answer.

Where should your evidence appear in your essay?

If you've mastered your material and included your answer at the start of your essay, providing support should be relatively easy. Every sentence that follows the first one should provide supporting ideas, facts, and details. Notice how natural this approach is. Your first sentence addresses the question directly, and the sentence that follows outlines the major points that support your answer. Then subsequent sentences—or paragraphs, if your essay is longer—will provide examples, details, and further evidence for your initial answer and its major points. When everything you write pertains to the first sen-

[1]Hugo Hartig, *The Idea of Composition* (Oshkosh, WI: Academia, 1974), p. 32.

tence, you cannot help but achieve unity; all your sentences will be both pertinent and cohesive.

Supporting General Opinions

Why do general opinions need support?

The evidence you supply should be factual, not opinionated. Even generally accepted opinions should be backed up with facts. According to Hartig:

> An opinion that is not supported by some kind of logical or factual evidence is not worth anything at all, even if it is absolutely correct. For example, if you make the statement: "*Huckleberry Finn* is a masterpiece of American literature," and do not give any good reason to show that the statement is true, you get a zero for the statement.[2]

> In the same way, you could expect to be marked down for writing "Seattle is usually cloudy." If, however, you wrote "According to the *Places Rated Almanac,* Seattle is either cloudy or partly cloudy an average of 308 days a year," you'd be adequately supporting that opinion.

Avoiding Personal Opinions

Why are personal opinions often discouraged in essay exams?

The opinions of experts have a place in an essay exam, but the same can't be said for your own opinions. All of us have personal opinions, but unless a question specifically asks for yours, leave it out. The grader is less interested in what you believe than in what you know. The purpose of essay exams, after all, is to see what you've learned and how you can apply it.

Operating Under Time Constraints

What should a good essay have at minimum?

As in all tests, time plays a key role in essay exams. Well-supported essays will earn you superior scores. But at the very least, use the available time to make certain your essay gets to the point, is carefully organized, and is neat.

Getting Right to the Point

Why is getting to the point so important in essay tests?

When you are writing an essay test, there's no time for obscuring facts in paragraphs filled with lavish adjectives or rambling discussions. Essay exams are written in a hurry and are often read in a hurry. You have to be concise!

Leave Off the Introduction

Why should you leave off your essay's introduction?

A good way to guarantee that your essay will get to the point is to skip writing an introduction. Don't even start off with a high-sounding sentence such as

---

[2]Ibid., p. 31.

"This is indeed a crucial question that demands a swift solution; therefore. . . ." Such a general approach scatters your ideas, thereby damaging the unity of your answer. An unfocused essay may contain all the right ideas, but if those ideas are scattered, your instructor may conclude that you don't know what you are talking about.

Put Your Answer at the Beginning

How do you put your essay's answer at the beginning?

Begin with a strong opening sentence that both repeats the question and provides the answer. Figure 14.2 shows how this principle works. The opening part of the first sentence restates but rearranges the question, while the second part supplies the answer. Such an approach keeps you honest and discourages partial or unfocused answers.

In Figure 14.3, the student has answered the question directly in the first sentence by naming three theories of forgetting. The rest of the essay follows a logical, predictable pattern in which she explains each theory in brief, then draws a conclusion about all of them.

Although the essay in Figure 14.4 is longer than the ones in Figures 14.2 and 14.3, its basic format is the same. In the opening sentence, the student answers the question directly by comparing and contrasting reciting and rereading. The next sentence states three reasons reciting is superior to rereading, and the paragraphs that follow develop those points.

Where does your answer belong in longer essays?

In longer essays, you don't have to include your answer in the first sentence. But you should make sure it is contained in the opening paragraph. Once your answer has been stated at the beginning, you can devote the rest of your essay to expanding on it. The ideas, facts, and details that follow all support your opening sentence or paragraph. As a result, your answer is both pertinent and unified.

Won't supplying your answer early "jump the gun"?

Don't worry that, by stating your answer so early in the essay, you will be "jumping the gun." There's no advantage to keeping a grader in suspense, not even for a few sentences. If your answer is not included in the first few lines, your point may never become clear. Even worse, if time runs out before you

Figure 14.2
A Direct Answer

Question: What does distributed practice involve?

Answer: Distributed practice involves dividing an assignment into several study sessions instead of one continuous session.

Figure 14.3
A Paragraph-Length Essay

Question: Identify three of the theories psychologists have suggested to explain forgetting.

Answer: Three of the theories that psychologists have suggested to explain how forgetting occurs include fading theory, retrieval theory, and reactive interference theory. Fading theory defines memories as paths or traces in the brain. According to the theory, if these paths aren't used (recalled) regularly, they fade until they eventually disappear (are forgotten). Retrieval theory claims that memories never really disappear; they simply get lost or misfiled, like important information buried under piles of paper on a messy desk. Reactive interference theory says that your attitude or emotions can interfere with your memory. If you are bored with or bothered by information, there's a greater chance that you will forget it. In certain cases, evidence seems to support all these theories of forgetting. But they remain only theories. None of them can be proved conclusively.

Figure 14.4
A Longer Essay Answer

Question: Compare and contrast reciting and rereading as methods of study.

Answer: Although reciting and rereading are both common methods of study, reciting is superior to rereading as a way of mastering your material. Unlike rereading, reciting (1) gets you involved, (2) supplies motivation, and (3) provides you with feedback on your progress.

1. Reciting gets you involved by compelling you to extract the meaning out of each paragraph you read. In contrast, it's possible to reread an assignment without understanding it.

2. Reciting supplies motivation because it encourages you to understand what you've read. If you had trouble grasping the meaning of one paragraph, you may be determined to have an easier time with the next one. If you understood a paragraph, you'll be motivated to continue your progress. But if you simply reread your assignment, you'll have no such incentive to succeed.

3. Because you know right away whether you've understood each paragraph, reciting provides you with immediate feedback on your progress. Potential trouble spots in your reading are brought to your attention right away. With rereading, the first real feedback you get is delayed until the test or quiz.

have finished your answer, that key concept you were carefully saving could go unused.

Avoid Wordy, Rambling Writing

What are the drawbacks of wordy, rambling writing?

Essays that are overstuffed with big words, unnecessary adjectives, and rambling philosophical discussions will leave the reader both confused and suspicious. Complex ideas don't have to be expressed in a complicated way. According to Hartig, "Quite difficult and subtle ideas can be expressed in straightforward and simple language."[3] You don't have to use large words and flowery language to prove that you are knowledgeable. In fact, as Hartig points out, a flashy essay may put your knowledge in question, instead of confirming it: "Any teacher who has read hundreds or thousands of papers becomes very sensitive to phoniness in student writing, because he sees so much of it."[4] Don't write answers that are deliberately difficult or disingenuous. You won't fool anybody. Strive for clarity, sincerity, and simplicity.

Organizing Your Essay Carefully

What aspects make organizing your essay easier?

Organization comes easier when you leave off an introduction, put your answer at the beginning, and aim for simplicity and sincerity in your sentences. These elements provide a solid foundation for your essay's structure. Even so, you may want to take some extra steps to guarantee that the logic of your essay is easy to follow.

Use a Recognizable Pattern

Why should you use a recognizable organizational pattern?

Instructors don't have time to treat each essay as a puzzle in need of a solution. Take the guesswork out of your essay. Make your answer clear and obvious by following a familiar organizational pattern.

What's the most straightforward way of organizing your essay?

The most straightforward way of organizing your essay is by using the decreasing-importance pattern (discussed in Chapter 10). Sometimes known as the inverted pyramid, this pattern starts off with the broadest and most important information and gradually gets narrower in scope. The advantage of this pattern is that it states the most important information at the outset so the reader can pick it up right away. It also eliminates the risk that time will run out before you've had a chance to fit in your answer.

How can you determine which organizational pattern is best?

Of course, not all essay questions are tailor-made for the decreasing-importance pattern. Key terms in the question can give you a clue about what sort of pattern is needed. If, for example, you are asked to summarize a particular event, you'll probably want to follow the chronological pattern, progressing steadily from past to present. Start off in one direction and keep moving that way until you reach

[3]Ibid., p. 32.
[4]Ibid.

the end of the essay. The same advice applies to essays that call for the spatial or the process pattern. In a descriptive essay, move systematically from one end of what you're describing to the other. Follow a process in an unbroken path from start to finish. And if the question asks you to compare or contrast, make sure you shift predictably between the things you're comparing or contrasting. Whether you use the decreasing-importance pattern or some other structure, it's crucial to move through your essay systematically and predictably.

Figure 14.5
Transitional Words and Expressions

The experienced essay uses "signposts," transitional words that provide directional clues for the reader and show the relationship between sentences in a paragraph. For example, the word *furthermore* says, "Wait! I have still more to say on the subject." So the reader holds the previously read sentences in mind while reading the next few sentences. The following list suggests other words and expressions that you might find valuable.

Transitional Words and Expressions	Intention or Relationship
For example, in other words, that is	Amplification
Accordingly, because, consequently, for this reason, hence, thus, therefore, if . . . . then	Cause and effect
Accepting the data, granted that, of course	Concession
In another sense, but, conversely, despite, however, nevertheless, on the contrary, on the other hand, though, yet	Contrast or change
Similarly, moreover, also, too, in addition, likewise, next in importance	No change
Add to this, besides, in addition to this, even more, to repeat, above all, indeed, more important	Emphasis
At the same time, likewise, similarly	Equal value
Also, besides, furthermore, in addition, moreover, too	Increasing quantity
First, finally, last, next, second, then	Order
For these reasons, in brief, in conclusion, to sum up	Summary
Then, since then, after this, thereafter, at last, at length, from now on, afterwards, before, formerly, later, meanwhile, now, presently, previously, subsequently, ultimately, since	Time

What is the benefit of
transitions?

Use Transitions

The transitions that help make textbooks and lectures easier to follow can play a similar role in your essays, as signposts that let the reader know just where you're headed. When transitions lead from one idea to the next, the reader finds the essay clear, logical, and refreshing. A number of transitional words are listed in Figure 14.5.

Why should you end your
essay with a summary?

End with a Summary

Summarize your essay in a final sentence or two. Finishing off your essay with a summarizing conclusion ties your points together and reminds the grader of the original answer that you've devoted the rest of your essay to supporting.

These suggestions for organizing your essay become even more compelling when you learn how essays are actually graded. Figure 14.6 takes a brief behind-the-scenes look at an essay exam grading session.

Figure 14.6
The Essay Grading Process

Behind the Scenes at an Essay Exam Grading Session

What happens after you finish your last essay, heave a sigh of relief, and hand in your exam? Although grading procedures may vary from school to school, here is how more than two hundred examination booklets in a popular introductory history course are graded at one college.

The day of the exam, each grader in the history department has time to scan, but not to grade, the answer booklets. Then at a meeting the next day, each grader reads aloud what he or she thinks is the one best answer for each question. A model answer for each question is then agreed on by the staff. The essential points in the model answers are noted by all the graders for use as common criteria in grading the responses.

Unfortunately, simply listing all the essential points in your essay won't automatically earn you a superior score. During the reading of the answers, one grader remarks, "Yes, this student mentioned points five and six . . . but I think he didn't realize what he was doing. He just happened to use the right words as he was explaining point four."

These comments reinforce the importance of crystal-clear organization in your essay. You may also want to underline the main point of the essay so it's obvious and mark off your subpoints with dark numbers. Don't forget to include transitional words to show how you got from one idea to the next. Make sure that no one thinks you just stumbled onto the correct answer.

Keeping Your Writing Neat

How does neatness affect your essay grade?

In a carefully controlled experiment, several teachers were asked to grade a stack of examination papers solely on the basis of content. Unbeknownst to these instructors, some of the papers were actually word-for-word duplicates, with one paper written in good handwriting and the other in poor handwriting. In spite of instructions, on average the teachers gave the neater papers the higher grades—by a full letter grade. Most instructors are unwilling to spend extra time interpreting sloppy papers. If your paper is messy, your meaning may be lost, and your grade could suffer. Take these precautions to ensure that your paper is neat.

Write Legibly

Why is important to write legibly?

Good ideas are all but useless if they can't be easily read. Most instructors specifically ask you to use pen, not pencil, so that the writing is bold and clear, not faint and smeary. If your penmanship is less than it should be, you should probably start using the modified printing style explained in Chapter 10. The modified printing style is easy to learn and should enable you to write your essays quickly but neatly.

Write on Only One Side of Each Sheet

Why should you write on only one side of each sheet of your essay test?

When you write on both sides of the paper, the writing usually shows through, resulting in an essay that looks messy and that may even be unreadable. Besides, if your essays are written in an exam booklet, writing on only one side of each page can provide you with some last-minute room. Should you need to change or add something, you can write it on the blank page and draw a neat arrow to the spot where you want it inserted on the facing page.

Leave Plenty of Space

What is the advantage of leaving extra space in the margins of your essay?

A little extra space in the margins (especially the left-hand margin) and between your essays provides room for the grader to make comments and for you to add an important idea or fact that occurs to you later. These "late entries" can be blended into your original answer by using an appropriate transitional phrase, such as "An additional idea that pertains to this question is. . . ."

Guard Against Careless Errors

Why is it so important to avoid careless errors?

Neatness goes beyond the readability of your handwriting and the appearance of your essay on the page. It includes an essay that is free of careless spelling and grammatical errors. As Hartig observes:

> If you misspell common words, and make clumsy errors in sentence structure, or even if you write paragraphs that lack unity and coherence, many of your

instructors are going to take it as a sure sign that you are sadly lacking in basic academic ability. Once a teacher thinks this about you, you will not get much credit for your ideas, even if they are brilliant.[5]

FINAL WORDS

What are graders looking for in your essays?

Writing is a skill that comes easily to some and is a struggle for others. If you worry that your writing is neither elegant nor eloquent, don't despair. Although students who are stylish writers may have an edge over those who aren't, the advantage is slight when it comes to scoring essay tests. Neatness counts, as we've seen, but graders will continue to place most of their emphasis on answers. If you master your material and can answer each essay question accurately and thoroughly, you will be rewarded for your efforts.

HAVE YOU MISSED SOMETHING?

SENTENCE COMPLETION

Complete the following sentences with one of the three words listed below each sentence.

1. In essay questions, you are graded on your _____.
   reasoning   opinions   decisions

2. Your answer to an essay question must demonstrate that you understand the _____.
   facts   dates   directions

3. Key points in an unfinished essay should be _____.
   outlined   combined   deleted

MATCHING

In each blank space in the left column, write the letter preceding the phrase in the right column that matches the left item best.

_____ 1. Suspense

_____ 2. Directions

a. Often provide specifics on how each question should be answered

b. Should be left off to ensure that your essay gets right to the point

[5]Ibid.

_____ 3. Simplicity

_____ 4. Space

_____ 5. Scope

_____ 6. Transitions

_____ 7. Handwriting

_____ 8. Introduction

c. Narrows gradually in an essay written in the decreasing-importance pattern

d. Unnecessary and undesirable in essay answers

e. Can be improved by using the modified printing style

f. Allows for late additions as well as for instructor's comments

g. Can be employed to make your logic more transparent

h. The best approach to writing essay answers

TRUE-FALSE

Write T _beside the_ true _statements and_ F _beside the_ false _statements._

_____ 1. You should develop a time plan for taking your test and always follow it strictly.

_____ 2. It's a good idea to read all the questions before you begin writing.

_____ 3. Leftover time should be used for double-checking your answers.

_____ 4. The appearance of your essay will have no influence on your grade.

_____ 5. Instructors prefer that you write in ink because it makes your answers easier to read.

MULTIPLE CHOICE

Choose the word or phrase that completes each sentence most accurately, and circle the letter that precedes it.

1. Jotting down notes on the back of the test sheet
   a. gets you involved right away.
   b. is usually not permitted in an essay exam.
   c. takes time that could be better spent.
   d. will often gain you partial credit.

2. In an essay test, it helps to start off with the question that is
   a. most difficult.
   b. first.
   c. last.
   d. easiest.

3. Keywords in an essay question should be
   a. paraphrased.
   b. circled.
   c. discussed.
   d. replaced.

4. You'll help prove that you write well under time constraints if your essay is
   a. concise.
   b. well organized.
   c. neat.
   d. all of the above.

5. In a sharply focused essay, a strong opening sentence
   a. restates the question.
   b. provides the answer.
   c. helps unify the answer.
   d. does all of the above.

SHORT ANSWER   *Supply a brief answer for each of the following items.*

1. Why are some students particularly nervous about taking essay exams?
2. What should you do if you are unable to finish an essay answer before time runs out?
3. What constitutes a "neat" essay?
4. How should opinions be treated in an essay answer?

WORDS IN CONTEXT

From the three choices beside each numbered item, select the one that most nearly expresses the meaning of the italicized word in the quote. Make a light check mark (✓) next to your choice.

We hold these truths to be *self-evident*, that all men are created equal, that they are *endowed* by their Creator with certain *unalienable* rights, that among these are life, liberty, and the *pursuit* of happiness.
—Thomas Jefferson (1743–1826), third president of the United States

| 1. *self-evident* | genuine | effective | obvious |
| 2. *endowed* | provided | developed | established |

3. *unalienable* rights	lawful	intrinsic	earned
4. *pursuit*	enjoyment	search	goal

Diplomacy is the art of saying "nice doggie" until you can find a rock.
—Will Rogers (1879–1935), American actor and humorist

| 5. *diplomacy* | trickery | cleverness | tact |

There is nothing *sinister* in so arranging one's affairs as to keep taxes as low as possible.
—Judge Learned Hand (1872–1961), American jurist

| 6. nothing *sinister* | illegal | easy | evil |

Capitalism is *humanitarianism.*
—Margaret Thatcher (1925–), former prime minister of Great Britain

| 7. *capitalism* | development | free enterprise | democracy |
| 8. *humanitarianism* | philanthropy | impermanent | materialistic |

THE WORD HISTORY SYSTEM

Deliberate
weighed in the scales

deliberate   de-lib′-er-ate *adj.*
1. Done with or marked by full consciousness of the nature and effects; intentional.
2. Arising from or marked by careful consideration. 3. Unhurried in action, movement, or manner, as if trying to avoid error.

A *deliberate* decision is one based upon a weighing of the facts and arguments involved—and that is the literal meaning of the word. *Deliberate* is derived from Latin *deliberatus,* past participle of the verb *deliberare,* from *librare,* "to weigh." *Librare* comes from *libra,* "a balance" or "pair of scales."

Reprinted by permission. From *Picturesque Word Origins* © 1933 by G. & C. Merriam Co. (now Merriam-Webster, Incorporated).

Appendix: Answers

Chapter 1 Settings Goals

HAVE YOU MISSED SOMETHING?

Sentence completion: 1. destination   2. experience   3. action

Matching: 1. f   2. d   3. e   4. g   5. h   6. a   7. c   8. b

True-false: 1. F   2. T   3. F   4. T   5. F

Multiple-choice: 1. d   2. a   3. c   4. c   5. a

WORDS IN CONTEXT: 1. perseverance   2. natural gift   3. high aptitude   4. vagrants   5. gorge   6. rewards

Chapter 2 Controlling Your Time

HAVE YOU MISSED SOMETHING?

Sentence completion: 1. game plan   2. daytime   3. term

Matching: 1. g   2. f   3. d   4. b   5. h   6. c   7. a   8. e

True-false: 1. F   2. T   3. F   4. T   5. T

Multiple-choice: 1. b   2. b   3. c   4. c   5. d

WORDS IN CONTEXT: 1. strength   2. sorrowfully   3. death   4. worth   5. inexplicable   6. associated   7. included

Chapter 3 Staying Focused

HAVE YOU MISSED SOMETHING?

Sentence completion: 1. thinking   2. steady   3. distraction

Matching: 1. g   2. h   3. a   4. b   5. c   6. d   7. e   8. f

True-false: 1. T   2. T   3. F   4. F   5. T

Multiple-choice: 1. a   2. b   3. b   4. a   5. c

WORDS IN CONTEXT: 1. corruptive   2. orderly   3. refinement   4. unappealing   5. despicable

Chapter 4 Defending Your Memory

HAVE YOU MISSED SOMETHING?

Sentence completion: 1. selectivity   2. DRAM   3. reciting

Matching: 1. c   2. e   3. g   4. h   5. a   6. d   7. f   8. b

True-false: 1. T   2. T   3. T   4. F   5. F

Multiple-choice: 1. b   2. b   3. b   4. b   5. c

WORDS IN CONTEXT: 1. new ideas   2. reword   3. possessed   4. disasters

Chapter 5   Managing Stress

HAVE YOU MISSED SOMETHING?

Sentence completion: 1. stressors   2. value
3. saturated

Matching: 1. f   2. g   3. b   4. e   5. a   6. h   7. d
8. c

True-false: 1. T   2. F   3. T   4. T   5. F

Multiple-choice: 1. c   2. d   3. b   4. c   5. d

WORDS IN CONTEXT: 1. stressed   2. gibberish
3. insinuations   4. untalkative   5. average people
6. nullified

Chapter 6   Improving Your Reading

HAVE YOU MISSED SOMETHING?

Sentence completion: 1. concept   2. fixations
3. phrases

Matching: 1. h   2. e   3. c   4. a   5. d   6. g   7. f
8. b

True-false: 1. F   2. T   3. T   4. F   5. T

Multiple-choice: 1. c   2. b   3. b   4. a   5. b

WORDS IN CONTEXT: 1. nonfeeling
2. disdainful   3. component   4. irritating

Chapter 7   Building a Lasting Vocabulary

HAVE YOU MISSED SOMETHING?

Sentence completion: 1. self-esteem
2. convenience   3. familiarity

Matching: 1. d   2. c   3. g   4. f   5. a   6. b   7. h
8. e

True-false: 1. T   2. T   3. T   4. T   5. F

Multiple-choice: 1. d   2. d   3. b   4. b   5. b

WORDS IN CONTEXT: 1. given new life
2. absolute   3. rewards

Chapter 8   Thinking Visually

HAVE YOU MISSED SOMETHING?

Sentence completion: 1. analytical   2. codes
3. symmetrical

Matching: 1. c   2. f   3. e   4. h   5. a   6. g   7. d
8. b

True-false: 1. F   2. T   3. T   4. T   5. F

Multiple-choice: 1. b   2. c   3. b   4. a   5. d

WORDS IN CONTEXT: 1. impresario   2. delegate
3. briefness   4. abundantly

Chapter 9   Adopting a Note-Taking Mindset

HAVE YOU MISSED SOMETHING?

Sentence completion: 1. context   2. ideas
3. anticipation

Matching: 1. c   2. e   3. b   4. g   5. d   6. a   7. h
8. f

True-false: 1. T   2. F   3. T   4. F   5. T

Multiple-choice: 1. d   2. d   3. a   4. c   5. d

WORDS IN CONTEXT: 1. dictionary   2. unbeatable
3. stern

Chapter 10   Taking Effective Notes

HAVE YOU MISSED SOMETHING?

Sentence completion: 1. forgetting   2. signposts
3. questions

Matching: 1. b   2. f   3. d   4. h   5. g   6. e   7. c
8. a

True-false: 1. F   2. T   3. F   4. T   5. T

Multiple-choice: 1. b   2. c   3. b   4. c   5.d

WORDS IN CONTEXT: 1. refinement   2. relieve
3. reasonable   4. dead end

Chapter 11   Mastering Your Notes

HAVE YOU MISSED SOMETHING?

Sentence completion: 1. recitation   2. reflection
3. ignored

Matching: 1. d   2. h   3. a   4. e   5. g   6. b   7. f
8. c

True-false: 1. T   2. F   3. T   4. T   5. T

Multiple-choice: 1. a   2. d   3. b   4. d   5. c

WORDS IN CONTEXT: 1. major   2. unrelated
3. abundantly   4. favorable   5. trite phrase
6. filled

Chapter 12   Managing Test Anxiety

HAVE YOU MISSED SOMETHING?

Sentence completion: 1. preparation
2. cramming   3. instructor

Matching: 1. g   2. d   3. e   4. a   5. f   6. h   7. b
8. c

True-false: 1. F   2. T   3. T   4. F   5. T

Multiple-choice: 1. d   2. d   3. d   4. d   5. a

WORDS IN CONTEXT: 1. confirmation   2. unfathomable
3. lingo   4. identification   5. hidden   6. reasons
7. continuation   8. haughty   9. nasty

Chapter 13   Answering Objective Tests

HAVE YOU MISSED SOMETHING?

Sentence completion: 1. circled   2. correct
3. overlooked

Matching: 1. g   2. d   3. h   4. a   5. e   6. c   7. f
8. b

True-false: 1. T   2. T   3. F   4. T   5. F

Multiple-choice: 1. c   2. c   3. d   4. a   5. b

WORDS IN CONTEXT: 1. damaging force   2. unseen
3. decreased value   4. inordinate   5. peculiarities
6. cautious   7. outdated

Chapter 14   Tackling Essay Tests

HAVE YOU MISSED SOMETHING?

Sentence completion: 1. reasoning   2. facts   3.
outlined

Matching: 1. d   2. a   3. h   4. f   5. c   6. g   7. e
8. b

True-false: 1. F   2. T   3. T   4. F   5. T

Multiple-choice: 1. a   2. d   3. b   4. d   5. d

WORDS IN CONTEXT: 1. obvious   2. provided
3. intrinsic   4. search   5. tact   6. evil
7. free enterprise   8. philanthropy

Index

abbreviations, for notes, 228
abridged dictionaries, 138–141
abstract ideas, concept maps for, 172–173
abstracts, rereading, 233
academic preparation, for tests,
        266–274
    asking for help, 267
    getting textbooks early, 184, 266
    organizing notes, 269–272
    organizing time, 267–268
    reading syllabus, 266–267
    staying on top of coursework, 267
    and systematic cramming, 272–274
    See also test anxiety management
action, goals and, 13–15
action-impact pattern, 223
active listening, 194, 196–197. *See also* listening skills
active participation, in note taking, 216–219
addition words, 224
adjustment, as listening skill, 197
advanced summary sheets, 270, 272, 273
advance organizers, 190–191, 199
advantageous learning, 270
aerobic exercise, 107–108
alarm clock
    and sleep deprivation, 101–102
    for time management, 25
alcohol, 105
altitude, determining, for reading, 121–122
Alzheimer's disease, 77
American Heritage Dictionary, The, 138–140
antonyms, 147

appendixes, textbook, 187
Archimedes, 254
Ashe, Arthur, 183
assignments
    completing before lectures, 199–200
    getting overview of, 120–121, 184
    master schedule for, 35, 36
    supplemental readings, 230–232
    surveying, 190–192
    weekly schedule for, 35–37
associations, memory and, 66–73
astronomy, mnemonic devices for, 71
attention, as listening skill, 196–197
attitude improvement, 91–97
    for effective listening, 195–196
    improving self-esteem, 94–95
    relaxation techniques for, 92–94
    and self-talk, 95
    and sense of control, 95–97
    and test anxiety management, 276–277
    See also health and well-being; stress management
Augustine, Norman R., 80
Ausubel, David, 126, 190
author's objective, 185
author's qualifications, 186

background knowledge
    basic courses for, 68
    for improving reading, 125–126
    and memory retention, 67–69
    and note taking, 184
    and surveying textbooks, 189, 190–191

backward interference theory, 61
bar graphs, 163–166
basic courses, and background, 68
Beecher, Henry Ward, 43
"belly breathing," 276
BEST (bright, even, steady), for proper lighting, 49
Bethe, Hans, 253
Bethlehem Steel Company, 34
bibliographies, textbook, 187
Bierce, Ambrose, 203
billboards, and vocabulary building, 134–135
Billings, Josh, 45
biology, mnemonic devices for, 71
Bloom, Kristine, 76
boldface, in textbooks, 221
bookmark method, in Q System, 247–248
bookstand, for studying, 50
Boone, Louis E., 110, 111
brain functions
    and improving understanding, 161
    and memory retention, 161
    and reading process, 119–120
    and visual thinking, 160–161
brainstorming, for goals, 15
breaks
    and concentration, 52
    value of, 25–26
breathing techniques, for relaxation, 93–94, 276
Brewster, Kingman, Jr., 280
Brody, Jane, 98
Brown, James I., 151–152
Bruner, Jerome, 64
bullets, in textbooks, 221
burnout, 7

cadence, in intonation, 219, 221
caffeine, 105, 106
calendar, mnemonic for, 70
calorie consumption, 99–100
Cambridge Psychological Society, 60
Camus, Albert, 203
carbohydrates, in diet, 99–100
career goals. *See* goals
category and cluster system, for memory, 66, 67
causal patterns, 223

cause-and-effect words, 224
cause-effect pattern, 223
CD-ROM dictionaries, 140–141, 142
chapters, surveying specific, 190–192, 231
Charlesworth, Edward A., 93
chronological pattern, 222, 314–315
Ciardi, John, 57
circadian rhythms
    and sleep patterns, 103–104
    and time management, 26
circle graphs, 163
Clemenceau, Georges, 81
climactic-order pattern, 223
clues, skimming for, 122
clustering
    for building vocabulary, 148, 151
    for memory retention, 66, 67
    page clustering, 124–125
    paragraph clustering, 123–124
    in reading process, 123–125, 190
    silent intonation for, 123
Cocks, Sir Barnett, 241
comparison patterns, 223, 315
comparison words, 224
completion, working to, 90
comprehension. *See* reading comprehension;
    understanding
computer technology
    diagram of modem, 170
    dynamic random access memory (DRAM), 75
    electronic dictionaries, 136–138, 140–141, 142
    personal digital assistants (PDAs), 52
    supplementary learning aids, 186
    See also Internet; technology
concentration, 45–54
    and alternative textbooks, 53
    balancing challenge with skill level for, 52–54
    BEST (bright, even, steady) lighting for, 49
    and circadian rhythms, 26
    defined, 46–47
    equipment for, 49–50
    external distractions and, 47–50
    flow and, 52–53
    internal distractions and, 50–51
    as listening skill, 196–197

lists for, 51–52
and multitasking, 88, 89
and noise distractions, 48
pencil technique for, 49–50
proper environment for, 47–50
setting realistic study goals and, 54
and sleep deprivation, 102
spider technique for, 49
taking breaks for, 52
tutors and study groups for, 53
and visual distractions, 48
worry pad for, 51
concentration scoresheet, 51
concept maps, 172–176
guidelines for creating, 173–175
for planning strategies, 175–176
for summaries, 175
for textbook passage, 171, 173, 174
concession words, 225
concluding sentences, function of, 123–124
conclusions, about visuals, 162, 167
connections, memory and, 66–73
consolidation
and memory, 75–76
and reading speed, 120
See also memory/memorization
context
in graphics, 168
in note taking, 184
and reflection, 255
and word meanings, 135–136, 143
contrast patterns, 315
contrast words, 224
control
impact of attitude on, 96–97
increasing sense of, 95–97
loss of, and procrastination, 86, 89
and out-of-control circumstances, 97
schedules for, 27
significance of feeling, 95–96
Coolidge, Calvin, 18, 142
Cooper, Dr. Kenneth, 108
Copernicus, Nicolaus, 301
Cornell System, 207–212
for combining notes, 257

cue column in, 207–208, 212
formats for, 208–212
margin questions in, 244–248
for marking textbooks, 212–216
note paper for, 207, 208
summary area in, 207, 208
cortisone, and stress, 96
count-of-three relaxation method, 93–94
Cousins, Norman, 95–96
cramming, 272–274
create-a-sentence mnemonic, 72–73
create-a-word mnemonic, 72
creativity, and reflection, 253, 254
CRF (corticotropin releasing factor), and
stress, 98
crowd psychology, and goals, 5–6
Csikszentmihalyi, Mihaly, 52, 97
cue column, in Cornell System, 207–208, 212
Cunningham, Anne, 118, 126
Czeisler, Dr. Charles, 102

daily activity log, 24–25
daily schedule, 28, 33
and concentration, 52
to-do list for, 37–38
data, distorting graph, 166–168
Davis, T. B., 76
decreasing-importance pattern, 223, 314
deductive pattern, 223
deep sleep, 104
deep thinking, 73
and listening, 196
and reflection, 254
definition notes, 210, 211
Deighton, Lee C., 135–136, 149
delta sleep, 104
depression, and exercise, 107
descriptive essays, 315
detail, in schedules, 29
diagrams, 170. *See also* visuals
dictionaries, 50
abridged desk, 138–141
electronic, 136–138, 140–141, 142
how to read, 136–138
pocket, 136–138

dictionaries (*cont.*)
  synonyms in, 138–140
  unabridged, 141–142
  usage notes in, 140
  for vocabulary building, 135–142
  word histories in, 140
diet. *See* eating habits
discussion classes, studying for, 29
distorted data, in graphs, 166–168
distractions
  discouraging internal, 50–51
  and effective listening, 194, 197
  and memory retention, 63
  reducing external, 47–50
  visual, 48
distributed practice, 75–76
divided context, in multiple-choice questions,
    287
documentation, of goals, 12, 15–16
Do It Now: How to Stop Procrastinating (Knaus), 86
Doyle, Sir Arthur Conan, 261
draft writing, massed practice for, 76
drawings. *See* visuals
dream sleep, 104
Drucker, Peter, 80, 303
dual coding, 161

eating habits, 98–101
  and calorie consumption, 99–100
  drinking water, 101
  eating dinner early, 91
  fats and carbohydrates, 99–100
  fruits and vegetables, 101
  impact of stress on appetite, 98
  routine meal schedules, 98–99
  and USDA's food pyramid, 99
  whole-grain foods, 100
Ebbinghaus, Hermann, 65, 206
Edfeldt, Åke, 119
Effective Listening (Murphy), 195
Eigen, Manfred, 261
80/20 rule, 38
Einstein, Albert, 57, 64
Ekman, Paul, 92
Elizabeth I (Queen of England), 22
Ellington, Duke, 39

e-mail
  as distraction from studying, 48
  limiting, for time management, 25
Emery, Albert W., 57
emotions, cause and effects of, 91
emphasis words, 225
endorphins, 108
enumeration, in textbook marking, 215, 216
enumeration words, 224
environment. *See* study environment
essay tests, 284, 305–318
  answering easiest questions first, 308
  answers at beginning of, 312–314
  correct answers in, 308–310
  ending with summary, 316
  evidence in, 310
  getting to the point in, 311–314
  grading process for, 316
  and instructor's "pet ideas," 310
  jotting general notes on back, 307
  keywords used in, 309
  neat handwriting for, 317–318
  opinions in, 311
  organization for, 314–316
  reading all questions first, 306–307
  reading directions first, 306
  skipping introduction in, 311–312
  spelling and grammar in, 317–318
  supporting material in, 310–311
  systematic approach to, 306–308
  time management techniques for, 307–308
  transitional words for, 315–316
  understanding questions in, 308
  using simple language in, 314
  writing cues beside questions, 307
evidence, in essay tests, 310–311
example words, 224
exam-week schedule, 268
excuses, verbalizing, 87
exercise
  and sleep, 105
  for stress management, 106–108
eye movements, in reading process, 116–118, 123

fading theory, of forgetting, 60
failure, fear of, and procrastination, 85

Faraday, Michael, 169–172
fats, in diet, 99–100
feedback, and recitation, 74
five-minute plan, 86
fixations, and speed reading, 116–118, 123
flexibility
    for devising plans, 13
    as listening skill, 197–198
    and reflection, 254
    and schedules, 28, 308
flow, and concentration, 52–53
focus. *See* concentration
Fordham University survey, 22
forgetting
    effect on reading and listening, 60
    motivated, 63–64
    and multitasking, 88
    pseudo-, 62, 89
    theories on causes of, 60–62
    See also memory/memorization
format, of graphics data, 167–168
forward interference theory, 61
Fourteen Master Words, 151–152
Fox, Edward W., 209
Frankl, Vicktor, 4
freedom, and schedules, 28
French vocabulary study, 25, 76
Friesen, Wallace V., 92
Frontier Vocabulary System, 145–148
    basic concepts of, 146–147
    and index card system, 148
    recognizing frontier words, 147
fruits and vegetables, in diet, 101
furniture, in study environment, 50

Galbraith, John Kenneth, 43, 261
geographical pattern, 222
George V (King of England), 142
Gibbon, Edward, 121
Gist, Marilyn, 84
gist, skimming for, 122
glossaries, textbook, 187
Glover, J. A., 76
glucocorticoids, and stress, 98
goals, 3–16
    action and, 13–15

being specific for, 87
brainstorming for, 15
changes in, 16
and crowd psychology, 5–6
defining, 10–12
devising plan for, 12–13, 15–16
documenting, 12, 15–16
and happiness, 7–9
imaging and, 6, 87
importance of, 4
major and minor, 10–12
and making money, 6–7
and marching to own rhythm, 4–9
master schedule for, 35, 36
and meaning, 4, 5
overcoming obstacles to, 14–15
publicizing, 86
quality vs. quantity in, 7–9
setting realistic study, 54
and success, 6–7
    See also GPA (goals, plans, actions)
Goldilocks technique, 294–295
Gould, Edson, 5
GPA (goals, plans, actions), 10–16
    example of, 11
    four-step process for, 15–16
    of success, 14
grading process, for essay tests, 316
grammatical clues, in objective tests, 297
Grant, Dr. Alexander, 105
graphics. *See* visuals
graphs, 162–168
    bar, 163–166
    circle, 163
    distortions in, 166–168
    line, 163–166
    using OPTIC system for, 166–167
"great recall" approach, to reading, 121
guessing, in objective tests, 298
Gurdjieff, George Ivanovitch, 157

Hall, Robert A., Jr., 118–119
Hand, Judge Learned, 321
handwriting, in essay tests, 317–318
Hanson, Dr. Peter, 96
happiness, and goals, 7–9

Hartig, Hugo, 310, 311, 314, 317–318
Hartmann, Dr. Ernest, 102
Hayakawa, S. I., 146
headings and subheadings
    previewing, 191, 192
    rereading, 233
    turning into questions, 218–219
health and well-being, 97–108
    and feeling in control, 95–96
    good eating habits for, 98–101
    improving sleep for, 101–106
    regular exercise for, 106–108
    role of happiness in, 7–8
    See also attitude improvement; stress management
Heilbroner, Robert L., 43, 56
hidden time, finding, 22–23
history
    illustrating notes for, 169
    mnemonic devices for, 71
History of England, The (Macaulay), 124
Holmes, Oliver Wendell, 3, 62
homestretch schedule, 268, 269
How to Lie with Statistics (Huff), 167
Huxley, Thomas, 21

Icahn, Carl, 129
Idea of Composition, The (Hartig), 310
Ikangaa, Juma, 265
illustrations, in note taking, 169–172. *See also* visuals
imaging, and goals, 6, 87. *See also* visualizations
importance patterns, 222–223
increasing-importance pattern, 223
index card system
    for studying for exams, 285
    for vocabulary building, 143–145, 148
indexes, textbook, 187–189
inductive pattern, 223
inner dialogue, rewriting, 94–95
insomnia
    and multitasking, 89
    and stress, 102
    See also sleep
interactive interference theory, 61
interest
    and effective listening, 194, 195
    and memory retention, 63

and vocabulary building, 132–135
interference theory, of forgetting, 61, 63
Internet
    as distraction from studying, 48
    limiting, for time management, 25
    supplementary learning aids on, 186
    See also computer technology
interrelationships, in graphics, 162, 167
intonation, 219–222
    in lectures, 219–221
    and meaning, 219
    silent, as reading skill, 123
    in textbooks, 221–222
    three components of, 219–221
introductions
    chapter, 192
    in essay tests, 311–312
    rereading, 233
    textbook, 187, 188–189
introductory courses, importance of, 68
inverted pyramid pattern, 223, 314
italics, in textbooks, 221

Jacobson, Edmund, 94
James, William, 85, 91
James-Lange theory, 91–92
Jefferson, Thomas, 320
Joy of Stress, The (Hanson), 96
Just, Dr. Marcel, 88

Katona, George, 190
Kennedy, John F., 10, 11
keyword mnemonic, 71–72
keywords, used in essay tests, 309
Knaus, William J., 86
Kobasa, S. C., 277
KPMG (Klynveld, Peat, Marwick, Goerdeler) poll, 7
Krug, D., 76

La Bruyére, Jean de, 179
Lange, Carl, 91
language, in essay tests, 314
La Rochefoucauld, François, Duc de, 179
laws and principles
    Ivy Lee principle, 34–35
    Pareto Principle, 38

Parkinson's Law, 25
learning plateau, 77
learning processes, characteristics of, 145
learning skills center, 53
LeBon, Gustave, 5
lecture classes, studying for, 29
lecture note taking
    and asking questions, 218
    basic guidelines for, 234
    combining with textbook notes, 256
    and effective listening, 194–198
    and end of lecture, 233
    and flexibility, 197–198
    and missed classes, 230
    Q System review for, 246, 247
    refining, 234
    reviewing past lecture notes, 199
    two-page system for, 230
    See also note taking
lectures
    asking questions during, 218
    intonations in, 219–221
    mentally recalling, 233, 234
    organizational patterns in, 197–198, 222–226
lectures, preparing for, 198–200
    completing reading assignments, 199–200
    reading syllabus, 199
    reviewing past lecture notes, 199
Lee, Ivy, 34–35
Levenson, Robert W., 92
library, for concentration, 47
lighting, bright, even, and steady, 49
line graphs, 163–166
listening, and memory retention, 60
listening skills, 192–200
    active listening, 194, 196–197
    capacity for adjustment, 197
    developing interest, 195
    exercising mind, 198
    listening for ideas, 196
    listening habits quiz, 193
    open mindedness, 198
    paying attention, 196–197
    positive attitude, 195–196
    and rebuttals, 196
    resisting distractions, 197

    ten keys to effective, 194
    triple-A listening, 194–198
    using thought speed, 197
lists
    for concentration, 51–52
    note taking, 210, 211
    for reading preparation, 121
    things to do, 37–38, 86
Loehr, Dr. James, 93
Logan, Richard, 96
logical connections, and memory, 67–69
logical patterns, 223
"loving kindness" meditation, 91
Lowes, John Livingston, 190

Macaulay, Thomas Babington, 124–125
"Magical Number Seven, Plus or Minus Two, The" (Miller),
    64
major goals, 11–12
Malcolm X, 132–133
Mann, Thomas, 243
Marden, Orison Swett, 202
Masefield, John, 159
Massachusetts Institute of Technology, 119
massed practice, 75–76
master schedule, 28, 29, 30
    task-based, 35, 36
matching questions, in objective tests, 289–291
McGuire, Al, 281
meals. *See* eating habits
meaning
    and goals, 4, 5
    and intonation, 219
    role of questions in, 217–218
medicine, mnemonic devices for, 71
melatonin, 105
memory/memorization, 59–77
    and Alzheimer's disease, 77
    associations and connections in, 66–73
    avoiding pseudo-forgetting, 62, 89
    and background knowledge, 68–69
    commercial methods for, 73
    conscious effort and intention in, 62–64
    consolidation in, 75–76
    and distributed practice, 75–76
    human vs. computer, 75

memory/memorization (*cont.*)
    impact of organization and amount on, 64–65
    and learning plateaus, 77
    limiting and selecting ideas for, 65
    and logical connections, 67–69
    meaningful clusters and categories for, 65–66, 67
    mnemonic devices for, 69–73
    motivated forgetting, 63–64
    and motivated interest, 63
    and multitasking, 88
    note taking for, 206–207
    recitation for, 73–75
    research on rates of forgetting, 60
    and sleep deprivation, 102
    and speed reading, 120
    strengthening, 66–75
    theories of forgetting, 60–62
    and understanding, 63, 68
    using whole brain, 161
    and visual thinking, 68–69, 161
Mencken, H. L., 241
mental images. *See* visual thinking
mental preparation, for managing test anxiety,
    274–277
Meyer, Dr. David, 88
Miller, G. A., 64–65
Miller, Gerald R., 70
minor goals, 10–11
mnemonic devices, 69–73
    classic, 70–71
    create-a-sentence, 72–73
    create-a-word, 72
    keyword, 71–72
modified printing style, 226, 227, 317
momentum, for preventing procrastination, 86–87
money, and goals, 6–7
Morgan, William, 107
motivation
    and distributed practice, 76
    impact on memory, 62–64
    and recitation, 74–75
movement patterns, 222
movies, line graphs as, 164, 165
multiple-choice questions, 286–289
    choosing "all of the above" for, 287

    choosing middle numbers in, 288–289
    converting to true-false format, 287–288
    differing formats for, 287
    discarding foolish options in, 288
    and divided context, 287
    stem in, 286
    varying directions in, 286
multitasking
    defined, 87–88
    impact on productivity, 88
    and increased stress, 89
    minimizing, 89–90
Murphy, Kevin J., 195
music, and concentration, 48

Nader, Ralph, 157
naps, 104
Nathan, Ronald G., 93
negatives, in objective tests, 295–296
newspapers, and vocabulary building, 133–134
noise distractions, and concentration, 48
nonacademic activities, scheduling for, 29
norepinephrine, 108
notepad
    for minimizing multitasking, 89, 90
    for time management, 26–27
    as worry pad, 51
note taking, 205–236
    active participation in, 216–219
    advanced summary sheets, 270, 272, 273
    and asking questions, 217–219
    avoiding outlines in, 209
    basic guidelines for, 234–236
    combining formats for, 212, 213
    combining lecture and textbook, 256
    Cornell System for, 207–212
    dealing with special cases, 227–232
    definition notes, 210, 211
    during essay tests, 307
    and exam preparation, 267, 269–272
    flexibility in, 197–198
    formats for, 208–212
    as handwritten textbook, 207
    as highly condensed summary, 231–232
    immediate review of, 244

lists for, 210, 211
and memory retention, 206–207
modified printing style for, 226, 227
paragraph notes, 210
paying attention to intonation for, 219–222
Q System for reviewing, 244–248
and recitation, 250–252
and recognizing organizational patterns, 197–198, 222–226
recording efficiently, 226–227
and reflection, 252–256
review process, 244–250
selective, 227, 230, 269
sentence notes, 209
Silver Dollar System for, 254–255
split-level summaries for, 250
standard summaries for, 248–250
summary sheets for, 269–272
for supplemental readings, 230–232
symbols and markings for, 212, 214, 228
telegraphic writing for, 209–210, 226–227, 228–229
textbook marking, 212–216
using illustrations, 169–172, 210, 212
wrap-up summaries for, 250
See also lecture note taking; textbook notes
note-taking preparation. *See* lectures, preparing for; listening skills; textbooks, previewing

obesity, 99–100, 101
objective tests, 283–298
choosing best option in, 296
clarifying ambiguous questions, 291–292
Goldilocks technique for, 294–295
grammatical clues in, 297
guessing in, 298
marking sure things first in, 297–298
matching questions, 289–291
multiple-choice questions, 286–289
noticing negatives in, 295–296
and Q System, 284
qualifiers in, 293–295
reading directions first, 293
reading questions carefully in, 293–296
sentence-completion questions, 291–292
study methods for, 284–285

"switch hitter" study for, 284–285
systematic approach to, 292–298
true-false questions in, 285–286, 295
See also multiple-choice questions
O'Connor, Johnson, 145–148
100 percent words, 294
open mindedness, as listening skill, 198
opinions, in essay tests, 311
OPTIC system, 162, 166–167
oral reports, concept maps for, 175–176
organization
advance organizers, 190–191
category and cluster system of, 66, 67
for managing test anxiety, 267–272
and memory retention, 64–66
poor, and procrastination, 86
See also clustering
organizational patterns, 222–226
causal patterns, 223
comparison patterns, 223
for essay tests, 314–315
importance patterns, 222–223
for lectures, 197–198
logical patterns, 223
movement patterns, 222
signposts for, 222, 224–226
organizational plan, of textbooks, 185–186
outlines
concept maps as, 176
disadvantages of, 209
overlearning, for vocabulary building, 143
overview
of finished reading assignments, 233
of reading assignment, 120–121, 184
of visuals, 162, 167
See also surveying; textbooks, previewing
Oxford English Dictionary (OED), 141, 142

PACE technique, for reading skills, 120–126
Padus, Emrika, 93
page clustering, in reading process, 124–125
Paivio, Allan, 161
paragraph notes, 210
paragraphs
elements of expository, 124

paragraphs (*cont.*)
  introductory, 192
  summarizing, in reading process, 123–124
  summary, 192, 231
  surveying, 191, 192
Pareto Principle, 38, 86
Pareto, Vilfredo, 38
Parkinson's Law, 25
participation, and recitation, 74
parts, of visuals, analyzing, 162, 167
Pascal, Blaise, 115
pauses, in intonation, 219, 221
Pavlov, Ivan Petrovich, 205
Peale, Norman Vincent
  on imaging, 6
  on positive thinking, 91–92
  on taking action, 14–15
peep-sight experiment, 116, 117
peg system, for memory retention, 73
pencil technique, 49–50
personal digital assistants (PDAs)
  dictionaries for, 136–138
  for schedules, 34, 52
Peter, Laurence J., 111
pictures, building memory with, 68–69. *See also* visual
  thinking
Picturesque Word Origins, 140, 153. *See also* word
  histories
pie chart, 163
place pattern, 222
place words, 225
plans
  for goals, 12–13, 15–16
  for minimizing multitasking, 90
  publicizing, 86
  using concept maps for, 175–176
plateaus, learning, 77
pocket dictionaries, 136–138
pocket work, 23
polar route, 13
positive attitudes. *See* attitude improvement
Positive Imaging (Peale), 6
prefatory material
  of supplemental readings, 231
  of textbooks, 184–187

prefixes, 148–152
  list of common, 150
preparation techniques
  mental preparation for tests, 274–277
  for reading, 120–121
  and test anxiety, 266
  See also academic preparation; lectures, preparing for;
    textbooks, previewing
previewing. *See* surveying; textbooks, previewing
prime time, studying during, 28–29
problem-cause-solution pattern, 223
problem-effect-solution pattern, 223
process pattern, 222, 315
procrastination, 85–87
  common sources of, 85–86
  and goals, 14–15
  methods for preventing, 86–87
  and multitasking, 89
programmed materials, as study aids, 53–54
progress checks, 86
progressive muscle relaxation (PMR), 94
pseudo-forgetting, 62, 89
purpose, and goals, 4

Q System, 244–248
  bookmarks for, 247–248
  and follow-up questions, 255
  formulating questions for, 244–246
  and recitation, 251
  separate notes for, 248
  sticky notes for, 247
  for studying for exams, 267, 284
qualifiers, in objective tests, 293–295
questioning method, 217
questions
  formulating while reading, 218–219, 236
  during lectures, 218
  in Q System, 244–248
  for reflection, 252–253, 255
  in SQ3R system, 220
  turning headings into, 218–219
  for unlocking meaning, 217–218

Random House Dictionary of the English Language, 141
rapid eye movement (REM) sleep, 104

Rau, John, 7
reactive interference theory, 61, 63
reading
     good and great books, 125–126
     and memory retention, 60
     pictures, 161–168
     and recitation, 73–74
     in SQ3R system, 220
     See also textbooks, previewing
reading comprehension
     and background knowledge, 125
     and distributed practice, 76
     and reading speed, 119–120
     and recitation, 74
reading skills, 116–126
     clustering techniques, 123–125
     and comprehension, 119–120
     and consolidation, 120
     determining altitude, 121–122
     expanding background knowledge, 125–126
     and eye movement, 116–118, 123
     limitations of speed-reading, 116–120
     PACE technique, 120–126
     page clustering, 124–125
     preparation techniques, 120–121
     reading with intonation, 221–222
     and silent speech, 118–119, 123
     skimming, 121–122
     summarizing paragraphs, 123–124
     vocabulary building, 126
Reagan, Ronald, 178
recitation
     from concept maps, 173
     for cramming, 274
     for mastering material, 267
     for memory retention, 73–75
     of notes, 250–252
     out loud, 251
     in SQ3R system, 220
     and textbook marking, 216
     for textbook reading, 236
     for vocabulary building, 143
     by writing, 251
recitation classes, studying for, 29
recorded study information, 23, 230

reference lists, textbook, 187
reflection, 252–256
     and advanced summary sheets, 270
     combining lecture and textbook notes, 256
     and context, 255
     and creativity, 253, 254
     flexibility of, 254
     importance of, 253–254
     questions for, 252–253, 255
     rearranging information for, 255
     Silver Dollar System of, 254–255
     and visual thinking, 256
relaxation
     and attitude improvement, 92–94
     breathing techniques for, 93–94, 276
     count-of-three method of, 93–94
     progressive muscle, 94
     schedules and, 27
     and test anxiety, 107, 276
remembering. *See* memory/memorization
repeat words, 225
reports, concept maps for, 175–176
retrieval theory, of forgetting, 60–61
reviewing
     past lecture notes, 199
     Q System for, 244–248
     scheduling time for, 268
     in SQ3R system, 220
     using summaries, 248–250
Rickenbacker, Eddie, 217
Ripley, George, 179
Robbins, Anthony, 39
Rogers, Will, 321
Roosevelt, Theodore, 129
roots, of words, 148–152
     list of common, 149

Sanskrit proverb, 40
Santayana, George, 59
Sapolsky, Dr. Robert, 98
scale, in graphs, 168
schedules, 27–38
     assignment-oriented, 35–37
     basic guidelines for, 28–29
     benefits of using, 27–28

schedules (*cont.*)
  breaks in, 25–26, 52
  and circadian rhythms, 26
  daily, 28, 33, 37–38
  exam-week, 268
  homestretch, 268, 269
  master, 28, 29, 30, 35
  for meals, 98–99
  for minimizing multitasking, 90
  nonacademic activities in, 29
  and Pareto Principle, 38
  sleep, 103–104
  task-based, 34–38
  for test anxiety management, 267–268
  three-part scheduling plan, 28–33, 35–38
  timer vs. clock-watching for, 87
  tools and utilities for, 34
  using time blocks, 28–34
  weekly, 28, 29–32, 35–37
  See also time management techniques
Schopenhauer, Arthur, 253–254
Schuller, Dr. Robert, 281
Schwab, Charles, 34–35
science, illustrating notes for, 169–172
selective note taking, 227, 230, 269
self-esteem
  and exercise, 106–107
  improving, 94–95
  and vocabulary building, 132–133
self-observation, concentration scoresheet for, 51
self-talk
  positive, 95
  and test anxiety management, 277
Selye, Dr. Hans, 83, 84
sentence-completion questions, 291–292
sentence notes, 209
sentences
  concluding, 123–124
  supporting, 123–124
  topic, 123–124
Sherman, James R., 87
Shorr, Dr. Joseph E., 68
Shuell, Thomas, 76
signposts, for organizational patterns, 222, 224–226

silent speech, in reading process, 118–119, 123
Silver Dollar System, 254–255, 270
skills, balancing work challenge with, 52–54
skimming
  for improving reading, 121–122
  as speed reading, 118
  for surveying assignments, 190–192
sleep
  and circadian rhythms, 26, 103–104
  drawbacks of naps, 104
  effects of sleep deprivation, 101–103
  and exercise, 105
  getting right amount of, 103
  guidelines for better, 104–106
  impact of multitasking on, 89
  regular schedules for, 103–104
  REM and deep, 104
  separate environment for, 91, 105
  waking up half-hour earlier, 90
snapshots, bar graphs as, 164, 165
Socratic method, 217
soft drinks, in diet, 101
spacing effect, 76
spare-time thinking, for studying, 23
spatial pattern, 222, 315
specific information, skimming for, 122
specificity, for procrastination, 87
speed-reading, limitations of, 116–120
spelling, mnemonic devices for, 70–71
spider technique, 49
split-level summaries, 250
SQ3R System, 219, 220
Stampfer, Meir J., 99, 100
statistics, distorted, 167–168
Stein, Gertrude, 283
Steinbeck, John, 280
Steinbrenner, George, 81
sticky-note method, in Q System, 247
Stop Procrastinating (Sherman), 87
strengths, listing, 15
stress
  defined, 84
  impact on health, 8, 96, 98
  two-sided potential of, 84

stress management, 83–108
  attitude improvement, 91–97
  discouraging procrastination, 85–87
  good eating habits, 98–101
  and happiness, 8–9
  improving sleep for, 101–106
  increasing sense of control, 95–97
  minimizing multitasking, 87–90
  for minor stress sources, 90–91
  regular exercise for, 106–108
  relaxation techniques, 92–94
  and self-esteem, 94–95
Stress Management (Charlesworth, Nathan), 93
Strunk, William, Jr., 305
study environment, 47–50
  eliminating noise in, 48
  and e-mail and Internet distractions, 48
  furniture and supplies for, 50
  minimizing visual distractions in, 48
  proper lighting for, 49
  for tests, 275–276
  using pencil technique in, 49–50
study groups, 53
study guides, supplementary, 186
subconscious
  and reflection, 254
  for saving time, 23
success
  building on past, 95
  fear of, and procrastination, 85
  and goals, 6–7
  and GPA, 10, 14
  vocabulary building for, 132–133
suffixes, 148, 150–151
summaries
  concept maps for, 175
  in essay tests, 316
  highly condensed, 231–232
  for improving reading, 123–125
  of notes, 248–250
  paragraph, 192, 231
  rereading, 233
  split-level, 250
  standard system for, 248–250
  wrap-up, 250

summary area, in Cornell System, 207, 208, 212
summary sheets
  advanced, 270, 272, 273
  for organizing notes, 269–272
  standard, 270, 271
summary words, 225
supplemental readings, note taking for, 230–232
supplementary learning aids, 186–187
supporting sentences, role of, 123–124
surveying
  and background knowledge, 189, 190–191
  in SQ3R system, 220
  textbook assignments, 190–192
  See also textbooks, previewing
surveys and studies
  on asking questions, 218
  on career goals, 7
  on effectiveness of advance organizers, 190–191
  on forgetfulness, 60
  French vocabulary study, 25, 76
  on imitating facial expressions, 92
  on memory, 62–63, 65, 206
  on multitasking, 88
  on reading comprehension, 119
  on silent speech, 119
  stress button experiment, 96
  on student use of time, 22
  on using mnemonic devices, 70
"switch hitter" study system, 284–285
swivel words, 224
syllabus
  reading before lectures, 199
  reading early in course, 266–267
symbols, for notes, 214, 228
synonyms, 135, 138–140
systems and techniques
  concentration scoresheet, 51
  Cornell System, 207–212
  five-minute plan, 86
  Fourteen Master Words, 151–152
  Frontier Vocabulary System, 145–148
  Goldilocks technique, 294–295
  GPA (goals, plans, actions), 10–16
  mnemonic devices, 69–73
  OPTIC system for visuals, 162

systems and techniques (*cont.*)
  PACE technique for reading, 120–126
  pencil technique, 49–50
  Q System, 244–248
  Silver Dollar System, 254–255
  spider technique, 49
  SQ3R System, 219, 220
  triple-A listening, 194–198
  worry pad, 51
Szent-Györgyi, Albert, 23
Szilard, Leo, 254

table of contents, surveying, 187, 231
task-based schedules, 34–38
  assignment-oriented, 35–37
  master schedule for, 35, 36
technical terms, 144
  symbols and abbreviations for, 228
technology
  for recording missed lectures, 230
  recording study information, 23
  scheduling tools, 34
  See also computer technology
Technostress (Weil), 89
telegraphic writing, for notes, 209–210, 226–227, 228–229
test anxiety management, 265–278
  and academic preparation, 266–274
  exam-week schedules for, 268
  exercise for, 107
  finding out about exam for, 275
  homestretch schedule for, 268, 269
  learning about test site, 275–276
  and mental preparation, 274–277
  and positive mental attitude, 276–277
  relaxation techniques for, 276
  reviewing past exams, 275
  and self-talk, 277
  summary sheets for, 269–272, 273
  and systematic cramming, 272–274
  and talking with instructor, 275
  visualizations for, 277
  See also academic preparation, for tests
test-taking strategies, 12. *See also* essay tests; objective
    tests
test words, 225

textbook marking, 212–216
  advantages of, 213–216
  avoiding overmarking in, 212–213
  disadvantages of, 216
  enumeration in, 215, 216
  symbols and markings for, 212, 214
  using recitation with, 216
textbook notes
  basic guidelines for, 235–236
  combining with lecture notes, 256
  concept maps for, 171, 173, 174
  and formulating questions, 218–219
  illustrating, 169–172
  Q System review for, 246–248
  textbook marking, 212–216
  See also note taking; textbook marking
textbooks
  finding alternative, 53
  formulating questions while reading, 218–219
  getting early, 184, 266
  organizational patterns in, 222–226
  overviewing finished readings, 233
  reading with intonation, 221–222
  supplemental readings to, 230–232
  typographical clues in, 221–222
textbooks, previewing, 184–192
  appendixes, 187
  author's objective, 185
  author's qualifications, 186
  bibliographies and references, 187
  of chapters, 190–192
  glossaries, 187
  headings and subheadings, 191, 192
  indexes, 187–189
  introduction, 187, 188–189
  organizational plan, 185–186
  for overcoming inertia, 191
  prefatory material, 184–187
  of set-apart information, 192
  supplementary learning aids, 186–187
  surveying specific assignments, 190–192
  table of contents, 187
  unique qualities, 186
  of visuals, 192
  as warm-up activity, 191

Thatcher, Margaret, 321
thinking
    spare-time, 23
    and vocabulary, 132
    See also visual thinking
Thoreau, Henry David, 4–5
thought speed, and listening, 197
three-part scheduling plan, 28–33, 35–38, 268
time, lack of, and procrastination, 86
time-block schedules, 28–34. *See also* schedules
time-management techniques, 21–39
    changing time habits, 24–27
    daily activity log, 24–25
    defying Parkinson's Law, 25
    for essay tests, 307–308
    for exam preparation, 267–268
    finding hidden time, 22–23
    guidelines for, 39–40
    importance of, 22
    limiting e-mail and Internet time, 25
    obeying alarm clock, 25
    pocket work, 23
    for saving time, 22–27
    schedules, 27–38 (*see also* schedules)
    spare-time thinking, 23
    studying in short periods, 25–26, 75–76
    taking "time out," 25–26, 52
    understanding circadian rhythms, 26
    using mind when it's free, 23
    using notepad, 26–27
    using recorded study information, 23
    using subconscious, 23
"time outs," 25–26. *See also* breaks
time pattern, 222
timer, for scheduled tasks, 87
time words, 225
titles
    rereading, 233
    surveying chapter, 191, 231
    of visuals, 162, 167
to-do list, 37–38, 86
topical pattern, 222
topic sentence, purpose of, 123–124
transitional words, for essay tests, 315–316
travel time, allowances for, 90

triple-A listening, 194–198
true-false questions, 285–286, 295
true-false technique, 288
tunnel vision, 190
tutors, 53, 267
Twain, Mark, 126, 131
two-page system, for lectures, 230
typographical intonations, in textbooks, 221–222

unabridged dictionaries, 141–142
underlining, in text, 221. *See also* textbook marking
understanding
    and asking questions, 217–219
    and background knowledge, 68
    and memory retention, 63, 68
    paying attention to intonation, 219–222
    recognizing organizational patterns, 222–226
    using whole brain, 161
usage notes, in dictionary, 140
USDA's food pyramid, 99

Valéry, Paul, 111
verbal step, for keyword mnemonic, 72
video learning aids, 186
visual distractions, in study environment, 48
visualizations
    at end of lectures, 233
    of goals, 6
    for procrastination, 87
    for test anxiety management, 277
visuals
    concept maps, 172–176
    graphs, 162–168
    illustrating notes, 169–172, 210, 212
    surveying, 192
    See also concept maps; graphs
visual step, for keyword mnemonic, 72
visual thinking, 160–176
    and brain functions, 160–161
    and concept maps, 172–176
    and distorted data, 166–168
    illustrating notes, 169–172
    language of graphs, 162–168
    OPTIC system for, 162, 166–167
    reading pictures and visuals, 161–168

visual thinking (*cont.*)
    and reflection, 256
    for strengthening memory, 68–69
    writing in pictures, 169–176
vocabulary building, 131–154
    and antonyms, 147
    and billboards, 134–135
    dictionaries for, 135–142
    Fourteen Master Words for, 151–152
    Frontier Vocabulary System for, 145–148
    Hayakawa's view of, 146
    index card system for, 143–145
    keyword mnemonic for, 72
    learning roots and prefixes, 148–151
    and newspapers, 133–134
    and power of interest, 132–135
    and reading speed, 126
    recitation for, 143
    and self-esteem, 132–133
    and suffixes, 148, 150–151
    and synonyms, 138–140
    for technical terms, 144
    and usage notes, 140
    using context, 135–136, 143
    and word familiarity, 146
    and word histories, 140, 152–154
    See also dictionaries
vocalization, in reading process, 118–119, 123
volume, in intonation, 219, 221

Warburg, James P., 303
water, in diet, 101
weaknesses, assessing, 15
Webb, Dr. Wilse, 101
Webster, Daniel, 121
Webster's New Collegiate Dictionary, 138
Webster's New World College Dictionary, 4th ed., 138
Webster's Third New International Dictionary of the English Language, 141
Webster's II New Riverside Pocket Dictionary, 136

weekly schedule, 28, 29–32
    assignment-oriented, 35–37
Weil, Michelle, 89
Wellness Letter, 95
"What Do You Want to Be When You Grow Up?"
    (Williams), 7–9
White, Dr. Paul Dudley, 106
Whitehead, Alfred North, 253
whole-grain foods, 100
Willett, Walter C., 99, 100
Williams, Dr. David, 7–9
Wilson, Ian E., 240
word histories
    examples of, 129
    locating books on, 153–154
    and vocabulary building, 140, 152–154
    acumen, 57
    anecdote, 240
    arrive, 260
    bedlam, 111
    bonfire, 129
    broker, 80
    calculate, 203
    congregation, 179
    curfew, 281
    deliberate, 321
    enthrall, 302
    neighbor, 157
    scholar, 153
    sophomore, 153
    tally, 42
    tantalize, 19
words. *See* vocabulary building
workbooks
    as study aids, 53–54
    supplementary, 186
workshop, for studying, 47–48
worry pad, 51
    for minimizing multitasking, 90
wrap-up summaries, 250